Matthias Arnold

HENRI DE TOULOUSE-LAUTREC

1864–1901

The Theatre of Life

Benedikt Taschen

FRONT COVER:
Detail from: Loge with Golden Mask, 1894
Colour lithograph, 37.2 x 37.2 cm
New York, The Metropolitan Museum of Art

FRONTISPIECE:
The Clowness Cha-U-Kao at the Moulin Rouge, 1895
Oil on canvas, 75 x 55 cm
Oskar Reinhart Collection, Winterthur

© 1987 Benedikt Taschen Verlag GmbH & Co. KG
Balthasarstrasse 79, D-5000 Köln 1
English translation: Michael Hulse
Cover design: Peter Feierabend, Berlin
Printed in Germany
ISBN 3-8228-0278-6

Contents

6
Problems, and How to Inherit Them
1864 - 1885

18
A New Style
1886 - 1891

28
A Kaleidoscope of Stars

48
Life is a Cabaret
1892 - 1898

80
Mastery and Self-destruction
1899 - 1901

92
Henri de Toulouse-Lautrec
1864 - 1901: A Chronology

Problems, and How to Inherit Them
1864 - 1885

An early and virtuoso self-portrait of a great artist: a young man is seen standing somewhat apprehensively looking into a mirror (left). The entire inventory of his feudal family home, at once costly and irrelevant, has been built up like a barricade between himself and his image – and the artist himself appears to have become part of the still-life. The light touches only his back and the nape of his neck. His face is in shadow. It is as if the young painter were reluctant to show it to the viewer or to himself, and the message is clearly one of self-doubt and scepticism: Is painting really my vocation? Will I make it? What about my body? Why have I been so terribly cursed with withered legs and a face that grows ever more ugly, with thick red lips and a weak chin which a first growth of beard is at last beginning to give some cover to? The man who posed these questions in his painting stood on the threshold of a unique career that was to establish him among the major artists in history. His name was Henri de Toulouse-Lautrec. And he was about to make his great leap from a cloistered dynastic background to the easy-going world of Parisian pleasures.

The counts of Toulouse can trace their family back to the times of Charlemagne, and they played a prominent part in the Crusades, but by the 19th century they were no longer making any kind of important contribution to the course of history. Instead, they were living an isolated life of plenty at their various estates in the south of France. It was a life of wealth and leisure, of hunting, animal breeding, party-giving, and musical dilettantism. To keep the family fortune as intact as possible it had long been tradition for relatives to intermarry within the family, and this, along with the agreeable financial advantages, brought with it rather less agreeable problems of genetic inheritance.

Count Alphonse de Toulouse-Lautrec-Monfa married Countess Adèle Tapié de Céleyran on 9th May 1863. Their mothers were sisters, the count and countess first cousins, and their marriage therefore tainted with the familiar incestuousness. It is worth mentioning that the bride's brother and the bridegroom's sister similarly entered on a union of this problematic nature, and paid for it with a number of still-born or mentally retarded children who were referred to in family correspondence, with a belittling kind of reticence, as "weak" or

Page from a school exercise book, ca. 1876–1878
Pen, 23 x 18 cm
Musée Toulouse-Lautrec, Albi

"To think I would never have painted if my legs had been just a little longer!"
TOULOUSE-LAUTREC

LEFT:
Self-portrait at the mirror, ca. 1880
Oil on cardboard, 40.3 x 32.4 cm
Musée Toulouse-Lautrec, Albi

"susceptible". As for Countess Adèle, on 24th November 1864, at the Hôtel du Bosc at Albi (the family's mediaeval town residence), she gave birth to a first child, a son, who was named Henri. A second son born four years later died at one year old.

The two cousins' illusions were also short-lived. Their marriage was one of convenience; and soon the differences in their characters drove them to go their separate ways, though the formal bond remained. Henri was brought up by his mother, who coped with the loss of her second child and the failure of her marriage by seeking refuge in the Catholic faith and in caring for the little son that was left to her. For a long time, commentators portrayed Countess Adèle in a too rosy light, as a self-sacrificing and loving (albeit rather bigoted) mother who did everything she could for her Henri. However, family letters which had evidently long been suppressed and which have only recently come to light tell a different story: of a woman close to religious mania, a

Count Alphonse de Toulouse-Lautrec Driving His Mail Coach in Nice, 1881
Oil on canvas, 38.5 x 51 cm
Musée du Petit Palais, Paris

LEFT:
Groom with Two Horses, 1880
Oil on cardboard, 32.5 x 23.8 cm
Musée Toulouse-Lautrec, Albi

9

hypochondriac and clinically hysterical, and in practical affairs with a good business head but mean. Her one real mistake was her passing love for Count Alphonse. Even her son, who loved her dearly, came to see this fact in the course of time: "My mother, Virtue personified! But she couldn't resist those red cavalry trousers!" (He is referring to the officer's uniform his father wore.)

For the young Henri, Countess Adèle was the most important person in his life; at times, on account of his weak constitution, she tutored him herself, and in all things he was the apple of her eye. Inevitably, as the child later grew to manhood, motherly dominance and care as problematic and oppressive as Countess Adèle's prompted reactions and the attempt to achieve the independence the young Henri had been denied. Toulouse-Lautrec's extreme career, from elitist aristocracy in the family château to the bohemianism of Montmartre cabarets and clubs, is perfectly understandable if we bear this background in mind: if he was to find himself and make his own way, the son had to put his possessive, didactic mother well behind him. Toulouse-Lautrec's dive into the bright world of the belle époque has hitherto been viewed as a consequence of his physical shortcomings, and no doubt they played a part, but psychologically it is likely that the need for emancipation from the maternal superego was of even greater significance. In order to find himself, Toulouse-Lautrec was prepared to go to any lengths, and ultimately even self-destruction. There was hardly any alternative.

Count Alphonse has traditionally been portrayed as a forceful and quaint eccentric, and doubtless the image is correct. But he may well have been the more natural, sensual figure in this disrupted family, all the subjectively-coloured reports to the contrary notwithstanding. In addition he was given to erotic dissipation, and had a passion for hunting that was almost grotesque. When Henri was twelve, his father gave him a book inscribed with words that the boy was to remember later in his worst health crisis: "Always remember, my son, that the only truly healthy life is a life out in the daylight and open air. Whatever is robbed of its freedom withers away and soon dies. This little book on falconry will teach you to value life out in the free open spaces of Nature. If ever you should become acquainted with the bitter side of life, a horse will be your best friend, and your dog and falcon will stand by you too, all of them loyal companions to help you overcome the injuries you suffer."

Henri no doubt inherited his father's unbridled temperament but nevertheless was later to eschew life out in the daylight and open air just as thoroughly as he rejected the kind of life advised by his mother. He put up deliberate opposition to his father too, though for different reasons. Count Alphonse rejected his son out of disappointment over the physically weak and retarded constitution of the boy, which would forever prevent him being the kind of horseman, hunter and soldier as he himself was. This must have hit young Henri hard, since he dearly loved horses, dogs and other animals; it may well have been a more

The Artist's Mother, Countess Adèle de Toulouse-Lautrec, ca. 1883
Charcoal, 62 x 40 cm
Brooklyn Museum, Brooklyn (N.Y.)

LEFT:
The Artist's Mother, Countess Adèle de Toulouse-Lautrec, at Breakfast at Château Malromé, ca. 1881–1883
Oil on canvas, 93.5 x 81 cm
Musée Toulouse-Lautrec, Albi

Young Routy at Céleyran, 1882
Charcoal, 63 x 48 cm
Musée Toulouse-Lautrec, Albi

"All day I am very much on my own, I read a little but if I keep it up for long I get a headache. I draw and paint as much as I can without tiring myself out, and when it grows dark I wonder if cousin Jeanne d'Armagnac will come to my bed! Sometimes she turns up and wants to play with me, and I listen to the things she says, but I am unable to look at her. She is so tall and handsome! And I am neither tall nor handsome."   TOULOUSE-LAUTREC

Young Routy at Céleyran, 1882
Oil on canvas, 61 x 51 cm
Musée Toulouse-Lautrec, Albi

bitter pill to swallow than the realisation that physically he was not up to scratch.

At the ages of thirteen and fourteen, Henri broke first one leg and then the other in accidents, and confirmed what had already been apparent but had been ignored by the family as long as possible or glossed over: the lad was suffering from a hereditary bone disease (pyknodysostosis), the major symptoms of which became evident around the age of ten. All his life long, Toulouse-Lautrec's bone structure remained sensitive and weak. After the first leg had been broken, in 1878, Countess Adèle tried cures and other more dubious methods of healing; but Henri's fractured thighbone was probably not treated as well as it might have been, and all the cures and other methods were of no avail. His legs stopped growing. As a youth, then as a man, Toulouse-Lautrec never grew taller than 152 cm (5' 1").

Lengthy spells in a sanatorium, and enforced rest and reclining, were very boring for a boy, but they had one positive side effect. Since he was six, he had shown an obvious talent for drawing, and now it became even more developed. While he was waiting in vain for the wished-for recovery, he filled school exercise books, sketch books, and any scraps of paper he could find, with drawings of everything that came into his head, whether he had seen it or only imagined it – people and animals, mainly. What drawings are preserved from Toulouse-Lautrec's childhood show that he was no prodigy but nonetheless plainly talented. This talent was not, however, rated any higher than a pastime. Toulouse-Lautrec's father, and his uncles Charles and Odon, all dabbled in painting as a hobby, and for the men of the aristocracy hunting, drawing and gourmet eating were all essential pleasures. As Toulouse-Lautrec's grandmother once put it: "When my sons shoot a wild duck they take a threefold pleasure in it: with their guns, their pencils, and their forks."

The fourteen-years-old's first oil paintings show the family property, a hunting and courtly milieu with horses, carriages, riders and dogs. A deaf-mute friend of Henri's father, René Princeteau, who specialized in painting animals, introduced the boy to the rudiments of painting when he was staying in Paris, and this teacher's speciality, together with Henri's own love of animals, naturally determined the choice of subjects in these early paintings. If the lad could not ride horses well, at least he was going to paint them well! It may be that these pictures were also a means of impressing his father.

It took Henri two tries and great effort, but in November 1881 he passed the first part of his school-leaving exams and, now aged seventeen, decided to lose no time. He wanted to be a painter. When we read the biographies of artists we often find parents offering fierce opposition, but in the case of Toulouse-Lautrec this was not so, and when later he had trouble with his family it was not because he was a painter but because of his choice of subjects and treatment. Initially, of course, the pictures the young artist showed his family were of horses and dogs, and scarcely likely to ruffle an aristocratic milieu.

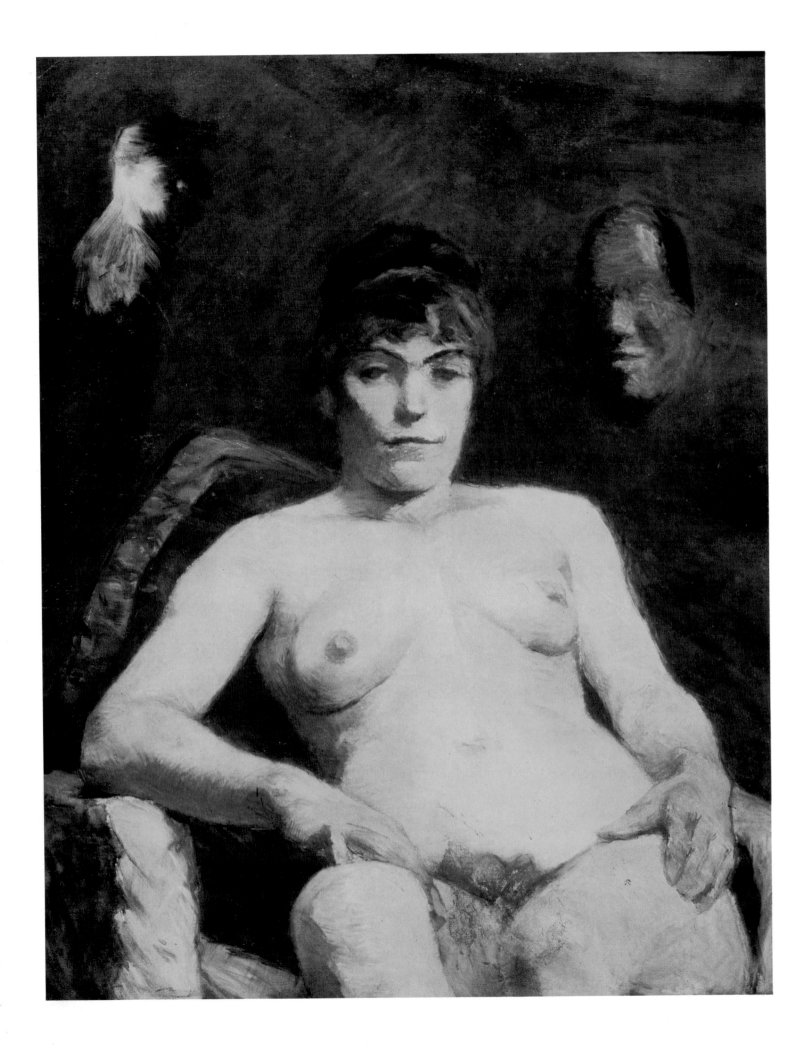

Count Alphonse consulted his painter friends Princeteau, John Lewis Brown, and Jean-Louis Forain, and they advised that his son needed academic training. On Princeteau's recommendation, and the personal introduction of Henri Rachou, a fellow-Albingensian, Toulouse-Lautrec entered the Parisian studio of Léon Bonnat, a fashionable painter, on 17th April 1882. A few weeks later, the young art student reported Bonnat's comments on his work as follows: "He told me: 'Your paintings are not at all bad, which is splendid, but, well, it just means they are not at all bad, and as for your drawings they are atrocious!'" Not many years later, Bonnat was to pronounce a similarly unfair judgement on his pupil Edvard Munch. In 1882, it is true, Toulouse-Lautrec was by no means mature as an artist; but his work at that date gives unmistakable evidence of great talent both as painter and as draughtsman. In later years, Bonnat was to stick to his antipathy towards his former pupil.

We need hardly be surprised that when Bonnat, not long afterwards, was given a position at the Ecole des Beaux-Arts, he did not take his unfavoured pupil to his classes there. So Toulouse-Lautrec found himself looking for a new teacher. The new teacher was Fernand Cormon, a salon artist who (like Bonnat) is now of no importance but who was at least of a more liberal disposition. "Above all," Toulouse-Lautrec wrote home, "he likes my drawings." And so the young artist was confronted with two totally contradictory academic opinions in the space of a few months. Not that this new praise was incentive enough: "When Cormon corrects me, he does it in a much gentler fashion than Bonnat; he takes a look at everything you show him and is very encouraging. You may be baffled by this, but in fact I find it less to my taste. When my first boss lashed me, the lashes hurt, and I didn't spare myself. But here I feel weakened and I need courage to produce a well-crafted drawing when a less good one would satisfy Cormon just as easily."

Naturally the young student submitted to the regulations and conventions of the academy, albeit only pro forma; but evidently he had his own ideas about painting and drawing right from the start. Beginning with his earliest oils, we are confronted with a technique and free artistic approach that are the very opposite of what then prevailed in the salons. Princeteau, Brown and Forain, as well as (from an early stage) the Impressionists, exerted a far stronger influence than Bonnat or Cormon. The paintings Toulouse-Lautrec did around 1880, as a sixteen-year-old, are composed in so easy-going and unconventional a manner that we can see them without reservation as his first wholly independent works (p. 8).

His pictures of horses, so dynamically expressive and with an energy in the brushstrokes that he may have learnt from Eugène Delacroix, show Toulouse-Lautrec already adept at what was later to become his unique hallmark: the recreation of a spontaneous, forceful and characteristic moment. The painting of his father in control of a brisk four-in-hand (p. 9) can meaningfully be compared with the artist's later

"Yes, what disturbed me especially was his disorderly form. Poor Henri! Every morning he came to my studio; at the age of 14, in 1878, he copied my studies and painted portraits; mind you, I trembled with horror. During the vacation he painted portraits, horses and dogs from nature, and soldiers on manoeuvre. During the winter, in Cannes, he painted ships, the sea, and women horseriders. Henri and I would go to the circus together on account of the horses, and to the theatre because of the decoration. He knew a great deal about horses and dogs." RENÉ PRINCETEAU

"Perhaps you are not aware of Bonnat's way of encouraging me. He told me: 'Your paintings are not bad — which is fine, though it still means they are simply not bad — but your drawings are utterly appalling.' And then you have to take your courage in both hands and start again: onward, breadcrumb!..." TOULOUSE-LAUTREC

"Cormon gave me a favourable reception. My drawings appealed to him best of all. My new master is the thinnest man in all Paris. He often comes to see us, and prefers us to paint outside the studio as often as possible." TOULOUSE-LAUTREC

Fat Maria, 1884
Oil on canvas, 80.7 x 64.8 cm
Von der Heydt Museum, Wuppertal

The Laundress, 1888
Charcoal, 65 x 50 cm
Musée Toulouse-Lautrec, Albi

"Nothing for it, nothing for it, I must play the deaf mute and batter my head against the walls – yes – and all for an art that eludes me and will never encompass all the terrible things I have endured for its sake... Ah, dear grandmother, you are wise not to give yourself over to painting as I do. It is more awful than Latin if you take it as seriously as I do." TOULOUSE-LAUTREC

The Laundress, 1884
Oil on canvas, 93 x 75 cm
Private Collection, Paris

obsession with dance movements. The background, rendered as if it were coloured cotton wool, is merely a backdrop in such paintings. The young Toulouse-Lautrec painted charming, sketchy landscapes in his home region, landscapes that are marked by a very vigorous technique, patches of colour linked up at lightning speed and tree-trunks or outlines gouged out of the paint with the handle of the brush. They are deeply-felt, visionary images of Nature, and we must almost regret the artist's later concentration on the human figure.

Subsequent to the early self-portrait, Toulouse-Lautrec repeatedly produced successful portraits of people in his immediate circle: Countess Adèle, for example, patiently sat for her son again and again. There are few painters who have paid such artistic homage to their mothers. The light-coloured portrait of his mother (p. 10), done in a virtuoso Impressionist style, is particularly good at conveying not only a quiet moment at the coffee table but also the mother-fixation of the young painter. The sparing use of colour – the concentration on bright, creamy shades of yellow and brown, with a few reddish and greenish highlights – already announces the delicacy of colour that was always to be at Toulouse-Lautrec's disposal.

In 1882 Toulouse-Lautrec portrayed a young farmworker called Routy (p. 13), who worked on the Céleyran estate, sitting on a low garden wall and carving a piece of wood. It is an unusual composition: the lower portion consists purely of a ground loosely applied (ploughed, as it were) with brush and spatula, and if it were not for the figure and landscape in the upper half it could be an abstract painting. This creates a kind of spatiality that draws our attention all the more strongly to the young man. The figure, and the landscape visible in the background too, has been done in broad patches of colour, and the painting dispenses almost entirely with outline. What results is a colour harmony in adjacent shades of grey, blue and green, with the odd highlight in brown. A number of preliminary drawings preceded this composition (p. 12), as indeed did another painting of young Routy out in the open, a half-length portrait which is qualitatively quite the equal of our picture and which is now in the Neue Pinakothek in Munich.

In 1884 Toulouse-Lautrec did a large-scale parody of the idealistic mural "The Sacred Grove" by Pierre Puvis de Chavannes, then much in demand. This parody was the twenty-year-old artist's farewell to that hollow, lying art of officialdom and bourgeois salons which was being imposed on him as an example to be followed. That same year, at least in terms of his domicile, Toulouse-Lautrec began to cut the apron strings and establish a circle of his own, friends and work that had nothing to do with his mother. He sensed the need of this, though it was not easy. What he wrote to his family was perhaps not wholly the fact of the matter: "Of course Papa would think me an outsider... It has cost me an effort, and you know as well as I do that leading a Bohemian life goes against the grain and taxes my will sorely in the attempt to get used to it, since I still bear with me a load of sentimental considerations that I shall have to throw overboard if I am to get anywhere..."

A New Style
1886 - 1891

A bar in Paris. Toulouse-Lautrec is twenty-three. Across from him sits his fellow-artist Vincent van Gogh, aged thirty-four – and with a few feeling strokes of his chalk the younger man produces what is far and away the most sensitive and revealing portrait we have of the Dutch painter (left). This is how others saw the passionate van Gogh: as an animal sitting in wait, with his absinthe, at a table, ready to spring at any moment. Van Gogh's self-portraits have their own expressive and artistic power, but this portrait by Toulouse-Lautrec is a masterpiece of psychological insight in its recreation of the phenomenon we label "van Gogh". It is the first time we find the young Frenchman's empathy giving us a full, essential human image. The style of the picture is still Impressionist, but its content goes far beyond mere mood and atmospherics. The dynamism and obsessive passion of the man van Gogh are fixed and at the same time the picture achieves an astounding physiognomic fidelity. None of the van Gogh self-portraits or photographs shows him in profile – it was left to Toulouse-Lautrec to render his friend this service. The portrait is not only profound in its psychology, it also shows us the receding brow and hooked nose which were typical of the van Gogh family.

The two painters, so very different in background and temperament, probably became acquainted in February 1886, when van Gogh had just arrived in Paris from Holland and Antwerp, was living with his brother Theo (who was an art dealer), and had joined Cormon's studio. Outsider Henri scented outsider Vincent and, communicative as he was, made contact with him. No doubt he also helped ease contact between the new studio member and other Cormon cronies: we know that Toulouse-Lautrec's friends Charles Laval, Eugène Boch, François Gauzi, Louis Anquetin and Emile Bernard were van Gogh's too within a short space of time.

Cormon, a liberal-minded salon artist, kept an atelier that was a major centre of Post-Impressionism, or rather, to be precise, of that splinter-group of Post-Impressionist style known as cloisonnism, from the French "cloisonné", an enamelling procedure. Several of Cormon's pupils imitated the techniques of this craft, among them Bernard, Anquetin, van Gogh, occasionally Toulouse-Lautrec, and indeed (through Bernard's

Quadrille on a Louis XIII Chair, 1886
Pen and pencil, 50 x 32 cm
Musée Toulouse-Lautrec, Albi

LEFT:
Portrait of Vincent van Gogh, 1887
Pastel on cardboard, 54 x 45 cm
Rijksmuseum Vincent van Gogh, Amsterdam

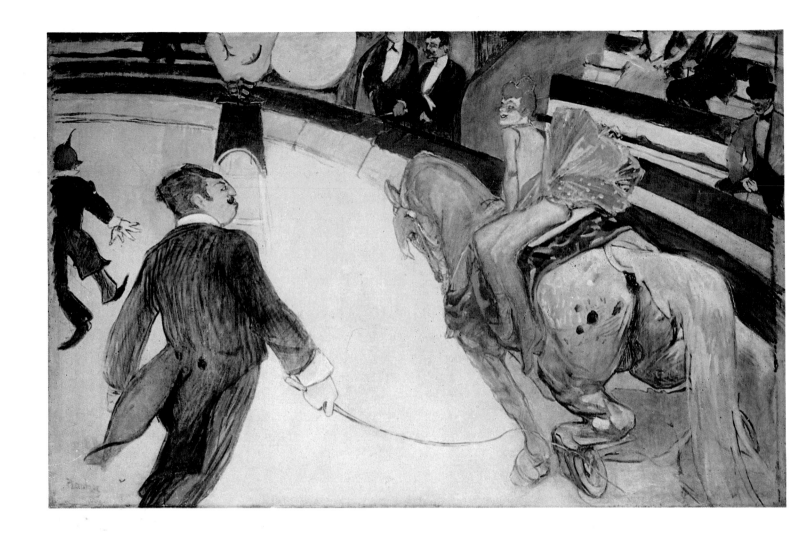

**Cirque Fernando: The Equestrienne,
1888**
Oil on canvas, 100.3 x 161.3 cm
Art Institute of Chicago, Chicago

offices as go-between) the outsider Paul Gauguin: the technique
involved highly abstract zones of colour, often contained in dark outlines
and clearly defined. In the art of enamels, or indeed in the lead framing
of stained glass, outlines of this kind had self-evident technical reasons,
but the cloisonnists made a virtue of the autonomous artistic value of the
formal process. Emphasized contours and the stylized approach of
Japanese woodcuts confirmed their sense that stylistic means of this kind
had an independent significance which could simplify and intensify (even
through distortion) expressive effects. Toulouse-Lautrec retained
"Japanese" elements in his mature style: the absence of shadows,
diagonal lines in the composition, surprisingly sectional approaches to
pictures, and certain decorative arabesques.

Not long before he left for Arles, van Gogh observed
Toulouse-Lautrec at work on "Rice Powder" (Stedelijk Museum,
Amsterdam): the painting, which shows a woman making up at her
dressing table, was done in an Impressionist style and completed in 1888,
and was bought privately by Theo van Gogh. That same year
Toulouse-Lautrec painted his first masterpiece, "Cirque Fernando: The
Equestrienne" (p. 20). The composition and arrangement of the painting
betray a strong Japanese inspiration, but nonetheless it bears the fully

individual stamp of the French artist, who – like his fellow-artists – had by now quit Cormon's studio. The motif of the circus was popular at the time: in 1879 Edgar Degas had painted his "Miss Lala at the Cirque Fernando" (National Gallery, London), which shows a trapeze artiste at a heavily foreshortened angle from below and is similarly influenced by Japanese art.

The motif of the circus rider, though, was Toulouse-Lautrec's own original idea; Georges Seurat and Pierre Bonnard were both to emulate him in due course. But none of them, Degas included, had Toulouse-Lautrec's ability to convey so suggestively the fleeting physical impression of power given by the horse along with the side-show excitement of the clowns. The painter's secret lies not in any kind of academic realism, not in Impressionist means, but in his unique approach to formal questions of colour and composition. The horse is seen at an angle, from the rear, galloping from the lower right into the heart of the

"He wears my clothes, but cut down to his own size."   EDGAR DEGAS on Toulouse-Lautrec

"I prefer Lautrec."   PAUL CEZANNE, asked about Degas

"A la Mie", 1891
Oil and gouache on cardboard,
53.5 x 68 cm
Museum of Fine Arts, Boston

EDGAR DEGAS:
**Marie Dihau at the Piano,
ca. 1869–1872**
Oil on canvas, 39 x 42 cm
Musée d'Orsay, Paris

"Lautrec's picture, the portrait of a woman musician, is quite astounding and has moved me deeply."   VINCENT VAN GOGH

**Mademoiselle Marie Dihau
Playing the Piano, 1890**
Oil on cardboard, 69 x 49 cm
Musée Toulouse-Lautrec, Albi

picture, the way ahead marked by the red ranks of seats. The diagonal dynamic which splits the picture into two sections was a favourite device with Japanese artists too. Toulouse-Lautrec retains empty space in the centre of his canvas, a startling effect for contemporaries used to compositions with a central focus. The two asymmetrical parts are linked through dynamic gestures and movements: the horse is moving forward and to the left into the open space of the circus ring, while the master of ceremonies on the left is cracking his whip across the empty space of the central foreground. This action of the ringmaster's creates a bridge to the horse and rider. The clown fooling about on the left and a second one on a platform further back, as well as the seated audience, are cut away by the edges of the painting – another "Japanese" trick. The Japanese habit of allowing the sectional view to appear dictated almost by chance had fascinated Degas and inspired him to imitation, and Toulouse-Lautrec too, in this his first work of genius, borrowed the technique.

Undoubtedly Degas was the most important influence and exemplar among the younger painter's older contemporaries. His academic teachers Bonnat and Cormon had given Toulouse-Lautrec a technical foundation, but his own stylistic beginnings were dictated by the Impressionists and those associated with them. Understandably, it was the painters who emphasized figural work who most inspired the young lover of animals and people; and Degas's subjects in particular became Toulouse-Lautrec's subjects, though the stress was often shifted. Women seen at the milliner's or at the dressing-table, in music-cafés or brothels, laundry-women and dancers – all of them met the criteria Charles Baudelaire and Emile Zola had set up for an art that would reflect modern life.

Toulouse-Lautrec was living in Montmartre in the same house where Degas had his studio, and so were the three Dihau sisters, who were in fact distant relatives. About 1870 Degas had painted a portrait of the pianist Marie Dihau, seated at the piano and turned to the viewer (above left), and in 1890 Toulouse-Lautrec followed suit with a painting of this woman playing the piano in her apartment (right). In the background to the right we can make out Degas's painting on the wall – subtle homage to Toulouse-Lautrec's idol. The portrait is in a mixed style between Impressionism and cloisonnism and, like the pastel of van Gogh, it succeeds in showing not only a spontaneous moment but also the character and essence of the subject. We see Marie Dihau amid stacked and opened scores, concentrating on her playing; the pictures on the wall, one of which Toulouse-Lautrec has used to bear his own signature, symbolize the cultured ambience of the family. By using a sparing yet rich palette, the artist has created shimmering colour effects.

The younger painter's admiration for Degas tended to be one-sided. Degas, who was in any case widely thought a misanthropist, adopted a patronizing tone towards his stunted junior. This may have been the result of a competitive instinct, though: for example, if we compare Toulouse-Lautrec's unachieved masterpiece "A la Mie" (p. 21)

The Morning After (Suzanne Valadon), 1889
Indian ink and blue crayon, 49.3 x 63.2 cm
Musée Toulouse-Lautrec, Albi

"The last day or so I've had a lot of fun at the 'Chat Noir'. We set up an orchestra and got the people dancing. It was very entertaining and no one went to bed till five in the morning."   TOULOUSE-LAUTREC

The Actor Henry Samary, 1889
Oil on cardboard, 75 x 52 cm
Musée d'Orsay, Paris

with Degas's "Absinth" of 1876 (Musée d'Orsay, Paris), a painting with great thematic and atmospheric similarity, we see that beyond the obvious resemblances there are also clear differences that lead us today to think Toulouse-Lautrec's the finer work. Degas's is a bold painting, but it has a somewhat formalist flavour, with its "Japanese" diagonals and its cut-off edges. The actual subject of the picture – two people in a mood of tired, melancholy togetherness – has been pushed aside into the upper right-hand corner. The various areas of the painting are gently and elegantly handled and the pastel colours have a certain reticence, so that what is in fact a well-observed, Naturalistic slice of modern Parisian life loses some of its edge and impact: form wins out over content.

In Toulouse-Lautrec's picture, on the other hand, we have not only the interior of a bar with a couple sitting at a table but also a shrewdly-realised character scene. The happy tipsiness of the man (the artist's friend Maurice Guibert sat for him) is countered by the bad mood of the red-haired slut who is turning away from him. The model for this female character, as also for "Rice Powder", was Suzanne Valadon, mother of Maurice Utrillo and herself a perfectly good painter later on. It is typical of Toulouse-Lautrec's incorruptible gift for observation that he will doggedly pursue what he has once seen in a model, and has a fine memory for the atmospherics of such a scene and will reproduce it in a painting. What conveys to us the condition of this grouchy couple on the skids is both the predominance of aggressive shades of red (colour used as a signifier of meaning) and the restless, at points sketchy and raw manner of the execution. For Toulouse-Lautrec, content needed the aptest form. In French art, so geared to harmony and decorative values, only certain caricatures and paintings by Honoré Daumier can appropriately be compared; and among later artists only the early Pablo Picasso and Käthe Kollwitz achieve a similar socio-critical bite, partly, no doubt, through following Toulouse-Lautrec's example.

It is true that Toulouse-Lautrec does not always have this empathy himself. The born aristocrat with monarchist views never took part in the daily round of political life, and was far from being a republican of Daumier's ilk. Nonetheless, in the Bohemian world of Montmartre's bars and meeting places, free of restraint and open to lovers and outsiders and all who left convention behind, he found his world, and himself. Among the quaint and curious, the painter attracted less attention than he would have done in the milieu he was born to, with people who did not care to face truths and preferred to cling to the dream of their caste rather than acknowledge that times had changed. In reaction to the lie his family was living, Toulouse-Lautrec opted for a trivial, brutal, everyday reality.

Dance clubs exercised a special fascination. At first he tried to record the abandoned amusement of the crowd at the "Elysée Montmartre", in a sketchy-cum-Impressionist manner; then, in the late 1880s, he came to prefer the "Moulin de la Galette", a cabaret club that had been set up in an old windmill in the Rue Lepic and enjoyed

At the Moulin de la Galette, 1889
Oil on canvas, 88.9 x 101.3 cm
Art Institute of Chicago, Chicago

long-lived popularity. Pierre-Auguste Renoir had already painted the garden of the "Moulin" in 1876, and the work, one of his best, shows the Impressionist manner at its least stiff (Musée d'Orsay, Paris). Toulouse-Lautrec, painting in 1889 (below), gives us the interior. As in the circus painting, a diagonal (the side of the dance-floor) jags across the picture, leading the eye to the background. Women wanting to dance are lined up at the rail, and beyond them a man in a hat is leaning on his table. They are all gazing in different directions, which creates a set of imaginary horizontals that (as it were) gives a psychological dimension to the foreground, suggesting spiritual isolation, friendly camaraderie, brooding emptiness, a whole tangle of polarities. In the background people are dancing and one group is talking. The diagonal of the rail,

leading to the right, is matched by other floor-level diagonals leading to the left. Indeed, the whole picture takes its life from these tensions between foreground and background, right and left. The oil paint has been applied very thinly at points as if it were watercolour, and at times very sketchily or runnily, and the background in particular is no more than a shimmer of brushstrokes. In all, the painting gives a perfect impression of the atmosphere of the moment in a dance-club.

One year later, Toulouse-Lautrec did a big painting of night-life in another dance-club, one which had opened in 1889 and was soon to steal the thunder and customers of the "Moulin de la Galette", the "Moulin Rouge". The painting was "At the Moulin Rouge: The Dance" (above) and it is a far more complex and mature composition than the previous year's work. Spatial depth is largely suggested by the positioning of figures. At centre left, surrounded by onlookers, La Goulue (the Glutton) and Valentin-le-Désossé (Valentin the Snakeman) are dancing, two cabaret artistes who, like the "Moulin Rouge" itself, were to enter art history through Toulouse-Lautrec.

At the Moulin Rouge: The Dance, 1890
Oil on canvas, 115.5 x 150 cm
Philadelphia Museum of Art, Philadelphia

A Kaleidoscope of Stars

In the great hall of the "Moulin Rouge", in the light of yellow lamps and surrounded by the black silhouettes of customers hungry for fun, La Goulue and Valentin-le-Désossé are dancing (left). They are the star attractions of the cabaret, opened just two years before, and both are at the peaks of their careers. In the foreground we see the half-figure of Valentin in a shimmering grey-green side-view silhouette, the effect of which is at once both muted and heightened by the flat colouring and a stylized, curved use of the line. His shadowy, sketchy figure partly conceals his partner, swirling about behind him – the only person in the picture who is portrayed as anything other than a silhouette. She too, though, is artistically simplified, and is very cleverly fitted into the painter's composition, not fully visible to us but instead cut off by Valentin at the right and with her fluttering white dessous hidden at left by a set of lamps. The spatial depth of the hall is conveyed by two main perspective devices: the lines of the floorboards lead to the rear, and the figures differ in size. Red and black lettering above it all tells us what is being advertised: the club where La Goulue performs and where there is a ball every evening.

When the poster went up in the streets of Paris, Toulouse-Lautrec became a celebrity overnight. In his laconic way, he wrote to his mother in October 1891: "My poster was pasted up on the walls of Paris today, and I shall soon be doing a new one." Toulouse-Lautrec's entry into graphic printing was electrifying. Previously he had provided material for magazine illustrations, but the printing was mechanical so that the result was not original graphic art; now, at the age of twenty-seven, and after a relatively long period of hesitation at the outset of what was to be his last decade of life, he plunged into work in a medium that was to prove his natural artistic element. Apart from a few ventures into etching, which were far from satisfying him, Toulouse-Lautrec was from now on to consider monochrome or coloured lithographs his most vital expressive medium. The catalogue of his work lists some 350 lithographs in all, about thirty of them posters; not all of these are works of the first rate, but a dozen are among the very best that utilitarian art has produced.

When Toulouse-Lautrec began to produce lithographs in 1891,

La Goulue Waltzing with Valentin-le-Désossé, 1894
Monochrome lithograph, 31.4 x 25.7 cm
Museum of Modern Art, New York

LEFT:
Moulin Rouge – La Goulue, 1891
Coloured lithograph (poster), 191 x 117 cm
Civica Raccolta di Stampe Bertarelli, Milan

Reine de Joie
par Victor Joze
chez tous les libraires

Imp. Edw ANCOURT & Cie PARIS

lithography had a century of history behind it: Alois Senefelder had invented the technique of printing from stone in Munich in 1796. Senefelder had found that if one drew on porous limestone with fatty chalk, moistened the areas that had not been drawn on, and covered the whole with fatty coloured printing ink, the moistened parts do not absorb the ink and in...

...start of the 19th century, lithographic printers started up business in Paris, initially concentrating on the reproduction of written texts or musical scores; by degrees, artists discovered the technical and material potential of lithography.

By 1820 the first lithographic masterpieces had been created, by Théodore Géricault, Richard Parkes Bonington, Francisco de Goya and Delacroix, among others. There were also specialists such as the Frenchman Nicolas-Toissaint Charlet and his pupil Denis-Auguste-Marie Raffet, who were less well-known than these painters. Before Toulouse-Lautrec, the most significant of French lithographic artists were Paul Gavarni and Daumier. Both of them did most of their work for illustrated magazines – editors had been quick to perceive the uses of lithography for illustrative purposes. This kind of work generally consisted of commentary on current affairs, whether in a more neutral, realistic manner or in exaggerated, caricaturist vein: both Garvani and (above all) Daumier have rightly reaped praise for the high artistic quality of their work in caricatures, which they employed to plead the cause of a more just society.

By Toulouse-Lautrec's day, other methods, cheaper though not necessarily better in quality, were coming to replace the original methods of stone-printing; and photograpy also looked like a promising means of illustration. This had the effect of making Toulouse-Lautrec independent of illustrative journalism in a way that had not been true of Daumier. He was free to make lithographic posters his own special province, along with lithographic work expressing his own concerns; the posters were his starting-point.

Studies and sketches which have been preserved show us clearly how carefully the artist prepared the "Moulin Rouge" poster. He used paintings, watercolour and pastel drawings, sketches, and even lithographs (p. 29) to vary his theme of dancing at the "Moulin Rouge" and of La Goulue and Valentin. After the sensational success of this poster, the artist did further coloured prints of the "Moulin Rouge", such as his two masterpieces of 1892, "'La Goulue' and her Sister at the 'Moulin Rouge'" and "The Englishman at the 'Moulin Rouge'".

In the first "Moulin Rouge" poster, Toulouse-Lautrec again used the Japanese and cloisonnist approaches he had first used in 1888 in the circus picture: heavily simplified figurative zones, an unusual composition based on cut-offs at the picture edges, silhouetted figures on a bright ground, and linear contours so that even at a distance the poster is effective. Extreme reduction and stylized presentation of this order – a limited conjunction of lines, spaces, colours and lettering – is

"Reine de Joie", 1892
Study for the poster
Charcoal on canvas, 152 x 105 cm
Musée Toulouse-Lautrec, Albi

LEFT:
"Reine de Joie", 1892
Coloured lithograph (poster),
136.5 x 93.3 cm
Musée Toulouse-Lautrec, Albi

PAGE 32:
"Ambassadeurs": Aristide Bruant, 1892
Study for the poster
Gouache on cardboard, 140.5 x 95 cm
Stavros Niarchos Collection, Paris

PAGE 33:
"Ambassadeurs": Aristide Bruant, 1892
Coloured lithograph (poster), 150 x 100 cm
Private Collection

Aristide Bruant, 1893
Monochrome lithograph, 26.8 x 21.5 cm
Musée Toulouse-Lautrec, Albi

"I have just returned from the opening of my exhibition at the Cercle, where my fumbled efforts, even though they have been hung so badly, have had a good press. All in all the papers have been very nice to me since my poster. 'Le Paris', which is a very republican journal (so do not mention it to my family), went so far as to devote two columns to an assessment of me, with not a single detail left out."

TOULOUSE-LAUTREC

"Divan Japonais", ca. 1892/93
Coloured lithograph (poster), 80.8 x 60.8 cm
Private Collection

characteristic of his poster work and points up the contrast with his other lithographic work: the posters are the end result of a process of crystallizing that has gone through numerous stages and are no longer intended to have the vitality of a fresh sketch or a painting rifted with intuition. They have been done for a different purpose and are distilled versions of something concrete which has been seen and is a symbol of the thing advertised.

The "Moulin Rouge" poster must be the most famous poster in art history, and rightly so. Toulouse-Lautrec was hard put to reach once again the standard he had set himself, and in subsequent posters he came close a couple of times but never quite brought it off. About a dozen of the thirty posters he did are of comparable quality. If we want to see why his "Moulin Rouge" poster aroused such excitement, we have only to compare it with the poster for the same club which Jules Chéret, acknowledged king of this particular kind of utilitarian art in Paris during the 1870s and 1880s, produced two years earlier: it shows a baroquely crowded and pompous confusion of costumed dancing girls riding donkeys (see p. 94, lower right). Toulouse-Lautrec valued Chéret highly and Chéret valued him. But all Toulouse-Lautrec could do was look for a completely new and original solution, and in finding one he far surpassed the earlier poster, and created a poster style which was quickly imitated and to this day remains influential.

In 1891 Pierre Bonnard made a poster for "France-Champagne" (there is no alternative but to call it kitsch) which some art historians have wrongly thought to have been an inspiration for Toulouse-Lautrec's "Moulin Rouge" poster; he then – following Toulouse-Lautrec's success – tried his hand the next year at another "Moulin Rouge" poster, but it was never completed. Bonnard, like Edouard Vuillard (who similarly was a member of the "Nabis" or prophets, a group of artists), profited from Toulouse-Lautrec's example in the posters and lithographs, as did the Norwegian Munch as well.

In 1892 more posters followed. Together with Bonnard, Toulouse-Lautrec undertook the advertising for Victor Joze's novel "Reine de Joie", which had just been published. Bonnard designed the book-jacket, and it was relatively weak; Toulouse-Lautrec did the poster, his second major work in the genre (p. 30). We see a coquettish woman at a dinner table, kissing a portly and ugly but plainly well-to-do bald man on the nose. Once again, as in his first poster, we find Toulouse-Lautrec applying a touch of "Japanese cloisonnism" in his arrangement of areas and contour lines and highlighting colour.

In the case of the lettering, it is important to distinguish between the script the artist deliberately integrated into his posters and other graphic work (i.e. script he had done himself) and other lettering that was overprinted later at the request of the advertiser and without consulting the artist. From an artistic point of view, only the lettering Toulouse-Lautrec himself designed is of interest. It may not always strike us now as being equal in quality to the picture, and "Reine de Joie" is a

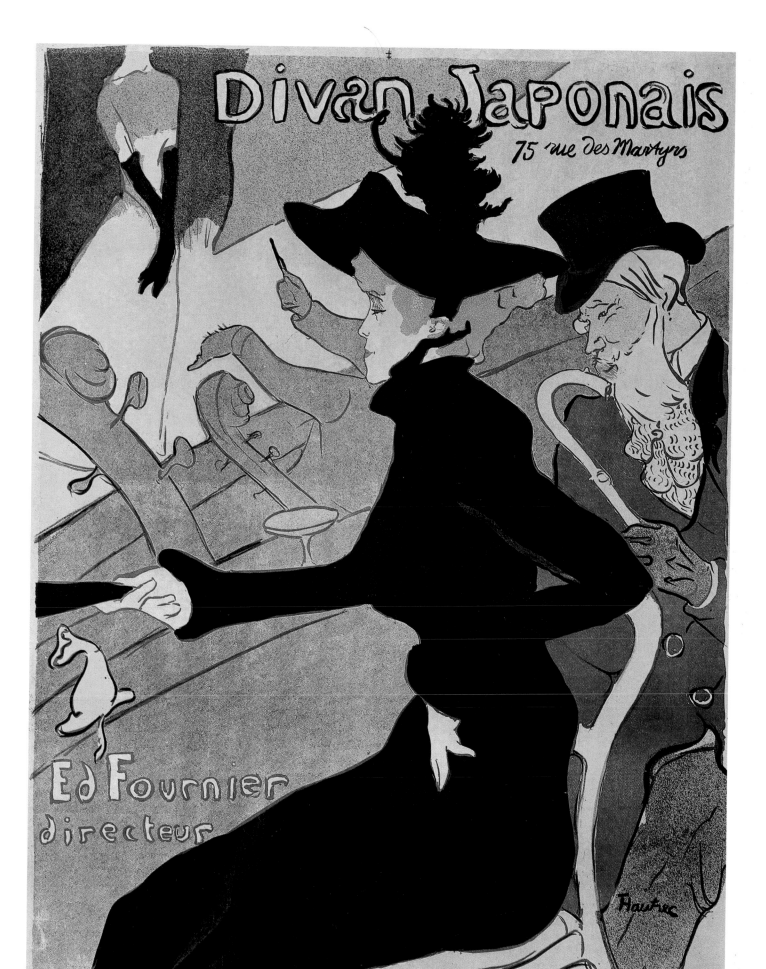

case in point, with its uneven characters, now big and now small, looking in their shakiness as if a child had written them. We can guess what was in the artist's mind when he opted to draw the letters in this way: he was aiming to integrate lettering and image into a single unified manner. But he was only rarely able to achieve this aim – best of all in the "Moulin Rouge" poster.

In the same year (1892) there followed the poster advertising the chanson singer Aristide Bruant (p. 33). It represents another attempt to give life to the genre by using idiosyncratic lettering; but what is far more interesting is the pictorial effect created by spatial reduction and the use of only the three prime colours red, yellow and blue. The result is highly evocative; and a preliminary study (p. 32) has an even livelier effect than the poster, thanks to its relaxed brushwork, and gives us an illuminating glimpse of the artist's working methods.

Toulouse-Lautrec had met Bruant some years before. Bruant had a cabaret club on Montmartre, "Le Mirliton", where he would abuse his audiences night after night, and get a great reception. But what particularly attracted both the working class and the artists and intellectuals were his chansons about life in working-class suburbs (a kind of early "chanson réaliste"). He sang in a razor-sharp voice, as recordings made around 1910 prove, and wore costumes of his own devising: atop black velvet suit and high boots, for instance, he would wear a black cape and scarlet scarf, and a broad-brimmed black hat. He often leapt up on a table and went on singing and scolding from there. He liked to affect a cane, to provide emphatic punctuation for his message.

Toulouse-Lautrec had a fine sense of artistic and human originality and was one of Bruant's early admirers. Apparently he was already entertaining fellow-students at Cormon's studio by singing Bruant's popular songs; and in the 1880s he painted a number of pictures for Bruant's cabaret, pictures that referred to the goings-on in the club or to the proprietor's hard-hitting chansons. With other Montmartre artists, such as Théophile Steinlen and Adolphe Willette, he also provided illustrations for Bruant's in-house newsletter, also called "Le Mirliton". When Bruant commissioned the first of four posters from Toulouse-Lautrec in 1892, the chansonnier had long made his name as a star and at times appeared at other, bigger venues; and the first poster was meant for one such guest appearance, at the "Ambassadeurs". The artist has neatly allowed the hat Bruant is wearing to cover part of the lettering of "Ambassadeurs", a trick that remains popular to this day. When Bruant gave a guest performance at the "Eldorado" cabaret, Toulouse-Lautrec simply altered the name of the club and printed the image the other way round. But the first version is without doubt the more effective. There were two further posters of Bruant in 1893 and 1894, one showing him at an angle and one from behind, one a half-figure with cape, hat and red scarf, the other a full-length in suit and boots standing on cobblestones.

Yvette Guilbert, 1894
Charcoal, coloured ink, 186 x 93 cm
Musée Toulouse-Lautrec, Albi

LEFT:
Yvette Guilbert Taking a Curtain Call, 1894
Gouache on cardboard, 48 x 28 cm
Musée Toulouse-Lautrec, Albi

PAGE 38:
Jane Avril dancing, 1893
Study for the poster for the "Jardin de Paris"
Gouache on cardboard, 99 x 71 cm
Stavros Niarchos Collection, Paris

PAGE 39:
Jane Avril at the "Jardin de Paris", 1893
Coloured lithograph (poster), 130 x 95 cm
Private Collecton

Yvette Guilbert, 1893
Monochrome lithograph, 25.3 x 22.3 cm
Private Collection

"But for heaven's sake don't make me so terribly ugly! Not quite so much...! A lot of people let out horrified screams when I showed them the coloured sketch... Not everybody sees the artistic angle only... and a lady!!! A thousand thanks from your very appreciative Yvette."   YVETTE GUILBERT

Misia Natanson: "Tell me, Lautrec, why do you always make your women look so ugly?"
Toulouse-Lautrec: "Because they are ugly!"

"Confetti", 1894
Coloured lithograph (poster), 54.5 x 39 cm
Private Collection

Yvette Guilbert, who performed in a variety of music cafés and cabaret clubs and at times sang chansons by Bruant, was another celebrated star. She too was able to make recordings, which show that she was also of the school of chanson realism which in our own time we are familiar with from the singing of Jacques Brel, Leo Ferré, Georges Brassens or Edith Piaf. As with Bruant, whose dress style became a trademark, Toulouse-Lautrec stylized Yvette Guilbert's appearance, rendering her in "silhouette" (his own expression). In his 1892 poster advertising the "Divan Japonais" (p. 35), the main subject of which is the dancer Jane Avril (seated in the foreground), the artist paid his first homage to his much-admired Yvette Guilbert, who appears in the upper left, singing a chanson on the club stage. Her head has been cut away by the top edge of the picture, but she is recognisable from her slenderness and her long black gloves, which Toulouse-Lautrec later made famous in the lithographs he devoted to the artiste. In her memoirs, the singer noted that this stylized image was if anything a product of chance and necessity: "At the start I was very poor, and since black gloves don't cost much I opted for black gloves. But whenever I could I wore them with bright dresses, and pulled so high up that they emphasized the slenderness of my arms and gave elegance to my shoulders and my long thin neck."

The relationship between Guilbert and Toulouse-Lautrec is typical of the repellent impression the artist made on first acquaintance, both physically and artistically. When she first met him, the diva was shocked by the man's stunted stature. Only one feature she found compelling – his dark brown eyes, which other contemporaries also noted: "They are beautiful, large, and gleaming with warmth and spirit. I can't take my eyes off them, and Lautrec, who well knows his only strong point, hastily takes off his pince-nez to give me a better look. As he does so I notice his droll dwarf's hand, a broad and angular hand at the end of a singular little marionette's arm... He wanted to fix a day the following week to make sketches, portraits and silhouettes of me... Three weeks later he turned up with all his little drawing things and said: 'I know I'm not expected, but I'm doing an exhibition of drawings, and I can't not have Yvette Guilbert, can I?' So I sat for him."

Toulouse-Lautrec made a great many drawings, gouaches and lithographs of Yvette Guilbert. There were plans for a poster, but they fell through, probably because the sitter, accustomed to the prettifiying approach of other portrait artists, was too hesitant over giving Toulouse-Lautrec a definite commission. A number of letters the singer wrote in 1894 clearly tell us how shocked she was by the artist's way of seeing and depicting her. But in the end she became convinced of his value. Now, of course, we know that it was only because of Toulouse-Lautrec's works that Guilbert achieved any kind of immortality, and she did so because he reproduced what was essential in her and did without the decorative adornments which other Guilbert portraitists and poster-makers added.

He made two series of black-and-white lithographs devoted

entirely to Yvette Guilbert. The first album was published in Paris in 1894. It includes a commentary by the art critic Gustave Geffroy which unfortunately often covers the lithographs. There are, however, copies without the printed text. The second album appeared in London in 1898 and is therefore known as the English Series. In it, Toulouse-Lautrec preferred close-ups of the artiste, mostly head-and-shoulders or half-figure studies, whereas the first album had focused on the overall phenomenon of Guilbert, the "silhouette". "Let us go and define Yvette," Toulouse-Lautrec once remarked as he set out to visit the singer. His definitions are vivid and highly original, not solely because of his simplified and epigrammatic presentation but also because of a quality in the sensitively-observed moment, that moment (for instance) when she spread her gloved fingers while singing (p. 37) or took her bow afterwards (p. 36). Not even the recordings or films that preserve Guilbert for us convey so memorable an impression of the singer as Toulouse-Lautrec's genius manages in these pictures.

He immortalized other stars on his posters too, most of them women, such as Jane Avril, who performed at the "Moulin Rouge" and elsewhere. The poster Toulouse-Lautrec designed for the "Jardin de Paris" in 1893 (p. 39) shows the dancer doing the cancan on the club stage; here once again, the flatly stylized figure contrasts with the spontaneous ease of a preliminary study (p. 38). An orchestra musician's double bass provides the picture with an asymmetrical, rounded frame which anticipates art nouveau decoration; Toulouse-Lautrec then got to know art nouveau mannerisms in England and Belgium, and the influence is particulary apparent in the second Jane Avril poster (right), done in 1899, with its ornamental use of space and of course the spiral pattern of the snake curled around the dancer's body.

In 1895, Toulouse-Lautrec did posters of the Irish singer May Belfort and the American dancer May Milton. He also pictured another American dancer, Loie Fuller, swirling the white swathes of her costume through the air; this picture was made available in delicately varied coloured lithographs sprayed with gold dust. He preserved the image of an unknown fellow-traveller he had fallen in love with on board a ship from Le Havre via Bordeaux and Portugal to Africa in his coloured lithograph "The passenger in Cabin 54" (left). Later, with lettering added, she was to serve as the poster for an exhibition. But we can easily see that this picture, so complex in its composition, was not originally intended to be a poster: it has greater immediacy, atmosphere, and intimacy, and draws its power from extremely personal and possibly desperate experience. Toulouse-Lautrec was making himself an image of what remained unattainable for him: a beautiful and sophisticated woman who personified the real life that he was largely excluded from.

Usually a lengthy series of preliminary studies preceded Toulouse-Lautrec's lithographs. Once he was attracted by a particular subject, stages on the way to the final litho might include a spontaneous sketch, a more thorough drawing, a watercolour study, or a study in tempera or oil (usually on cardboard), through to the picture proper,

Jane Avril, 1899
Coloured lithograph (poster), 91 x 63.5 cm
Private Collection

"Without a doubt I owed him the fame I enjoyed from that very first moment his poster of me appeared." JANE AVRIL

The Passenger in Cabin 54, 1896
Coloured lithograph, 60 x 40 cm
Private Collection

Femme au Tub, 1896
Coloured lithograph from the "Elles" album,
40 x 52.5 cm
Private Collection

which at times might be painted on canvas. On the other hand, it sometimes happened that Toulouse-Lautrec, once at the printroom, would rely on his excellent visual memory and draw straight on to the stone without any preliminaries. Perhaps his greatest strength was his rapid and unerring stroke – in the very moment of creation it both abstracted the simple essentials and clarified the subject. In the Parisian printrooms of Chaix, Verneau, and especially Ancourt and Stern, Toulouse-Lautrec was a familiar and welcome client through the 1890s. He tried out various coloured inks on papers of different colours, experimented with technical procedures, and had trial copies and then the whole editions of his lithographs printed.

As well as posters, a large proportion of Toulouse-Lautrec's black-and-white lithographs were devoted to the theatre and to stars. He was a great fan of comedies and operettas and would often go to see the same show repeatedly. At times he went to preposterous lengths,

Country Outing, 1897
Coloured lithograph, 40.5 x 52 cm
Private Collection

as when he went to see the operetta "Chilpéric" some twenty times, much to the agony of those who had to accompany him, apparently because he was infatuated with Marcelle Lender's low-cut dress. Marcelle Lender was the star of this Merovingian show, and Toulouse-Lautrec recorded her snapshot-style in various scenes from the operetta in a number of lithographs. He also painted a large canvas (Whitney Collection, New York) which shows Lender in mediaeval costume dancing the bolero. In format and execution the picture constitutes an exception in the artist's œuvre. Quite possibly the huge painting was a preliminary for a coloured lithograph in a comparatively small format, a lithograph which is among his finest and today fetches a very high price: the half-length portrait of Lender which was done in 1895 and first published in the German art magazine "Pan". Julius Meier-Graefe, the editor responsible for printing, lost his job as a result.

Other stage stars of the time besides Lender appear on Toulouse-Lautrec's lithographs, either acting in scenes or portrayed half-length in pictures that may in part have been done from photographs and are thus a species of superior fan-pics. In the artist's day, these pictures were bought on account of the stars shown, as is shown, for example, by the fact that the two Guilbert albums were signed not only by the artist but also by the singer. No one has ever captured theatrical scenes as well as Toulouse-Lautrec. His theatre lithographs may well be the best way of demonstrating his witty, feeling and epigrammatic art; formally as well as in subject matter, they owe a good deal to Japanese woodcuts of theatre people. No doubt his passion for the theatre can be explained by his romantic southern French tendency towards the dramatic, but equally the world of the theatre provided him with a substitute world. Like some voyeur, he drank down the scenes he saw on stage, just as in real life he drew sustenance from the scenes he experienced.

In 1896 Toulouse-Lautrec's album "Elles" was published in Paris by Pellet. It consists of coloured lithographs showing the everyday life of prostitutes in a brothel (p. 44). This series was revolutionary not only in its thematic material but particularly in its extremely sensitive and subtle use of the lithographie medium. Unlike in his strongly-coloured and contrastive posters, which were designed to catch the eye, Toulouse-Lautrec opted for delicate intermediate tones of colour which he combined with great originality. The gradations of light and dark and the structuring of planes are amplified by hatching and by areas consisting of countless little blots and blobs. The "Elles" album constitutes a landmark in the history of coloured lithography. Fellow-artists, the "Nabis" and Munch in particular, quickly followed suit with coloured lithographs of their own which are likewise of great importance.

The last coloured lithograph of major significance that was done separtely from poster work was "Elsa, called 'La Viennoise'" (right). Thematically it is related to the "Elles" series, but in the finesse of its tonal nuances it surpasses all Toulouse-Lautrec's previous work in multi-coloured printing. The hatching clusters round the figure like iron filings round a magnet; cloudy zones of blue and chestnut brown create a tender, flowing ambience. The wit of the picture lies in the fact that Toulouse-Lautrec is portraying a prostitute fully clad – we cannot even guess at her body beneath this clothing. All we are offered is her face, fashionably made up and rather on the vacuous side.

Elsa, called "La Viennoise", 1897
Coloured lithograph, 58 x 40.5 cm
Musée Toulouse-Lautrec, Albi

Life is a Cabaret
1892 - 1898

An Englishman, armed to the teeth with cane, top hat and winning charm, is flirting with two coquettes at the "Moulin Rouge". The formality of his clothing and bearing is contrasted with the merely suggested subtlety of the women's rig-out. Yet a handful of sketched-in details – the black neck-band, the low-cut back of the dress, the postures of the women (who are seen half from the rear) and the animal slant of their eyes, and the pert strand of hair on the forehead of one of the women – leave us in no doubt as to the nature of these ladies. The artist has found it necessary to provide greater detail in the case of the Englishman, with his elegant front: his demeanour suggests he is lying in wait, his ears have a reddish look, his hand lacks its wedding ring, and his facial expression, that of a pleasure-seeker putting on a debonair, easy-going show (caught in a few vigorous lines), all betray the deal he is intent on negotiating, and the sensual anticipation that characterizes this wolf in sheep's clothing.

The preliminary study (left) has a spontaneity that is close to genius. In the coloured lithograph of the same subject, by contrast, Toulouse-Lautrec presents the Englishman as a violet silhouette with only a few lines picking out his jacket, and uses this silhouette technique to express the contrast between the figures, which in the lithograph is conceived as a poster and is not necessarily more successful. In the stylized graphic version (see the monochrome state at right), too much has become over-definite and stiff, while the study preserves the vital spontaneity of the moment.

Toulouse-Lautrec was so fascinated by the night life of Montmartre that after 1884 he made his home in that part of the city, at the very source of his material, as it were. Reacting against the pretensions and arrogance of his family, he preferred the natural ordinariness of the people, from all walks of life, who lived out their instinctive lives in Montmartre. In this sense, the picture of the Englishman at the "Moulin Rouge" can be seen as a kind of indirect self-portrait. The aristocrat well knew the sensuality and lust that were concealed behind the lordly façade of the man of the world. The artist had scant success with women, on account of his stunted physical form, and necessarily took something of an outsider's view of those healthy fortunates who had fun,

The Englishman at the Moulin Rouge, 1892
Monochrome lithograph, 47 x 37.3 cm
Private Collection

"I don't give a fig for the play. No matter how bad the show, when I go to the theatre I always enjoy myself."　TOULOUSE-LAUTREC

LEFT:
The Englishman at the Moulin Rouge, 1892
Oil and gouache on cardboard,
85.7 x 66 cm
Metropolitan Museum of Art, New York

At the Moulin Rouge, 1892
Oil on canvas, 123 x 140.5 cm
Art Institute of Chicago, Chicago

RIGHT:
**La Goulue Entering the Moulin Rouge
Accompanied by two Women, 1892**
Oil on cardboard, 79.4 x 59 cm
Museum of Modern Art, New York

enjoyed their youth and money, and relished the pleasures of the flesh. Toulouse-Lautrec's addiction to the clubs and bars of Montmartre was partly a matter of taking his mind off things and numbing the loneliness that so easily arose once he confronted his extreme situation.

Cabaret life had become his main subject, and he fed his visual appetite every evening with new stimuli and scenes, always with people at their centre, people who tended to reveal their true natures only under the influence of alcohol or on the dance floor. Toulouse-Lautrec enjoyed watching vitality and energy, beautiful women, the flashing lights and colours of a world that was so artificial and yet, at a deeper level, perhaps truer and more honest since it was less inhibited. He found what he was after in places that other artists rejected or thought

Carmen Gaudin, 1884
Oil on cardboard, 23.9 x 15 cm
Musée Toulouse-Lautrec, Albi

"I was always struck by the way Lautrec changed his way of talking when art was being discussed. On any other subject he was cynical and witty, but on art he became totally serious. It was like a religious belief for him."   EDOUARD VUILLARD

At the Moulin Rouge:
The Start of the Quadrille, 1892
Oil and gouache on cardboard,
80 x 60.5 cm
National Gallery of Art, Washington

scandalous. In the spirit of Zola and with a meticulously dissecting gift of vision, he sought out the places and situations that had never before been thought worthy of treatment by artists.

In the early 1890s, the "Moulin Rouge" and its stars provided Toulouse-Lautrec with a near-inexhaustible source of inspiration for masterpieces. In one painting now in New York (p. 51), La Goulue, whom he had immortalized the year before on his first poster, is seen entering the "Moulin Rouge" wearing a daringly décolleté dress. The edges of the picture cut away the two companions she has linked arms with: as was probably the case in life as well, they merely serve to provide the dancer with support as she makes her entry. A bulldog-like man in a top hat is crossing behind them and , together with the lamps receding in the mirror, he adds a sense of depth perspective. The picture is composed wholly in cool and carefully graded tones of blue-green, with only a few highlights of brown and orange. The painting is totally dominated by La Goulue's bearing and facial expression, as if to say: Look here, this is a star arriving.

A similarly striking moment is captured in another picture of 1892, "At the 'Moulin Rouge': The Start of the Quadrille" (right). Legs apart and dress gathered up, a dancer (La Goulue?) is all set to perform, while in the foreground a couple of customers, who have clearly just arrived, are crossing the floor for a place. The position of the dancer's legs and arms, and her somewhat stupid facial expression, doubtless signal the beginning of the quadrille but also a certain displeasure at the delay as well as frivolous self-confidence.

Toulouse-Lautrec has here captured a highly ambiguous moment with great skill. It is a moment snatched from the confusion of green and orange lighting, a moment that would strike a less alert eye es unremarkable; Toulouse-Lautrec has caught movement, registered the unrepeatable event as if in a snapshot, and through artistic exaggeration has given permanence to the whole. He has even anticipated certain shots that were to become familiar through film camerawork. Technically speaking, this, like so many other oils by the artist, is marked by an economy that has something of genius about it: indeed, the shades of orange have largely been provided by unpainted areas of cardboard (which today has probably darkened with the years). The coat that the woman in the foreground is wearing (we see her at an angle from the rear) is suggested by just a few blue and brown brush-strokes together with unpainted surfaces, and the effect is a very neat characterization. The intermediate area and background are brought alive with unpainted areas too, which contrast attractively with the predominant pale green.

Another large composition done the same year (and later added to and improved by extra pieces joined on at the bottom and right) shows a different location and mood: the "promenoir" of the "Moulin Rouge" (p. 50). It is painted on canvas and is one of the artist's most thoroughly achieved works. Customers, acquaintances of the artist's, are sitting at a diagonal bar that crosses the foreground at left, talking at a

Cartoon self-portrait at the easel
Pen drawing
Musée Toulouse-Lautrec, Albi

"Ugliness always and everywhere has its enchanting side; it is exciting to hit upon it where no one has ever noticed it before."
TOULOUSE-LAUTREC

At the Moulin Rouge:
Two Women Dancing, 1892
Oil on cardboard, 93 x 80 cm
Národní Gallery, Prague

table – two women and three men. To the right in the foreground the face of a woman dressed in dark clothes (Jane Avril?) is dazzled by the light, and the green shadows in the upper part make the face appear like a mask. In the background La Goulue and a woman friend are doing up their hair in a mirror, while behind them little Toulouse-Lautrec and his tall cousin and friend Gabriel Tapié de Céleyran, a perfect Sancho Panza and Don Quixote, are crossing the room.

Toulouse-Lautrec loved making comic appearances in bars with this relative of his. Of course he could scarcely have seen himself in the position he is seen in here, in this most detailed of compositions – in profile. But he imagined the way he looked to others and painted it, and in doing so was merciless towards himself. At the same time, his position among the other people in this picture is typical of his role in life: while the others have fun and chat, Toulouse-Lautrec hovers on the fringe, simply an outsider in the scene, an extra, even a voyeur to be put up with.

In the years following its opening in 1889, the "Moulin Rouge" became the most popular night-spot in Montmartre, thanks to the stars it billed and its lavish and wittily original décor. The red mill, which still stands on its side at the Place Blanche and which was originally designed by Willette, was merely a façade and as such alluded to the many real windmills that had previously existed in Montmartre, one of which, the "Moulin de la Galette", had become a dance club. In the garden of the "Moulin Rouge" there was an outsize elephant, bought at the 1889 Paris World Exhibition, in the inside of which curios were displayed. As you entered the club, you saw Toulouse-Lautrec's "Cirque Fernando: The Equestrienne" hung against red velvet. The heart of the club was the dance hall with its galleries, where the performances took place. A table was permanently reserved for the artist there, and most evenings he was to be seen at it. What amused him was the mixture of trivia and art, elegance and sensuality.

La Goulue (the glutton) had been given her stage name because of her supposed habit of draining guests' glasses. Some of her less well-known colleagues had nicknames which were even cruder or more ambiguous: La Torpille (Electric Ray), Grille d'égout (Drain-cover), Nana-la-Sauterelle (Nana the Grasshopper), Georgette-la-Vadrouille (Georgette the Tramp), Demi-Siphon (Half-Siphon) and Rayon d'or (Ray of Gold). One name that was a direct contrast to the vulgarity of La Goulue's nickname was that of her distinguished colleague Jane Avril, who was known as La Mélinite (High Explosive), not so much on account of her personal charms as her stage act. At first she was part of the quadrille line at the "Moulin Rouge" but then she established her own act, and proved her talent not only in her performing and choreographic artistry but also in her own designs for costumes.

Jane Avril and Toulouse-Lautrec were good friends. In addition to the posters, he made a number of paintings showing the dancer during or after her "Moulin Rouge" act. One is a vertical-format piece showing the slender artiste dancing, caught at the moment

Jane Avril leaving the Moulin Rouge, 1893
Oil and gouache on cardboard,
84.3 x 63.4 cm
Wadsworth Atheneum, Hartford (Conn.)

"Only the figure exists. Landscape merely is, and must not be anything more than an addition: the pure landscape painter is a barbarian. Landscape should only serve to help us understand the character of the figure better. Corot is great only on account of his figures, and the same is true of Millet, Renoir, Manet and Whistler. When figural painters do landscapes they treat them as they would treat faces. Degas's landscapes are incredible because they are human masks! Monet has abandoned the figure, but what might he not have achieved with it!"   TOULOUSE-LAUTREC

when, standing on one leg and gathering up her white dress, she is kicking up her other leg in the **port de bras**. Her surroundings are merely suggested by loose brush-strokes. Once again, perspectival depth is implied by lines running diagonally and by a couple of onlookers in the background where the sight-lines converge. Another of Toulouse-Lautrec's devices, one which he often employs elsewhere, is apparent here with particular clarity: the vanishing-point, customarily located around the centre of a picture, is re-located at one side, indeed sometimes he places it beyond the edge of a picture. This device, adopted from Japanese practice, was a novelty in European art and made it possible to use abrupt perspectives and unusual angles of vision in order to lend greater emphasis to the subject. In other works, such as the "Moulin Rouge" picture (p. 50), Toulouse-Lautrec even went so far as to incorporate two different and diametrically opposed perspectives in a single picture, with the effect of suggesting great space and the liveliness of the club.

Also in 1892, he painted two of the more private pictures of Jane Avril. One (Courtauld Institute, London) shows her with coat, hat and gloves at the cloakroom. With a relaxed and introvert air she is getting ready to go home. The other (right) shows her lost in thought as she leaves the "Moulin Rouge" and the merry hustle and bustle. Her sobre, lady-like attire, dark and unrevealing, done by the artist in vertical strokes, contrasts with the tawdriness of her surroundings; Toulouse-Lautrec succeeds brilliantly in conveying the polarity of an individual's inner mood and the outside atmosphere. The artist's personal involvement and sympathy come across clearly. Indeed, these pictures are declarations of love – in paint – for a woman who was perhaps understood by no one but Toulouse-Lautrec, with his highly sensitive alertness to what was essential and unique in people. These two people, physically so unlike, were at one in their melancholy.

Toulouse-Lautrec was at his remarkable best with portraits when he knew his sitters well, as friends. At the start, when he had yet to make his mark, he portrayed professional models or girls he saw on the streets, in the most various of settings. And in the 1880s he painted masterly portraits of Carmen Gaudin (p. 52), who was known as La Rosse (The Slut), Rosa-la-Rouge (Red Rosa), Hélène Vary and Suzanne Valadon (p. 24). The painting of Justine Dieuhl (p. 61), done in 1890 in "Père" Forest's Montmartre garden, is a later example of this kind of portrait. One or two other portraits were painted in the same place, among them that of Désiré Dihau. What is unusual in these, given that they are works of the artist's maturity, is the landscape background and the fact (as photographs show) that Toulouse-Lautrec painted out of doors.

Some years later, he visited the châteaux of the Loire with friends who drew his attention to the natural beauty of the scenery there (no doubt to encourage him to try his hand at landscape painting), but Toulouse-Lautrec vehemently rejected the landscape art of the Impressionists. In his rigorous concentration on the human figure, Toulouse-Lautrec remains one of the most extreme (and consistent) artists

**La Goulue Dancing with
Valentin-le-Désossé, 1895**
Oil on canvas, 298 x 316 cm
Musée d'Orsay, Paris

"Ha! I should like to see the woman on
this earth who has a lover uglier than me."
TOULOUSE-LAUTREC

of any age. His preference for the figure testifies to the high standards he set himself. Like Degas, whom he admired, he viewed his few pastel landscapes as exceptions to his own rule, and when he departed from the human figure, he preferred to do so only to paint animals, preferably horses.

Thus the portrait of Justine Dieuhl is something of an exception, though the landscaped garden background is by no means merely a backdrop but rather, in a manner that almost anticipates the

Expressionists, serves to amplify our grasp of the sitter's character. Toulouse-Lautrec liked in general to show his subjects in a typical setting, especially if they were friends. Thus he pictured his cousin Gabriel as a full-length figure, elegantly dressed, pacing the foyer of the Comédie Française during the interval, lost in thought, leaving the gossiping crowd behind (p. 63); or the actor Henry Samary on stage (once again the picture has two vanishing-points!), doing his act in front of a painted backdrop (p. 25). He showed his other cousin, lady's man Louis Pascal, as

La Goulue Dancing ("Les Almées"), 1895
Oil on canvas, 285 x 307.5 cm
Musée d'Orsay, Paris

"One is ugly oneself, but life is beautiful."
TOULOUSE-LAUTREC

Maxime Dethomas at the Opera Ball, 1896
Oil on cardboard, 67.5 x 52.5 cm
National Gallery of Art, Washington

Justine Dieuhl, 1890
Oil on cardboard, 74 x 58 cm
Musée d'Orsay, Paris

a dandy in a top hat and carrying a cane, all set to go out (Musée Toulouse-Lautrec, Albi).

Once he told his painter friend Maxime Dethomas: "I shall record your immobility amidst the fun of the dance." The painting that resulted (left) is a masterpiece, showing the painter's friend in a dark coat and hat sitting stiffly with his stick watching the bright, colourful creatures at the opera house ball. The artist must have known his subject intimately to reproduce his character so well in paint. The portrait of another friend, Tristan Bernard (private collection, New York), a writer and manager of two Parisian cycling racetracks, shows the subject on the track of one of the velodromes. That of the young critic Paul Leclercq (who was later to write on the artist) shows him in a wicker chair in the studio (Musée d'Orsay, Paris). As for the scandalous Oscar Wilde, who refused to sit for Toulouse-Lautrec, he appears – in a portrait done from memory – as a bloated monster with a pretentious and sour gaze: the artist has taken his revenge for the writer's churlish refusal (private collection, Beverly Hills).

Toulouse-Lautrec undoubtedly suffered greatly from his physical condition, and as a sort of self-defence he developed a special kind of irony directed at himself. His appearance was certainly unusual, as many photographs and portraits by artist friends show, but it was by no means as frightful as he saw himself in numerous cartoons (p. 54). In conversations and in his letters, too, he generally referred to himself in sarcastic and disillusiond tones. It was a way of getting in ahead of potentially hurtful remarks and robbing them of their edge: he owned up to all his weaknesses himself and thus deprived sadistic mockers of their ammunition. No doubt his predilection for masks and costumes also resulted from his desire to be (or at least appear) other than he was. When we look at photos of the artist in the 1880s in particular we find him time after time at costume balls, often dressed in bizarre style as a choirboy, a woman, or a squinting Japanese in a kimono. At the same time he loved and admired everything that for him remained unattainable: beauty, physical strength and mobility, acrobatic skill. If anything was beyond him he aimed to feel his way into it, through his art, and so creativity for Toulouse-Lautrec represented a substitute for the life he could not lead himself. And precisely because he was excluded from so much, his sensitivity was all the more intense, his eye all the clearer.

His friends are unanimous in their testimony to his ready wit. To win social acceptance in spite of his physical appearance, Toulouse-Lautrec cultivated a vein of amusing originality that issued in characteristic turns of phrase and funny word-play, and in a love of the trivial and even the obscene. He recognised very few taboos among friends, and frequently shocked people (especially simple, petit bourgeois people) with his subtly adopted pose of naive openness. Sociable and something of a gourmet, Toulouse-Lautrec was amusing and readily amused, quick to see unintended humour or paradox in a situation. Only one thing was sacred to him: art. Art was the very heart of his existence. He needed art

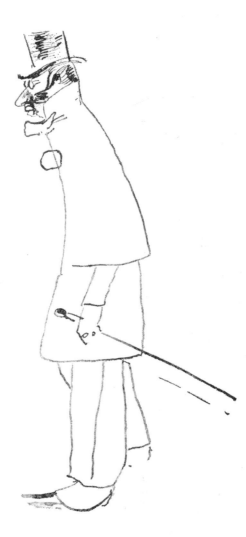

An Interne: Gabriel Tapiè de Céleyran, 1894
Pen, 33 x 22 cm
Musée Toulouse-Lautrec, Albi

"If I were not a painter, I should like to be a doctor or a surgeon." TOULOUSE-LAUTREC

Dr. Gabriel Tapié de Céleyran, 1894
Oil on canvas, 109 x 56 cm
Musée Toulouse-Lautrec, Albi

to live – and, conversely, he was greedy for the life he needed to use in his art.

Toulouse-Lautrec attended his theatre of life not only in cabarets and café-concerts but also in the bars he visited most nights. Two of his favourite bars, the "Weber" and the "Irish and American Bar", were not in Montmartre but in the Rue Royale. There he could meet not just artists but also sportsmen: famous jockeys attracted him and he showed them in a number of painted and graphic works. The most important of these is probably the monochrome lithograph "The Jockey" (1899), which also exists in a number of versions hand-coloured by the artist (p. 83). The impact of this picture, dynamic enough with its two riders galloping away on horseback, is further increased by the energetic colours. This lithograph, one of Toulouse-Lautrec's masterpieces, is finer even than Degas's fine pictures of jockeys.

What drew the artist to the jockeys was of course their physical ability and power, and similar reasons attracted him to circus artistes and entertainers. He could meet them in the "Irish and American Bar". One pair of clowns, Footit and Chocolat, intrigued him in particular, and he showed them performing their act in numerous lithographs, drawings and studies. The black (known for obvious reasons as Chocolat) is seen in one drawing (p. 64) performing an elegant dance, lithe as a cat, in the "Irish and American Bar". With the bony, macabre silhouette of Valentin, this exotic figure, pictured with an exaggeratedly ape-like quality, is one of Toulouse-Lautrec's few male models that have any of the memorability of his countless women. The scene is also striking for its anticipation of the socio-critical art of a later time, especially in Germany – it could be straight out of Bertolt Brecht's **Threepenny Opera**.

Other types caught the artist's attention in the bars of Paris, such as the corpulent drinker with the sandy walrus moustache seated next to the anaemic barwoman (p. 67). This oil study, done with sure brush-strokes on cardboard, is reminiscent of Daumier or Heinrich Zille. The old Dutch subject of the unmatched couple had attracted Toulouse-Lautrec in his early masterpieces "A la Mie" and "Reine de Joie"; here, what he emphasizes is not so much the aggression that alcohol prompts, or the marketability of love, but rather convivial tipsiness and indifferent business sense viewed side by side.

What we have now come to call a sub-culture was Toulouse-Lautrec's preferred field. For instance, a number of lesbian establishments that normally kept their doors closed to men welcomed the artist in. One-eyed Madame Armande, who presided over the takings at "Le Hanneton" (The Cockchafer) in the Rue Pigalle, was immortalized in a coloured lithograph of 1897, while Palmyre, the owner of "La Souris" (The Mouse), kept a bulldog called Bouboule which dog-lover Toulouse-Lautrec depicted in drawings, oil sketches and lithos.

The subject of lesbian love seemed to exert a special power over the artist, who was indeed generally interested in departures from the sexual norm. The clowness Cha-U-Kao, who appeared at the "Moulin Rouge", and whom Toulouse-Lautrec repeatedly portrayed (p. 2),

doubtless fascinated him because her departure from the norm was twofold: on the one hand a woman was playing the classic male role of clown, and on the other she was a woman who loved women. A more private picture, as it were, shows her dancing a waltz with a woman friend, in a work of feeling and intimate character (p. 55). Toulouse-Lautrec's "Elles" series of coloured lithographs opens with Cha-U-Kao the female clown, quasi-programmatically, as if to insist that these too are women: a lesbian clowness and brothel girls.

Toulouse-Lautrec's models, whether famous or unknown, all led their own lives; and when the stars – such as Bruant, Guilbert or Avril – grew old, they wrote their memoirs, and often had things to say about the painter. Some of them were in the limelight for only a few years. La Goulue's fall from stardom to obscurity was especially rapid, and as early as 1895, grown fat, she was to be seen doing her turn at fairgrounds. In that year she approached Toulouse-Lautrec with a request for two large painted curtains for the booth where she performed, and the artist rose to the occasion with two immense, square, unprimed canvases showing La Goulue yesterday and today: in one (a variant on the "Moulin Rouge" poster) she is dancing with Valentin, in the other she is seen performing her new act, a Moorish dance (pp. 58 and 59). In the latter picture, with their backs to us, we can identify Oscar Wilde, Jane Avril, Toulouse-Lautrec himself, and the critic Félix Fénélon among the audience – which doubtless flattered La Goulue and briefly buttressed her collapsing reputation. These two "functional" works of art naturally suffered during years of fairground wear and tear, wind and rain; and, as if that were not enough, a businesslike art dealer later cut the two curtains into a number of pieces to be sold separately. It is little short of a miracle that the Louvre conservation team was able to piece the puzzle back together again.

Few other artists so faithfully reproduced the life of the people and places around them. For Toulouse-Lautrec, life was one big theatre to be passionately enjoyed, a cabaret, a circus, a fairground, where the variety and contradictions, the instincts and the inhibitions, the limitations and the ambition of genius, goodness and wickedness, exhibitionism and introversion, sophistication and naivety, youth and age, happiness and melancholy, were all to be found. It was reality that Toulouse-Lautrec so hungrily sought and absorbed, reality that he so vitally and persuasively expressed. Weak in constitution and health, he was addicted to energy: "Ah, life, life!" he is said to have often exclaimed. His appetite for the diverse scenes of life was matched by his appetite for great works of art – though few painters of the past or present met with the approval of this sternest of critics. When he visited a gallery (such as in Brussels) Toulouse-Lautrec could stand before a single picture for hours and ignore everything else on show. His love of life and art alike was passionate.

His family fortune gave him financial independence, so Toulouse-Lautrec had no need for success and sales. With the exception of a handful of enlightened critics (such as Arsène Alexandre, Gustave

Behind the Scenes at the "Folies Bergère", 1896
Indian ink and blue chalk, 65 x 50 cm
Musée Toulouse-Lautrec, Albi

Chocolat Dancing in the "Irish and American Bar", 1896
Indian ink, crayon and opaque water colour on paper, 65 x 50 cm
Musée Toulouse-Lautrec, Albi

Geffroy or Roger Marx), most people rejected his work in tones of indignation, incomprehension or ridicule. In 1896 Maurice Joyant, the artist's old school friend and an art dealer, organized a major exhibition at his Paris gallery. It was at this show that Toulouse-Lautrec for the first time exhibited (admittedly in a separate room to which only friends had access) a series of the pictures he had painted in Parisian brothels in 1893 – pictures which were considered risqué in subject matter and, as one outraged uncle informed his nephew, dishonoured the family name.

The subject of prostitutes and brothels did in fact have a tradition behind it, with the Impressionists and cloisonnists: we need only think of Manet's "Olympia" (1863; Musée d'Orsay, Paris) and "Nana" (1877; Kunsthalle, Hamburg), Degas's brothel monotypes (done around 1879), brothel pictures by Anquetin and Bernard dating from the late 1880s, and the interest van Gogh had already shown in prostitutes in his Dutch period. This is largely due to the influence of the Naturalist novelists Zola and the brothers Goncourt, and of Guy de Maupassant; all of them had turned to the subject before the painters did. A further influence on Toulouse-Lautrec, open as he was to all things Japanese, may have been Kitagawa Utamaro's pictures of courtesans.

Toulouse-Lautrec was delighted by the naturalness, lack of posing, naive triviality, sentimentality and humour of the prostitutes. He was able to win their confidence and was thus in a position to observe them in the brothels undisturbed. For a time he even moved into a bawdy-house, which outraged a number of acquaintances who came to visit, such as the prudish art dealer Paul Durant-Ruel. Though the artist loved pranks of this kind, his true reason for this change of scene was no doubt of an artistic nature: only if he grew intimately familiar with the whores' everyday life could he give a truthful and unprettified account of it in his art. As with the cabarets, he first needed to know the thing he wanted to paint.

His paintings, lithographs and drawings show prostitutes in various ways, always credible and without denunciatory or mocking tones. He showed them at ordinary business, killing time before or after a "customer": eating, playing cards, engaged in lesbian tenderness with each other. Tellingly, he never (apart from a handful of very private cartoons) showed them at their actual trade of selling love. For one thing, we can assume that the artist was scarcely welcome as an onlooker (another exclusion! – though an understandable one), and for another he did not want to risk being thought a producer of pornography. Brothels were tricky and scandalous enough as a subject; and plainly Toulouse-Lautrec knew he was ahead of his time with these pictures, which he carefully preserved for posterity. When he presented prostitutes or nudes, the images were not so much erotic as honest. What mattered more to him than a woman's seductive charms was to discover her nature and portray her everyday moods and way of life.

In 1893, as a sort of prelude, Toulouse-Lautrec painted a fairly harmless brothel interior: "Monsieur, Madame and the Dog". It shows the couple that run a house of pleasure, sitting on a red settee in

In the Bar, 1898
Oil on cardboard, 81.5 x 60 cm
Kunsthaus Zürich

The Couch, 1894
Oil on cardboard, 63 x 81 cm
Metropolitan Museum of Art, New York

"All I hear is brothels! What of it? There's nowhere I feel more at home."

TOULOUSE-LAUTREC

front of a mirror which reflects both them and the vague figure of one of the house's girls seen from behind. What is exciting here is not so much the actual theme as the novel artistic treatment, with its message. The bright red-green contrasts render human types in brush-strokes of a seismographic expressiveness, with a ready largesse that was not to be attained again until Munch grasped it and took it further. Yet this painting, so close to caricature, is also the picture which most clearly shows Toulouse-Lautrec's debt to Daumier: we are reminded of his great predecessor's waiting-rooms and third-class railway compartments, where a similar mute resignation and petit bourgeois idiosyncrasy reign.

Because parts of the picture were left empty, works such as this made an unfinished and therefore aesthetically unacceptable and invalid impression on contemporaries trained in an academic tradition. The artist countered this oft-repeated reproach with pithy, pointed arguments that underline what was new in his aesthetic viewpoint. He once said to his cousin Gabriel: "These people get on my nerves. They want me to finish my works. But that is how I see things, so I paint them that way. After all, it is so easy to finish things. I can do you a Bastien-Lepage with no problem at all." And then, when he had promptly done a "finished" picture of this kind on the nearest canvas to hand, he turned back to his vis-à-vis and said: "See, that's how easy it is! There's nothing simpler than to finish a painting in an external sense. It's the very glibbest of lies."

The example of the old masters Rembrandt and Frans Hals (who in their own day were as much outsiders on account of their technique as Toulouse-Lautrec was in his), and unconventional pioneers such as Goya, Daumier and van Gogh, promted Toulouse-Lautrec to that realisation that was to revolutionize twentieth century art: that in distortion, and the use of approaches that had been seen hitherto as unaesthetic (such as leaving pictures "unfinished"), there were more suggestive and unplumbed possibilities and opportunities for conveying the truth than in

"I am pitching my camp in a brothel."
TOULOUSE-LAUTREC

Monsieur, Madame and the Dog, 1893
Oil on canvas, 48 x 60 cm
Musée Toulouse-Lautrec, Albi

"Just imagine...When you see the way they love... eh? The technique of tenderness."

TOULOUSE-LAUTREC

In Bed, ca. 1893
Oil on cardboard, 54 x 70.5 cm
Musée d'Orsay, Paris

any form of accurate realism. On the other hand, the formal exaggeration and abstraction of a scene can indeed show its true essence, though more symbolically. Post-Impressionist Paul Cézanne held at that time that art was a "harmony running parallel to Nature". In the age of photography the task of painting can no longer be to provide an objective record of a thing or person. The work of art must show with greater intensity what the great old masters had already shown (in addition to merely reproducing given reality): a self-contained, independent world, a world of thought and feeling.

Toulouse-Lautrec devoted an entire series of works to the tender intimacies of whores. In what is perhaps the most successful of them, "In Bed" (pp. 70/71), we see the heads of two people in a double bed, almost totally covered by sheets and blankets and thus not immediately identifiable as two women. Yet what we see here is in fact two prostitutes lying cosily in bed, contented and secure together, gazing happily at each other. For prostitutes, sexually exploited by men and treated as commodities, lesbian relationships provided an outlet for the

Women in a Brothel, 1893
Oil on cardboard, 60.3 x 80.5 cm
Szépmüvészeti Múzeum, Budapest

The Inmate of the Brothel, 1894
Oil on cardboard, 49 x 34 cm
Private Collection, New York

"And you imagine you're talking about love? You're only talking about what happens between the sheets... Love is something else..." TOULOUSE-LAUTREC

The Salon in the Rue des Moulins, 1894
Oil on canvas, 111.5 x 132.5 cm
Musée Toulouse-Lautrec, Albi

The Modern Judgement of Paris, 1894
Lithograph, 5.6 x 7.3 cm
Private Collection

"If a woman is simply a redhead, but really a redhead, a proper redhead – give her the full Venetian treatment!" TOULOUSE-LAUTREC

Woman Adjusting her Garter, 1894
Gouache on cardboard, 61.5 x 44.5 cm
Musée Toulouse-Lautrec, Albi

feelings of tenderness they too had. In formal terms, the picture's structure, tending to abstraction and with areas whose decorative values exceed their textural content, relates it to work done at the same period by the "Nabis", though Toulouse-Lautrec does not neglect his content in the way that Bonnard or Vuillard often did. The sparing but highly sophisticated colouring of this painting appears three years later in the lithographic cycle "Elles", also concentrating on life in the brothels.

In other pictures of whores (p. 68) Toulouse-Lautrec conveys the emotional relations of his models more unambiguously: the embraces and kisses and intimate chat of two women, often quite different in age and type, are presented without any reservations in all their human innocence. One or two large-scale individual portraits (p. 72) take their place in a grand artistic tradition. Toulouse-Lautrec was an admirer of painters of the early Renaissance such as Piereo della Francesca and Domenico Veneziano, among whose masterworks were a number of female portraits. Rembrandt too affords examples of the kind of portrait that Toulouse-Lautrec, unusually for his time, took up in such works.

He had already produced first-rate work of this kind in his early Carmen portraits of the 1880s and the 1888 portrait of Hélène Vary (Kunsthalle, Bremen). When in 1893 he was asked to adorn the salon of a brothel in the Rue d'Amboise he hit upon the idea of providing portrait medallions in Louis XVIII style, which had the effect of unmasking the courtly pretentiousness of French style while also placing prostitutes in an exalted milieu which was at the same time satirized. In the individual portraits of prostitutes, Toulouse-Lautrec makes no distinction between his models and the "good citizens" who were their customers or affected superiority. In general, the girls felt flattered that "Monsieur Henri" wanted to portray them. One of them, Mireille, even brought flowers when she visited Toulouse-Lautrec's studio, which touched the artist. His comment on the girls was : "They have a good heart. True education is a matter of the heart, and that is good anough for me." Like his idol Degas, Toulouse-Lautrec was of course also fascinated by the basic earthiness of the prostitutes: "Professional models always seem to have been stuffed, whereas these girls are alive… I shouldn't dare offer them 100 sous for sitting for me, but God knows they're worth it. They loll and stretch on the divans like animals… They are utterly without affectation.„

Around 1500 the Venetian Renaissance master Vittore Carpaccio had already painted a brothel picture (Museo Correr, Venice), a reproduction of which hung in Toulouse-Lautrec's studio. The French artist's most famous work may well be an allusion to Carpaccio's. After a number of preliminary studies, some of which seem fresher and more immediate than the final product, he painted "The Salon in the Rue des Moulins" (pp. 74/75), a very thoroughly executed piece by Toulouse-Lautrec's standards. We see a number of prostitutes waiting for customers, sitting lightly-clad on red velvet sofas; the woman in a pink gown on the right, probably the propietress of the establishment, seems an odd one out. She provides the artist with a contrast to his lolling, stretching animals. He has worked with a sure eye for faces and

physical positions. He was also exceptionally good at showing them routinely getting dressed (p. 77).

A number of nudes, unique in French art, round off Toulouse-Lautrec's brothel paintings in the late 1890s. "Nude Woman Standing at the Mirror" (right) is one of his least-known but most accomplished paintings and symbolically summarizes all his pictures of prostitutes. We see a whore standing in front of her reflection in a mirror; she is wearing the typical dark stockings, and holding the blouse she has just taken off. She stands revealed, the moment of truth has come; as Jean Cocteau once said, "Every day when I look in the mirror I see Death going about his business." We can view Toulouse-Lautrec's picture in the same way. The girl's body is still young and fresh, but for how much longer? What then? Who will still want the woman then? She will no longer be up to selling love (hinted at by the rumpled bed visible in the background).

It may be that this paintings, which we can certainly see in such symbolic terms, was inspired by baroque **vanity** pictures; but it was Toulouse-Lautrec's strength that his works resist being seen in one way only. The insensitive might see in this masterpiece no more than a delicate and accomplished nude of the kind that Degas, Renoir and Matisse made a French speciality, but we should not allow what looks at first sight like images of sensual serenity to distract our attention from Toulouse-Lautrec's message. These are pictures created by a wounded heart and a wasting body, where a spirit still alert intuits its coming end.

Nude Woman Standing at the Mirror, 1897
Oil on cardboard, 63 x 48 cm
Haupt Collection, New York

Mastery and Self-destruction
1899 - 1901

A whore looking into her mirror… How much more a picture like this expresses than all of Renoir's and Degas's paintings of women dressing put together! The subject, treated superficially by most other painters, has deeper significance in Toulouse-Lautrec's treatment (left). The composition and the melancholy import close the circle to his youthful self-portrait, with the still-life in the foreground on the dressing-table, the inward pause at an everyday task, the glance in the mirror. As in "Nude Woman Standing at the Mirror", painted two years earlier, what is celebrated here is neither beauty not eroticism but immutable transience. These women raise questions: Who am I? What will become of me? What is the point of it all?

It is no accident that these works were painted on the brink of Toulouse-Lautrec's decline. They may have been done with Dutch **vanitas** pictures in mind that he probably saw on two trips to Holland and which use symbolic props to indicate the vanity of all human endeavour. This imagistic expressivity, so totally beyond mere decorativeness or formality, marks Toulouse-Lautrec as an outsider in French art; his late work in particular, done in the space of two short years, anticipated the achievements of the Expressionism that was soon to follow in Germany. A muted minor-key note prevails in his artistic mastery.

Toulouse-Lautrec had for years been living beyond his physical means, and it began to catch up with him. Constitutionally he was in any case weak, and he had not spared himself, with his all-night bar-hopping, downing increasingly vast amounts of alcohol. From a certain time on, not even the warnings of friends or of his constantly worried mother helped. Nor was it possible to assist him by providing other amusement; indeed, the alcoholic had grown suspicious and often saw through plans and rejected them. He came to affront even his closest friends, and only succeeded in making his isolation all the greater. He took up with the worst kind of company: light women who drained the pleasure-seeker of his money, and some rather unsavoury men who served as his drinking companions. In the end this artist, intelligent and gifted though he was, let himself go and more or less deliberately sought his own downfall.

At the Circus: Clown, Pony and Baboon, 1899
Pencil and crayon, 35.5 x 25 cm
Art Institute of Chicago, Chicago

"One has to be able to put up with oneself."
TOULOUSE-LAUTREC

LEFT:
Madame Poupoule Dressing, 1898
Oil on wood, 60.8 x 49.6 cm
Musée Toulouse-Lautrec, Albi

Jockey on his Way to the Scales, 1899
Monochrome lithograph, 38.5 x 28.2 cm
Musée Toulouse-Lautrec, Albi

"Lautrec loved animals too. The animals along the avenues of the Bois, the animals at the circus or in the menageries... He loved sport, all kinds of sport, and everything about sport."   THADÉE NATANSON

The Jockey, 1899
Lithograph with oil and water colour,
51.5 x 36.3 cm
Private Collection

Toulouse-Lautrec's final years of life resemble a chronicle of gradual self-destruction. In addition to his inherited debility he had syphilis, which in his day was incurable. His friend, Dr. Henri Bourges, advised spells at the sea and other trips, to ease his illness. The 19th century saw many of its artists struck by syphilis, among them Franz Schubert, Friedrich Nietzsche, Manet, Gauguin and probably van Gogh. Toulouse-Lautrec drank more and more to dull his body and spirit, to numb the pain and to forget his lot as a man excluded from normal life. But the alcohol, to have the desired effect, needed to be consumed in ever greater quantities. It became a vicious circle. The artist's personality changed. He suffered from paranoid obsessions, became tyrannical and unpleasant, and devised devious ways of avoiding the means which well-wishing friends and relatives thought up to keep him from drink.

Then at the beginning of 1899 Toulouse-Lautrec collapsed in the street. In a state of delirium, he was taken (apparently at his family's request) to a mental hospital at Neuilly near Paris. Deprived of alcohol, he gradually recovered his senses, realised he was in an asylum, and flew into a rage, fearing he would be locked away for good. At the age of thirty-five, in this situation, he recalled the words Count Alphonse had written in his weak little son's falconry book, and sent his father a letter crying out for help: "Papa, this is your chance to act humanely. I have been imprisoned, but everything that is imprisoned dies!" His father, however shied away from his responsibility. Friends (Joyant especially) visited Toulouse-Lautrec, and again and again he requested help and freedom; but they hesitated to take over-hasty steps, and soothed their consciences by remembering the doctors' diagnostic warnings. The doctors, of course, had a vested interest in keeping a well-to-do patient in their hands as long as possible. In the end, Toulouse-Lautrec could see only one way out: he himself had to prove that he was once more in a normal condition. He asked Joyant for the tools of his trade: "Once I have done a certain number of drawings they will not be able to keep me here. I want to get out, they have no right to lock me up."

Working from memory, he did a series of drawings on the subject of the circus, on coloured chalk – drawings that are rather overworked by Toulouse-Lautrec's standards. But then, they were done primarily with the aim of convincing the Neuilly doctors that he had pulled himself together again; he was out to show that he was in command of his trade. Masterly as they are, these drawings, with their echoes of a subject he had liked at an earlier time, strike us as uncanny. The strong emphasis on shadows and his (not always successful) attempt to get the proportions of figures "right", as well as the presentation of clowns and animals shown in front of ranks of terribly empty circus seating, give us insight (his efforts at exactness notwithstanding) into his inner turmoil, the unsteady world he was now living in, his melancholy and desolation.

The Parisian press had meanwhile launched an ugly campaign against him. They had got wind of his confinement and were out to establish the nastiest of links between Toulouse-Lautrec's art and his

The English Girl from "The Star" at Le Havre, 1899
Red crayon, 62 x 47 cm
Musée Toulouse-Lautrec, Albi

"Let's go and see the puppets dance. They're really good, they're marvellous... No, don't worry about it, drinking doesn't do me any harm... What, I'm so close to the ground? What of it? I drink only the best. How can it be bad?"   TOULOUSE-LAUTREC

The English Girl from "The Star" at Le Havre, 1899
Oil on wood, 41 x 32.8 cm
Musée Toulouse-Lautrec, Albi

mental condition. When he was discharged on 17th May, liberty was the finest present he could have been given. He felt he had "fled from prison" and told his friends repeatedly: "I bought my way out with my drawings."

Toulouse-Lautrec had been discharged on condition that he would not be left alone, for fear of a relapse. A distant relative from Bordeaux, Paul Viaud, volunteered to be his constant companion. After a short stay in Albi, Toulouse-Lautrec set off on his travels with Viaud. From Le Havre he wrote to Joyant, who by agreement was taking care of the artist's financial affairs and whom Toulouse-Lautrec therefore addressed ironically as his "guardian": "Dear Sir, we are glad to confirm that the art materials have arrived safely. I have done a red chalk drawing of an English girl in the 'Star' which I shall send off by registered mail tomorrow..." (left). "Dear Sir, yesterday I sent you a canvas showing the head of the barmaid at the 'Star', by registered mail. Please have it dried and framed. My thanks for the news of my finances. I hope my guardian is satisfied with his ward."

From an artistic point of view, Joyant had cause to be satisfied. "The English Girl from 'The Star' at Le Havre" (right) is a masterpiece of portrait art. Using relaxed but precise brush-strokes that betray no sign of his recent breakdown, he painted the image of the English barmaid in a seaport bar, a young creature who is open to life and carefree. The colouring is of a notable delicacy, with gentle shades of pink effecting the transition from the blue of the dress to the yellow of the girl's hair. The greens in her brightly-coloured blouse are taken up in the architectural background and varied with blues. The oil paint is applied thinly, in a linear and picturesque way; the painting is like a mosaic composed of different patterns of lines and dots. The effect is fresher and livelier than the red chalk drawing done as a preliminary.

Toulouse-Lautrec brought off a similar and arguably more significant achievement around the turn of the year 1899/1900 in his painting "In a Private Room at the 'Rat Mort'" (p. 87). We see an expensive bar, with a somewhat sketchy man cropped by the right edge, and his little lady friend, garishly turned-out, sitting at a set table behind a virtuoso still life. Bright and doll-like, the coquette seems almost to be a part of this arrangement of fruit – delicious enough to eat, as it were. The cherry red of her made-up mouth, and the yellow used for her face, re-appear in the pear of the still life. What gives life to the painting is not only the contrast of light and dark (stronger here than in his earlier work) but also the carefully thought-out balance of colour values: the red of that doll-like mouth suggestively provides the background too, with the effect that the warmer colour seems to be pushing the cooler colours of the figures and objects in front towards us.

Toulouse-Lautrec also painted a very fine late portrait of a milliner (left) with whom he enjoyed an almost childish friendship. Here once again is the emphatic contrast of dark and light: we see a strawberry blonde young woman in profile, her eyes downcast and half closed, wearing a shimmering yellow green blouse, wholly absorbed in her

The Milliner, 1900
Oil on cardboard, 61 x 49.5 cm
Musée Toulouse-Lautrec, Albi

work, among dark hats on display and the rear wall with window. We are reminded of Jan Vermeer's dreamy girls standing at windows, though this picture, with its varied colour and the deeply moving mood of gentle sadness, is filled with tender introversion. It is a consolatory farewell. Some months later, before he set off on his last journey of all, Toulouse-Lautrec was to take his leave from the milliner for ever with a similarly calm serenity: "Let us embrace, you will not be seeing me again. When I am dead I shall have Cyrano's nose."

In the last but one year of his life, Toulouse-Lautrec also painted his friend Joyant, in yellow oilskin and sou'wester, standing aboard a sailing-boat, his gun raised for duck-shooting (p. 88). Against a sketchy background that allows the grain of the wood on which the picture was painted to show through, the stoutly-built man, seen almost full-length and from the side, is established in bold yellow and chestnut brush-strokes. Only his pinkish-yellow face and purplish-red hands break with the overall colour scheme. This kind of painting, explosive and rapid and uncorrected afterwards, might have been inspired by "Professor" Hals, from whom Toulouse-Lautrec had occasionally taken "lessons" in Holland. A certain wildness in the style marks this work out from the draughtsmanly hatching and reticent colouring in earlier paintings. Perhaps this rapidity of execution was dictated by the slackening of his constitutional powers: sheer lack of endurance and patience caused Toulouse-Lautrec to slap his work down quickly, and in this way he anticipated much that was later to come in the Expressionist and subsequent movements in modern art – anticipated and, in terms of quality and accuracy, excelled. Knowing of the collapse of his health, critics sometimes rate Toulouse-Lautrec's late work lower and find it wanting; but in fact they are wrong to do so. During the last stage of illness, the artist drew upon reserves of creative energy and went back to the very heart of his talent and concerns, offering us a distillation of all he had seen and felt.

In the winter of 1900/1901 Toulouse-Lautrec rented a studio and apartment in Bordeaux, his companion's home town. His passion for the theatre reawoke with visits to Jacques Offenbach's operetta "La Belle Hélène" and Isidore de Lara's opera "Messalina", for a last time. In a letter to Joyant in Paris he wrote: "My dear Maurice, have you seen any photos, good ones or bad, of Lara's 'Messalina'? The show quite engages me; and the more I know about it, the better my work will go." Plainly he was intending to paint various pictures showing this opera; six of the "Messalina" series have survived, all done on canvas. Though they vary in quality, all of them are attractive in their colouring and unconventional in their approach to form. It is possible that these pictures draw not only on sketches and recollections of performances but also on photographs that his friend Joyant perhaps sent him. This might explain unusual features in the composition. Though no doubt Toulouse-Lautrec, normally an artist who valued the spontaneity of impressions, would have had reservations about such a process of creation, it must have

**In a Private Room at the "Rat Mort",
ca. 1899/1900**
Oil on canvas, 55 x 45 cm
Courtauld Institute Galleries, London

had the advantage of helping the weakened memory of the painter, and enabling him to concentrate on technique and colour values.

The Zurich picture, "Messalina with two extras" (p. 91), is a particularly virtuoso piece of craftsmanship, wholly thriving on the interplay of the three prime colours, blue, red and yellow. Here once again the red background has the effect of pushing the cooler foreground further forward. This painting also shows a new mastery in the loose, sketchy application of paint that replaces the earlier dominance of the line in Toulouse-Lautrec's art: the great draughtsman, significantly no longer at work on lithographs, emerges as a great expressive painter in his last paintings.

After a final visit to Paris, to clear up his studio and put his artistic estate in order and sign a few things, and destroy others, Toulouse-Lautrec travelled to the sea as he did every year. In mid-August, in Taussat, he suffered a stroke which left him partially paralysed. Countess Adèle, who knew that he was going to die, took him to Château Malromé on 20th August. During a brief period of recovery, Toulouse-Lautrec painted his last and (in terms of format) largest surviving picture (Museu del Arte, São Paulo), which he conceived as a mural for a room in the castle. It shows his companion Viaud, in an admiral's uniform and wig in 18th century style, with the sea in the background and a frigate in trouble in a gale out on the horizon. The background of the picture is unfinished and there are trickles where the paint has run (a visual effect which has become ugly normal practice among the Neo-Expressionists of our own time).

His family was well aware of the seriousness of the situation; and towards the end Toulouse-Lautrec also abandoned his lifelong self-protective mask of irony and sarcasm. On 9th September 1901 at 2.15 in the morning, not yet aged 36, Henri de Toulouse-Lautrec died, in full possession of his faculties, in the presence of his parents, his companion Viaud, and his cousin Gabriel, who had hurried to his deathbed at the painter's express wish.

At the time of his death, Toulouse-Lautrec was well-known, mainly through his posters, but the calibre of his artistic achievment was not merely disputed but was in fact wholly dismissed by the official art world for many years. As early as 1902, his mother founded a complete collection of the graphic art, along with a great many trial printings, in the Bibliothèque Nationale in Paris. After lengthy deliberation the Louvre accepted a Toulouse-Lautrec as a gift. In 1904 the family gave four pictures to the Toulouse Museum. In 1914 more of his works were made over to the Louvre under the will of an eminent collector, Camondo. Abroad, especially in Scandinavia and Germany, collectors and museums gradually began acquiring Toulouse-Lautrecs. Then in 1922, with the co-operation of the family and on the initiative of Joyant (who some years later wrote the first and basic biography of the artist), the Musée Toulouse-Lautrec was opened at Albi, and remains to this day the most important collection of his works.

Toulouse-Lautrec was always overshadowed by his great

**Head of an Old Man
(Patient at Neuilly Hospital), 1899**
Coloured crayon, 35 x 30.4 cm
Musée Toulouse-Lautrec, Albi

"Mama, only you! Dying is damned hard!"
TOULOUSE-LAUTREC's last words

Maurice Joyant, 1900
Oil on wood, 116.5 x 81 cm
Musée Toulouse-Lautrec, Albi

Mademoiselle Cocyte in "La Belle Hélène", 1900
Drawing for the watercolour, 40 x 29 cm
Musée Toulouse-Lautrec, Albi

Messalina with two extras, ca. 1900/1901
Oil on canvas, 92.5 x 68 cm
E.G. Bührle Collection, Zurich

contemporaries Cézanne and van Gogh, but he need not fear comparison. Unlike other Post-Impressionists who are today no longer so highly rated as was the case even a few years ago – Gauguin or Seurat, for instance – Toulouse-Lautrec's reputation is still growing firmer. What distinguishes his art is not the supposed frivolity that alienated conservative art-lovers and in some quarters is still thought the basis of his work, but an incomparable capacity for empathy. Nowadays Toulouse-Lautrec's great significance as an artist of humanity is finally being assessed in exhibitions and books; Toulouse-Lautrec the lithographer and poster-artist has (unjustly) been rated above Toulouse-Lautrec the painter, but there are signs that hidden treasures are now being discovered among his 600-odd paintings.

He was reluctant to theorize about art, but he once made a comment to his cousin Gabriel that revealingly indicates his creative approach: "The first human being to invent a mirror put it upright, for the simple reason that he wanted to look at himself full-length. A mirror of that kind is all well and good, because it is useful and need be nothing more than useful. To invent it was a necessity, and everything that happens from inner compulsion is good, and justified. Later, other people came and said: Up till now people have set up their mirrors perpendicularly without ever wondering why they did so. They found that mirrors can be put horizontally on their sides – naturally – though the question is whether there is any point in doing so. They did it because it was novel, and it was the novelty that appealed to them; but nothing is ever beautiful merely because it is novel. In our time there are many artists who go for novelty, and see their value and justification in novelty; but they are wrong – novelty is hardly ever important. What matters is always just the one thing: to penetrate to the very heart of a thing, and create it better."

Henri de Toulouse-Lautrec 1864 - 1901: A Chronology

1864 Henri-Marie-Raymond de Toulouse-Lautrec-Monfa is born on 24th November at the Hôtel du Bosc at Albi, the eldest son of Count Alphonse de Toulouse-Lautrec-Monfa and his wife, Countess Adèle-Zoë-Marie-Marquette Tapié de Celeyran. His parents are first cousins.

1868 His brother Richard-Constantine, born on 28th August 1867, dies at the age of one. Henri grows up on the family estates in the south of France and at Albi, as well as Céleyran. From 1868 his parents are separated.

1872 Countess Adèle with Henri in Paris. Living at the Hôtel Parey, Cité du Rétiro 5. Henri goes to the highly thought-of Lycée Fontanes (later Condorcet) along with his cousin Louis

Pascal and Maurice Joyant, who is later to be his closest friend, dealer, and biographer. Sketches and caricatures in school exercise books. Contact with painter friends of his father's; the deaf mute René Princeteau, specialist in paintings of animals, is particularly helpful.

1875 Return to the family home, Because of his poor health, Henri is educated privately.

1878 Henri breaks his left thigh-bone in Albi. He convalesces at Amélie-les-Bains and Nice. At Barèges he strikes up a friendship with Etienne Devismes, for whom he illustrates a tale three years later.

Young Henri, nicknamed "petit bijou", at the age of about three

1879 Henri breaks his right thigh-bone at Barèges. From this time on, both legs stop growing.

1880 In need of therapeutic relaxation, he spends most of his time drawing and painting. Convalescence at Nice.

1881 In Paris in July, Henri fails his school-leaving examinations, but passes them in November when he re-takes them in Toulouse. Then in Paris with Princeteau. His decision to become a painter is supported by painter friends of his father's.

1882 Joins Léon Bonnat's Paris atelier. When it is closed he becomes Fernand Cormon's student in September. Among his fellow-students are Henri Rachou, René Grenier, Eugène Boch, Charles Laval,

The artist's father: Count Alphonse-Charles-Marie de Toulouse-Lautrec-Monfa wearing a Scottish costume

The artist's mother: Countess Adèle-Zoë-Marie-Marquette Tapié de Céleyran

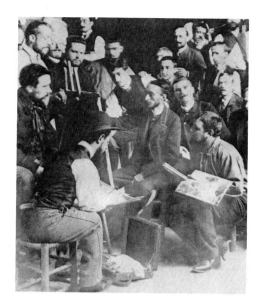

Toulouse-Lautrec (foreground left) in the studios of Fernand Cormon (at the easel), ca. 1885

François Gauzi, Louis Anquetin. He paints "Young Routy at Céleyran" (p. 13).

1883 Countess Adèle buys Château Malromé near Bordeaux; from this time Toulouse-Lautrec normally spends the late summer there after his annual spell by the sea (he is a keen sailor). Academic studies.

1884 Moves to Montmartre. First he lives in Lili and René Grenier's house at Rue Fontaine 19, where Edgar Degas has a studio. Increasingly he leaves academic approaches behind. The young Emile Bernard joins Cormon's studio. Toulouse-Lautrec exhibits in a group show at Pau, for the first time. Paints "Fat Maria" (p. 14) and the Carmen portraits (p. 52).

Because his head was over-sensitive, Toulouse-Lautrec would often wear a hat indoors. Ca. 1894

Posing cross-legged on an Arabian armchair

1885 He frequents clubs and bars in his quarter ("Elysée Montmartre", "Moulin de la Galette") and is a welcome guest at Aristide Bruant's cabaret club "Le Mirliton", where he exhibits paintings. Stays with Anquetin in Etrepagny and with the Greniers in Villiers-sur-Morin. Takes an apartment at Henri Rachou's, Rue Ganneron 22. "Portrait of Emile Bernard" (Tate Gallery, London).

1886 At Cormon's he meets and becomes friends with Vincent van Gogh. Summer at Villiers-sur-Morin, Malromé, Arcachon and Respide. In the autumn,

Forty winks after lunch

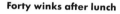

Drinking wine with friends in the garden of the Moulin de la Galette

Toulouse-Lautrec leaves Cormon and rents a studio at 27 Rue Tourlaque, at the corner of Rue Caulaincourt. He meets Suzanne Valadon, who is both his model and lover. First drawings published in magazines.

1887 Takes an apartment together with Dr. Henri Bourges at Rue Fontaine 19. Exhibits in a group show in Toulouse (using the anagram pseudonym "Treclau"). Together with van Gogh, Anquetin and Bernard he founds cloisonnism. Studies Japanese coloured woodcuts. His friends exhibit in cafés and restaurants. "Portrait of Vincent van Gogh" (p. 18).

1888 In February exhibits with the "Vingt" in Brussels. Theo van Gogh buys "Rice Powder" and takes other works on

"Monsieur Toulouse painting Monsieur Lautrec-Monfa." Photo-montage, ca. 1890

Toulouse-Lautrec in 1892

The Moulin Rouge at the Place Blanche. Ca. 1890

Toulouse-Lautrec, head shaven posing as Valentin-le-Désossé in front of a sketch for the Moulin Rouge poster. Ca. 1891

commission for Goupil. Autumn at Villiers-sur Morin. Separation from Suzanne Valadon. "Cirque Fernando: The Equestrienne" (p. 20).

1889   From now on he exhibits almost every year in the Salon des Indépendants and in the Cercle artistique et littéraire Volnay. He paints a series of portraits in "Père" Forest's garden in Montmartre. The "Moulin Rouge" is opened and

The artist with a model in his studio with his painting "The Salon in the Rue des Moulins" and other pictures. Ca. 1894

Toulouse-Lautrec becomes a regular. "At the Moulin de la Galette" (p. 26)

1890   Travels to Brussels with Paul Signac and Maurice Guibert for the opening of the "Vingt" exhibition. His school-friend Joyant becomes Theo van Gogh's successor as manager of Goupil's. Summer vacation at the seaside resort of Taussat and then in Spain. "Marie Dihau at the Piano" (p. 23), "At the Moulin Rouge: The Dance" (p. 27).

1891   Moves with Bourges to the house next door (Rue Fontaine 21). His favourite

cousin Gabriel Tapié de Céleyran comes to Paris to study medicine. Joins an Impressionist and Symbolist exhibition at Le Barc de Boutteville. "A la Mie" (p. 21). First printed graphic works, including the Moulin Rouge poster (p. 28).

1892   Travels to Brussels and London. Late summer in Taussat. Posters for Bruant (p. 33) and Jane Avril. Series of

With Charles Zidler, manager of the Moulin Rouge, in front of Jules Chéret's Moulin Rouge poster. Ca. 1891

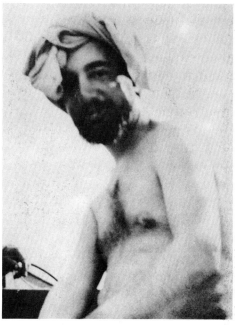

Maurice Joyant carrying his friend Henri on board ship at Crotoy

Taking a breather on the deck of the "Cocorico", after a swim

With his married friends Thadée and Misia Natanson at the seaside resort of Etretat. Ca. 1896

lithographs. "The Englishman at the Moulin Rouge" (pp. 48/49).

1893 First major solo exhibition at Goupil's. Exhibits with the "Vingt" in Brussels again. Stays with Bruant in Saint-Jean-les-Deux-Jumeaux. Takes an apartment in the building where he has his studio. Countess Adèle moves to the Rue de Douai nearby. Poster for the "Jardin de Paris" (p. 39). Greatly interested in theatre; also lives and paints in a brothel. Joint exhibition with the "Peintre-Graveurs".

1894 New apartment at Rue Caulaincourt 27. Travels to Brussels, Harlem and Amsterdam (with Anquetin). Exhibits with the Salon de la Libre Esthétique in Brussels, and at a show in Toulouse. In summer trips to Spain and then Malromé. Two stays in London. First album of Yvette Guilbert lithographs. The cultural journal "La Revue Blanche" attracts not only Toulouse-Lautrec but also the "Nabis" (among them Pierre Bonnard, Edouard Vuillard, Félix Vallotton). For a time he lives in a brothel. "The Salon in the Rue des Moulins" (pp. 74/75).

1895 Moves once again, to Rue Fontaine 30. Travels to Brussels for the Libre Esthétique exhibition. In London he meets Oscar Wilde and James Whistler, and exhibits in a show of posters. Trips to northern France; from there he travels by sea via Bordeaux to Lisbon ("The Passenger in Cabin 54", p. 42). Returns via Spain. Decorations for La Goulue's fairground booth (pp. 58/59); posters for May Belfort and May Milton.

1896 Exhibition at Joyant's. Le Havre, Bordeaux, Arcachon. Travels to Brussels, where he meets Henry van de Velde. Villeneuve-sur-Yonne, Spain, Arcachon. Visits the castles of the Loire. The "Elles" album of coloured lithographs (p. 44).

1897 Exhibits with the Libre Esthétique. New studio at Rue Frochot 5. In the early summer with Maxime Dethomas in Holland, afterwards at Villeneuve-sur-Yonne. Increasing problems with alcohol. "Nude Woman Standing at the Mirror" (p. 79).

1898 Exhibits at Goupil's London studio. Because of his growing health

problems his output declines in terms of quantity, though not of quality. Summer in Arromanches and Villeneuve-sur-Yonne. The second album for Yvette Guilbert is published in London. Nine etchings.

1899 Illustrations for Jules Renard's "Histoires Naturelles". After a breakdown he is confined for three months to an asylum at Neuilly. A polemical campaign against Toulouse-Lautrec is launched in the newspapers. Draws a circus series from memory (p. 81)..After he is discharged he recovers on the coast of Bordeaux and at Le Havre. In spite of Paul Viaud's watchfulness, Toulouse-Lautrec's alcohol intake goes up again. Evolves his late style: "The English Girl from 'The Star' at Le Havre" (p. 85), "In a Private Room at the 'Rat Mort'" (p. 87).

1900 Money squabbles with his family. Exhibitions in Paris and Bordeaux. Protracted spell by the sea in summer. Winter in Bordeaux. "The Milliner" (p. 86), "Maurice Joyant" (p. 88).

1901 Theatre visits in Bordeaux (six pictures based on "Messalina", (p. 91). Signs of paralysis in his legs. From mid-April he spends a last three months in Paris, putting his affairs in order, then returns to the sea. After a stroke in Taussat he is paralysed on one side. On 20th August he removes to Malromé, where he dies on 9th September. He is buried in Saint-André-du-Bois; the body is later transferred to Verdelais. Final pictures: "The Medical Examination", "Admiral Viaud".

LIST OF CONTRIBUTORS

Dr AC Fry MRCP(UK)
SpR in Nephrology
Department of Renal Medicine
Addenbrooke's Hospital
Cambridge

Dr JD Gillmore MD PhD MRCP(UK)
Senior Lecturer and Honorary Consultant Nephrologist
National Amyloidosis Centre
Royal Free Hospital and University College Medical School
London

Professor PH Maxwell DPhil FRCP FMedSci
Chair of Nephrology
Imperial College London
London

Dr CA O'Callaghan DPhil FRCP
Reader and Consultant Nephrologist
Nuffield Department of Medicine and Oxford Kidney Unit
University of Oxford and Churchill Hospital Oxford
Oxford

Dr SA Summers MRCP(UK)
Clinical Fellow and PhD Student
Centre for Inflammatory Diseases
Monash University
Melbourne
Australia

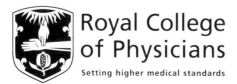

Royal College
of Physicians
Setting higher medical standards

© 2008 Royal College of Physicians of London

Published by:
Royal College of Physicians of London
11 St. Andrews Place
Regent's Park
London NW1 4LE
United Kingdom

Set and printed by Graphicraft Limited, Hong Kong

First edition published 2001
Reprinted 2004
Second edition published 2008

ISBN: 978-1-86016-274-9 (this book)
ISBN: 978-1-86016-260-2 (set)

Distribution Information:
Jerwood Medical Education Resource Centre
Royal College of Physicians of London
11 St. Andrews Place
Regent's Park
London NW1 4LE
United Kingdom
Tel: +44 (0)207 935 1174 ext 422/490
Fax: +44 (0)207 486 6653
Email: merc@rcplondon.ac.uk
Web: http://www.rcplondon.ac.uk/

CONTENTS

List of contributors iii
Foreword vi
Preface vii
Acknowledgements ix
Key features x

NEPHROLOGY

PACES Stations and Acute Scenarios 3

1.1 History-taking 3
1.1.1 Dipstick haematuria 3
1.1.2 Pregnancy with renal disease 5
1.1.3 A swollen young woman 8
1.1.4 Rheumatoid arthritis with swollen legs 11
1.1.5 A blood test shows moderate renal failure 13
1.1.6 Diabetes with impaired renal function 16
1.1.7 Atherosclerosis and renal failure 18
1.1.8 Recurrent loin pain 20
1.2 Clinical examination 22
1.2.1 Polycystic kidneys 22
1.2.2 Transplant kidney 23
1.3 Communication skills and ethics 23
1.3.1 Renal disease in pregnancy 23
1.3.2 A new diagnosis of amyloidosis 24
1.3.3 Is dialysis appropriate? 25
1.4 Acute scenarios 26
1.4.1 A worrying potassium level 26
1.4.2 Postoperative acute renal failure 30
1.4.3 Renal impairment and a multisystem disease 33
1.4.4 Renal impairment and fever 36
1.4.5 Renal failure and haemoptysis 38
1.4.6 Renal colic 41
1.4.7 Backache and renal failure 43
1.4.8 Renal failure and coma 47

Diseases and Treatments 49

2.1 Major renal syndromes 49
2.1.1 Acute renal failure 49
2.1.2 Chronic renal failure 51
2.1.3 End-stage renal failure 58
2.1.4 Nephrotic syndromes 60
2.2 Renal replacement therapy 64
2.2.1 Haemodialysis 64
2.2.2 Peritoneal dialysis 66
2.2.3 Renal transplantation 69
2.3 Glomerular diseases 72
2.3.1 Primary glomerular disease 72
2.3.2 Secondary glomerular disease 79
2.4 Tubulointerstitial diseases 81
2.4.1 Acute tubular necrosis 81
2.4.2 Acute interstitial nephritis 82
2.4.3 Chronic interstitial nephritis 82
2.4.4 Specific tubulointerstitial disorders 83
2.5 Diseases of renal vessels 86
2.5.1 Renovascular disease 86
2.5.2 Cholesterol atheroembolisation 88
2.6 Postrenal problems 89
2.6.1 Obstructive uropathy 89
2.6.2 Stones 90
2.6.3 Retroperitonal fibrosis or periaortitis 91
2.6.4 Urinary tract infection 92
2.7 The kidney in systemic disease 92
2.7.1 Myeloma 92
2.7.2 Amyloidosis 93
2.7.3 Thrombotic microangiopathy (haemolytic–uraemic syndrome) 94
2.7.4 Sickle cell disease 95
2.7.5 Autoimmune rheumatic disorders 95
2.7.6 Systemic vasculitis 97
2.7.7 Diabetic nephropathy 99
2.7.8 Hypertension 101
2.7.9 Sarcoidosis 102
2.7.10 Hepatorenal syndrome 102
2.7.11 Pregnancy and the kidney 103
2.8 Genetic renal conditions 104
2.8.1 Autosomal dominant polycystic kidney disease 104
2.8.2 Alport's syndrome 106
2.8.3 X-linked hypophosphataemic vitamin-D resistant rickets 106

Investigations and Practical Procedures 108

3.1 Examination of the urine 108
3.1.1 Urinalysis 108
3.1.2 Urine microscopy 109
3.2 Estimation of glomerular filtration rate 109
3.3 Imaging the renal tract 110
3.4 Renal biopsy 114

Self-assessment 116

4.1 Self-assessment questions 116
4.2 Self-assessment answers 125

The Medical Masterclass Series 131
Index 147

Since its initial publication in 2001, *Medical Masterclass* has been regarded as a key learning and teaching resource for physicians around the world. The resource was produced in part to meet the vision of the Royal College of Physicians: *'Doctors of the highest quality, serving patients well'*. This vision continues and, along with advances in clinical practice and changes in the format of the MRCP(UK) exam, has justified the publication of this second edition.

The MRCP(UK) is an international examination that seeks to advance the learning of and enhance the training process for physicians worldwide. On passing the exam physicians are recognised as having attained the required knowledge, skills and manner appropriate for training at a specialist level. However, passing the exam is a challenge. The pass rate at each sitting of the written papers is about 40%. Even the most prominent consultants have had to sit each part of the exam more than once in order to pass. With this challenge in mind, the College has produced *Medical Masterclass*, a comprehensive learning resource to help candidates with the preparation that is key to making the grade.

Medical Masterclass has been produced by the Education Department of the College. A work of this size represents a formidable amount of effort by the Editor-in-Chief – Dr John Firth – and his team of editors and authors. I would like to thank our colleagues for this wonderful educational product and wholeheartedly recommend it as an invaluable learning resource for all physicians preparing for their MRCP(UK) examination.

Professor Ian Gilmore MD PRCP
President of the Royal College of Physicians

PREFACE

The second edition of *Medical Masterclass* is produced and published by the Education Department of the Royal College of Physicians of London. It comprises 12 textbooks, a companion interactive website and two CD-ROMs. Its aim is to help doctors in their first few years of training to improve their medical knowledge and skills; and in particular to (a) learn how to deal with patients who are acutely ill, and (b) pass postgraduate examinations, such as the MRCP(UK) or European Diploma in Internal Medicine.

The 12 textbooks are divided as follows: two cover the scientific background to medicine, one is devoted to general clinical skills [including specific guidance on exam technique for PACES, the practical assessment of clinical examination skills that is the final part of the MRCP(UK) exam], one deals with acute medicine and the other eight cover the range of medical specialties.

The core material of each of the medical specialties is dealt with in seven sections:

- Case histories – you are presented with letters of referral commonly received in each specialty and led through the ways in which the patients' histories should be explored, and what should then follow in the way of investigation and/or treatment.

- Physical examination scenarios – these emphasise the logical analysis of physical signs and sensible clinical reasoning: 'having found this, what would you do?'

- Communication and ethical scenarios – what are the difficult issues that commonly arise in each specialty? What do you actually say to the 'frequently asked (but still very difficult) questions?'

- Acute presentations – what are the priorities if you are the doctor seeing the patient in the Emergency Department or the Medical Admissions Unit?

- Diseases and treatments – structured concise notes.

- Investigations and practical procedures – more short and to-the-point notes.

- Self assessment questions – in the form used in the MRCP(UK) Part 1 and Part 2 exams.

The companion website – which is continually updated – enables you to take mock MRCP(UK) Part 1 or Part 2 exams, or to be selective in the questions you tackle (if you want to do ten questions on cardiology, or any other specialty, you can do). For every question you complete you can see how your score compares with that of others who have logged onto the site and attempted it. The two CD-ROMs each contain 30 interactive cases requiring diagnosis and treatment.

I hope that you enjoy using *Medical Masterclass* to learn more about medicine, which – whatever is happening politically to primary care, hospitals and medical career structures – remains a wonderful occupation. It is sometimes intellectually and/or emotionally very challenging, and also sometimes extremely rewarding, particularly when reduced to the essential of a doctor trying to provide best care for a patient.

John Firth DM FRCP
Editor-in-Chief

ACKNOWLEDGEMENTS

Medical Masterclass has been produced by a team. The names of those who have written or edited material are clearly indicated elsewhere, but without the support of many other people it would not exist. Naming names is risky, but those worthy of particular note include: Sir Richard Thompson (College Treasurer) and Mrs Winnie Wade (Director of Education), who steered the project through committees that are traditionally described as labyrinthine, and which certainly seem so to me; and also Arthur Wadsworth (Project Co-ordinator) and Don Liu in the College Education Department office. Don is a veteran of the first edition of *Medical Masterclass*, and it would be fair to say that without his great efforts a second edition might not have seen the light of day.

John Firth DM FRCP
Editor-in-Chief

KEY FEATURES

We have created a range of icon boxes that sit among the text of the various *Medical Masterclass* modules. They are there to help you identify key information and to make learning easier and more enjoyable. Here is a brief explanation:

> **Iron-deficiency anaemia with a change in bowel habit in a middle-aged or older patient means colonic malignancy until proved otherwise.**

This icon is used to highlight points of particular importance.

> **Dietary deficiency is very rarely, if ever, the sole cause of iron-deficiency anaemia.**

This icon is used to indicate common or important drug interactions, pitfalls of practical procedures, or when to take symptoms or signs particularly seriously.

NEPHROLOGY

Authors:

AC Fry, JD Gillmore, PH Maxwell, CA O'Callaghan and
SA Summers

Editor:

PH Maxwell

Editor-in-Chief:

JD Firth

1.1 History-taking

1.1.1 Dipstick haematuria

Letter of referral to the renal outpatient clinic

Dear Doctor,

Re: Mr Charles Oatway, aged 43 years

This airline pilot was found to have a positive urine dipstick test for blood at an insurance medical. Repeat testing confirms this and also shows a trace of protein. He has no symptoms. His BP is 142/94 mmHg and there are no other abnormalities on examination. I would be grateful for your advice regarding diagnosis and management.

Yours sincerely,

TABLE 1 DIFFERENTIAL DIAGNOSIS OF HAEMATURIA[1]			
Type of pathology	Source of bleeding	Common	Other causes
Benign	Kidney	Glomerulonephritis, especially IgA nephropathy Thin membrane disease/benign familial haematuria	Interstitial nephritis Adult polycystic kidney disease Alport's syndrome Loin pain haematuria syndrome Papillary necrosis
	Urinary tract/ bladder	Urinary tract infection Benign prostatic disease Urinary stone	
Malignant	Anywhere in urinary tract	Bladder cancer	Hypernephroma Papillary renal carcinoma

1. Also consider trauma and gynaecological bleeding.

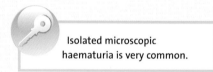

Isolated microscopic haematuria is very common.

The clinical approach depends on the age of the patient (Fig. 1):

- In a young person, haematuria is usually glomerular in origin –

Introduction

Everyone has some red blood cells in their urine. Urine dipstick tests are very sensitive and are capable of detecting concentrations of red blood cells at the upper limit of the normal range for red cell excretion. Positive urine dipstick tests for blood occur in 2.5–13% of men, and in most cases this is not associated with significant disease. Recognised causes of haematuria are shown in Table 1.

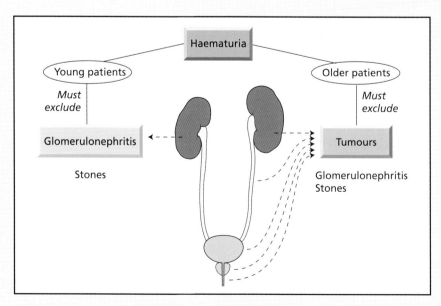

▲**Fig. 1** The approach to the investigation of haematuria depends on the age of the patient.

most frequently as a result of IgA nephropathy – and tumours are rare.

- In an elderly patient, tumours within the kidney or urinary tract are an important cause.

- Stones can cause haematuria at any age.

> - In older patients (>45 years) with haematuria, the first priority is to identify or exclude malignancy in the urinary tract.
> - In younger patients, malignancy is very infrequent and a glomerular cause (eg IgA nephropathy or thin membrane disease) is more likely.

History of the presenting problem
Although the patient is said to be asymptomatic, it is worth asking about the following symptoms.

Have you ever seen blood in your urine, and if so when?
Blood present at the start of micturition usually comes from the urethra or prostate; that at the end of the stream from the bladder. Blood clots are unusual with glomerular bleeding. Episodes of frank haematuria, especially occurring at the same time as, or just after, a mild upper respiratory tract infection, suggest IgA nephropathy, as does frank haematuria followed by persistent microscopic haematuria. However, remember that frank haematuria also occurs with stones and tumours.

Have you had any pain in the loins, abdomen, groins or genitalia?
Ask about previous pain in the loins, abdomen, groins and external genitalia. Pain is consistent with stones or tumours, polycystic kidney disease, loin pain haematuria

syndrome, renal infection or infarction. Painless haematuria is consistent with tumours, glomerulonephritis, interstitial nephritis or a bleeding disorder.

Other relevant history

General history
Ask about the following.

- Recent trauma or heavy exercise, which can cause haematuria on dipstick testing.

- Joint pains or skin rashes, which would suggest a multisystem disorder (eg systemic vasculitis).

- A sore throat or other recent infection, raising the possibility of a postinfective glomerulonephritis (when haematuria typically occurs 2 weeks after the sore throat, rather than at the same time).

Urinary symptoms
Ask about any dysuria or increased urinary frequency, which would suggest infection. Also ask about poor urinary stream or hesitancy, or poor flow and dribbling, either of which suggest prostatic or bladder pathology. Ask the patient if he has ever passed stones, grit or gravel in the urine.

Family history
Ask if anyone in the family has had kidney problems (eg polycystic kidney disease or Alport's syndrome). Other important inherited causes of haematuria include sickle cell disease and sickle trait. Many patients with haemophilia or von Willebrand's disease experience microscopic or frank haematuria.

Travel history
Ask if the patient has travelled to areas where *Schistosoma haematobium* is prevalent. Infection

can cause urinary tract granulomas and tumours.

Drug history
Ask specifically about analgesics, which can cause papillary necrosis and therefore haematuria. However, note that this does not happen with occasional use of painkillers and has become very uncommon since phenacetin was withdrawn from compound analgesic preparations. The typical story, now rarely encountered, would be of chronic headache or back pain, with the patient consuming 10–20 or more analgesic tablets per day for many years.

Plan for investigation and management
After explaining to the patient that under normal circumstances you would examine him carefully to confirm that there are no physical abnormalities apart from the raised BP, you would then plan further investigations as follows.

Dipstick urinalysis and microscopy
Proteinuria combined with haematuria suggests intrinsic renal disease, especially glomerulonephritis. Interstitial nephritis is less likely. If there is dipstick proteinuria, as in this case, then quantify this by measuring the urinary albumin/creatinine ratio or protein/creatinine ratio in a spot urine sample (or with a 24-hour collection).

Dysmorphic red cells on microscopy suggest glomerular bleeding, but morphological changes can occur as artefacts after collection of the sample; the distinction between dysmorphic cells (from the kidney) from non-dysmorphic cells (from the urinary drainage system) requires special expertise and is not a routine or reliable test in most centres. If seen, red blood cell casts indicate active glomerular inflammation.

> Red cell casts indicate active glomerular inflammation.

Blood tests

Check plasma urea and creatinine. Note or calculate the estimated glomerular filtration rate (eGFR, now routinely reported by many laboratories) based on sex and age (see Section 3.2). Remember that there can be a substantial fall in GFR before serum creatinine rises out of the normal range. If renal function is normal, BP is normal and there is no significant proteinuria, significant medical renal pathology is very unlikely.

Imaging

Image the renal tract to exclude stones and assess renal size and anatomy. The best way of doing this is to perform both of the following.

- Plain radiograph (kidneys, ureter and bladder): to look for stones.

- Ultrasonography of the urinary tract: to measure renal size (preferably length of each kidney in centimetres; don't describe as 'normal' or 'small'), look for renal masses and carefully examine the bladder wall.

Other imaging approaches can be useful in some cases: intravenous urogram to determine whether small calcific lesions are urinary stones and whether stones are causing obstruction; and CT with contrast (CT urogram) can be useful to look at the entire urinary tract for causes of haematuria.

Urine cytology and cystoscopy

In an older person (eg >45 years), arrange cystoscopy to look for a tumour in the lower urinary tract. Urine cytology may be useful if there is suspicion of malignancy, but cannot be used instead of cystoscopy since it is not sufficiently sensitive to rule out a tumour.

Renal biopsy

If there is hypertension, proteinuria and impaired renal function, glomerular disease is likely and renal biopsy may be performed to make a precise diagnosis. However, note that in cases of isolated haematuria with normal renal function a renal biopsy is not recommended since it will not lead to a change in management.

> Renal biopsy is usually indicated if there is significant proteinuria, renal impairment or unexplained systemic symptoms.

Review

See the patient in clinic with the results of the investigations and recheck renal function.

Further discussion

In many cases of microscopic haematuria, no specific diagnosis will be made unless a renal biopsy is undertaken, and even then no diagnosis will be established in 50% of cases. However, the commonest recognised cause in a young, otherwise well patient is IgA nephropathy, for which there is no specific treatment.

Any patient with persistent microscopic haematuria should have annual monitoring of BP and measurement of serum creatinine to enable calculation of eGFR. If this monitoring shows significant decline in renal function, then further investigation (eg renal biopsy) may be appropriate.

It is important to consider that giving the patient a 'renal diagnosis' may adversely affect his ability to obtain life insurance and may have implications for employment. Clearly this patient has hypertension (if the value of 142/94 mmHg is confirmed on other readings) and the fact that he has haematuria increases the argument for treating this, because strict control of BP slows the progression of renal damage in patients with renal disease. In addition, renal disease increases the risk of vascular disease and therefore the likely benefit of antihypertensive therapy.

1.1.2 Pregnancy with renal disease

Letter of referral to nephrology outpatient clinic

Dear Doctor,

Re: Mrs Patricia Redwood, aged 30 years

Please would you see this woman who has just discovered that she is pregnant for a second time. She had what was thought to be pre-eclampsia at 34 weeks in her first pregnancy 3 years ago and was induced at about 35 weeks. I am pleased to say that her baby boy is quite well. About 2 months ago we saw her for contraceptive advice because she was considering going back onto the oral contraceptive pill. Her blood pressure was 142/86 mmHg (confirmed on repeated measurement), she had positive urinalysis for protein and her creatinine was slightly elevated at 122 µmol/L. Following discussion she decided to continue to use barrier contraception and is now pregnant.

> I think she almost certainly has mild chronic kidney disease and would be grateful for your advice.
>
> Yours sincerely,

> **A creatinine outside the normal range is often dismissed as mildly elevated: remember that it equates to loss of about 50% of normal glomerular filtration rate (GFR) for age and weight.**

Introduction

Pre-eclampsia is the most common medical complication of pregnancy, affecting 5–7% of previously healthy women. Pre-existing renal disease increases the risk of pre-eclampsia, and in women with pre-eclampsia it is easy to overlook evidence of pre-existing renal disease.

Pregnancy in women with kidney disease may result in a worsening of renal function and is associated with increased fetal morbidity and mortality. When counselling women with renal impairment, one has to consider the risk to both the mother and the fetus/baby.

Risk of maternal renal disease to the fetus

Almost 60% of infants born to women with a baseline serum creatinine >125 µmol/L are premature and they are usually small for gestational age. There is a progressive increase in the risk of prematurity and reduced size with more marked renal insufficiency. However, advances in neonatal intensive care have improved fetal outcomes so that the survival of babies is now routine, even when born as early as 27 weeks' gestation. Chances of a successful pregnancy are around 65–85% if the pre-existing creatinine is below 175 µmol/L and 20–30% if over 250 µmol/L.

Risks of pregnancy to the mother with renal disease

As a woman's degree of renal insufficiency increases, the risk that renal function will worsen during pregnancy rises sharply, a tendency exaggerated by the presence of hypertension. Broadly, among women with renal impairment, about 15% of those with a pre-existing serum creatinine <125 µmol/L, about 40% of those with a pre-existing serum creatinine of 125–175 µmol/L and about 65% of those with a pre-existing serum creatinine >175 µmol/L experience a decline in pregnancy. As many as one in three women in the latter group require dialysis during or shortly after pregnancy. Among women with moderate or severe renal disease, the deterioration in renal function is usually irreversible.

History of the presenting problem

Was there any evidence of renal disease in the past, especially early in the course of her first pregnancy? BP and urinalysis would have been checked at the time of the first pregnancy: significant proteinuria early in the pregnancy would prove that she had renal disease before she had pre-eclampsia. It is also important to ask directly whether she has ever had her urine or blood tested at any other times. If there were urinary abnormalities in the past, this would constitute strong evidence of underlying chronic renal disease. In contrast, if the urine had been tested and showed no blood or protein, this would be consistent with a more acute renal problem.

Renal impairment of the degree described in this case is very unlikely to cause symptoms, but there may be clues that renal function is not normal, and an appropriate history may reveal clues as to what has caused renal damage. Ask the following.

- Do you have to get up at night to go to the toilet? This suggests lack of urinary concentrating ability and commonly occurs in people with renal impairment. Of course it is also quite common in people with normal kidney function, and prominent nocturia in elderly men is much more likely to be related to the prostate.

- Did you have infections in your urine as a child? Did you have trouble with wetting the bed? Either could suggest reflux nephropathy.

- Have you ever passed blood in your urine? Episodes of macroscopic haematuria would suggest IgA nephropathy.

- Does anyone in your family have a kidney problem or high BP? This could suggest autosomal-dominant polycystic kidney disease.

- Do you ever take medicines, herbal remedies or painkillers? Interstitial nephritis or (much less likely) analgesic nephropathy are possibilities (see Section 1.1.1).

- Have you had any skin rashes, trouble with your joints or eye problems? These might suggest systemic lupus erythematosus (SLE), vasculitis or interstitial nephritis.

- Have you had any other pregnancies? Spontaneous abortions might suggest an anticardiolipin antibody syndrome.

Other relevant history

The patient's feelings about her pregnancy should be gently explored. This should not be a main focus in Station 2 of PACES, although counselling a woman with significant renal disease about the risks of pregnancy could certainly feature in Station 4. However, if the conversation is led in this direction by the patient (or by the examiner), then it will be important to explain that at this level of kidney function the risks to the patient and the baby are slightly increased, that more intensive monitoring than usual will be recommended but also that the likelihood of a successful outcome for the baby is very high. At this level of renal function the pregnancy is unlikely to result in an acceleration in the course of kidney disease. Indeed, if the woman knows she wants more children in the future, then she needs to understand that kidney disease generally progresses over time, and that if her kidneys were worse the risks would be higher.

Plan for investigation and management

Investigation

Investigation of the patient (not including standard renal and obstetric investigations that have already taken place) should include the following.

- Urine dipstick for haematuria, proteinuria and glycosuria.

- Urine microscopy and culture for infection (asymptomatic bacteriuria occurs in up to 7% of pregnancies).

- Spot urinary protein/creatinine ratio or albumin/creatinine ratio for quantification of proteinuria.

- Serum creatinine to estimate GFR (remember GFR normally increases and creatinine falls in pregnancy) (Fig. 2).

- Baseline liver function tests, serum urate and lactate dehydrogenase: this patient is at increased risk of pre-eclampsia and haemolysis, elevated liver enzymes and low platelets.

- FBC and blood film: platelet count and evidence of haemolysis.

- Renal ultrasound: this might show scars, which would establish a diagnosis of reflux nephropathy, or cysts.

The history may suggest other investigations (eg immunological tests if there is any suggestion of SLE or a systemic vasculitis). Note that renal biopsy can be performed safely in pregnancy if necessary.

Investigation of the fetus (not including standard obstetric tests) should include close monitoring for intrauterine growth retardation with serial ultrasonography.

Management

Management of known renal disease in pregnancy involves:

- meticulous BP control, using drugs known to be safe in pregnancy (this will often require alteration of medication);

- avoidance of salt;

- low-dose aspirin;

- heparin if there is a high risk of thrombosis (eg nephrotic syndrome);

- antibiotic prophylaxis in those with recurrent urinary tract infections.

Further discussion

Pre-eclampsia

Pre-eclampsia is more common in first pregnancy, when with a new partner and in multiple pregnancies. It is also more common in those with renal impairment. The definitive management of pre-eclampsia is delivery of the baby, and the balance to strike is between risk to the baby (prematurity and intrauterine death) and risk to the mother (convulsions and irreversible renal impairment).

Reflux nephropathy

The incidence of vesicoureteric reflux is as high as 1 in 4 in the children of patients with reflux nephropathy. It is therefore

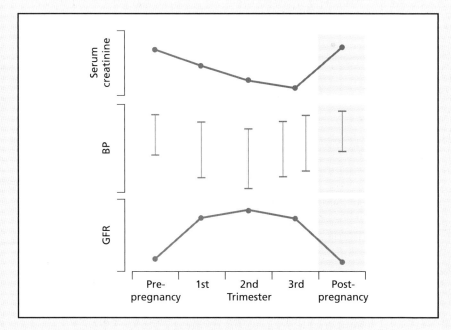

▲ **Fig. 2** Schematic diagram illustrating the changes in BP, serum creatinine and GFR during pregnancy.

recommended that children of a patient with reflux nephropathy should be screened for vesicoureteric reflux soon after birth, usually with a micturating cystogram.

Pregnancy in patients on renal replacement therapy

Pregnancy is uncommon among dialysis-dependent patients. The likelihood of successful pregnancy is substantially higher if the patient becomes pregnant before needing dialysis than if she conceives while on maintenance dialysis. The management of the pregnant dialysis patient involves increasing both dialysis dose and frequency, minimising cardiovascular instability and fluid shifts, and monitoring anticoagulation carefully. Careful monitoring of intrauterine growth is required. Renal transplantation restores fertility.

1.1.3 A swollen young woman

Letter of referral to nephrology outpatient clinic

Dear Doctor,

Re: Miss Gemma Blyth, aged 21 years

Thank you for seeing this young woman who is usually fit and well. She presented to the practice last week complaining of breathlessness and increasingly swollen legs over the past fortnight. On examination she had bilaterally oedematous legs. A urine dipstick showed proteinuria of 3+ but no haematuria. I would be grateful for your further assessment.

Yours sincerely,

TABLE 2 CAUSES OF THE NEPHROTIC SYNDROME IN ADULTS

Condition	Common	Less common
Primary glomerular disease	Minimal-change nephrotic syndrome Focal segmental glomerulosclerosis Membranous glomerulonephritis	Other glomerulonephritides[1]
Secondary glomerular disease	Diabetes mellitus Systemic lupus erythematosus (SLE) Amyloidosis Drugs, eg gold, penicillamine, NSAIDs, captopril	Malignancy related Other autoimmune rheumatic disorders Infection related[2]

1. Other glomerulonephritides are common (eg IgA nephropathy is the commonest form of glomerulonephritis) but do not typically present with nephrotic syndrome.
2. Infections are not common causes of nephrotic syndrome in the developed world, but are in other parts of the world (eg malaria).

Introduction

There are many causes of breathlessness and ankle swelling in a young woman, including cardiopulmonary conditions such as cardiomyopathy and primary pulmonary hypertension. However, in this scenario urinalysis by the GP, a very simple test, indicates that the patient is likely to be nephrotic.

Nephrotic syndrome

- Proteinuria of >3 g in a 24-hour urine collection: in the absence of the other features, this is referred to as nephrotic-range proteinuria.
- Hypoalbuminaemia: serum albumin <35 g/L.
- Peripheral oedema.

Complications of the nephrotic state include the following.

- Oedema, pleural effusions and ascites.

- Hypercoagulability: increased risk of venous and arterial thromboembolism, including renal vein thrombosis.

- Increased susceptibility to bacterial infection.

- Hypercholesterolaemia.

- Increased risk of acute renal failure, often because these patients have intravascular volume depletion.

The nephrotic syndrome results from glomerular disease and has many potential causes, as shown in Table 2.

History of the presenting problem

From the brief information in the referral letter, which describes a young woman with no past medical history, a primary glomerular disease would appear to be the most likely cause of the nephrotic syndrome. However, the patient should clearly be asked about previous personal or family history of renal disease before pursuing the history of the nephrotic state.

- Oedema: detectable oedema implies at least a 2-L increase in extracellular fluid. In the nephrotic syndrome there is often a 10-L increase in extracellular fluid volume. How long has the patient noticed this? Did it come on suddenly? Rapid onset of severe oedema is more common in minimal-change nephrotic syndrome. Has her weight changed and by how much?

- Urine: has the patient noticed a change? Heavy proteinuria causes frothy urine and this can help to date the onset of problems.

Other relevant history

Are there any clues to the cause of the nephrotic syndrome, especially the secondary glomerular diseases listed in Table 2?

- SLE: an important consideration in a young woman. Is there anything in the history to suggest this? (See *Rheumatology and Clinical Immunology*, Sections 1.1.8 and 2.4.1.)

- Minimal-change nephrotic syndrome: this often relapses and remits. Has she ever had this problem before? It may also follow an upper respiratory tract infection.

- Drugs: a range of over-the-counter and prescribed medications can cause the nephrotic syndrome (eg NSAIDs), as can intravenous drug abuse.

- Possibility of amyloidosis: any chronic inflammatory condition can be associated with secondary amyloid, eg rheumatoid arthritis or bronchiectasis.

- Possibility of malignancy: this would be a most unlikely cause of the nephrotic syndrome in a young patient, but could be in someone older. Is there any history suggestive of underlying malignancy? Carcinoma can cause membraneous nephropathy; lymphoma is associated with minimal-change nephrotic syndrome.

- Family history: Alport's syndrome (see Section 2.8.2) can be associated with nephrotic-range proteinuria, and familial forms of other glomerulonephritides are recognised (eg focal segmental glomerulosclerosis).

Is there evidence of any complications of the nephrotic state, in particular of venous thromboembolism? Ask the patient if one leg has been more swollen than the other or if she has experienced breathlessness, chest pain or haemoptysis.

Plan for investigation and management

Bedside tests

Repeat dipstick urinalysis: check proteinuria and see if microscopic haematuria is present. The latter can occur in minimal-change nephrotic syndrome, but if heavy (>1+) it suggests another diagnosis. The urine should be sent for microscopy of the spun deposit: red cell casts point to active glomerular inflammation.

> Oedema and dipstick proteinuria occur in other settings besides nephrotic syndrome, eg in congestive cardiac failure.

Blood biochemistry

Check renal and liver function and serum cholesterol.

- Serum creatinine: may be high in some types of nephrotic syndrome, eg membranous glomerulonephritis, and in elderly patients with minimal-change glomerulonephritis or renal vein thrombosis.

- Serum albumin: this is low (by definition) in those with nephrotic syndrome, and especially so in less well-nourished patients (eg the elderly), those with systemic disease (hepatic albumin synthesis reduced) and in those with gross proteinuria (eg >10 g per 24 hours).

- Cholesterol: this will be elevated and may be very high (>10 mmol/L) when proteinuria is gross.

> Nephrotic syndrome results in hypercholesterolaemia.

Quantitation of proteinuria

This is traditionally performed by measurement of the protein content of a 24-hour urinary collection but can also be estimated from a spot urine sample, either by measuring the protein/creatinine ratio or albumin/creatinine ratio (ACR). The normal ACR in adults is less than 2.5 mg/mmol (men) or 3.5 mg/ mmol (women); those with nephrotic-range proteinuria will have a value above 300 mg/mmol.

Other blood tests

- Inflammatory markers: C-reactive protein and erythrocyte sedimentation rate.

- Evidence of SLE: antinuclear factor, double-stranded DNA and further specific tests if indicated.

- Serum complement levels: C3 and/or C4 may be depressed in some forms of glomerulonephritis, particularly SLE.

- Immunoglobulins (although myeloma is extremely unlikely at this age): reduced levels of IgG and IgA are non-specific findings in those with heavy proteinuria.

- Antineutrophil cytoplasmic antibodies (ANCA): patients with ANCA-positive vasculitides can occasionally present with the nephrotic syndrome, but this would be very unusual.

- FBC and clotting screen: a renal biopsy will be needed to establish a precise diagnosis.

- Blood glucose.

Radiological tests

- CXR: this may show pleural effusions and may also reveal an underlying malignancy in elderly patients that is associated with membranous nephropathy.

- Renal ultrasonography: in most cases renal size will be normal or increased, the latter caused by oedema or infiltration (eg amyloid).

Renal biopsy

Renal biopsy is almost always recommended in order to determine the cause of nephrotic syndrome in adults. The situation is different in children, where minimal-change disease accounts for over 90% of cases and biopsy is reserved for those with renal impairment, failure to respond to corticosteroids, frequent relapses or an atypical clinical course.

Renal biopsy in the nephrotic syndrome

- In children with nephrotic syndrome, 90% of cases are due to minimal-change disease, and renal biopsy is reserved for those who do not respond to steroids and those with renal impairment or an atypical course.
- In adults, the range of causes is much wider and renal biopsy is almost always recommended.

Management

Management of any patient with the nephrotic syndrome is based on general treatment measures that can be started before a precise diagnosis is established. Once this is known, specific treatment for the underlying renal condition can be started.

General treatment measures include the following.

- Salt-restricted diet: occasionally fluid restriction is also necessary.

- Loop diuretics: usually oral furosemide or bumetanide, which may be better absorbed from the oedematous gut mucosa. Dose escalation is often needed and resistant cases may require the addition of oral metolazone or admission for intravenous diuretics, very occasionally combined with infusion of intravenous 20% human albumin.

- Daily measurement of the patient's weight is the best means of assessing fluid balance, the usual aim being to titrate diuretic dosage to achieve a loss of 0.5–1 kg per day.

- If the nephrotic patient is immobile, prophylactic subcutaneous low-molecular-weight heparin is indicated.

Specific treatment measures for the underlying kidney problem may be instituted once the result of the renal biopsy is known. In this particular clinical scenario, minimal-change disease is at the top of a list of likely diagnoses, but biopsy confirmation is necessary before steroid therapy is commenced. See Section 2.3 for details of individual conditions and their treatment.

Further discussion

Would you anticoagulate this patient?

Anticoagulation and antiplatelet agents are often used to reduce the risk of thromboembolic complications, but these should not be commenced before renal biopsy has been performed. As a general rule of thumb, low-dose aspirin (75 mg daily) is appropriate if the serum albumin is >20 g/L, and anticoagulation with warfarin (INR 2.0–3.0) would be advocated by many nephrologists if it is <20 g/L. However, note that it is not necessary to commence warfarin therapy if a rapid response to treatment is predicted, as would be the case in minimal-change disease.

Should the patient be treated for hypercholesterolaemia?

Statin therapy is often used to treat the hypercholesterolaemia of patients with nephrotic syndrome but, as with warfarin, there is little point in doing this if the underlying condition is expected to respond rapidly once treatment is initiated. However, if the nephrotic state is expected to persist for months or years (eg focal segmental glomerulosclerosis), and particularly if the patient has other cardiovascular risk factors, then statin therapy is appropriate. Statins may also have an additional antiproteinuric effect.

How can patients monitor their condition?

Usefully, many patients can be taught how to weigh themselves daily and make appropriate adjustment to diuretic dosage. They can also be supplied with urinalysis reagent strips to enable them to monitor their proteinuria. This is particularly useful for patients with minimal-change disease as it enables them to reduce their steroid dose once they are in remission (absence of protein on urine dipstick) and also to monitor for relapses.

The patient is hypertensive: how should this be treated?

The management of fluid overload by dietary salt restriction and diuretics may be adequate for treating hypertension. If the nephrotic state persists and hypertension is still present, then the agents of choice are angiotensin-converting enzyme (ACE) inhibitors because of their additional effect in reducing proteinuria. Angiotensin receptor blockers have a similar effect and can be used if ACE inhibitors are not tolerated. A BP target of 125/75 mmHg or less is appropriate as it reduces the risk of progressive loss of renal function.

Why are nephrotic patients more susceptible to infection?

The loss of antibodies (especially IgG) and complement components in the urine impair the response of the host to infection, particularly to encapsulated bacteria. Bacteria also thrive in areas of oedematous tissue where skin fragility allows easy entry.

1.1.4 Rheumatoid arthritis with swollen legs

Letter of referral to nephrology outpatient clinic

Dear Doctor,

Re: Mrs Edna Smith, aged 60 years

Thank you for seeing this woman with a long-standing history of rheumatoid arthritis, for which she has had various treatments. Over the last 2 or 3 months she has noticed progressively increasing swelling of her ankles. On dipstick urinalysis she has proteinuria 3+ (on two occasions). I have checked her biochemistry: her creatinine is elevated (170 µmol/L) and her albumin is low (17 g/dL). Both were normal 2 years ago. I would be grateful for your advice as to the cause of this and regarding her management.

Yours sincerely,

Introduction

This woman almost certainly has nephrotic syndrome, which could be confirmed by measuring her 24-hour urinary protein excretion or estimating the protein/creatinine or albumin/creatinine ratio in a spot sample. Many different pathological processes in the glomerulus can cause this clinical syndrome (see Table 2), and in adults a renal biopsy will almost certainly be indicated to establish which of these is present in order to guide prognosis and to determine whether specific treatment (eg corticosteroids for minimal-change nephrotic syndrome) is possible. The history provides clues as to the underlying glomerular process and is crucial in determining what therapeutic interventions and investigations will be indicated before the biopsy.

An immediate issue in this case is that the patient clearly has impaired renal function: is this stable or is it deteriorating? It may be that previous monitoring indicates that the problem is long-standing and stable, but a diagnosis needs to be made rapidly if it is not. If you are not sure about this, then you should either arrange for the serum creatinine to be measured again (to ensure there is no acute deterioration) or see the patient promptly to arrange investigation.

Renal failure is best avoided

Remember that a single measurement of creatinine does not tell you whether renal function is stable or deteriorating rapidly. If there is any doubt, re-check the creatinine a few days later; if it is rising, then the tempo of the investigation should be very rapid.

History of the presenting problem

Most of the issues discussed in Section 1.1.3 are equally applicable

here, but there should be particular emphasis on the following.

- Is there anything to suggest chronic renal disease? As mentioned above, a previous serum creatinine measurement would be invaluable, but have there been any previous abnormalities on urinalysis? A history of hypertension might also suggest a long-standing renal problem.

- Drugs: what medications is the patient taking now and what has she taken in the past? Ask specifically about over-the-counter drugs: patients do not always count them as medicines. In a patient with rheumatoid arthritis, remember particularly that NSAIDs can cause minimal-change nephrotic syndrome (and also acute and chronic interstitial nephritis, although these are not causes of nephrotic syndrome) and that penicillamine and gold can both cause membranous nephropathy.

- Activity of arthritis: how bad and for how long? As a generalisation, the longer and the more active the arthritis, the greater the chance of secondary amyloidosis.

- Features that might suggest malignancy: nephrotic syndrome, particularly when caused by membranous glomerulonephritis, can be a complication of malignancy in the older patient. Is there any evidence of this? Has there been any weight loss? Has her bowel habit changed?

- The presence of worsened constitutional symptoms with joint pains, rashes or night sweats might indicate the development of a vasculitis as a complication of rheumatoid arthritis.

Plan for investigation and management

The investigations described in Section 1.1.3 will be relevant in this case, with particular note of the following.

- Is creatinine rising? If it is, then renal biopsy is needed without delay.

- Serum immunoglobulins, serum and urine electrophoresis: myeloma and other plasma cell dyscrasias are common in this age group.

- Renal ultrasonography: are there two normal-sized unobstructed kidneys? If both kidneys are small (<9 cm in length), this indicates chronic disease and biopsy is much less likely to reveal a treatable diagnosis.

- CXR: any suggestion of malignancy?

- Does the patient have a low threshold for investigation of gastrointestinal symptoms? This might indicate malignancy.

- Check iron status and faecal occult bloods, pursuing gastrointestinal investigation if there is evidence of iron deficiency and/or gastrointestinal blood loss.

- Renal biopsy will certainly be required to establish a diagnosis in this case.

Although a renal biopsy will almost certainly be required in a patient with nephrotic syndrome, a proper history and examination are still essential.

General management of the nephrotic syndrome will be as described in Section 1.1.3; specific management will be determined by the precise diagnosis.

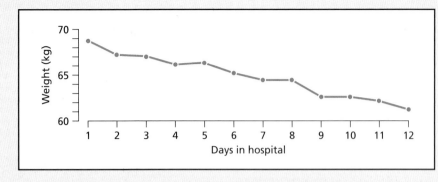

▲ **Fig. 3** Weight chart of a patient with nephrotic syndrome treated with intravenous diuretics (furosemide 160 mg once daily). Weight decreases at a satisfactory rate (8 kg over 12 days in hospital).

Further discussion

Diuretics

Massive oedema cannot be ignored and needs relief, but note the dangers of overdiuresis, particularly in older patients who can easily feel totally exhausted, develop postural hypotension with risk of falls and suffer acute deterioration in renal function.

- Aim for 0.5–1.0 kg weight loss per day (Fig. 3).

- Reduce the diuretic dose if this is being exceeded.

- Tell patients, particularly those given the powerful diuretic metolazone, to check their weight daily at home and omit/stop diuretics if they lose more than 1 kg/day.

Furosemide is sequestered by albumin in the renal tubule, so high doses are often required in the nephrotic syndrome.

Angiotensin-converting enzyme inhibitors

Any patient with proteinuric renal disease and renal impairment will benefit from an angiotensin-converting enzyme inhibitor to reduce proteinuria and the rate of

progression of renal failure (see Section 2.1.2).

Statins

Lipids are invariably deranged in nephrotic syndrome, but the relationship to cardiovascular risk is not yet clear. There are animal experiments to suggest that lipid-lowering drugs may alter the course of progressive renal failure, but there are no reliable human data concerning this. Statins reduce cholesterol effectively and should be considered if the nephrotic state persists.

Anti-inflammatories and analgesics

Remember that NSAIDs cause a predictable fall in glomerular filtration rate. This does not generally cause clinical problems in those with normal renal function, but can do so when kidney function is impaired. If at all possible, this woman should avoid using them and take regular simple analgesics, eg paracetamol, for her musculoskeletal pains. Also note that opiates can accumulate in those with renal impairment, and regular doses of co-proxamol and similar agents could lead to nausea and drowsiness in this case.

Thrombotic tendency

There should be a high index of clinical suspicion when symptoms that could represent a thrombotic complication occur. Of particular note is renal vein thrombosis, which can present with:

- flank/back pain;

- increasing proteinuria;

- haematuria (increased microscopic and sometimes macroscopic);

- rising creatinine.

If suspected, the diagnosis can be made by Doppler ultrasonography (requires considerable technical skill), CT or renal arteriography (looking at the venous phase). If any thrombosis does occur, then anticoagulation should continue for as long as the patient remains nephrotic.

1.1.5 A blood test shows moderate renal failure

Letter of referral to nephrology outpatient clinic

Dear Doctor,

Re: Mr Peter Ward, aged 38 years

This garage mechanic came to see me with a vague history of fatigue a week ago. He was hypertensive (160/104 mmHg). His blood tests showed Na$^+$ 134 mmol/L, K$^+$ 4.8 mmol/L, urea 21 mmol/L, creatinine 370 µmol/L, haemoglobin 10.1 g/dL, mean cell volume (MCV) 89 fL, white blood cell count (WBC) 4.2 × 10^9/L and platelets 254 × 10^9/L.

Please consider investigation of his stage 4 chronic kidney disease and advise concerning further management.

Yours sincerely,

Introduction

The emphasis in the history-taking station of PACES is clearly on conditions that present to medical outpatient clinics, but how do you know that this is chronic renal failure? The answer is that you cannot be sure from the information provided: this could be acute renal failure that is potentially reversible and you must recognise this in your approach to, and discussion of, the case.

How will you establish whether the renal failure is acute or chronic?

- Further values of creatinine are required: any previous blood tests would be useful, and urgently obtain a current creatinine sample to check that renal function is not deteriorating rapidly.

- Renal ultrasound is very important: reduced renal size would prove that there is chronic kidney disease, but if this is the case there may still be an element of acute-on-chronic renal failure.

> Take an exhaustive approach before concluding that renal failure is chronic.

History of the presenting problem

How long has the patient had renal failure?

Renal failure does not produce dramatic symptoms. Ask specifically about the following.

- Energy: many patients with advanced renal failure simply notice that they are exhausted all the time.

- Concentration: uraemia causes mental dulling.

- Breathing: anaemia may cause breathlessness on exertion and

fluid retention can cause pulmonary oedema.

- Appetite, nausea or vomiting: uraemia causes anorexia and, when advanced, nausea and vomiting.

- Nocturia: the normal kidneys elaborate concentrated urine at night; they cannot do this when they fail and this leads to nocturia, a significant symptom in a young man or woman (prostatism being a much more common cause in older men).

- Itching: a symptom of uraemia.

How long has the patient had a renal problem?

Are there any clues from the past? Take a detailed history of any contact with medical services. Approach this from several angles by asking the following questions.

- Have you ever had kidney disease or swelled up in the past?

- Has anyone ever taken your BP before and told you it was high?

- Have you ever had your urine tested?

- Have you ever had a medical for work or insurance purposes?

- Have you ever had a blood test or had blood taken? (Knowing that the creatinine was normal or abnormal 3 months ago would be a crucial piece of information.)

What is the cause of renal failure?

Explore all avenues that might suggest a diagnosis or aetiological factor; in particular note the following.

- Recent illnesses such as diarrhoea or upper respiratory tract infection, which in retrospect may have heralded the start of the illness, would favour an acute aetiology.

- Multisystem disease: any previous rashes, painful or swollen joints, eye pain, haemoptysis, numbness, weakness or tingling may point to a systemic inflammatory illness such as vasculitis (see Section 2.7).

- Urinary tract symptoms: childhood recurrent infections or enuresis suggest reflux nephropathy (see Section 2.4). Recurrent haematuria associated with upper respiratory tract infections could point to IgA nephropathy (see Section 2.3). Has the patient had urinary stones?

- Drug history: this should include over-the-counter medications,

illicit drugs, and traditional and herbal remedies, because all of these have been known to cause renal failure.

- Family history of kidney disease or of deafness (see Section 2.8).

Plan for investigation and management

Investigations
The key issue is to determine whether the renal failure is acute or chronic, which can only reliably be done on the basis of previous measurements of renal function or ultrasonographic demonstration of small kidneys (Fig. 4).

Certain chronic renal failure If renal failure is chronic, then the investigations shown in Table 3 are required. Further pursuit of a specific diagnosis is likely to have a poor yield, make little difference in terms of subsequent management and potentially risk complications. In particular, a renal biopsy would not be useful.

A renal biopsy is contraindicated in patients with small kidneys; it is technically difficult, has a high complication rate and the pathological findings are non-specific.

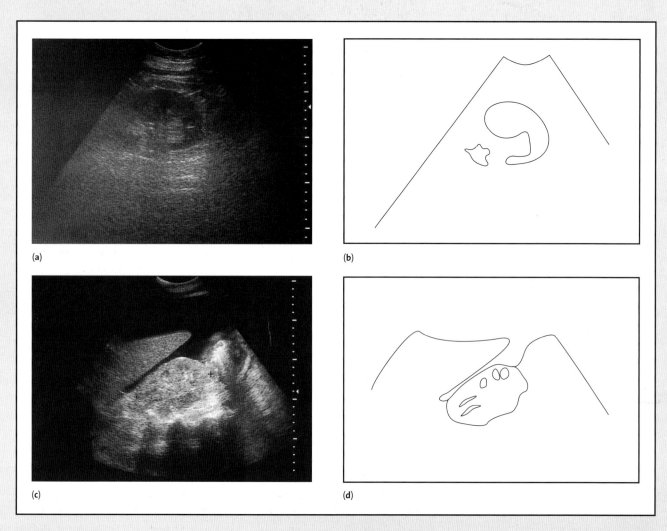

(a)

(b)

(c)

(d)

▲ **Fig. 4** Renal tract ultrasonography showing (**a**, **b**) a normal kidney and (**c**, **d**) a small hyperechoic kidney without clear corticomedullary differentiation consistent with chronic renal failure.

TABLE 3 INVESTIGATIONS IN THE EVALUATION OF CHRONIC RENAL FAILURE

Investigation	Purpose
FBC and haematinics	Evaluation of contributory factors to anaemia
Calcium, phosphate and PTH	Assess degree of secondary or tertiary hyperparathyroidism
Lipid profile	Cardiovascular disease is accelerated by CRF and is the main cause of death
Hepatitis B and C serology, HIV testing (after counselling)	Positive patients will need specific haemodialysis arrangements. All patients who are HBsAg-negative should be vaccinated against hepatitis B
ECG and CXR	Evidence of LVH and/or IHD

CRF, chronic renal failure; IHD, ischaemic heart disease; LVH, left ventricular hypertrophy; PTH, parathyroid hormone.

TABLE 4 INVESTIGATIONS TO HELP EXCLUDE A POSSIBLE ACUTE AETIOLOGY

Investigation	A normal result is likely to exclude the following diagnoses
FBC and blood film	Haemolytic–uraemic syndrome
CRP	Any inflammatory disease
Serum and urine electrophoresis	Myeloma
Anti-GBM	Anti-GBM disease
ANCA ± ELISA for anti-MPO or anti-PR3	ANCA-associated vasculitides
C3, C4, autoantibody screen	Connective tissue diseases, SLE, MCGN, cryoglobulinaemia, infection-related glomerulonephritis

ANCA, antineutrophil cytoplasmic antibodies; CRP, C-reactive protein; ELISA, enzyme-linked immunosorbent assay; GBM, glomerular basement membrane; MCGN, mesoangiocapillary glomerulonephritis; MPO, myeloperoxidase; PR3, proteinase 3; SLE, systemic lupus erythematosus.

Uncertain diagnosis In some cases it is not certain whether renal failure is acute or chronic. It is then necessary to carry out tests to exclude potentially reversible diagnoses (Table 4), and in some cases a renal biopsy may be indicated even if the kidneys are reduced in size.

If there is any doubt about the findings on ultrasonography or if they seem at odds with the clinical setting, ask an experienced radiologist to repeat the study or consider CT, which is less operator dependent (Fig. 5).

Management

There is no specific treatment for chronic renal failure, but particularly note the following.

- Angiotensin-converting enzyme inhibitors and angiotensin receptor antagonists slow the progression of chronic renal disease, but remember to check serum creatinine 7–10 days after initiating treatment to ensure there is no acute deterioration (a rise of up to 20% can be tolerated, but a more substantial rise suggests the possibility of renal arterial disease and should lead to the drug being stopped and consideration given to imaging the renal vessels). Also remember that these drugs may exacerbate the common tendency to hyperkalaemia in those with advanced chronic kidney disease.

- Cardiovascular morbidity and mortality are extremely high in patients with renal impairment. All require a full cardiovascular risk assessment, followed by attempts to deal with reversible factors such as smoking, hypertension and lipids.

- Treatment of anaemia, usually with erythropoietin (see Section 2.1).

- Treatment of hyperparathyroidism (see Section 2.1).

- Dietary advice: may be appropriate and is most commonly to restrict potassium intake.

Further discussion

Telling a patient that he or she has chronic renal failure and will need long-term renal replacement therapy can be devastating. The reaction is often similar to that seen in bereavement, with progression through shock, grief and denial before reaching acceptance. Accurate information and continued support are essential and best provided by a team that includes doctors, dietitians and specialist nurses. Breaking of bad news such as this may feature in PACES Station 4, but it will also be important to demonstrate an appropriately sympathetic way of talking to the patient in a Station 2 scenario such as this (as is certainly the case in routine clinical practice).

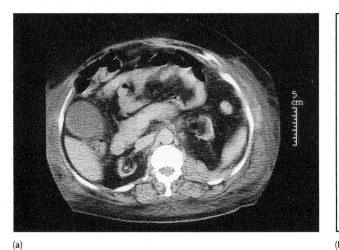
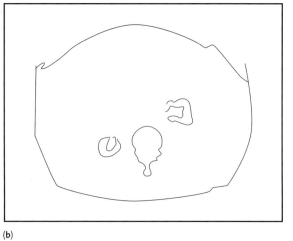

(a)   (b)

▲**Fig. 5** Abdominal CT scan demonstrating small kidneys with little renal cortex, consistent with chronic renal failure.

1.1.6 Diabetes with impaired renal function

Letter of referral to nephrology outpatient clinic

Dear Doctor,

Re: Mr David Marshall, aged 55 years

Please would you see this man who has had diabetes for the last 10 years, treated with metformin and gliclazide. He is not a frequent attender at the surgery, but he came in last week to consult me about erectile dysfunction. I did some blood tests which showed that his creatinine was elevated at 160 μmol/L. I would be grateful for your advice about his management.

Yours sincerely,

Introduction

Diabetic nephropathy is the commonest cause of end-stage renal failure in the Western world and its incidence is increasing. In the USA, more than 35% of people with end-stage renal failure have diabetes, and up to 20% of type 1 diabetics eventually develop end-stage renal disease. Only about 10% of patients with type 2 diabetes develop end-stage renal disease, but due to the higher prevalence of type 2 diabetes (5–10 fold) they are the commonest diabetics treated for renal failure. Genetic factors appear to play an important role in the development of diabetic nephropathy and some ethnic groups, particularly African-Americans, persons of Hispanic origin, Native Americans and Indo-Asians, are predisposed to renal disease as a complication of diabetes. Interestingly, the likelihood of developing new diabetic nephropathy declines 20 years after the onset of type 1 diabetes, suggesting that some individuals are relatively protected.

The initial aim in dealing with this case must be to determine whether the overall history is consistent with diabetic nephropathy or if there are any features to suggest an alternative diagnosis. Between 10 and 30% of patients with diabetes who have renal disease are discovered to have a non-diabetic cause of nephropathy.

The duration of diabetes is important. In general, the risk of diabetic nephropathy is higher when the duration of diabetes is up to 20 years, although type 2 diabetics may have had the condition for several years before becoming aware of it. Renal impairment is preceded by hyperfiltration, microalbuminuria and macroalbuminuria. Hypertension is usually present early in the course of the disease. Diabetic nephropathy is more common if diabetic control has been poor, and the condition is unusual in the absence of any diabetic retinopathy.

> Diabetic nephropathy is very common, but diabetics with renal impairment may have another diagnosis, for example obstructive uropathy, plasma cell dyscrasia or renovascular disease.

History of the presenting problem

Related to renal disease

Although the referral letter suggests that the patient has no systemic symptoms other than erectile dysfunction and the strong suspicion is that he has diabetic nephropathy, it is important to probe the history thoroughly as he may have renal failure due to a cause other than diabetes. Crucially, this might be acute and potentially reversible. The questions relating to past medical history and potential causes of renal failure listed in Section 1.1.5 would all be appropriate in this case.

Related to diabetes

It is important to ask about the following.

- Monitoring of diabetes: how is the patient assessing his diabetic control? Occasional patients are still using urine testing, which is certainly inappropriate in the presence of renal disease. How often is he checking his blood sugar, at what times of day and what values have been obtained? Part of the management of diabetic nephropathy is to optimise diabetic control.

- Hypertension: has his BP been checked regularly and does he know what readings have been obtained? Obtaining good control of BP will be crucial in this case, whatever the cause of renal impairment.

- Retinopathy: has the patient ever been told there is a problem with his eyes? Are his eyes checked regularly for signs of diabetic damage? Has he ever had laser treatment?

- Neuropathy: does he get any numbness, pins and needles or funny feelings in his toes and/or fingers, which would indicate peripheral neuropathy?

- Macrovascular disease: has he suffered from angina/myocardial infarction, transient ischaemic attacks/amaurosis fugax/stroke or intermittent claudication? If these are prominent features, then renovascular disease requires consideration.

- Feet: has he had ulcers, which could be caused by neuropathy, ischaemia or both?

> Diabetic nephropathy with renal impairment is almost always associated with some diabetic retinopathy. If this is not present, you need to seek another renal diagnosis.

Other relevant history

It will be important to obtain a proper smoking history: the combination of diabetes, renal impairment and smoking is devastating to health.

Plan for investigation and management

Investigations aim to determine whether diabetic nephropathy is the most likely cause of the renal impairment and should include the following.

Urine tests

Dipstick testing would typically reveal significant proteinuria (2+ or more) but no haematuria in a patient with renal impairment due to diabetic nephropathy. Microscopic haematuria and the absence of proteinuria are both unusual in diabetic nephropathy, and either of these findings should raise the possibility of another diagnosis. If microscopic haematuria is observed, then urine microscopy should be performed: the presence of red cell casts would strongly suggest that diabetic nephropathy was not the diagnosis. Quantitate proteinuria by estimation of urinary albumin/creatinine ratio (or protein/creatinine ratio or 24-hour urinary protein excretion).

Blood tests

- Serum creatinine to determine the current level of renal function and rate of decline (if previous values are available).

- Cholesterol and triglycerides to help quantitate cardiovascular risk.

- HbA$_{1c}$ to determine medium-term glycaemic control.

- FBC: deficiency of erythropoietin and renal anaemia often occur relatively early in the course of diabetic renal disease.

To rule out other causes of renal impairment, consider serum (and urine) protein electrophoresis (plasma cell dyscrasias are a common cause of renal impairment in this age group) and also immunological tests including antineutrophil cytoplasmic antibodies, antinuclear factor and complement to exclude immunologically mediated renal disease (but note that hypocomplementaemia may be a feature of cholesterol embolisation syndrome).

Urinary tract ultrasonography

In contrast with most other causes of chronic renal failure, renal size is often normal in patients with diabetic nephropathy. Disparity in renal size (>1.5 cm difference in kidney length) may suggest renovascular disease or reflux nephropathy, and irregular renal outlines may indicate congenital dysplasia/reflux nephropathy/chronic pyelonephritis. Check that the patient's bladder empties properly: neglected obstruction is a common cause of renal impairment in elderly men.

Other tests

- Perform an ECG to look for evidence of previous myocardial infarction or left ventricular hypertrophy.

- Conduct magnetic resonance angiography if the history, examination findings or ultrasonography suggest renovascular disease, but only if you would proceed to angiography and renal artery angioplasty/ stenting if renal artery stenosis is demonstrated.

- Consider renal biopsy if there are any features to suggest a non-diabetic cause of the renal impairment other than renovascular disease, eg an absence of previous proteinuria or retinopathy, sudden onset of nephrotic syndrome or the presence of red cell casts on urine microscopy.

> If the history and clinical findings are consistent with diabetic nephropathy, it is usually not appropriate to undertake a renal biopsy.

Management

Aside from issues common to all diabetics, eg regular eye and foot checks, issues of particular importance in this case include the following.

- Review of current drug therapy: metformin can cause lactic acidosis in advanced renal impairment and should probably be discontinued in this case.

- BP control: the most important determinant of the rate of progression of diabetic renal impairment. BP should be maintained as low as tolerated (<125/75 mmHg if achievable without unacceptable side effects) using an angiotensin-converting enzyme (ACE) inhibitor followed by an angiotensin II receptor blocking agent in combination. Other antihypertensive agents may need to be added. Modest restriction of salt intake can help to achieve BP targets.

- Management of cardiovascular risk: encourage the patient to stop smoking (if necessary) and take exercise; reduce cholesterol using a statin.

- Glycaemic control: improvement may slow the progression of early diabetic nephropathy but is less important than BP control.

> Management of diabetic nephropathy is with ACE inhibitors and angiotensin II receptor blockers, often in combination, aiming for BP <125/75 mmHg.

> Management of cardiovascular risk and macrovascular arterial disease is essential in patients with diabetic nephropathy.

Further discussion

Blockade of the renin–angiotensin axis

Even in the absence of hypertension, there is evidence that progression of diabetic renal failure is slowed by ACE inhibitors and angiotensin II receptor blockers. Their use in combination is more effective than either class of agent alone.

Renovascular disease

Renovascular disease may coexist with diabetic nephropathy and should be considered in all diabetic patients with renal impairment. Hence, as stated in Section 1.1.5, it is always important to check renal function 7–10 days after starting an ACE inhibitor or angiotensin II receptor blocker to ensure there is no acute deterioration. The decision to undertake angioplasty and stenting of stenotic lesions in renovascular disease needs careful consideration and is the subject of ongoing trials.

Prognosis of diabetic nephropathy

Diabetic nephropathy is usually inexorably progressive and patients with diabetes have a reduced survival rate compared with other causes of renal failure. Once renal replacement therapy is instituted, mortality among type 2 diabetics is up to 25% per year.

1.1.7 Atherosclerosis and renal failure

Letter of referral to nephrology outpatient clinic

Dear Doctor,

Re: Mr Harry Scott, aged 65 years

Please would you see this man? He is a heavy smoker and has been hypertensive for 10 years. One month ago he was admitted to hospital with chest pain and a suspected acute coronary syndrome. His troponin was not elevated, he was started on an angiotensin-converting enzyme (ACE) inhibitor and he was put on the waiting list for a coronary angiogram (not yet done). I was asked to check his renal function, and this shows that his creatinine, which was normal when he was discharged from hospital, is now markedly elevated at 260 μmol/L. What should be done about this?

Yours sincerely,

peripheral vascular disease, so probe carefully for symptoms suggesting intermittent claudication, amaurosis fugax or transient ischaemic attacks.

> The best predictor of renovascular disease is evidence of peripheral vascular disease.

Introduction

Renovascular disease is an important cause of renal dysfunction and resistant hypertension. In patients with atherosclerotic renovascular disease there is usually evidence of cardiovascular, cerebrovascular and peripheral vascular disease.

History of the presenting problem

Renovascular disease

It is very likely that this man has this condition, which produces no specific symptoms. However, it is worth asking the following questions.

- Has he felt dizzy and been hypotensive since starting the ACE inhibitor? Hypertension related to renovascular disease often responds dramatically to ACE inhibitors.

- Has he had episodes of sudden-onset severe shortness of breath suggesting 'flash pulmonary oedema'? Renovascular disease can cause such problems, which may have been better since starting on the ACE inhibitor, but this is uncommon and episodes of breathlessness are generally much more likely to have a cardiac explanation.

Other vascular disease

There is a strong association between renovascular disease and

Other causes of acute renal impairment

It is very important to consider other possible causes by pursuing the following aspects of the history.

- Prerenal failure: find out if the patient has had any illness since discharge from hospital that would predispose him to this, for example diarrhoea/vomiting or any symptoms that suggest volume depletion (eg postural dizziness).

- Urinary obstruction: has he had any difficulty passing urine, any back pain, any haematuria or passed any stones?

- Renal inflammatory condition: has he felt unwell in any way? Systemic features (fever, etc.) are not expected with renovascular disease and could support a diagnosis of prerenal failure or a renal inflammatory condition. Has he noticed any skin rash, particularly on the feet? This may suggest cholesterol emboli, or if it is more widespread may be due to drug hypersensitivity associated with acute interstitial nephritis. Relating to the latter, has he taken any other new drugs (including over-the-counter medicines, the commonest cause of acute interstitial nephritis)? Has he had aching muscles? He will almost certainly be on a statin and could have developed rhabdomyolysis. Has he had any symptoms that

might suggest a multisystem disorder (eg joint pains or nasal/sinus problems)?

Other relevant history

Patients at risk of renal atherosclerosis have the same risk factors as patients with atherosclerosis at other sites: he smokes, but is he diabetic?

Plan for investigation and management

Given the high index of clinical suspicion that this patient has renovascular disease with acute deterioration in renal function caused by the ACE inhibitor, your immediate action should be to stop this drug, which may lead to improvement in renal function.

Urinalysis

Significant proteinuria (more than 1+) and/or haematuria (more than trace) would not be expected in renovascular disease; if present, consider cholesterol embolism or other renal inflammatory condition.

Blood tests

- Check renal function: is this getting worse, has it stabilised or is it improving?

- Check FBC and clotting screen (this man may require an interventional procedure).

- Inflammatory markers and myeloma/autoimmune/vasculitis screens depending on clinical suspicion.

Urinary tract ultrasonography

This is the first-line imaging test in any instance of unexplained acute deterioration in renal function. In this case look particularly for a discrepancy in renal length >2 cm, which is strongly predictive of renovascular disease. Ultrasound will also exclude obstruction.

Urinary tract ultrasonography should be performed urgently in any patient with unexplained acute deterioration in renal function.

Imaging for renal artery stenosis

The standard screening test is magnetic resonance angiography, proceeding to angiography, which remains the gold standard for diagnosis and also enables therapeutic angioplasty/stenting.

Management

The following are essential.

- Stop smoking: aside from general vascular considerations, smoking is an independent risk factor for the progression of renal disease.

- Aspirin and cholesterol lowering (statin) to reduce cardiovascular risk, although it is not proven that they influence progression of renovascular disease.

If renovascular disease is proven, then consider dilatation and/or stenting.

Further discussion

Which patients should have occlusive renal artery lesions dilated and stented?

This is controversial. Although benefit is unproven, it is technically feasible to dilate and to stent discrete stenoses in the renal artery. Most nephrologists would recommend angioplasty for:

- bilateral stenoses with acute deterioration in renal function, especially in the context of ACE inhibition;

- small kidney on one side and tight stenosis affecting the opposite kidney;

- episodes of flash pulmonary oedema not explained by left ventricular dysfunction.

1.1.8 Recurrent loin pain

Letter of referral to nephrology outpatient clinic

Dear Doctor,

Re: Mr Lawrence Perkins, aged 46 years

This man, with no past medical history of note, has had several episodes over the past few years of severe right-sided flank pain, following which he has sometimes noticed gravel in his urine. He recently had a particularly severe attack when away on holiday that took him to the Emergency Department of the local hospital, where he required diclofenac and pethidine to ease the pain. Stimulated by this, he came to see me. I would be grateful for your advice as to what we should do about his kidney stones.

Yours sincerely,

Introduction

Urinary tract stones are a common problem. They typically present when they enter the ureter, causing colic and/or obstruction. If present in the renal pelvis, they make urinary tract infection much harder to eradicate. Aside from confirming the history of loin pain and passage of gravel/stones in this case, the history must focus on the well-recognised predisposing factors for stone formation. In deciding on the correct treatment, it will be very important to determine the chemical composition of the patient's stones

(if possible) because different types of stone require different treatments.

History of the presenting problem

To confirm that the patient has had pain from urinary stones

Renal colic is usually of sudden onset and very painful; it occurs typically in the loin, radiating to the suprapubic area, and is often spasmodic in nature, occurring in waves lasting from 30 minutes to 1 hour. Nausea and vomiting are common symptoms. The patient may notice haematuria, and dysuria is common when stones are in the bladder or passing through the urethra. Strong analgesia may be required. As in this case, an episode of pain followed by passing a stone or grit in the urine establishes the diagnosis.

Previous episodes

There will often be a previous history of urinary stone disease, as seems to be the case here. Ask the patient directly whether he has had any tests done for these in the past: 'Have you ever had X-rays or scans done to look at the kidneys or bladder? Have you ever seen an urologist or a kidney doctor?' In routine clinical practice it would be not at all uncommon for a patient not to have mentioned these to the GP, and in PACES the instruction to the patient could well say 'Do not mention this unless asked directly'.

Other relevant history

Ask about the following risk factors for urinary stones.

- Fluid intake: ask the patient what he drinks over 24 hours on a typical day. Go through this carefully: 'When you get up, what do you drink at breakfast, and then during the morning, and at lunch?' Low fluid intake is a major risk factor for formation of all types of stones.

- Diet: high oxalate intake (spinach, tea, nuts and chocolate) and high protein intake predispose to calcium stones (the commonest sort).

- Time in hot climates: increased perspiration leads to decreased urine output, hence stones are much commoner in hot climates. This might be relevant in this case if the man had spent 10 years working in the tropics. Once stones form, they are very slow indeed to resolve, even if the precipitating factor is removed.

- Hypertension.

- Urinary tract infections: these predispose to stones and are also more likely in those with stones.

- Gout, suggesting increased uric acid production and excretion, is a risk factor for uric acid stones.

- Drugs promoting crystalluria can rarely cause stones, eg triamterene, indinavir.

- Family history of stone disease: if many family members are affected, then obviously consider genetic causes, including medullary sponge kidney.

Also consider the following.

- Are there other symptoms suggesting hypercalcaemia and/or hyperparathyroidism (such as thirst, polyuria, abdominal pain, depression or aching bones)?

- Increased oxalate absorption from short bowel syndrome: has this patient had any intestinal surgery?

Plan for investigation and management

Examination of the urine

- Spot urine sample: check urinary pH, specific gravity and microscopy for crystals, and then

send for culture. A pH >7 with phosphate crystals is suggestive of magnesium ammonium phosphate/calcium phosphate 'infection stones'; hexagonal cystine crystals are diagnostic of cystine stones.

- Two 24-hour urine collections are required: one in a container with acid preservative for analysis of volume and excretion of creatinine, calcium, magnesium, sodium, potassium, phosphate, oxalate and citrate; the other in a plain container for analysis of volume, creatinine, pH, protein, urate and a qualitative test for cystine.

Chemical examination of the stone (if available)

Ask the patient if he has saved a stone: sometimes people do but may not volunteer this information, only revealing it if asked directly. Expect to find one of the following:

- calcium oxalate/phosphate (common and not specific);

- uric acid (uricosuria);

- cystine (cystinuria);

- magnesium ammonium phosphate, usually with calcium phosphate, suggests stones caused by chronic infection with urea-splitting bacteria.

> Always ask patients if they have saved any stone/gravel that they have passed: analysis is crucial to direct specific treatment.

Blood tests

- Check creatinine and calculate estimated glomerular filtration rate.

- Estimate sodium, potassium, calcium, magnesium, phosphate,

bicarbonate, urate, albumin and alkaline phosphatase.

- Consider measuring parathyroid hormone.

Imaging

The test to perform at the first outpatient attendance would be an abdominal radiograph of the kidneys, ureter and bladder, which would show any radio-opaque stones. The single most useful test to look for stones within the urinary tract would be an unenhanced CT of the kidneys, ureters and bladder. An intravenous urogram would offer a reasonable alternative to CT. Ultrasonography of the kidneys would be the appropriate test if obstruction were suspected, but there is nothing in the letter of referral to suggest that this is likely in this case.

Management

The management of patients with urinary stones includes general measures and specific measures based on the type of stone, where this is known.

General measures to decrease stone formation Ensure the patient:

- drinks enough water to increase urinary output at over 2000 mL daily;

- decreases animal protein intake;

- reduces dietary oxalate (spinach, tea, nuts and chocolate).

> Whatever the cause of urinary stones, get the patient to drink more.

Specific measures for specific stones These include the following.

- Calcium oxalate/phosphate stones: potassium citrate and thiazide diuretics.

- Urate stones: potassium citrate and allopurinol.

- 'Infection stones' require eradication of urinary sepsis: prolonged antibiotic therapy (3–6 months) is often required. Note that these stones are associated with alkaline urine and are not helped by giving alkalis such as potassium citrate.

- Cystine stones: penicillamine, captopril or α-mercaptopropionylglycine.

Underlying medical causes of stones, such as hyperparathyroidism, need to be treated, and chronic renal failure (if present) would require management along conventional lines (see Section 2.1).

Further discussion

What happens if a symptomatic stone doesn't pass?

Urinary obstruction must be relieved, usually by percutaneous antegrade nephrostomy. Stone removal can be effected by percutaneous endoscopic or ureteroscopic procedures, or by external shock-wave lithotripsy, depending on the site, size and type of stone and on the availability of technical expertise. Open surgery to remove urinary stones is rarely required, but remains the best option in some cases.

1.2 Clinical examination

1.2.1 Polycystic kidneys

Instruction

This patient has noticed abdominal swelling. Please examine the abdomen.

General features

Is there any evidence of renal failure or renal replacement therapy? Look in the root of the neck and below the clavicles for tunnelled dialysis catheters, or scars indicating that these may have been inserted in the past: they typically enter the internal jugular vein low down in the neck and exit the skin 3–8 cm below the clavicle in the mid-clavicular line. Look for arteriovenous fistulae in the arms to indicate treatment with haemodialysis, or scars over the forearms and in the elbows that might be due to attempts to create such fistulae.

Has the patient had neck surgery, perhaps a parathyroidectomy?

Abdominal examination

The instructions state that the abdomen will be swollen: is this symmetrical? Does it look like fluid, suggesting ascites and (most probably) a hepatological case?

Is there a Tenckhoff catheter *in situ*, indicating peritoneal dialysis treatment? Look carefully for scars: these may be from previous Tenckhoff catheters, which are inserted in the midline about 5 cm below the umbilicus and tunnelled to exit laterally, or may be related to renal transplant operations, which leave a 'hockey-stick' incision in either the right or left iliac fossa.

The most likely finding is bilateral abdominal masses, in which case it is essential to have a logical technique for distinguishing between bilateral polycystic kidneys and hepatosplenomegaly. Remember the five clinical features that can be used to do this.

1. Can you get above the masses? If yes, this indicates that they are renal; you cannot get above a liver or spleen.

2. How do the masses move on respiration? A kidney moves 'up and down'; a spleen moves 'down and across' (towards the right iliac fossa).

3. Are the masses ballotable? A kidney, being a retroperitoneal structure, will move forwards when pushed forward by fingers pressing firmly in the renal angle, but a liver or spleen will not be affected.

4. Percussion note: kidneys are resonant (usually), but the liver and spleen are dull (always).

5. Can you feel a notch? This is a feature of some spleens.

Remember that polycystic enlargement of the liver is a common finding in polycystic kidney disease, so do not be concerned if you can feel what you think is a kidney on the left side and what you think is a liver on the right: you are probably correct. Also examine the patient for inguinal hernias (or evidence of previous repair) since these are associated with polycystic kidney disease.

If asked whether you would like to extend your examination of the patient, say that you would want to check BP and perform fundoscopy looking for signs of end-organ hypertensive damage.

Polycystic kidneys range in size from barely larger than normal kidneys to being so large that they distend the abdomen. In the latter case they can be confused with ascitic distension and may be hard to feel as distinct masses.

Remember that patients with polycystic kidneys, particularly women, can have a very large polycystic liver.

Further discussion
For further discussion see Section 2.8.

1.2.2 Transplant kidney

Instructions to candidate

Examine this patient's abdomen (with hockey-stick scar in iliac fossa).

General features
Look for evidence of the following.

- An underlying condition causing renal failure: treatment or complications of diabetes, hearing impairment (Alport's syndrome), facial rash (systemic lupus erythematosus) or collapsed nasal bridge (antineutrophil cytoplasmic antibody-associated vasculitis).

- Previous renal replacement therapy: arteriovenous fistula (haemodialysis) or an abdominal scar (continuous ambulatory peritoneal dialysis catheter).

- Complications of long-standing renal impairment: parathyroidectomy scar and carpal tunnel release (dialysis-related amyloid).

Numerous features are commonly found in the general examination of transplant recipients, many of which are the direct consequence of immunosuppressive drugs.

- Steroids: 'moon face', 'buffalo hump', central obesity, acne, bruising, thin skin and striae.

- Ciclosporin: gingival hyperplasia and hirsutism.

- Sirolimus (rapamycin): mouth ulcers and acneiform rash.

- Long-standing immuno-suppression: 'field change' in skin of sun-exposed areas, typically face and backs of hands; warts; actinic keratoses; and scars from removal of squamous/basal cell carcinomas.

Abdominal examination
The typical sign is a scar in the right or left iliac fossa beneath which there is a palpable smooth mass, which may feel very superficial or may be quite deep: this is the transplanted kidney. Look carefully at the other iliac fossa for another transplant, which may be small and shrunken (a previous failed graft).

Palpate carefully for polycystic kidneys (see Section 1.2.1).

Further discussion

What are the common causes of renal failure?

- Diabetes mellitus is the commonest cause of end-stage renal failure in the UK (20–30% and increasing).

- Biopsy-proven glomerulonephritis (15%), with IgA disease the single commonest form.

- Congenital dysplasia/reflux nephropathy/chronic pyelonephritis (10–15%).

- Autosomal dominant polycystic kidney disease (5%).

- Obstruction (5%).

- Renovascular (5%).

- Multisystem autoimmune/vasculitis (5%).

- Cause unknown (20–30%).

1.3 Communication skills and ethics

1.3.1 Renal disease in pregnancy

Scenario

Role: you are a junior doctor in a nephrology outpatient clinic.

Mrs Jean Booth is a 27-year-old woman who is known to have reflux nephropathy with moderate renal impairment. She is hypertensive and taking lisinopril 10 mg daily. She attends the nephrology clinic every 6 months for review. Her routine pre-clinic investigations demonstrate proteinuria (1.2 g per 24 hours) and creatinine 196 µmol/L (estimated glomerular filtration rate 28 mL/min). Her BP is 156/90 mmHg.

She tells you that she is planning to start a family. This is something that she has said before and a previous letter in the notes from the renal consultant to the patient's GP has documented that there would be considerable risks: at least a 50% chance of significant rapid deterioration in the patient's renal function and at least a 50% chance of fetal loss.

Your task: to explain the implications of pregnancy with regard to the patient's renal condition.

Key issues to explore
What is her understanding of the risks of pregnancy to her own health, and what does she think the chances are of her having a healthy

baby? What does she understand about the risks to pregnancy caused by her medication?

Key points to establish

- Pregnancy poses a very significant risk to her own health.

- There is a high chance that pregnancy will not be successful.

- Angiotensin-converting enzyme inhibitors (lisinopril) are contraindicated in pregnancy.

- That you will try to give her the best care, whatever she decides about pregnancy.

Appropriate responses to likely questions

Patient: I feel perfectly well, so I must be fit enough to have a child.

Doctor: it's obviously good that you feel well, but I am afraid that this does not mean that there aren't any problems. Kidney disease does not make people feel ill until it is very bad indeed; but the fact that your blood pressure is high, that you have protein in the urine and the blood test showing that kidney function is about 30% of normal all mean that the risks of pregnancy would be very high.

Patient: what do you mean by very high?

Doctor: I mean that there's at least a 50% chance that the stress of pregnancy would make your kidneys get significantly worse, and at least a 50% chance that the pregnancy would not go well, so you would not end up with a healthy baby.

Patient: you and all the other doctors are just trying to frighten me, aren't you?

Doctor: no, we're trying to give you the proper facts. I'd like to be able to tell you that there aren't any

problems, but that wouldn't be true. The risks of pregnancy for you are much higher than they are for a woman who doesn't have kidney problems, and it's important that you understand this.

Patient: if I do get pregnant, then what would you do?

Doctor: we would try and look after you as well as we can. We would want to see you in clinic as soon as you knew you were pregnant, and we would monitor your blood pressure and kidney function very carefully. And if things were going wrong, we would talk to you about it.

Patient: if I am going to get pregnant, should I do anything before?

Doctor: we should try and get better control of your blood pressure and we should change the blood pressure tablet, because lisinopril – the one you're taking at the moment – can cause problems in pregnancy.

Patient: if I have a child, will it develop the same kidney problems as me?

Doctor: it's not inevitable, but it is possible that they might. If this was a concern, then the baby could have scans done to see.

1.3.2 A new diagnosis of amyloidosis

Scenario

Role: you are a junior doctor working on a renal ward.

Mr Stephen Foster is an anxious 45-year-old man who was admitted for investigation of nephrotic syndrome (oedema, proteinuria of 16 g per 24 hours and serum albumin 15 g/L). His plasma creatinine is normal. He has a history of long-standing

ankylosing spondylitis and the renal biopsy showed deposits of AA amyloid.

His case was discussed on the renal ward round. Treatment of his ankylosing spondylitis may reduce inflammation and thereby his tendency to form amyloid, but this is unlikely to have a dramatic effect and it is expected (1) that he will require continued symptomatic treatment for his oedema and proteinuria; (2) that his renal function is likely to deteriorate with time, even to the point where he requires dialysis, but this is not predictable; and (3) that his amyloid may cause problems with function of other organs in the future, but this also is not predictable.

Your task: to explain the diagnosis of amyloidosis to the patient and discuss what this means for his future.

Key issues to explore

What is his understanding of the situation?

Key points to establish

- The link between ankylosing spondylitis and amyloidosis.

- The multisystem and progressive nature of amyloidosis.

- That control of the underlying inflammatory disease can halt/slow progression of amyloidosis.

- That symptomatic treatments can help his renal symptoms.

Appropriate responses to likely questions

Patient: what is amyloid? I've never heard of it.

Doctor: it's quite a rare problem so that isn't very surprising. When we get infection or inflammation in the body, the body makes special proteins to try and fight the infection or inflammation, which is a good thing. But if the inflammation goes on for a very long time, as in your case with the ankylosing spondylitis, the body finds it difficult to get rid of the proteins designed to fight inflammation and they get deposited in the tissues. In your case at the moment this is happening in the kidneys, and once the proteins are there it's very hard for the body to dissolve or break them up.

Patient: what's wrong with my kidneys?

Doctor: at the moment your kidneys are actually doing their main job of removing waste from the blood normally. The problem is that they are 'leaky', so some of the protein in your blood is being lost into the urine. When this happens the kidneys try to make up for it by hanging onto more salt and water than usual, which is why your ankles are swollen. We can help the ankle swelling with diuretics, 'water tablets', and we can reduce the amount of protein leaking with a particular sort of blood pressure tablet, an angiotensin-converting enzyme inhibitor.

Patient: is there anything that will get rid of the amyloid?

Doctor: no, I'm afraid that it's extremely unlikely that it will be possible to get rid of it. But if the inflammation caused by the ankylosing spondylitis can be reduced, then the rate at which it increases can be slowed down and it may even improve a little. I am not an expert in this area, but we will discuss things with our colleagues in the rheumatology department and see if they can recommend any treatments to do this. This is something I am sure you'll want to talk about with them in clinic.

Patient: what happens if the amyloid in my kidneys get worse?

Doctor: there is a chance that over time the kidneys will work less well and stop cleaning the blood properly, so we will keep an eye on this with blood tests in the clinic. If the kidneys do fail because of amyloid, this will not happen suddenly; it will be a gradual process over many months and years, and we will let you know what is happening so that we can plan treatment. It may be that you will need dialysis – that's treatment to do the work of the kidneys – in the future. You might not, but it is a possibility.

Patient: does amyloid affect anything besides my kidneys? I had a quick look on the internet and read something about amyloid in the heart being very serious.

Doctor: you are right that amyloid can cause trouble in other places, especially the bowel and liver. But these are less affected than the kidney and I'm pleased to say that, although some other kinds of amyloid do affect the heart, the kind that you have almost never causes heart trouble.

Patient: am I going to die from this?

Doctor: you're right to think that this is a serious condition, and some people with amyloid do die earlier than they would have done otherwise. But at the moment the problem you have is not life-threatening and many people with this problem will not get worse for years and years.

1.3.3 Is dialysis appropriate?

Scenario
Role: you are a junior doctor working on a renal ward. A 78-year-old retired lecturer was found to have metastatic carcinoma 3 months previously. No primary site has been identified and previously he declined further investigation and treatment. He has been more short of breath for the last week and confused for about 2 days. He has chronic renal failure, cause unknown. Previous imaging has shown that both of his kidneys are of reduced size and his serum creatinine was 300 µmol/L 2 months ago. He is brought to the emergency department by his son who was visiting him. His BP is 70/50 mmHg. Blood tests show creatinine 670 µmol/L, urea 38 mmol/L and potassium 7.2 mmol/L. You are called to give advice on the management of his renal failure. You discuss this with the renal consultant who is on call and she says that dialysis would not be appropriate and that he should be managed conservatively. **Your task:** to explain the management plan to the patient's son, who is upset.

Key issues to explore
What is the son's understanding of his father's condition? Does he know about the diagnosis of malignancy, and does he know that his father declined further investigation and treatment?

Key points to establish

- The background of malignancy.

- The patient's wishes are more important than anyone else's: he is confused now, but when competent to make decisions he declined intervention.

- The patient is dying and heroic medical interventions would not change that, as well as being contrary to his wishes.

- That you will ensure that the patient is not distressed, and will look after him until he dies.

Appropriate responses to likely questions

Son: *why is my father so ill?*

Doctor: it's difficult to be sure what has caused the recent deterioration, but it's quite clear that his kidneys, which weren't working normally before, have got worse – he has advanced kidney failure. The kidneys control the levels of salts in the blood and also remove toxins and the level of toxins and salts in your father's blood are now very abnormal. They are at a level that might be responsible for his confusion, and also the fact that the heart is not pumping properly. I'm afraid I think he is dying.

Son: *I thought kidney failure could be treated with dialysis.*

Doctor: you are right, it can be. We can do the job of the kidneys with a dialysis machine, and this is something we do for lots of people every day. However, dialysis treatment tends to lower the blood pressure, and his blood pressure is already very low. He would not be strong enough for the treatment, and if we tried to give it I think he might die more quickly. I think we ought to concentrate on making him as comfortable as possible.

Son: *but there must be something you can do, some tests.*

Doctor: yes, there are obviously a lot of tests we could do, but I don't think they'd do any good. We know that your father has got widespread cancer, which we cannot cure. Furthermore, a few months ago he was quite clear that he didn't want more tests and treatments, and it's important that we all respect that view. We cannot make him better, and it would be wrong to put him through lots of tests that won't alter anything when he's dying. We must make sure that he is as comfortable as possible.

Son: *but don't you think that's wrong? I can't understand why he didn't want to be treated.*

Doctor: I understand why you find that difficult, but people are very different and he has a cancer which he knew we couldn't cure. Perhaps that's why he was so clear that he did not want more tests and treatments. Even people who are well in other ways often find some of the tests and treatments we do very draining.

Son: *what is going to happen if you don't give my father treatment for his kidney failure?*

Doctor: I think whatever we do he is going to pass away quite soon, and it's likely to be within the next few hours.

Son: *is he suffering?*

Doctor: no, I don't think so. The toxins in the blood affect the brain, which is why he is confused. As they build up he is likely to become sleepy, but if he seems to be distressed in any way, we can give him some medicine to make him more comfortable. If his heart stops, we won't go jumping up and down on him to try and resuscitate him, we will let him die peacefully.

1.4 Acute scenarios

1.4.1 A worrying potassium level

Scenario

A previously fit 74-year-old man presents to his GP after feeling unwell for 4 weeks with anorexia and more recently nausea, vomiting and breathlessness. He is found to have crackles at both lung bases and a grossly enlarged bladder. He is referred to the surgical admissions unit where blood tests identify renal failure: Na^+ 134 mmol/L, K^+ 8.9 mmol/L, urea 72 mmol/L and creatinine 1208 µmol/L. A urinary catheter is inserted. You are called to give an urgent medical opinion.

Introduction

What should you check immediately?

This patient has severe hyperkalaemia, a life-threatening complication of renal failure that requires urgent treatment. An ECG should be performed immediately and treatment should be instituted without delay, before an extensive history-taking or full examination.

Assessment of severity of hyperkalaemia The main risk of hyperkalaemia is cardiac arrest, and the ECG is the best guide of the severity of hyperkalaemic toxicity. There are progressive ECG changes as serum potassium rises: first, tenting of T waves, followed by diminished P waves with lengthening of the PR interval

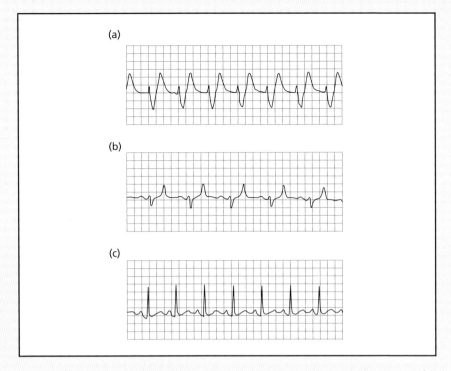

▲**Fig. 6** ECG in a patient with hyperkalaemia. (**a**) Initial ECG with [K⁺] 8.9 mmol/L, showing a sine-wave pattern: peaked T waves, broad QRS complex and absent P waves. (**b**) ECG after 40 mL 10% calcium gluconate: the P waves have returned and the complexes are starting to narrow. (**c**) Normal ECG after serum potassium had been restored to normal by dialysis.

and broadened QRS complexes, and finally a sine-wave pattern before the onset of either asystole or ventricular fibrillation. This patient's ECG showed a sine-wave pattern (Fig. 6a) requiring immediate treatment.

Treatment of hyperkalaemia
Treatments for hyperkalaemia are shown in Table 5.

Severe ECG changes Calcium counteracts the cardiotoxicity of hyperkalaemia by stabilising the

myocardium. It acts as soon as it reaches the heart, and its effect lasts for about 1 hour. It should be given intravenously in 10-mL aliquots and repeated as necessary until the ECG improves significantly (Fig. 6b). Calcium does not affect serum potassium concentration.

After calcium, give insulin and dextrose or nebulised β-agonist (they do not have an additive effect): either of these should lower serum potassium by about 1.5 mmol/L within 1–2 hours.

The effects of calcium and of insulin and dextrose will last for 3 or 4 hours: unless the patient has a form of renal failure that is likely to recover quickly (as might be possible in this case with the relief of obstruction), use this time to arrange transfer to renal/intensive care unit (ICU) services for dialysis/haemofiltration.

> If the ECG shows severe changes of hyperkalaemia (tented T waves with diminished P waves or broadened QRS complexes), give intravenous calcium immediately.

Less severe ECG changes If the only ECG manifestation of hyperkalaemia is tenting of T waves, then it is not necessary to give intravenous calcium. Give insulin and dextrose or nebulised β-agonist.

Note that none of the treatments mentioned above actually remove potassium from the body. This can be accomplished by renal excretion (if kidney function can be restored), by dialysis or to a limited degree by ion-exchange resins. In obstructive nephropathy relief of the obstruction will often lead to an immediate diuresis with potassium removal, but when hyperkalaemia is severe then dialysis will often be necessary.

TABLE 5 TREATMENT OF HYPERKALAEMIA		
Treatment	**Dosage**	**Effect**
Intravenous calcium	Calcium gluconate 10% in 10-mL aliquots iv by 'slow push' (2 min)	Stabilises myocardial cells and counteracts cardiac toxicity of hyperkalaemia
Intravenous insulin and dextrose	10–20 units soluble insulin in 50 mL 50% dextrose infused over 20 min	Insulin induces cellular uptake of K⁺ by activating Na⁺/K⁺-ATPase. Dextrose prevents hypoglycaemia
Nebulised β-adrenergic agonist	Salbutamol 5 mg	Induces cellular uptake of K⁺ by activating Na⁺/K⁺-ATPase
Oral or rectal ion-exchange resins	Calcium resonium 15 g oral tds	Removes K⁺? from the body by binding in the gastrointestinal tract (1 g of resonium binds 1 mmol of K⁺)
Haemodialysis	For 2 hours using dialysis fluid with low (or zero) K⁺	Removes K⁺ from the body by diffusion across semi-permeable membrane

What else should you check?

The man is breathless, most likely due to pulmonary oedema, so before embarking on details of history and examination, make sure that he does not require urgent attention for this. Check his airway, breathing and circulation: which of the four categories (well, ill, very ill or nearly dead) describes the patient? If nearly dead, call for ICU help immediately: don't wait for cardiac arrest. After this, note the following.

- Can he talk? If so, how many words at a time?

- Is he using his accessory muscles to breathe?

- Is he exhausted?

- Cyanosis.

- Vital signs: pulse rate, respiratory rate (beware the patient with a normal respiratory rate who is exhausted as death may occur soon) and BP.

- Peripheries: are they cold and shut down?

- Cardiac examination: JVP (likely to be grossly elevated) and gallop rhythm.

- Chest examination: crackles or wheeze.

If the patient is very ill or worse:

- sit the patient upright, assuming that pulmonary oedema and not hypotension is the main problem;

- give high-flow oxygen via reservoir bag;

- attach pulse oximeter (to monitor oxygen saturation);

- connect to cardiac monitor;

- establish intravenous access.

What are the likely diagnoses in this patient?

The combination of renal failure with clinical evidence of urinary retention is usually the result of long-standing bladder outflow obstruction. This is most often caused by benign prostatic hypertrophy, although other possibilities should be considered (Table 6).

Bladder outflow obstruction with renal failure is a common clinical scenario, accounting for up to 30% of cases of acute renal failure in community-based studies. In such cases there is often a long history of urinary outflow symptoms and presentation is notoriously late.

History of the presenting problem

After immediate treatment for hyperkalaemia and pulmonary oedema has been given, take a full history concentrating on the following.

Symptoms relating to renal failure

There is often a non-specific prodrome with malaise, fatigue and sometimes nausea. As renal failure advances, these rapidly progress with the development of vomiting, confusion and eventually coma.

Symptoms related to urinary outflow obstruction

Chronic retention is usually painless, in contrast to the restless agony of acute retention. Ask about frequency (most common and earliest symptom), urgency and difficulty with micturition (poor stream).

Symptoms related to specific pathology

If obstruction is caused by a pathology other than benign prostatic hypertrophy, then specific symptoms may be reported. Prostate or bladder malignancy may be indicated by loss of weight, haematuria or bone pain. Although almost certainly not the explanation in this man, kidney/bladder stones may be a problem in others.

Symptoms related to infection

Urinary tract infection is present in at least 50% of patients presenting with renal failure caused by bladder outflow obstruction.

Examination

General features

Before you started to take a history, you rightly made a general assessment of this patient and initiated any necessary emergency treatment.

Abdominal system

When the patient's condition permits, look for evidence of causal pathologies (see Table 6) especially the following.

TABLE 6 DIFFERENTIAL DIAGNOSIS OF RENAL FAILURE WITH A LARGE BLADDER

Frequency	Diagnosis
Common	Obstructive nephropathy caused by benign prostatic hypertrophy
Less common	Obstructive nephropathy caused by prostatic carcinoma Incidental acute urinary retention with another cause for renal failure
Uncommon	Obstructive nephropathy caused by a neurogenic bladder (eg spinal cord compression) Obstructive nephropathy caused by other bladder outflow pathology (eg urethral stricture)

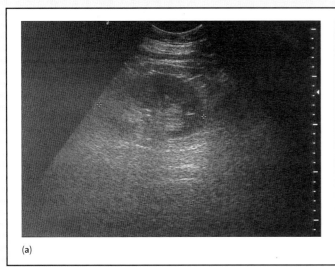
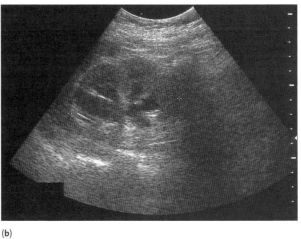

(a)   (b)

▲ **Fig. 7** Renal ultrasonography: (**a**) normal kidney; (**b**) hydronephrotic kidney with marked pelvicalyceal dilatation.

- Lymphadenopathy and hepatomegaly, suggesting malignancy.

- Rectal examination: benign prostatic hyperplasia or malignancy.

- Neurological signs in the legs: this is unlikely to be bladder outflow obstruction resulting from spinal cord pathology, but it is a bad mistake to miss it.

Record the residual urine volume from catheterisation and the rate of urine output.

Investigations

> If available, past biochemistry results indicate the chronicity of renal damage and the level of recovery to expect: check the notes, check the pathology records, and ask the GP.

Blood tests

- Repeat electrolytes and renal function.

- FBC.

- Clotting screen.

- Liver and bone function tests.

- Prostate-specific antigen.

- Blood cultures (if suspicion of sepsis).

CXR

To assess for pulmonary oedema, and also (although much less likely) for secondaries in lungs or bones.

Ultrasonography of urinary tract

This is required urgently in any patient with an unexplained acute deterioration in renal function. A large residual bladder volume in combination with bilateral hydronephrosis (Fig. 7) is diagnostic of obstructive nephropathy caused by bladder outflow obstruction.

Management

Pulmonary oedema

The spectrum ranges from mild breathlessness on exertion to respiratory failure leading to respiratory arrest. All patients should receive high-flow oxygen and be sat upright. Those who are severely compromised with increasing respiratory rate, fatigue and hypoxia require transfer to the ICU and (probably) ventilation. In others, intravenous nitrates may be sufficient until fluid can be removed by either diuresis (perhaps after relief of obstruction in this case) or dialysis with fluid removal by ultrafiltration.

Hyperkalaemia and fluid overload causing pulmonary oedema are the most common indications for urgent dialysis; others are given in Table 7.

Volume depletion and fluid replacement

Although this man's initial problem is pulmonary oedema, relief of obstructive nephropathy is often followed by excessive diuresis associated with sodium, potassium, bicarbonate, calcium and magnesium wasting. This happens because the tubules have 'forgotten' how to concentrate the urine and thus there is a risk of the patient becoming volume depleted, which could compromise recovering renal function. Note the following.

- Fluid status (postural hypotension, JVP and weight) and biochemistry should be checked frequently (usually daily).

- Care needs to be taken with the sodium content of intravenous fluid; alternating physiological (0.9%) saline and 5% dextrose is usually an appropriate choice.

- Large quantities of potassium may need to be given (20–40 mmol/L); this requires close monitoring.

TABLE 7 INDICATIONS FOR URGENT DIALYSIS

Condition	Indication
Hyperkalaemia	Different patients respond differently to hyperkalaemia: if there are severe ECG changes, then intervention is required
Pulmonary oedema	This is the commonest life-threatening manifestation of salt and water overload in acute renal failure. All patients should receive high-flow oxygen and be sat upright. Other holding measures while preparations for dialysis are made include intravenous nitrates, low-dose morphine and (in extreme circumstances) venesection
Uraemia	Severe uraemia (urea >50 mmol/L) is a relative indication. When associated with encephalopathy or pericarditis, then urgent dialysis is required
Severe acidosis	This is usually a reflection of the severity of metabolic derangement and it is difficult to suggest a particular value for blood pH that demands intervention. A pH <7.2 should certainly prompt early intervention and dialysis

- It is sometimes helpful to measure urine biochemistry to determine the specific losses.

If the patient is polyuric and passing more than 3 L of urine daily, give a total fluid input equal to the measured output of the day before. This will achieve a gentle negative balance; you will need to monitor volume status carefully.

> **Don't chase your own tail!**
> Avoid driving a postobstructive diuresis with huge volumes of replacement fluid.

If urine output does not continue

The urethral catheter has drained the bladder, but there may be coincident ureteric obstruction. This is particularly common in prostate carcinoma, which can spread to encase the ureters. Repeat ultrasonography to determine whether the hydronephrosis has been relieved. Consider CT to look at the retroperitoneum and involve the urology team.

Other possibilities are that the kidneys may have been chronically damaged by obstruction, or there may be acute tubular necrosis (see Section 1.4.2) resulting from the combination of hypoxia, sepsis and poor perfusion. Also consider other causes of renal failure: how convincing was the evidence of obstruction and what was the residual urine volume?

1.4.2 Postoperative acute renal failure

Scenario

A 73-year-old man presents with a Duke's B carcinoma of the descending colon for which he has had a hemicolectomy. Preoperatively his serum creatinine was normal (103 µmol/L), but his urine output has been low since he left the operating theatre recovery suite. This was managed by the surgical team with intravenous fluids and boluses of furosemide, but 24-hours postoperatively you are asked to see him to give a medical opinion because his urine output is 10 mL/hour and his creatinine has risen to 180 µmol/L.

Introduction

The most common cause of postoperative acute renal failure (ARF) is acute tubular necrosis (ATN). ATN may be the end-result of a variety of insults to the kidneys, many of which cause hypoperfusion and initially cause prerenal ARF (Table 8). By definition, prerenal ARF will be corrected immediately when normal perfusion is restored.

Management of ARF depends on identification and correction of the cause, treating life-threatening complications (eg hyperkalaemia and pulmonary oedema) and providing supportive treatment, including renal replacement therapy, when required.

History of the presenting problem

When confronted with a patient with impaired renal function, it is always important to establish whether this is acute or chronic. In this case the preoperative creatinine clearly indicates an acute deterioration. In dealing with this patient consider the following.

Consider causes of hypoperfusion (prerenal)

These may lead to ATN.

- Intraoperative haemodynamic details (usually from anaesthetic charts), including blood loss, fluid replacement, BP, urinary output (if measured) and time on bypass (if relevant).

- Postoperative haemodynamic details, including blood loss, fluid replacement, urinary and other fluid outputs (gastrointestinal losses and drains, etc), and BP.

- Evidence of hypoxia (eg low oxygen saturation or dyspnoea).

- Details of all medications, particularly NSAIDs, ACE

TABLE 8 CAUSES OF ATN[1]

Haemodynamically mediated ATN	Toxic ATN
Reduced circulating volume: blood loss, excessive gastrointestinal fluid loss (eg diarrhoea), burns	Drugs toxic to renal epithelial cells: gentamicin, amphotericin
Low cardiac output	Rhabdomyolysis
Systemic sepsis	Radiocontrast nephropathy
Drugs inducing renal hypoperfusion: NSAIDs, ACE inhibitors, angiotensin II receptor blockers	

1. Note that many patients suffer more than one of these insults.
ACE, angiotensin-converting enzyme.

inhibitors, angiotensin receptor antagonists and nephrotoxic antibiotics.

- Evidence of sepsis, eg fever, hypotension, acute-phase response and wound discharge.

- Evidence of cardiac dysfunction, eg postoperative chest pain may go unnoticed but be an indication of myocardial infarction.

Consider causes of postrenal renal failure

- Bladder outflow obstruction, particularly in elderly men due to prostatic enlargement: is the catheter properly positioned and draining freely?

- Bilateral ureteric obstruction is very uncommon but may occur postoperatively due to retroperitoneal haemorrhage or inadvertent ligation of the ureters (eg during hysterectomy).

Consider intrarenal renal failure

These would be very unlikely in this case.

- Acute tubulointerstitial nephritis, usually due to drugs.

- Disease of small blood vessels, eg thrombotic microangiopathy associated with drugs.

Examination

As always, the first priority is to make an overall assessment of the patient (ie well, ill, very ill or nearly dead) (see Section 1.4.1 for discussion). Check in particular for features to support the diagnosis of renal hypoperfusion or postrenal problems.

Evidence of likely renal hypoperfusion

- Hypotension and postural hypotension (lying and sitting).

- Low JVP.

- Presence of sepsis: warm peripheries, bounding pulse, hypotension and wound infection.

- Evidence of low cardiac output: cold peripheries, thready pulse and hypotension.

- Murmur and/or chest crepitations may suggest low cardiac output/hypoxaemia.

- Blood or fluid loss, eg wound haematoma.

Evidence of postrenal renal failure

- Enlarged bladder due to outflow obstruction.

Evidence of fluid overload

In any patient who is acutely unwell or who has renal impairment, it is crucial to establish current volume status.

- Raised JVP.

- Gallop rhythm.

- Basal crackles in the chest suggesting pulmonary oedema.

- Peripheral oedema shows that there is an increase in overall body salt and water: even a trace of ankle oedema usually corresponds to at least 3 L of expansion.

Evidence of intravascular fluid depletion

The following suggest that renal hypoperfusion is likely.

- Hypotension/postural hypotension.

- Low JVP.

Evidence to support specific renal pathologies

- Loin pain: can occur with hydronephrosis, rarely with acute renovascular occlusion or embolisation, and more commonly with retroperitoneal haematoma.

- 'Trash feet' as part of cholesterol embolisation syndrome, particularly after vascular operations.

- Drug rash associated with tubulointerstitial nephritis.

- Enlarged bladder indicating urinary obstruction.

Investigations

The diagnosis of the cause of this man's acute deterioration in renal function is likely to be made on the basis of the history and physical examination. However, appropriate investigations will assist in making a diagnosis in some cases and be necessary to assess the severity of metabolic disturbance and progress in all.

Assessment of severity and progress

- Blood tests: electrolytes (watch for development of hyperkalaemia), creatinine, liver/bone function tests, C-reactive protein, FBC (consider postoperative bleeding) and clotting screen; also arterial blood gases (if the patient is very ill or worse).

- CXR: to look for features of pulmonary oedema and/or postoperative pneumonia.

Diagnosis of cause of ARF

- Urine dipstick for blood and protein: if the cause is prerenal ARF or ATN, one would not expect more than a score of 1+ for both protein and blood: evidence of greater haematuria or proteinuria in a non-catheter specimen should prompt consideration of a renal inflammatory cause of ARF, although this would be extremely unlikely in this context.

- Screen for sepsis: cultures of wound swab, blood, urine and sputum (if any).

- Ultrasonography of urinary tract (if a clinical diagnosis of hypovolaemia is not clear-cut): look for features of obstruction.

Note that measurement of urinary sodium concentration, urinary creatinine or urea concentration, and urine osmolality are of no value in this context: whether the patient has prerenal ARF or ATN will be determined by his response to resuscitation.

Other tests

- ECG: deterioration could have been caused by perioperative myocardial infarction.

Management

- Treat life-threatening complications (eg hyperkalaemia and pulmonary oedema), decide if urgent haemodialysis is required and assess whether the patient should be transferred to the intensive care unit (as described in Section 1.4.1).

- Optimise circulating volume, oxygenation and (hopefully) renal perfusion: the aim is to correct possible renal hypoperfusion while avoiding dangerous fluid overload and pulmonary oedema. If renal function improves immediately with fluid infusion, the diagnosis is prerenal ARF.

- Monitor fluid input and output carefully: a urinary catheter is required.

Fluid management of the patient with postoperative ARF associated with hypovolaemia

- Resuscitate: give intravenous 0.9% saline or colloid rapidly until the JVP is seen easily and postural hypotension is abolished.
- Maintain optimal intravascular volume: give fluid input equal to measured outputs plus 500–1000 mL/day; examine the patient twice daily for features of volume depletion (low JVP or postural fall in BP) or overload (tachypnoea or basal crackles) and then adjust fluid input appropriately.

In the patient with ARF, always look at the drug chart and stop drugs that have adverse renal haemodynamic effects when the circulation is disturbed (NSAIDs, ACE inhibitors and angiotensin receptor blockers) or which are nephrotoxic (eg aminoglycosides).

- Repeat measurements of serum electrolytes and creatinine regularly. Particular attention should be paid to the trend as well as the absolute values of abnormalities: if these are getting worse day by day, do not wait until they are extreme before seeking advice from renal services. Once the need for renal replacement therapy becomes clear, usually in the context of oliguria and worsening renal function, there is no point delaying its commencement until there is an emergency indication.

- Always consider sepsis and set a low threshold for commencing broad-spectrum (non-nephrotoxic) antibiotics.

- There is very little evidence that prognosis is altered by measures such as loop diuretics and dopamine, which increase urinary flow in people with normal kidneys.

- Nutritional support is frequently required and should be commenced early in ARF.

Management of ARF

- Treat life-threatening complications (may require urgent haemodialysis).
- Restore and maintain renal perfusion.
- Investigate and correct the cause while continuing supportive management.

Further comments

Haemodialysis or haemofiltration?

Intermittent haemodialysis is the renal replacement modality used on renal units for most patients with renal failure but without failure of other organs (isolated ARF). Patients who are haemodynamically unstable or who have failure of more than one organ require management in the intensive care unit, where continuous renal replacement therapies such as haemofiltration or haemodiafiltration are the norm. These techniques have the advantage of cardiovascular stability, optimal circulatory volume manipulation and the ability to create space for enhanced nutritional replacement. However, in randomised trials in a variety of settings there is no evidence that one treatment modality is better than the other.

Outcome of ARF

Although most patients with ATN have potentially recoverable renal function, the mortality of patients with this condition is high: 40–45% of those who require acute renal replacement therapy will die. This reflects the poor outcome of those who have ATN as a component of multiorgan failure: if a patient has failure of three or four organs, mortality is 80–90%. In contrast, mortality is less than 10% in patients with isolated ARF.

The renal outcome of those patients who survive is roughly that 60% will recover normal renal function, 30% are left with chronic kidney disease and 10% remain dialysis dependent.

1.4.3 Renal impairment and a multisystem disease

Scenario

A 26-year-old woman presents to the Emergency Department with several weeks of intermittent pleuritic chest pain and joint pain. She is found to have dipstick proteinuria, a creatinine of 225 μmol/L and anaemia with fragments on the blood film.

Introduction

What is the first priority in a young woman with pleuritic chest pain?

The first priority is to establish that the patient does not have pulmonary embolism (PE).

Features suggesting a multisystem disorder

Arthralgia, anaemia and impaired renal function all clearly suggest a multisystem disorder. History and examination are crucial in narrowing down the differential diagnosis. Considered analysis of the findings of simple tests such as urinalysis, plasma biochemistry and haematology will often give a clear lead to the underlying pathology, and is essential in determining the urgency of the situation. Joint and chest pains in a young woman with renal impairment raise a strong clinical suspicion of systemic lupus erythematosus (SLE) (see Section 2.7.5).

History of the presenting problem

Pleuritic chest pain

The differential diagnosis of intermittent pleuritic chest pain going on for some weeks includes PE, musculoskeletal pain, pericarditis and rarer causes of pleurisy such as autoimmune rheumatic disease. It is clearly very important to pursue the possibility of PE, so ask about previous thromboembolism, leg/calf pain or swelling, breathlessness and haemoptysis. If the patient has musculoskeletal pain, this may be positional. Do any particular movements bring it on? And does getting into any particular position lead to improvement? Pericarditis would be supported by any 'cardiac radiation' of the pain, and also if it were eased on sitting forward.

Joints

What is the pattern of joint involvement? Which joints are affected, is the distribution symmetrical and does this change over time? Is there a diurnal pattern? Is there swelling, stiffness or discoloration? Is the pain eased or worsened by movement? These features are important in the differential diagnosis of arthritis (see *Rheumatology and Clinical Immunology*, Sections 1.1.8 and 1.1.14).

Renal disease

Until renal impairment is far advanced, it is asymptomatic. Patients with the nephrotic syndrome may notice frothy urine and will (by definition) have oedema.

Other relevant history

Ask about other features that would support the diagnosis of SLE (Fig. 8).

- Skin rashes, especially ones that are photosensitive.

- Raynaud's syndrome.

- Myalgia.

- Neurological abnormalities: seizures or psychiatric disturbances.

- History of spontaneous abortion.

- Drugs: some (eg hydralazine) can precipitate a lupus-like illness.

Examination

Once again it is important to make an initial assessment as to how ill the patient is (see Section 1.4.1), but the details given here do not indicate that the patient is *in extremis*. Examination, as always, should be focused on confirming or refuting diagnoses suggested by the history, so apart from checking vital signs look for the following.

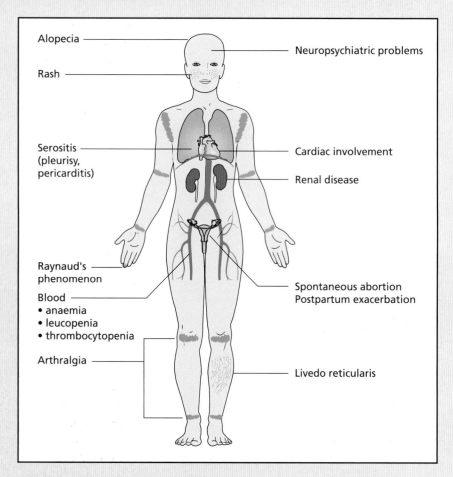

Labels on figure:
- Alopecia
- Rash
- Serositis (pleurisy, pericarditis)
- Raynaud's phenomenon
- Blood
  • anaemia
  • leucopenia
  • thrombocytopenia
- Arthralgia
- Neuropsychiatric problems
- Cardiac involvement
- Renal disease
- Spontaneous abortion Postpartum exacerbation
- Livedo reticularis

▲**Fig. 8** Manifestations of SLE. This figure illustrates the widespread potential manifestations of this multisystem disease.

Signs of PE/deep venous thrombosis

- Raised JVP, palpable right ventricle, loud P2, right ventricular gallop, pleural rub and pleural effusion.

- Warm swollen leg.

- Check pulse oximetry.

Signs of pericarditis/pericardial fluid

- Pericardial rub.

- Raised JVP and/or pulsus paradoxus (fall in systolic BP of more than 10 mmHg on inspiration) if there is sufficient pericardial fluid to cause haemodynamic compromise.

Signs suggesting SLE

- Skin: typically facial butterfly rash and/or alopecia; also livedo reticularis.

- Fingers and toes: are there signs of ischaemia caused by severe Raynaud's phenomenon?

- Joints: are these swollen or tender? Small joints are typically involved in SLE in a symmetrical and (usually) non-deforming manner.

- Cardiovascular: cardiac murmurs and peripheral oedema.

- Neurological, including ocular fundi. Neuropsychiatric lupus can present in a wide variety of ways: cranial nerve palsy, peripheral neuropathy, cerebrovascular accident, movement disorder and transverse myelitis.

Investigations

Exclusion of PE
Although it seems very likely that this woman has lupus, it would be unwise to completely dismiss PE on clinical grounds. A normal D-dimer would be reassuring but an abnormal result, which would be very likely in the case described and almost certainly be non-specific, should be followed by appropriate imaging, either lung ventilation–perfusion scanning or CT pulmonary angiography.

Urinalysis
Around 10% of adults presenting with lupus have protein or blood in their urine, which indicates renal involvement. Proteinuria should be quantified, most usually by meaurement of urinary albumin/creatinine ratio. Red cell casts confirm active glomerulonephritis.

Biochemistry
Check renal function (to ensure no further acute deterioration in this case) and liver blood tests. Lupus can affect any organ, but liver involvement is unusual. Patients may have low serum albumin as a result of proteinuria and/or chronic disease.

🔑 Renal involvement is common in SLE but does not cause symptoms, so it is very important to perform urinalysis, measure serum creatinine and estimate glomerular filtration rate.

Haematology
Check FBC, blood film, reticulocyte count, direct antiglobulin test (Coombs' test), clotting screen and haptoglobins. Lupus often causes anaemia, which is usually normochromic and normocytic but can be haemolytic. Haemolysis

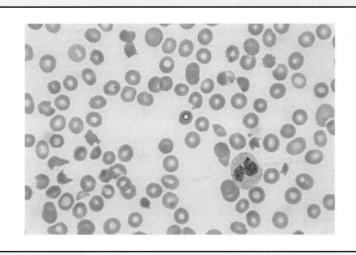

▲**Fig. 9** Blood film of microangiopathic haemolytic anaemia. This blood film shows the typical features of microangiopathic haemolytic anaemia, with abnormally shaped red blood cells and red blood cell fragments. Aside from SLE, this picture can be caused by pre-eclampsia or eclampsia, disseminated intravascular coagulation, prosthetic heart valves (especially if leaking or infected), thrombotic thrombocytopenic purpura, haemolytic–uraemic syndrome, accelerated-phase hypertension and scleroderma. (Courtesy of Dr J.A. Amess, St Bartholomew's Hospital.)

is suggested by polychromasia, reticulocytosis, low haptoglobin levels and a raised unconjugated plasma bilirubin. A positive Coombs' test would suggest autoimmune haemolysis. The presence of fragmented red blood cells on the blood film would indicate a microangiopathic process, as can be seen in SLE (Fig. 9). Up to two-thirds of lupus patients have leucopenia, with the main deficit being lymphopenia; there may also be mild thromocytopenia. This contrasts with the primary systemic vasculitides, which usually cause high white cell and platelet counts. Abnormalities of the clotting screen may be associated with antiphospholipid antibodies.

Inflammatory and serological markers

Check erythrocyte sedimentation rate (ESR)/C-reactive protein (CRP), antinuclear antibodies, anti-double-stranded DNA (dsDNA) antibodies and complement levels. The typical pattern of active lupus is a raised ESR with a low CRP, low levels of complement C3 and C4, antinuclear antibodies and antibodies to dsDNA. There may be other autoantibodies, especially antiphospholipid antibodies such as the lupus anticoagulants, which prolong the kaolin cephalin clotting time but paradoxically predispose to thrombosis.

Other investigations

- Renal ultrasonography to confirm that the patient has two anatomically normal kidneys.

- Renal biopsy to make a precise renal diagnosis to determine prognosis and inform treatment decisions (see Section 2.7.5).

Management

The managment of lupus is complex and depends on the precise clinical situation. Agents used for renal disease include steroids and cytotoxic drugs, principally azathioprine, mycophenolate mofetil and cyclophosphamide. There is recent interest in the anti-B cell monoclonal antibody rituximab.

The renal response to treatment depends on the histological appearances, eg lupus membranous nephropathy is not usually treated aggressively because it responds less well. Studies from the US National Institutes of Health have shown benefit from steroid therapy in patients with severe diffuse proliferative lupus glomerulonephritis (Fig. 10), with the benefit increased if pulsed intravenous cyclophosphamide is added every 1–3 months. Plasma exchange offered no additional benefit. Cyclophosphamide toxicity includes haemorrhagic cystitis, infection, bone marrow suppression, suppression of ovarian function and tumours. The use of 2-mercaptoethane sulphonate (mesna) helps protect against bladder toxicity. Drug toxicity should be discussed with the patient and, when practicable, storage of gametes should be considered before therapy is started.

Treatment of BP is important. Dialysis and/or renal transplantation may be required if the kidneys fail completely.

Further comments

Joint pains, pleuritic chest pain and renal abnormalities should always raise the possibility of lupus. Renal involvement in lupus is important and all patients with lupus should have their BP monitored, together with urine dipsitck analysis and serum creatinine measurement.

Lupus is unpredictable; it can remit and relapse frequently. It can be a mere nuisance or it can be a devastating illness. This is worrying for patients; uncertainty is difficult for them, their family and friends, and also for their doctors. Many of the treatments used are of limited efficacy and have side effects. All these issues need to be frankly

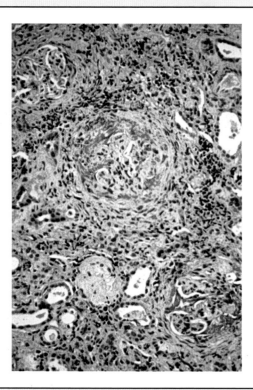

▲ **Fig. 10** Glomerulonephritis in SLE. This is a section of a renal biopsy showing a severe crescentic glomerulonephritis. The central glomerulus is full of inflammatory cells and shows a clear crescent caused by inflammatory cells in Bowman's space. (Courtesy of Dr J.E. Scoble, Guy's Hospital.)

discussed with the patient at the beginning.

With women, discuss the interplay between pregnancy and lupus (and hypertension or renal impairment if present, see Sections 1.1.2 and 1.3.1). Lupus can be exacerbated during pregnancy and for the first 2 months postpartum, and women with lupus have an increased incidence of abortion, perinatal death and preterm delivery.

1.4.4 Renal impairment and fever

Scenario

A 22-year-old man with no significant previous history is seen in the Emergency Department in the evening. He reports a 4-day history of fever, aching muscles and rigor.

His temperature is 39°C. Urinalysis shows proteinuria and haematuria. He is admitted for observation. The following morning his creatinine on the admission sample is noted to have been 275 µmol/L and you are asked to see him. The referring doctor wonders if the patient may have a systemic vasculitis because of the fever, urinary findings and renal impairment.

Introduction

What do you want to know next to guide your immediate management?

There are three key pieces of information.

- The state of the patient's circulation: the renal failure

may be due to circulatory shock. What are his vital signs?

- How much urine is he passing? Acute renal failure (ARF) is usually associated with oliguria or anuria. If he is passing less than 0.5 mL/kg per hour, his creatinine is likely to be rising rapidly and renal replacement therapy may be necessary within 24–48 hours. If he is unwell and it is not clear that he is producing good volumes of urine, then a catheter should be inserted to enable continuous monitoring of urine output.

- What are today's blood results? In particular, determine serum potassium (hyperkalemia may be life-threatening; see Section 1.4.1) and creatinine levels.

The possible causes of ARF can be usefully considered by thinking through the processes involved in renal physiology: blood perfuses the glomeruli, generating a primary filtrate that is modified by the tubular epithelium and which then passes through the ureters, bladder and urethra. Thus the possible causes of ARF can be categorised as follows.

- Prerenal disease: hypotension or reduced intravascular volume.

- Renovascular disease.

- Glomerular disease.

- Renal vasculitis.

- Tubular and interstitial disease.

- Postrenal obstruction: potentially in the renal pelves, ureters, bladder or urethra.

Which possible causes of ARF are most likely in this case?

- The short history and prominent constitutional features in a previously fit man suggest he could have reduced renal perfusion due to a severe systemic illness. The commonest cause of renal failure in this context would be acute tubular necrosis (ATN, see Section 1.4.2). However, the presence of proteinuria and haematuria would not be expected in a diagnosis of ATN and raise the possibility of a renal inflammatory process: an acute glomerulonephritis, a vasculitis or a tubulointerstitial nephritis.

- Another possibility to be considered is that he has unsuspected chronic renal impairment accounting for his raised creatinine and an unrelated acute illness.

What would you consider a normal glomerular filtration rate for a 22-year-old man, and what do you estimate this man's glomerular filtration rate to be?

A normal glomerular filtration rate (GFR) in a man of this age would be 80–150 mL/min. If his creatinine were stable at 275 μmol/L, this would give an estimated GFR of about 25 mL/min. But his GFR could be 0 mL/min: you only have a single value of creatinine, which may be climbing rapidly.

> Even when glomerular filtration has stopped completely, serum creatinine will rise only by about 200 μmol/L per day.

History of the presenting problem

Assuming the patient is not *in extremis*, you will clearly start to take the history along the lines of 'What did you first notice', but key issues to probe include the following.

- 'How long have you been unwell? When were you last completely well?' He says he became unwell

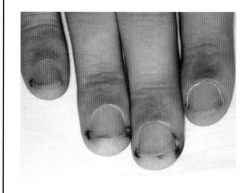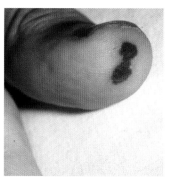

▲ **Fig. 11** Fingertip infarcts.

4 days ago, but the point is important enough to pursue; 22 year olds may be rather dismissive of more subtle symptoms and patients with systemic vasculitis have usually been unwell for weeks or months.

- Possibility of infection: has he had contact with anyone else who has been unwell, and has he been travelling recently (which brings in a wider infective differential)?

Other relevant history

Ask specifically about the following.

- Possibility of multisystem disorder: skin rash, arthralgia, trouble with ears or sinuses, pins and needles/numbness/focal weakness (mononeuritis) and haemoptysis (suggestive of pulmonary haemorrhage).

- Sore throat: may suggest IgA nephropathy or poststreptococcal glomerulonephritis, but both are unlikely in the scenario described.

- Drugs (prescribed or non-prescribed): some can trigger interstitial nephritis or (less commonly) vasculitic reactions.

Examination: general features

Look for signs that the patient is very unwell, as described in Section 1.4.1. If near death, call for

intensive care unit help immediately. Do not wait for cardiac arrest.

Next, on a quick head-to-toe screen, look for potential sources and signs of sepsis, for signs to support a diagnosis of vasculitis (skin rash, typically 'palpable purpura', and splinter haemorrhages) and perform a full physical examination.

Your examination reveals a temperature of 39°C and pulse 110/minute, regular. The patient's peripheries are strikingly warm and his BP is 90/60 mmHg. There are infarcts around his fingertips (Fig. 11) and widespread muscle tenderness. What are you considering now?

These findings are very worrying indeed. They would be most unusual in systemic vasculitis, as would the abrupt onset and the rigor. The picture is more suggestive of a septicaemic illness: nail-fold infarcts suggest acute endocarditis; and aching and tender muscles are common in *Staphylococcus aureus* septicaemia, which should lead you back to take further history about recent infections, trouble with boils or spots, an abscess anywhere, bad toothache or a visit to the dentist. Following such prompts, this man recalls that he had a spot on his elbow which burst a couple of days earlier. Examination suggests an infected olecranon bursa.

The possibility of staphylococcal endocarditis now leads you to repeat the cardiovascular examination: the pulse is too rapid to be sure of its character, but is there a decrescendo murmur?

> Severe acute aortic regurgitation may not be accompanied by an obvious diastolic murmur.

> Making a diagnosis in a sick patient often involves:
> - taking a history;
> - physical examination;
> - reviewing investigations;
> - repeating elements of the history;
> - repeating elements of the physical examination;
> - re-reviewing investigations;
> - and so on repeatedly.

Approach to investigation and management

Your clinical diagnosis is acute endocarditis, probably staphylococcal. You need to confirm the diagnosis, institute appropriate supportive treatment and start empirical antibiotic treatment.

Today the patient's creatinine is 400 µmol/L: what do you think is the cause of the renal failure? Renal failure is likely to be mainly due to hypotension and the sepsis syndrome, but it is probable that there is also active glomerulonephritis, as indicated by the proteinuria and haematuria. Bacterial endocarditis can be associated with glomerulonephritis (similar to postinfectious glomerulonephritis histologically), acute interstitial nephritis and embolic events.

Investigations

Laboratory tests from the day before show a low platelet count, a neutrophil leucocytosis and a C-reactive protein (CRP) of 300 mg/L. These are consistent with a diagnosis of septicaemia. The high CRP and neutrophil leucocytosis are consistent with bacterial infection or systemic vasculitis, but the low platelet count is a typical feature of sepsis and would be uncommon in systemic vasculitis (where the platelet count is often elevated).

The following investigations should be arranged.

- To pursue the diagnosis of bacterial endocarditis: blood cultures and an echocardiogram (which revealed aortic vegetation in this case).

- To assess severity and monitor for complications and progress: FBC, clotting screen, electrolytes, creatinine, liver/bone function tests and CRP, arterial blood gases, CXR, ECG.

- To consider vasculitic disease: antinuclear antibodies, complement levels (C3 and C4), antineutrophil cytoplasmic antibodies (ANCA). However, note that (i) the indirect immunofluorescence test for ANCA is not uncommonly positive in endocarditis and other infective conditions – the specific tests for antibodies against serum proteinase 3 and myeloperoxidase are much less likely to mislead; and (ii) C3 and C4 levels are commonly low in infection-related glomerulonephritis.

Management

> Keep the relatives informed: they need to know that this man could die.

In a life-threatening situation such as this, it is often essential to start treatment before the diagnosis is confirmed. The following are appropriate here.

- Supportive care: transfer him to the intensive care unit/high-dependency unit and ensure he receives high-flow oxygen, urinary catheterisation and close haemodynamic monitoring (central venous line and arterial line); ventilatory and inotropic support may also be required.

- Specific treatment: appropriate antimicrobials (initially the patient must be started on broad-spectrum cover, but given the suspicion of staphylococcal disease this must include high-dose flucloxacillin or vancomycin) and consideration of valve replacement (Fig. 12).

> ARF occurs in many severe illnesses. It is crucial to consider underlying diagnoses such as sepsis at an early stage. About one-third of a series of 200 patients with bacterial endocarditis developed ARF, which was more common in the elderly and those with *Staphylococcus aureus* infection.

1.4.5 Renal failure and haemoptysis

Scenario

A 66-year-old man presents with a 5-week history of malaise, myalgia, arthralgia and increasing breathlessness. In the week leading up to admission he begins to cough up blood and his GP performs blood tests that reveal creatinine 580 µmol/L and haemoglobin 8.4 g/dL. He immediately goes to the patient's house to reassess him, notices a purpuric rash and organises emergency admission.

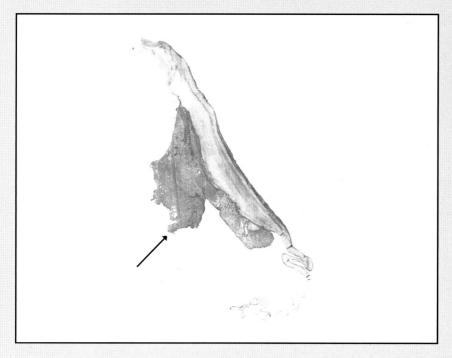

▲ **Fig. 12** Low-power view of section through resected aortic valve leaflet showing adherent vegetation (arrow).

Introduction

This man almost certainly has a pulmonary–renal syndrome, which is defined as a combination of diffuse pulmonary haemorrhage and glomerulonephritis. If not treated urgently this is usually fatal, and despite aggressive treatment mortality remains in the region of 25–50%.

Pulmonary–renal syndromes are usually caused by immunologically mediated diseases, with most cases due to:

- vasculitis, often positive for antineutrophil cytoplasmic antibodies (ANCA), such as microscopic polyangiitis or Wegener's granulomatosis;

- anti-glomerular basement membrane (GBM) disease (Goodpasture's disease);

- systemic lupus erythematosus (SLE).

Other causes of acute renal failure can be complicated by pulmonary

oedema, infection or an increase in capillary permeability that may not be easy to distinguish from pulmonary haemorrhage. Patients with severe pneumonia can develop acute renal failure as part of a sepsis syndrome, and these also need to be distinguished, in particular because their treatment is radically different.

> 🔑 Acute renal failure with blood/protein in the urine plus haemoptysis indicates a pulmonary–renal syndrome until proved otherwise. This is a medical emergency.

History of the presenting problem

A detailed medical history is crucial. The presence of systemic symptoms and abnormalities in other organ systems may indicate a systemic vasculitis, SLE or an alternative diagnosis. The initial symptoms of many conditions, ranging from pneumonia to vasculitis, are

relatively non-specific and include lethargy, fever, weight loss, arthralgia and a non-specific feeling of being 'unwell'. Probe for clues to the following diagnoses.

- Vasculitis: skin rash, abdominal pain and focal numbness or weakness (mononeuritis); this can be precipitated by some drugs, eg penicillamine, hydralazine.

- Wegener's granulomatosis: sinus and upper respiratory tract symptoms, which may have been investigated in the past; also symptoms of generalised vasculitis.

- Goodpasture's disease: can be triggered by inhaled hydrocarbons; pulmonary haemorrhage occurs almost exclusively in smokers.

- Churg–Strauss syndrome: asthma and nasal polyps; also symptoms of generalised vasculitis.

- SLE: arthralgia, alopecia and pleurisy; commonly in those of African, Asian or Afro-Caribbean ethnicity.

- Pneumonia or other severe sepsis: any obvious symptoms suggesting infection, eg rigors or dysuria; always ask about travel history.

Examination

As always, the first priority is to make an overall assessment of the patient: is he well, ill, very ill or nearly dead? (See Section 1.4.1 for discussion.) The description given here suggests that this man might be very ill or worse: if he is, call for help from the intensive care unit immediately. In addition to features indicative of the severity of his illness, note the following.

- Signs of active vasculitis: palpable purpura (Fig. 13), splinter haemorrhages, uveitis,

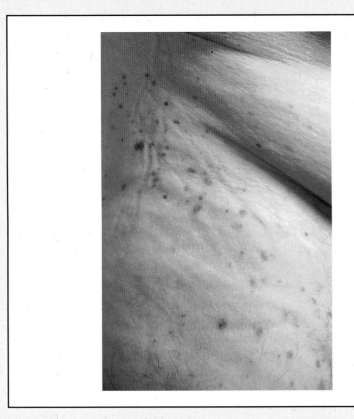

▲ **Fig. 13** Typical vasculitic rash in the axilla of a patient with microscopic polyangiitis.

mononeuritis multiplex and Roth's spots; a collapsed nasal bridge is very suggestive of Wegener's granulomatosis.

- Signs of SLE: alopecia, butterfly rash, arthritis and vasculitic skin lesions.

- Chest: there may be few abnormalities despite significant pulmonary haemorrhage.

Investigations

Blood and other routine tests

- To assess severity and monitor for complications and progress: FBC, clotting screen, electrolytes and creatinine, liver/bone function, C-reactive protein, erythrocyte sedimentation rate and ECG.

- To make a diagnosis of vasculitis/autoimmune disease: ANCA, anti-GBM antibodies, antinuclear antibodies, anti-

double-stranded DNA antibodies and complement (C3 and C4).

- To make a diagnosis of an infection-related syndrome: blood cultures and antistreptolysin antibody titres.

- To support treatment: blood cross-match.

Lung investigations

CXR should clearly be a first-line investigation in this case, looking for appearances suggesting diffuse alveolar haemorrhage (Fig. 14). Consider the following, depending on the fitness of the patient and clinical suspicion.

- Lung function tests: if the patient is well enough (which he may not be), looking for elevated Kco indicating pulmonary haemorrhage.

- CT scan of the chest: this may show appearances characteristic of alveolar bleeding; it is also good for demonstrating other pathology, eg pneumonia.

- Bronchoscopy and bronchoalveolar lavage: if infection is strongly suspected.

Renal investigations

Urine dipstick testing for proteinuria and haematuria, and urine microscopy for red cell casts are urgently required because they can establish the diagnosis of a renal

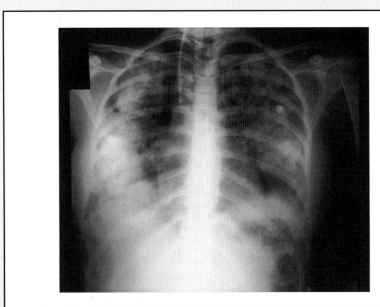

▲ **Fig. 14** CXR showing pulmonary haemorrhage in a case of pulmonary–renal syndrome.

inflammatory lesion. Urinary tract ultrasonography will be needed to demonstrate the presence of two normal-sized (and unobstructed) kidneys prior to renal biopsy, which will almost certainly be required to establish a definitive diagnosis of the particular type of pulmonary–renal syndrome. Key things to look for on the renal biopsy include the following.

- Vasculitis: glomeruli that contain crescents (cells/material within Bowman's space and outside the glomerular capillary tuft, which they may compress, hence 'crescentic glomerulonephritis') and areas of necrosis (pink amorphous material within the glomerular tuft on a standard haematoxylin/eosin stain, hence 'necrotising glomerulonephritis'), but no immunoglobulins or complement in the glomeruli (hence 'pauci-immune glomerulonephritis'). Not all glomeruli may be affected (hence 'focal glomerulonephritis') and within a glomerulus not all parts may be involved (hence 'segmental glomerulonephritis') (Fig. 15).

- Linear IgG deposition along the capillary basement membrane: Goodpasture's disease.

- Deposition of immunoglobulins and complement in the glomeruli: lupus/poststreptococcal glomerulonephritis.

Management

Supportive care
Patients with pulmonary haemorrhage are often very ill and require the following.

- Respiratory support: oxygen (high flow via reservoir bag if needed) to maintain adequate Po_2 levels (saturation >92%); ventilation if hypoxia does not respond to other measures.

- Haemostatic support: blood transfusion(s) if anaemic; correction of clotting abnormalities.

- Treatment of infection: low threshold for administration of antibiotics if infection is suspected.

- Renal replacement therapy: haemodialysis or haemofiltration if appropriate (see Section 1.4.1), and without heparin if possible.

Specific treatments
If pulmonary haemorrhage is secondary to vasculitis,

Goodpasture's disease or SLE, management should clearly be directed by an appropriate specialist, but the most commonly used initial treatment is a combination of the following.

- Steroids: usually initiated as intravenous methylprednisolone and then oral prednisolone.

- Immunosuppressant (cyclophosphamide).

- Plasma exchange/plasmapheresis: this is definitely indicated for the treatment of Goodpasture's disease with pulmonary haemorrhage, where the antibody is directly pathogenic. It is also used in pulmonary haemorrhage due to ANCA-associated vasculitis and SLE in some centres/cases.

A range of other immunosuppressants have been used with some success in individual cases.

Further comments
Anti-GBM disease (Goodpasture's) is almost always a 'one-hit' condition and does not relapse. In contrast, ANCA-positive vasculitis and SLE have a high incidence of relapse, and treatment is usually maintained for years. Repeated episodes of pulmonary haemorrhage can cause pulmonary fibrosis.

1.4.6 Renal colic

Scenario

A 47-year-old man presents to the Emergency Department with a 6-hour history of acute colicky loin pain, nausea, vomiting and haematuria.

Introduction
The diagnosis of renal colic is not usually difficult: typically there is

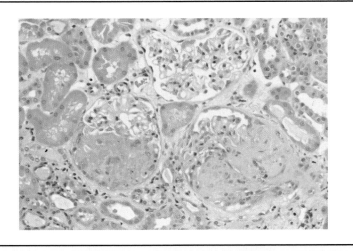

▲**Fig. 15** Renal histology in microscopic polyangiitis showing focal segmental necrotising glomerulonephritis with crescent formation.

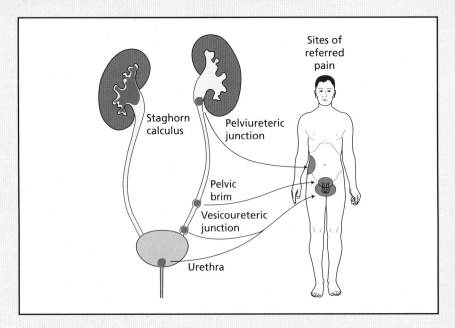

▲ Fig. 16 Sites where stones can lodge: the common sites at which urinary tract stones can lodge as they pass down the urinary system.

very severe colicky pain radiating from the flank. Sensory nerves from the ureter and renal pelvis enter the spinal cord at T11, T12, L1 and L2, and pain is referred to these dermatomes. Stones can lodge in the ureter at the pelviureteric junction, at the pelvic brim or at the ureterovesical junction. The renal pelvis refers pain to the loin and back, the lower ureter to the testis or labium majus, and the lowest pelvic part of the ureter to the tip of the penis or perineum (Fig. 16).

The priorities are to organise appropriate analgesia, confirm the suspected diagnosis of a ureteric stone and look for obstruction or infection. The possibility of an underlying stone-forming tendency needs to be considered after the acute problem has been dealt with.

History of the presenting problem

Ask about the following.

- Radiation of the pain: does this follow the pattern typical of renal/ureteric colic?

- Haematuria (present in this case).

- Passage of grit, gravel or stones in the urine, which clearly would confirm the diagnosis.

- Fevers, sweats and rigors: could there be infection, which with obstruction can be a very dangerous combination?

- Continued passing of urine: bladder stones can halt urine flow suddenly, with penile or perineal pain that is sometimes relieved by lying down.

The presence of haematuria in this case makes it nearly certain that the diagnosis is urinary stone, but if there is no history of blood in the urine and if the pain does not radiate in a typical manner, then consider the following.

- Musculoskeletal pain: not usually so severe, typically not associated with nausea or vomiting, may be exacerbated by movement, and the patient may be able to assume a comfortable position.

- Biliary colic: typically felt in the right upper quadrant and epigastrium; may be precipitated

by fatty food; and is also associated with nausea and vomiting, a past history of indigestion, dark urine and pale stools.

Other relevant history

Has the patient had any similar episodes previously? Ask carefully about predisposing factors: family history, bowel disease, diarrhoea and use of antacids or vitamin D-containing compounds.

Examination: general features

Once again it is important to make an initial assessment as to how ill the patient is (see Section 1.4.1), but the details given here do not indicate that the patient is likely to be very ill. Note particularly the following.

- Evidence of infection: is there a fever? Is the kidney tender?

- Are there any physical signs that might suggest a different diagnosis? In the spine and back, does movement exacerbate the pain? Is there local tenderness? In the upper abdomen, is there right upper quadrant or epigastric tenderness? Is this gallbladder pain?

Investigations

Blood and urine tests

- Urine dipstick (if there is not at least a trace of haematuria, then the diagnosis of renal colic is in doubt) and urine culture.

- FBC, electrolytes, creatinine, liver/bone function tests.

- Blood culture (if there is clinical suspicion of infection).

Imaging

To confirm the diagnosis of urinary stone disease, to demonstrate the site of any stone, to detect evidence (if any) of obstruction and to look for the presence of other stones.

- Plain radiography: ask for a radiograph of kidneys, ureter and bladder, which should reveal radio-opaque stones (containing calcium and cystine, but not urate).

- Ultrasonography: detects all stone types and will demonstrate obstruction, but is often difficult in the lower ureter.

- CT or intravenous urogram: defines the site of obstruction and the stone is usually visible as a filling defect in the ureter.

Urate stones are radiolucent.

Management

Immediate priorities

- Give adequate analgesia and antiemetics as the pain of renal colic is very severe: NSAIDs such as diclofenac are often used, alone or with opioids. If possible, avoid NSAIDs if there is significant renal impairment.

- Maintain adequate hydration, if necessary with intravenous fluids.

- If infected, treat vigorously.

Obstruction without infection

This is usually diagnosed when ultrasonography shows dilatation of the pelvicalyceal system but there are no clinical or laboratory features to suggest infection. Stones smaller than 6 mm in diameter usually pass spontaneously, but stones larger than 1 cm will probably not. If the patient's pain is controlled and the stone is small, observe carefully. If there is no progress over a few days or if the stone is large, then the obstruction must be relieved. A range of techniques is available to urologists for this purpose: extracorporeal shock-wave lithotripsy and endoscopic, percutaneous or open surgical removal (Fig. 17).

Obstruction with infection

This is an emergency requiring urgent (same-day) relief of obstruction, usually by anterograde percutaneous nephrostomy, and broad-spectrum intravenous antibiotics pending culture results.

Further comments

See Section 2.6.2 for details of the approach to making the diagnosis of the specific type of urinary stone and preventive treatment.

1.4.7 Backache and renal failure

Scenario

A 60-year-old man is referred to the medical admissions unit with general malaise and lower backache. On examination, he is dehydrated and there is tenderness over his lumbar spine. Initial investigations reveal serum calcium of 3.2 mmol/L and creatinine of 275 μmol/L.

Introduction

The priorities with hypercalcaemia are to rehydrate the patient, control the hypercalcaemia and establish a diagnosis. The main causes of hypercalcaemia are shown in Table 9. In this case, myeloma seems the most likely diagnosis (Fig. 18), but other malignancies with lumbar metastases should also be considered.

History of the presenting problem

Hypercalcaemia can cause many symptoms (Table 10). Ask about these: they may give a clue as to how long ago problems began.

Chronically high serum calcium levels cause neurological, gastrointestinal and renal symptoms (depressive moans, abdominal groans and renal stones).

Other relevant history

Ask in particular about the following.

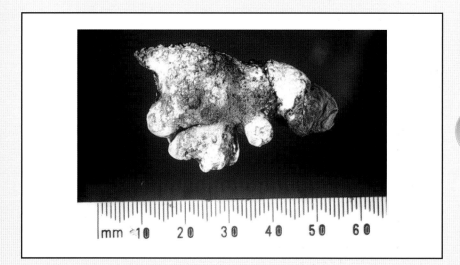

▲ **Fig. 17** A huge staghorn calculus that was surgically removed. (Courtesy of Dr J.E. Scoble, Guy's Hospital.)

TABLE 9 CAUSES OF HYPERCALCAEMIA

Common	Other
Malignancy: myeloma or metastases from solid tumour	Chronic renal failure with tertiary hyperparathyroidism
Primary hyperparathyroidism	Vitamin D excess
Sarcoid or other granulomatous conditions	Thiazide diuretics
	Immobilisation
	Thyrotoxicosis

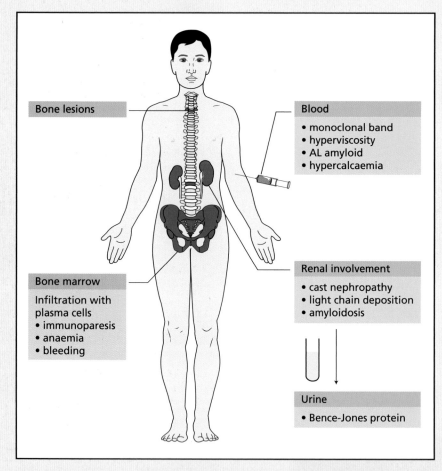

Bone lesions

Blood
• monoclonal band
• hyperviscosity
• AL amyloid
• hypercalcaemia

Bone marrow
Infiltration with plasma cells
• immunoparesis
• anaemia
• bleeding

Renal involvement
• cast nephropathy
• light chain deposition
• amyloidosis

Urine
• Bence-Jones protein

▲**Fig. 18** Clinical features of myeloma: the different ways in which myeloma can affect the patient.

- Weight loss: a general feature of malignancy.

- Pointers to a primary tumour, eg haemoptysis and rectal bleeding.

- Drug history: including over-the-counter medications (antacids and 'white medicine') and vitamin supplements (cod liver oil/vitamin D), which many patients do not regard as drugs.

Examination: general features

As always in an acute context it is vital to make an initial assessment as to how ill the patient is (see Section 1.4.1), but the details given here do not indicate that the patient is likely to be very ill. Note particularly the following.

- Fluid status: the details given state that the patient is dehydrated, but is there clear evidence of intravascular volume depletion (postural drop in BP and low JVP) and/or dehydration (reduced skin turgor and dry mucous membranes/axillae)?

- Evidence of malignancy: in particular, are any lymph nodes palpable? Are there any chest signs? Feel carefully for any abdominal mass or hepatomegaly, and do not forget rectal examination. Look for localised bone deformity or tenderness. In a woman, check the breasts.

> Hypercalcaemia increases urinary sodium and water loss. This causes dehydration and a fall in glomerular filtration rate, which further reduces urinary calcium excretion.

Investigations

Blood tests

- FBC and blood film: is there anaemia? Are there rouleaux suggesting myeloma? See Fig. 19.

- Sodium and potassium;

- Calcium and creatinine (to monitor for deterioration or improvement).

- Liver and bone function tests (may give clue to malignancy).

- Immunoglobulins, serum and urinary electophoresis: look for monoclonal band in serum, Bence Jones protein in urine and immunoparesis, all suggesting myeloma.

- Parathyroid hormone: will be suppressed by any cause of hypercalcaemia other than hyperparathyroidism, when it will be high or inappropriately

TABLE 10 SYMPTOMS AND SIGNS OF HYPERCALCAEMIA

	Symptom	Sign
Neurological	Drowsiness Lethargy Weakness Depression	Coma
Gastrointestinal	Constipation Nausea Vomiting Anorexia Peptic ulceration	
Renal	Nephrogenic diabetes insipidus and dehydration Urinary stones	Nephrocalcinosis/urinary stone
Cardiac		Shortening of the QT interval, sometimes with broad T waves and atrioventricular block
Others		Corneal calcification Tissue calcification may be detectable radiographically

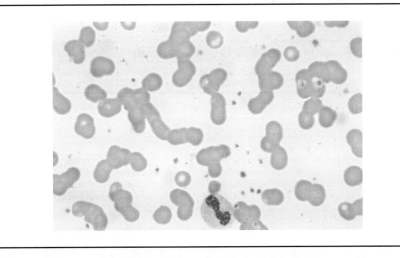

▲ **Fig. 19** Peripheral blood film of a patient with myeloma. The red blood cells have formed stacks known as rouleaux. (Courtesy of Dr J.A. Amess, St Bartholomew's Hospital.)

(given hypercalcaemia) at the upper limit of the normal range.

- Serum angiotensin-converting enzyme (if sarcoid is suspected).

Imaging

- CXR: bony secondaries and lung cancer.

- Skeletal survey: lytic lesions and features of myeloma.

- Kidneys, ureter and bladder radiograph: nephrocalcinosis and urinary stones.

- Ultrasonography of urinary tract: obstruction, nephrocalcinosis and renal stones.

Other investigations, as clinically indicated

- Examination of bone marrow: look for excess plasma cells diagnostic of myeloma (Fig. 20).

- Sepsis screen: urine, blood and other appropriate cultures.

- Renal biopsy: sometimes appropriate in myeloma with renal impairment to establish the nature and chronicity of damage, and hence the potential for reversibility.

Hypercalcaemia and myeloma

- Hypercalcaemia occurs in about 25% of patients with myeloma.
- Myeloma cells secrete osteoclast-mobilising and -stimulating cytokines, and osteoclasts secrete interleukin 6 which is a growth factor for myeloma cells.
- Bone destruction is caused by osteoclasts related to collections of myeloma cells.
- Osteoblastic activity is reduced, so bone scans are usually negative in myeloma.

Management

Fluid

Whatever the cause of hypercalcaemia, initial management is to correct volume depletion while carefully monitoring the patient and his urine output to ensure that you do not overload him in the (relatively unlikely) event that his renal function does not pick up with volume expansion.

- Correct volume depletion: this may require several litres of intravenous 0.9% ('normal') saline. Give 1 L over 1–2 hours and then reassess clinically; repeat until signs of hypovolaemia have been corrected (no postural drop in BP and JVP easily seen).

- Consider giving a loop diuretic (eg furosemide 40–80 mg iv) to increase urinary volume and calcium excretion if urine output

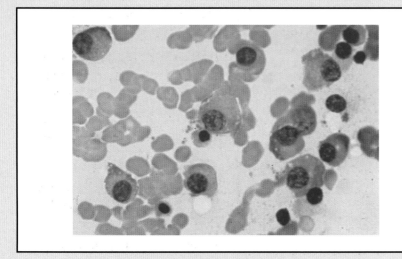

▲ **Fig. 20** Bone marrow appearances in myeloma. There are multiple nucleated plasma cells infiltrating the bone marrow. (Courtesy of Dr J.A. Amess, St Bartholomew's Hospital.)

is below 100 mL/hour (probably of little benefit if the patient is polyuric).

After restoration of circulating volume, further fluid management should be dictated by urinary output.

- Urine output satisfactory (>100 mL/hour): ensure that fluid input (oral or intravenous) is enough to sustain a urine output of 3 L/day, but monitor this closely and reduce input if urine output not maintained.

- Urine output not satisfactory: this indicates that volume depletion is not the sole explanation for renal impairment (prerenal renal failure) and other pathological processes are involved (eg myeloma kidney, acute tubular necrosis, urinary obstruction).

Fluid management in the patient with renal impairment

- Ensure adequate filling: no volume depletion (no postural drop in BP, no low JVP) and no volume overload (breathless, high JVP and basal crackles).

- Give input equal to all measured outputs plus 500–1000 mL/day for insensible losses.
- Examine patient at least once a day for signs of volume depletion or overload and adjust input as appropriate.

Other treatments for hypercalcaemia

If the patient's serum calcium remains very high (>3.0 mmol/L) or he continues to be symptomatic from hypercalcaemia, further therapy for hypercalcaemia might include bisphosphonates or steroids.

- Bisphosphonates: the P–O–P bond of pyrophosphate is cleaved by a phosphatase during bone mineralisation and in osteoclastic bone resorption. Bisphosphonates contain a P–C–P bond that is resistant to cleavage; they bind tightly to any calcified bone matrix, impairing both mineralisation and resorption. Disodium pamidronate is commonly used to treat this, up to a maximum of 90 mg by slow intravenous injection.

- Steroids, eg prednisolone 20 mg daily, are very effective in hypercalcaemia caused by sarcoidosis, and may be of some more limited use in hypercalcaemia caused by vitamin D intoxication or myeloma. They reduce calcium absorption in the gut, reduce the production of osteoclast-activating cytokines and can induce tumour lysis. They usually take 1 to 2 days to act.

Management of myeloma

See *Haematology*, Section 2.2.1. Note that the 1-year survival rate for patients with myeloma who require long-term dialysis is only 50%.

Further comments

Does renal impairment need investigation if there is hypercalcaemia? If renal impairment does not completely correct with rehydration and other measures to lower serum calcium, then it is essential to find out why. See Section 1.4.2 for further discussion, but the key elements include the following.

- Dipstick of urine and urine microscopy: proteinuria and haematuria would almost certainly indicate kidney myeloma, but could also indicate another renal inflammatory lesion, eg malignancy-associated glomerulonephritis.

- Renal ultrasonography: what is the renal size? Is there obstruction?

- Daily check of fluid input, urine output and patient weight: with appropriate fluid management to ensure that the patient does not become fluid depleted or volume overloaded.

- Daily measurement of renal function and serum calcium.

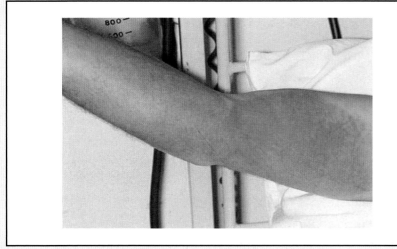

▲ **Fig. 21** Swollen arm caused by muscle damage. If ischaemic compression is suspected, an urgent orthopaedic opinion should be sought as fasciotomy or débridement may be limb-saving.

1.4.8 Renal failure and coma

Scenario

A 34-year-old man is found collapsed at home 18 hours after spending a night on a drinking binge with friends. You are the junior doctor on duty in the Emergency Department when he is brought to the resuscitation room. There is no other history available.

Examination

Your initial assessment is as for anyone in coma.

- *Airway, Breathing* and *Circulation* (ABC).

- *Disability* (neurological assessment): Glasgow Coma Scale (GCS) and pupillary responses.

For further details of how to deal with the comatose patient see *Acute Medicine*, Section 1.2.31.

The initial assessment reveals the following.

- The patient's airway is patent: he is breathing spontaneously with a respiratory rate of 12 breaths/min and his arterial oxygen saturation,

measured by pulse oximetry, is 99% on high-flow oxygen.

- His heart rate is 120 bpm, with BP 87/45 mmHg.

- His GCS score is 10/15, ie eyes 2, voice 3 and motor 5. His pupils are normal size, equal and reactive.

What is your next step? ABCD is followed by E (*Exposure*). Make a thorough examination of the patient, which reveals that he:

- looks dehydrated;

- has a tender tense swelling of the right arm, and the hand is discoloured but warm with palpable pulses (Fig. 21).

More information becomes available.

- He is catheterised by one of the nursing staff and passes a small quantity of dark-brown urine.

- The laboratory phones through the results of urgent blood tests, which demonstrate potassium 7.2 mmol/L, urea 15 mmol/L, creatinine 430 µmol/L, phosphate 3.6 mmol/L and corrected calcium 1.85 mmol/L.

The diagnosis is clear: rhabdomyolysis is responsible for his renal failure, with muscle breakdown originating from the right arm, which was injured by ischaemic compression during coma. The electrolyte results are typical: hyperkalaemia, hypocalcaemia and hyperphosphataemia. The causes of rhabdomyolysis are shown in Table 11: excess alcohol and drug overdose are common contributors, as seems very likely in this case.

Rhabdomyolysis

- Suspect in unexplained renal failure, particularly if associated with coma.
- Look carefully for evidence of muscle damage or limb ischaemia.

TABLE 11 CAUSES OF RHABDOMYOLYSIS

Frequency	Cause	Example
Common	Crush injury	Trauma or coma with compression
	Ischaemic injury	Femoral artery thrombosis or
	Prolonged epileptic fits	embolism
	Severe exercise	
	Snake bite (commonest cause in some parts of the world)	
Rare	Infections	Viral necrotising myositis and coxsackievirus
	Inflammatory myopathies	Polymyositis
	Metabolic myopathies	McCardle's syndrome
	Malignant hyperpyrexia	
	Drugs	Statins
	Hypothyroidism	

Investigations

As in Section 1.4.1, with particular note paid to the following.

- ECG: hyperkalaemia is often severe in renal failure associated with rhabdomyolysis.

- Urine dipstick and microscopy: with rhabdomyolysis the urine looks brown (like a cola drink) and registers strongly positive for haem on dipstick testing, although there are no red cells visible on microscopy.

- Creatine kinase: measure whenever rhabdomyolysis is suspected. A grossly elevated value (>10,000 U/L, with a normal upper limit of 180–200 U/L) establishes the diagnosis; a less elevated value is consistent with it but not diagnostic.

- Arterial blood gases: metabolic acidosis is expected.

- Toxicology: in the comatose patient and/or where drug overdose is a possibility.

- In rhabdomyolysis serum potassium rises rapidly and can be life-threatening.
- Phosphate rises rapidly and calcium is usually low.
- Creatine kinase is massively elevated, as are other muscle enzymes (aminotransferase and lactate dehydrogenase).

Management

- Close clinical monitoring: aside from regular checks of vital signs and urine output, keep a careful watch on the arm. Apart from the swollen tender muscles, examination should look for distal neurovascular compromise: skin colour and temperature, capillary refill, pulses and sensation (if and when the patient regains consciousness).

- Close biochemical monitoring: regular measurement (at least every 12 hours) of electrolytes and renal function tests. Hyperkalaemia can develop rapidly in this context.

The following are the immediate issues.

- Standard measures to manage the unconscious patient.

- Initial management of hyperkalaemia (see Section 1.4.1).

- Monitor hourly urine output (via urinary catheter).

- Aggressive fluid resuscitation to correct intravascular volume depletion, with the aim of achieving a urine output of >100 mL/hour (as described in Section 1.4.7).

Get surgical/orthopaedic help quickly: urgent fasciotomy or débridement may be needed to treat compartment syndrome and save the ischaemic limb. Compartment syndrome refers to ischaemic compression created by swelling within a muscle group that is constrained by fascial planes, resulting in necrosis of the muscle with or without compromise of the distal limb circulation.

Further comments

What about urinary alkalinisation?

Myoglobin is more soluble in alkaline urine (pH >6.5) and urinary alkalinisation has frequently been used in patients with rhabdomyolysis. This is achieved by intravenous infusion of isotonic (1.26%) sodium bicarbonate as part of the fluid regimen, but there is no controlled-trial evidence that this is better than resuscitation and maintenance of diuresis with 0.9% saline. However, bicarbonate infusion can worsen both hypocalcaemia and fluid overload, and is perhaps best reserved for hyperkalaemic, volume-replete patients with an adequate urine output.

When does the patient need dialysis?

Standard indications for dialysis apply (see Section 1.4.1), but note that metabolic disturbances can worsen more rapidly in patients with rhabdomyolysis than with other sorts of renal failure, so consult renal services sooner rather than later. Dialysis does not remove myoglobin.

Who should be investigated for an underlying muscle disorder?

An underlying muscle disorder should be considered if the patient presents without a clear precipitant, if there is a preceding history of increasing or intermittent muscle fatigue, or if there is a clinical picture suggestive of an inflammatory process. Diagnosis is usually by muscle biopsy.

2.1 Major renal syndromes

2.1.1 Acute renal failure

Abnormal renal function, identified by a high creatinine or oliguria (<30 mL/hour), is frequent and caused by a wide range of processes. When it develops over hours or days, the term 'acute renal failure' is used.

Aetiology/pathophysiology

Acute renal failure (ARF) can be caused by a problem anywhere from the renal artery to the urethra. It is useful to classify ARF according to where the principal problem is: prerenal, renal or postrenal (Fig. 22).

Epidemiology

Transient renal dysfunction occurs in up to 5% of hospital admissions. In the UK, severe ARF (a reversible increase in creatinine >500 μmol/L) has an incidence of about 140 per million population per year.

Clinical presentation

Usually ARF is diagnosed on the basis of elevated plasma creatinine, or when oliguria develops in a patient whose urine output is being monitored reliably (eg catheterised). Sometimes the presentation will be a direct consequence of the renal failure (eg fluid overload or acidosis), but usually features of the underlying condition predominate.

Immediate consideration must be given to whether dialysis (or another intervention) is required urgently. A circulatory assessment is essential.

In glomerulonephritis, there may be a nephritic presentation, ie the combination of oliguria, hypertension, oedema and haematuria.

> Renal failure does not usually cause specific symptoms. Have a high index of suspicion for any patient who is unwell for any reason and have a low threshold for measuring plasma creatinine.

Investigations

To assess severity/danger

The following are appropriate in all cases of ARF.

- Serum potassium and ECG (hyperkalaemia).

- Blood gases (Po_2 and pH; oxgenation and acidosis).

- CXR (pulmonary oedema and others).

To determine the cause of the renal failure

- Examine the urine (blood, protein and casts).

- Renal ultrasonography (obstruction).

- Obtain results of any previous blood tests to prove that renal failure is acute.

- Further investigations will be guided by the clinical setting.

Many cases of ARF will merit renal biopsy to establish the diagnosis.

Specific diagnoses

- Acute tubular necrosis (ATN): often the cause of ARF is prerenal failure/ATN. A renal biopsy will be performed only if there is doubt about the diagnosis.

- Obstructive uropathy will usually be diagnosed on ultrasonography. Be aware that occasionally rapid-onset obstructive uropathy, especially if the patient is volume depleted, may not result in hydronephrosis.

- Suspected renovascular disease/occlusion or renal vein thrombosis: magnetic resonance angiography or digital subtraction X-ray angiography is the preferred investigation if a case of renal failure might be the result of renal artery occlusion/stenosis or renal vein thrombosis (usually in a patient with nephrotic syndrome).

- Blood tests will be helpful in certain settings, and in some circumstances will mean that a biopsy is not required, eg haemolytic–uraemic syndrome, disseminated intravascular coagulation and rhabdomyolysis.

Treatment

Urgent attention is given to maintaining oxygenation and circulation. Determine whether immediate renal replacement is required.

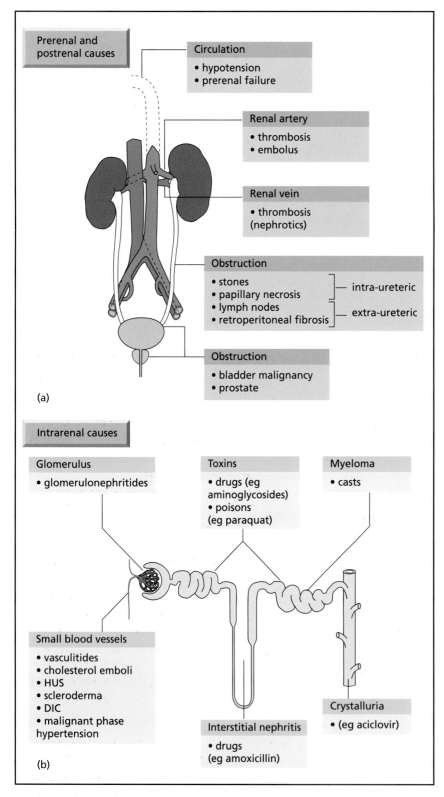

(a)

(b)

Indications for renal replacement therapy

- Hyperkalaemia (K^+ >6.5 mmol/L): seriousness is best evaluated by ECG (Fig. 23).
- Fluid overload not responsive to diuretic.
- Acidosis.
- Generally if urea >40 mmol/L (certainly if >50 mmol/L).

ARF is frequently a manifestation of a very serious systemic illness. Sometimes, for instance in the setting of disseminated malignancy, dialysis is technically feasible but may not be appropriate.

Supportive treatment

- Optimise the circulation: if the lungs are clear on auscultation give fluid rapidly until the JVP is seen easily, then stop and review the situation.

- Treat infection.

- Avoid further renal insults (eg hypotension and nephrotoxic drugs).

- Maintain nutrition (enteral or parenteral if necessary).

- Monitor fluid balance: input/output charts and daily weighing.

- Monitor renal function: biochemistry and urine output.

- Renal replacement if necessary.

Treat underlying cause
See Sections 2.3–2.7.

Prognosis
The mortality rate is about 40% in those requiring renal replacement therapy for ARF. It is much better

▲ **Fig. 22** Selected causes of acute renal failure: (**a**) prerenal and postrenal; (**b**) intrarenal. DIC, disseminated intravascular coagulation; HUS, haemolytic–uraemic syndrome.

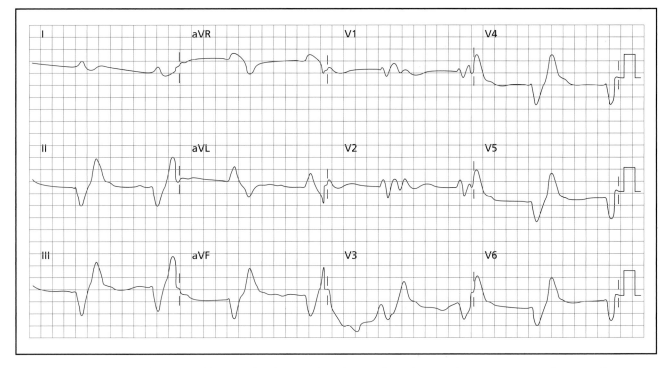

▲ **Fig. 23** ECG showing changes of severe hyperkalaemia. Widened QRS complexes slur into tall tented T waves. There are no P waves. Cardiac arrest will occur soon if appropriate action is not taken immediately (see Section 1.4.1).

when renal failure is not associated with other organ failure.

2.1.2 Chronic renal failure

Chronic renal impairment is the irreversible loss of glomerular filtration rate (GFR). This is important for two main reasons:

- there may be direct consequences of impaired renal function;

- loss of GFR tends to be progressive, ultimately leading to end-stage renal failure.

Normal young adults have a much higher GFR (approximately 10-fold) than that needed for life, so substantial decrements in GFR often cause few (if any) symptoms.

> Do not dismiss a slightly elevated creatinine level as a minor problem. In chronic renal impairment, lost nephrons cannot be recovered and an elevated creatinine score represents a loss of about 50% of GFR.

Aetiology/pathophysiology

Diverse primary processes result in the loss of GFR (see Sections 2.3–2.7). The following are the most common causes in the UK:

- diabetes mellitus;

- glomerulonephritides (most common is IgA nephropathy);

- congenital dysplasia/chronic pyelonephritis/reflux nephropathy;

- obstructive uropathy;

- autosomal dominant polycystic kidney disease;

- vascular disease/hypertension.

Loss of renal function tends to be progressive, probably as a result of the following:

- continuing loss of nephrons from the primary process (eg glomerulonephritis);

- glomerular hypertension in remaining glomeruli, which increases GFR per nephron but in doing so leads to loss of further

nephrons (the hyperfiltration hypothesis).

Epidemiology

Normal GFR in the population varies with age (Fig. 24), falling as patients get older. Since muscle bulk (and thus creatinine production) also decreases with age, the normal range for plasma creatinine remains the same. An elevated creatinine will be outside the normal range of GFR at any age, and usually represents a loss of about 50% of GFR. In elderly people, a slightly elevated creatinine may represent a GFR of only 30 mL/min.

Investigation and interventions need to be considered in those who are outside the normal range for GFR and have risk factors for progression (hypertension or proteinuria), or when renal function is changing, even if the absolute value lies within the normal range (Table 12). Prevention of progression is clearly most effective if started early, well

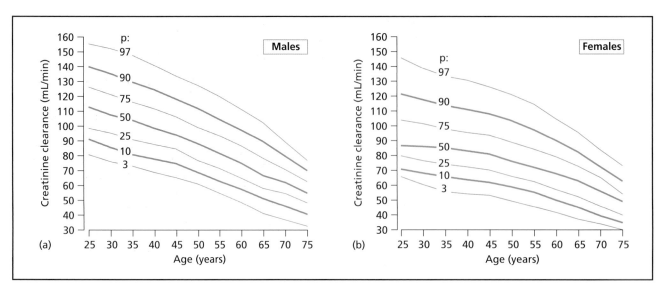

▲**Fig. 24** Percentiles (p:) of creatinine clearances according to age and sex, calculated using the method of Cockcroft and Gault. (Redrawn with permission from M.M. Elseviers *et al. Lancet* 1987; 329: 457.)

CKD stage	GFR (mL/min per 1.73 m^2)	Interventions
I	≥90, with urinary markers or imaging indicating kidney damage	Control blood pressure and cardiovascular risk factors
II[2]	60–89, with urinary markers or imaging indicating kidney damage	Control blood pressure and cardiovascular risk factors
III	30–59	Control blood pressure and cardiovascular risk factors
IV	15–30	Plan for renal replacement therapy (RRT) if appropriate. Likely to need erythropoietin, dietary restriction of phosphate and potassium, and vitamin D analogue
V	≤14	Likely need to commence RRT (or conservative management if RRT is inappropriate)

TABLE 12 STAGES OF CHRONIC KIDNEY DISEASE[1] (CKD) AS DEFINED IN THE AMERICAN KIDNEY DISEASES OUTCOME QUALITY INITIATIVE (KDOQI)

1. 'Chronic' is defined as markers of kidney damage or GFR <60 mL/min per 1.73 m^2 persisting for at least 3 months. In all cases consideration should be given to identifying any potentially treatable cause of continuing renal damage (eg systemic vasculitis and tubulointerstitial nephritis).
2. Note that a patient should *not* be described as having CKD stage II just on the basis of having a GFR in the range 60–89.

- Symptoms/findings attributable to loss of renal function are often present in those with more severe renal impairment, but they are relatively non-specific, eg fatigue, anaemia and disturbed taste.

- A significant number of patients will have previously unrecognised end-stage renal failure at presentation.

> ⚠ Signs and symptoms pointing to chronic renal impairment rather than acute renal failure are commonly quoted but are very unreliable. Assume that any patient has acute (ie potentially reversible) renal failure until you can prove that it is chronic, for example by finding a blood test showing a similar level of renal function months or years previously, or reduced renal size.

> 🔑 Symptoms attributable to loss of renal function usually only occur when there is severe renal impairment (GFR <25 mL/min). This has two implications:
>
> - check creatinine in high-risk populations (people with diabetes or hypertension, or those with protein or blood on a dipstick test);
> - in patients with moderately elevated creatinine (<300 μmol/L), symptoms need another explanation.

before there are any symptoms attributable to renal failure.

Clinical presentation

- Most often with the incidental finding of a raised creatinine, abnormal urinalysis or hypertension.

- Sometimes with symptoms related to underlying process (eg macroscopic haematuria or outflow obstruction).

Investigations

To guide interventions

- Biochemistry: potassium, creatinine, calcium and phosphate.

- Haematological parameters.

Identify cause of renal impairment

If possible, identify the cause of renal impairment, especially treatable conditions. All patients should have:

- urinalysis and microscopy;

- renal ultrasonography.

Further tests are guided by these and the probable underlying cause in the particular patient. The choice of tests is also influenced by whether or not a treatable condition could be identified.

- Older patients should usually have serum and urine electrophoresis (Fig. 25).

- Patients with normal-sized unobstructed kidneys without scars should usually have a renal biopsy.

- Those with small kidneys should usually not be biopsied: the hazards are substantial and no useful information can be obtained.

- Monitoring renal function over time is important. Once creatinine is elevated (usually indicating loss of about 50% of normal GFR for age), serum creatinine alone gives a simple and reliable measure.

- Some drugs (eg trimethoprim and cimetidine) decrease creatinine secretion, causing a reversible rise in plasma creatinine. This can be mistaken for a deterioration in renal function.

> Once an individual's creatinine is elevated, this gives a sensitive and straightforward indicator of changes in renal function, and it is not usually necessary to measure creatinine clearance. This avoids the inaccuracies and inconvenience of 24-hour urine collections: many patients fail to collect all urine for precisely 24 hours. If you try it for yourself, you will understand why!

> Often a reciprocal plot of creatinine against time is linear (Fig. 26), representing a constant rate of loss of GFR. This plot is useful in:
>
> - predicting when end-stage renal failure is likely to be reached;
> - determining whether a new value of creatinine is consistent with the expected trend – if a new value indicates a faster than expected deterioration, it may prompt a search for another cause (eg prostatic obstruction, urinary tract infection or an NSAID).

Complications and treatment

Aims are to:

- prevent progression of CRF;

- prevent secondary complications.

Where possible, the underlying cause of the renal damage should be treated or corrected (eg analgesic nephropathy, systemic lupus erythematosus, paraproteinaemia).

Progression of CRF

As stated previously, irrespective of cause, there is a tendency for CRF to progress.

> The amount of proteinuria correlates well with the risk of progression of CRF (Fig. 27).

Many interventions alter the course of CRF in animal models, including the following.

- Antihypertensives, especially angiotensin-converting enzyme (ACE) inhibitors and angiotensin receptor blockers (ARBs). These have a preferential action on the efferent arteriole, lowering glomerular pressure more than systemic BP.

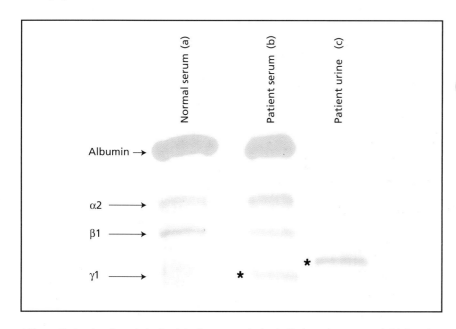

Albumin →

α2 ——→

β1 ——→

γ1 ——→

Normal serum (a) Patient serum (b) Patient urine (c)

▲ **Fig. 25** Electrophoretic analysis of proteins in serum and urine. In the normal serum sample (**a**), there is a broad gamma band containing IgA, IgG and IgM. In the sample from the patient (**b**), there is a monoclonal band (indicated by asterisk), which is an IgG κ paraprotein. In the urine (**c**), there is a band which represents free κ light chain. (Courtesy of Dr S. Marshall, Oxford Radcliffe Hospitals.)

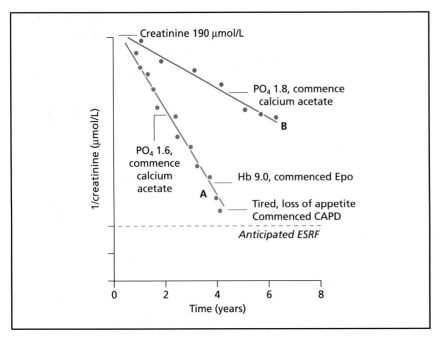

▲**Fig. 26** Reciprocal creatinine plots against time for two patients with progressive chronic renal failure (CRF). Patient A had IgA nephropathy, with protein excretion of 3 g per 24 hours. Patient B had autosomal dominant polycystic kidney disease. CAPD, continuous ambulatory peritoneal dialysis; Epo, erythropoietin; ESRF, end-stage renal failure.

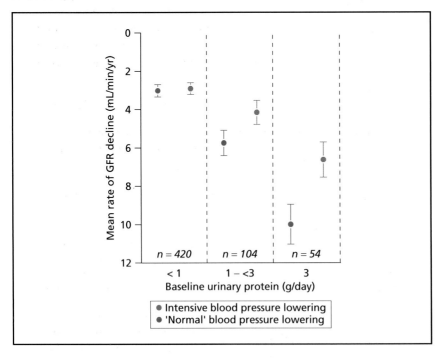

▲**Fig. 27** Rate of loss of renal function (mL/min per year) in a randomised study comparing a target mean arterial pressure of 107 mmHg with one of 92 mmHg. The patients were categorised according to the amount of proteinuria (g per 24 hours).

- Protein restriction.

- Lipid-lowering agents.

- Antiplatelet agents.

- Immunosuppression.

- NSAIDs.

Antihypertensives, particularly ACE inhibitors and ARBs, are the only treatment that has been proved to influence the progression of CRF in convincing clinical trials in humans (see below).

In diabetics, good glycaemic control should be encouraged. Successful pancreatic transplantation has been shown to reverse the histological changes of diabetic nephropathy.

Antihypertensive agents

Diabetes

In one study, 409 patients with type 1 diabetes were randomised to captopril or placebo. Other antihypertensives (but not calcium channel blockers or other ACE inhibitors) could be added. After 4 years of similar BP control, the group given captopril had a slower rate of increase in plasma creatinine and less likelihood of end-stage renal failure or death. In those with creatinine >132 µmol/L, the annual rate of rise in the placebo group was 123 µmol/L versus 53 µmol/L in the captopril-treated group. Importantly, there was benefit in normotensive patients. In nephropathy due to type 2 diabetes the largest trials have been of ARBs, which were shown to protect renal function (RENAAL and IDNT studies).

Non-diabetic CRF

The Modification of Diet in Renal Disease was a 2 × 2 study of 840 patients that examined the effect of protein restriction; it also compared aggressive and standard BP control. Achieved mean arterial pressure in the groups was 91 and 96 mmHg (corresponding to 125/75 and 130/80 mmHg, respectively). The benefit was greatest in those with more proteinuria (>3 g/day) and moderate renal impairment (see Fig. 27).

Subsequent large randomised trials have shown that ACE inhibitors offer greater protection of renal function compared with placebo or other antihypertensive agents in patients with significant proteinuria (eg Ramipril Efficiency In Nephropathy trial). There is some evidence for further benefit with the addition of an ARB to an ACE inhibitor (COOPERATE study).

TABLE 13 FOODS AND DRINKS HIGH IN POTASSIUM AND SOME OF THEIR ALTERNATIVES

Foods and drinks high in potassium	Alternatives
Coffee	Tea
Fruit juice	Squashes
Beer, cider, sherry, wine	Spirits
Bananas, grapes, oranges	Apples, pears, satsumas
Chips/french fries, jacket potatoes	Rice, pasta
Baked beans, mushrooms, tomatoes	Carrots, cabbage, lettuce
Chocolate	Boiled sweets
Crisps and nuts	
Salt substitutes (eg Lo Salt)	

Contolling BP is the only intervention that has been proved to slow the progression of chronic renal impairment in humans. In patients with heavy proteinuria (>3 g per 24 hours), a BP of 125/75 mmHg is more beneficial than one of 130/80 mmHg (see Fig. 27).

Hypertension

A high proportion of patients with CRF (80% as end-stage renal failure approaches) will have hypertension. Treating hypertension slows CRF progression, especially in those with proteinuria (see above), and is also presumed to reduce cardiovascular risk.

Treatment strategy When planning, remember the following.

- Most patients are salt sensitive so it is appropriate to decrease salt intake.

- Many patients will require multiple antihypertensive drugs. The first-choice antihypertensive is an ACE inhibitor (based on animal studies and studies of people with diabetes), except in those with renovascular disease.

- Loop diuretics (eg furosemide) are useful adjunctive agents, especially if there is evidence of sodium overload (oedema).

- In patients with proteinuria >3 g per 24 hours or diabetes, the target BP should be <125/75 mmHg.

Hyperkalaemia

Hyperkalaemia will cause symptoms only at near-lethal levels. Serum potassium should be monitored by blood tests (not symptoms!) and, acutely, ECG.

Treatment strategy Plan as follows:

- dietary restriction of potassium intake (Table 13);

- avoid potassium-sparing diuretics;

- consider changing from ACE inhibitor/ARB;

- correct acidosis;

- in diabetes, improve diabetic control;

- for emergency management, see Section 1.4.1.

Acidosis

Metabolic acidosis is usually a clinical problem only at or near end-stage renal failure, and may contribute to feelings of malaise and breathlessness. It is identified and monitored by measuring venous bicarbonate.

Treatment strategy Remember to take account of the following:

- avoid excessive protein intake;

- consider oral sodium bicarbonate (but a sodium load may exacerbate hypertension);

- some patients will need dialysis.

Bone and mineral metabolism

As CRF progresses, phosphate excretion is insufficient and plasma phosphate rises, stimulating parathyroid hormone (PTH) secretion (Fig. 28). Also, 1α-hydroxylation of vitamin D (proximal tubule mitochondria) is impaired, which:

- derepresses PTH;

- reduces calcium absorption and serum calcium, further stimulating PTH.

Consequences of elevated PTH In normal individuals this produces marked phosphaturia. However, in those with CRF this does not occur and phosphate rises as a result of increased bone turnover, further stimulating PTH. This results in the following:

- bone loss and risk of fractures;

- Progressive parathyroid hyperplasia, and eventual autonomy;

- itching and calcinosis cutis;

- pyrophosphate arthropathy.

Treatment strategy This should include the following.

- Dietary restriction of phosphate.

- Phosphate binders, eg calcium acetate before food. The use of calcium is often limited by hypercalcaemia. Aluminium compounds are effective, but can cause toxicity as a result of accumulation. Sevelamer hydrochloride is a relatively new treatment that reduces these problems but it is expensive.

- Alfacalcidol or calcitriol: corrects deficiency in activated vitamin D

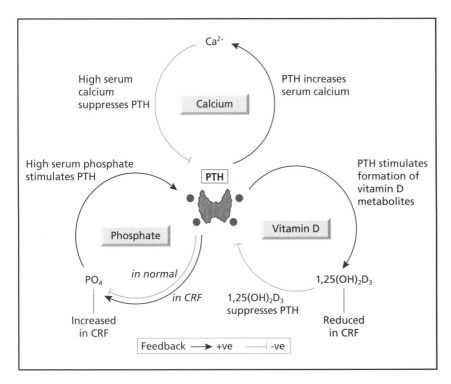

▲ **Fig. 28** The central role of the parathyroid gland in bone and mineral homeostasis, and the principal effects of chronic renal impairment.

(Fig. 29). Its use may be restricted by hypercalcaemia, and it also tends to increase plasma phosphate.

- Cinacalcet: stimulates the calcium-sensing receptor, leading to decreased PTH secretion.

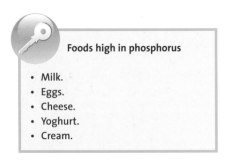

Foods high in phosphorus

- Milk.
- Eggs.
- Cheese.
- Yoghurt.
- Cream.

Anaemia

In renal disease, the renal cortical and outer medullary fibroblasts produce less erythropoietin for a given haematocrit. Consequently, the haemoglobin set point falls as GFR falls. The resulting anaemia is normochromic and normocytic (Fig. 30). Always consider other contributory factors, eg iron

deficiency or ongoing inflammation. Consequences include fatigue and left ventricular hypertrophy (LVH).

Treat with recombinant erythropoietin, which is usually not necessary until creatinine is above 350 μmol/L. Aim to maintain haemoglobin >10.5 g/dL.

Cardiovascular risk and LVH

There is high cardiovascular mortality in those with CRF; even after correction for diabetes, age, sex and race, it is at least 10 times greater than that of the general population once end-stage renal failure has been reached. Probable aetiological factors include hypertension, dyslipidaemia and elevated homocyst(e)ine.

LVH is an independent risk factor for cardiovascular mortality and, as renal impairment progresses, the percentage of patients with LVH rises to 45% when GFR is <25 mL/min. Major factors are hypertension and anaemia.

Treatment strategy This should include the following.

- Attention to other cardiovascular risk factors (smoking and exercise).

- Meticulous treatment of hypertension (also important in preventing progression of CRF).

- Possibly a lower threshold for preventive measures (antiplatelet agents, lipid-lowering drugs and folic acid). This may be appropriate, but is not proved. Potentially these interventions could also influence the progression of CRF (based on animal studies). Human studies are in progress (eg Study of Heart And Renal Protection).

Gout

Gout is common. Reduced urate excretion and diuretics are the major factors. It is often confused with pseudogout (pyrophosphate). Generally, treat acute episodes with colchicine (avoiding NSAIDs). Prevention is with allopurinol (if urate is high or after an episode).

⚠ Remember to reduce the dose of allopurinol in those with renal impairment.

Pregnancy in chronic renal impairment

As renal function declines, so does the ability to conceive and to carry a pregnancy successfully. In some women with chronic renal impairment, pregnancy results in additional deterioration in renal function superimposed on the predicted course of their chronic renal impairment.

The chance of successful fetal outcome and risk to maternal

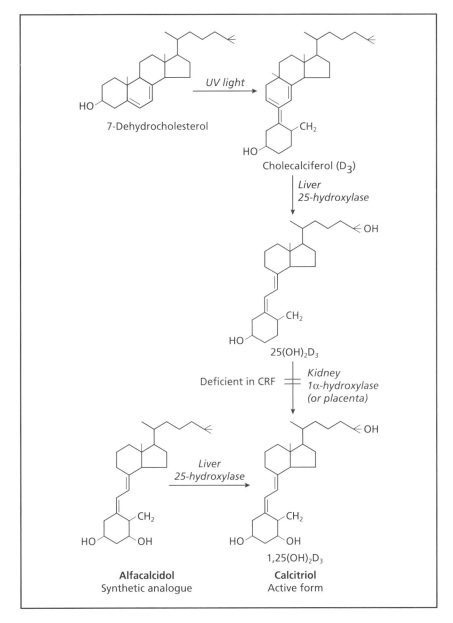

Prognosis

The effect of chronic renal impairment on morbidity and mortality is uncertain. The tendency to progress correlates closely with the following:

- amount of proteinuria;
- amount of interstitial damage on the renal biopsy;
- higher in men than in women.

The likelihood of end-stage renal failure obviously increases as functional reserve decreases. The most useful guide is the trend in GFR.

▲ Fig. 29 Principal pathway of vitamin D metabolism. Alfacalcidol or calcitriol are used to treat patients with renal impairment.

renal function can be stratified on the basis of renal impairment, hypertension and proteinuria. Normal pregnancy is rare with creatinine >275 µmol/L. See Section 2.7.11 for further discussion.

Drugs

Dose adjustments are required for many medications. Take care to avoid nephrotoxic drugs. If in doubt, consult the *British National Formulary*.

Preparation for renal replacement therapy

Once it is clear that the patient will develop end-stage renal failure, preparation for renal replacement therapy should be made well in advance (eg formation of arteriovenous fistula for haemodialysis). You should also consider whether a transplant would be appropriate before the patient reaches end-stage renal failure.

FURTHER READING

Atkins RC, Briganti EM, Lewis JB, *et al.* Proteinuria reduction and progression to renal failure in patients with type 2 diabetes mellitus and overt nephropathy. *Am. J. Kidney Dis.* 2005; 45: 281–7. (IDNT study)

Brenner BM, Cooper ME, De Zeeuw D, *et al.* Effects of losartan on renal and cardiovascular outcomes in patients with type 2 diabetes and nephropathy. *N. Engl. J. Med.* 2001; 345: 861–9. (RENAAL study)

Klahr S, Levey AS, Beck GJ, *et al.* The effects of dietary protein restriction and blood-pressure control on the progression of chronic renal disease. *N. Engl. J. Med.* 1994; 330: 877–84. (MDRD study)

Lewis EJ, Hunsicker LG, Bain RP and Rohde RD. The effect of angiotensin-converting enzyme inhibition on diabetic nephropathy. *N. Engl. J. Med.* 1993; 329: 1456–62.

Nakao N, Yoshimura A, Morita H, *et al.* Combination treatment of angiotensin-II receptor blocker and angiotensin-converting-enzyme inhibitor in non-diabetic renal disease: a randomised controlled trial. *Lancet* 2003; 361: 117–24. (COOPERATE study)

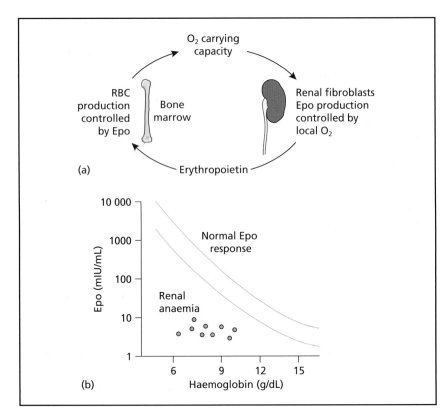

▲ Fig. 30 (a) Control of erythropoietin secretion. (b) Patients with renal impairment (red dots) have a relative deficiency in erythropoietin secretion, with reduced levels of circulating erythropoietin compared with the normal response for a given level of haemoglobin.

2.1.3 End-stage renal failure

End-stage renal failure is the point at which an individual's renal function is no longer sufficient for normal life as a result of irreversible loss of renal function, ie the point at which renal replacement therapy should be commenced (if appropriate for the patient).

Aetiology/pathophysiology/pathology

At a certain level of glomerular filtration rate (GFR), the accumulation of molecules that are usually excreted by the kidney reaches a level at which they prevent or endanger normal physiological functions. The principal problems are:

- potassium;

- salt and water;

- hydrogen ions;

- uraemic toxins.

The term 'uraemic toxins' refers to the vast numbers of chemicals that accumulate in the blood as the kidneys fail. Urea and creatinine are the two measured in clinical practice, but they do not correlate very strongly with uraemic symptoms (those made better by dialysis). Elderly people and those with less muscle mass will have a lower GFR for any given creatinine than is normal, and will reach end-stage renal failure with a lower creatinine (eg 450 μmol/L as opposed to 850 μmol/L).

> ⚠️ As patients approach end-stage renal failure, they frequently become malnourished because of loss of appetite, resulting in muscle wasting and deceptively low creatinine. The correct treatment is dialysis and attention to nutrition.

Epidemiology

The take-on rate for renal replacement therapy in the UK is approximately 100 per million population per year. End-stage renal failure is much more common in elderly than in young people. Causes are the same as for chronic renal failure (CRF).

Clinical presentation

Symptoms are sensitive, but not very specific:

- tiredness and difficulty concentrating;

- loss of appetite;

- nausea and vomiting.

If these symptoms are present in a patient with creatinine >450 μmol/L, serious consideration should be given to commencing dialysis unless there is another cause (eg anaemia contributing to tiredness). In severe cases, presentation may be with pericarditis, uraemic encephalopathy or neuropathy. In other instances, the need for dialysis will be precipitated by acidosis, hyperkalaemia or fluid overload resistant to diuretics and sodium restriction.

> 🔑 Monitoring patients with renal impairment as they approach end-stage renal failure should enable them to be commenced on dialysis at a time when symptoms are minimal but they will feel a clear benefit.

> 🔑 Early referral to a renal unit enables emphasis to be placed on delaying the progression of end-stage renal failure, avoiding complications and making the appropriate physical and psychological preparations for renal replacement therapy.

Physical signs

- Commonly, there are no physical signs when a patient reaches end-stage renal failure.

- Less commonly, pericardial rub or metabolic flap may be present.

- Peripheral neuropathy, uraemic frost and fits are rare.

Investigations

- Identify the cause of the renal damage if possible (as for CRF).

- Establish that the diagnosis is CRF: look for small kidneys on ultrasonography and evidence of previous renal impairment. If kidneys are normal size and not obstructed, a renal biopsy will usually be indicated.

- Consider whether there is a reversible factor causing acute-on-chronic renal failure: volume depletion or hypotension, nephrotoxic drugs (eg NSAIDs) or prostatic obstruction.

- Test for hepatitis B and C: potentially infectious patients will require special dialysis arrangements. Others should be immunised against hepatitis B.

Treatment

- Commence renal replacement therapy: if the need is urgent, haemodialysis will usually be used initially.

- If there is cardiovascular instability, haemofiltration may be preferred to begin with.

- Emergency treatment for hyperkalaemia (see Section 1.4.1) may be indicated pending transfer for dialysis.

> It is unwise to defer dialysis: if in doubt, dialyse first and ask questions later.

> It is important to appreciate that dialysis is equivalent to only a low level of GFR, in the region of 6 mL/min. Although sometimes patients (and occasionally their doctors) will suggest dialysis in the context of less severe renal impairment, this would represent a relatively small increment in clearance compared with the patient's own renal function. This is unlikely to lead to clinical benefit, would be at considerable financial cost and would also be a major inconvenience to the patient.

Complications

These are as listed for chronic renal impairment (see Section 2.1.2).

The following are particular problems in patients with end-stage renal disease treated by dialysis:

- increased cardiovascular mortality (Fig. 31);

- autonomous hyperparathyroidism, requiring parathyroidectomy (Fig. 32);

- accumulation of β_2-microglobulin amyloid with carpal tunnel syndrome and arthropathy (Fig. 33);

- specific complications of the renal replacement therapies (see Section 2.2).

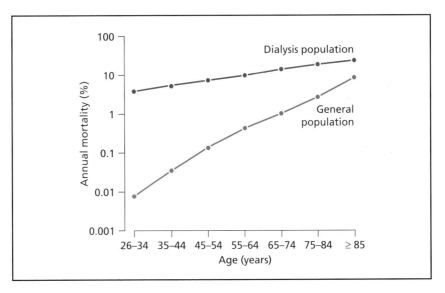

▲ **Fig. 31** Annual mortality in the general population and dialysis patients (data from the United States Renal Data System 1994–1996). Mortality is increased over 100-fold in younger dialysis patients.

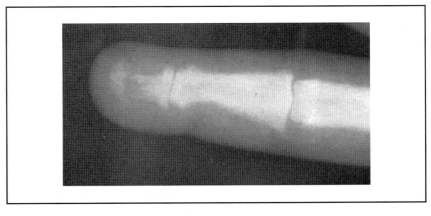

▲ **Fig. 32** Radiograph of the finger of a haemodialysis patient with severe hyperparathyroidism. There is subperiosteal resorption and osteo-acrolysis.

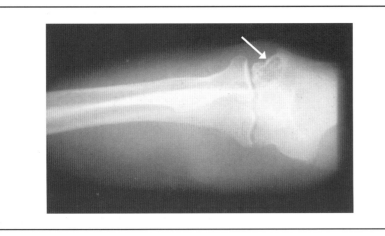

▲ **Fig. 33** Radiograph of the wrist of a long-standing haemodialysis patient. The radiolucent area (arrow) is an amyloid deposit.

Prognosis

In appropriate patients dialysis can usually be performed relatively smoothly and safely, especially when adequate practical and psychological preparation is made.

On renal replacement therapy, mortality is much higher than in a population matched for age, diabetes, etc. (Fig. 31).

Prevention

- Measures to prevent progression of CRF (see Section 2.1.2).

- If there is sufficient advance planning, transplantation (from either a living or cadaveric donor) before end-stage renal failure is reached may avoid the need for dialysis.

2.1.4 Nephrotic syndromes

Nephrotic syndrome is the combination of:

- proteinuria (usually >3 g per 24 hours);

- hypoalbuminaemia (<35 g/L);

- oedema.

Aetiology/pathophysiology/pathology

Proteinuria

The underlying defect is increased glomerular permeability to protein. Some of the leaked protein is absorbed and catabolised by the tubular cells; the remainder is passed in the urine. The normal glomerulus selects which molecules can pass from the circulation to the tubular space based on size and electrical charge.

Size selectivity relates to:

- fenestrae in the endothelium;

- pores in the basement membrane;

- slit diaphragms between the foot processes of the epithelial cells (podocytes).

Charge selectivity is the result of electrostatic repulsion of negatively charged proteins by negative charge on the basement membrane and endothelium.

In some patients with congenital nephrotic syndrome a specific protein (eg nephrin or podocin) is absent from the slit diaphragm because of an inherited genetic defect. In other settings the precise mechanism(s) resulting in the substantial filtration of protein is not well understood, although it is clear that there is altered size selectivity, usually enabling passage of considerable amounts of IgG (radius about 5.5 nm) in addition to albumin. There is also reduced charge selectivity. Classification of causes of the nephrotic syndrome is by histological appearance; some respond to immunosuppression.

Hypoalbuminaemia

The circulating albumin concentration does not correlate tightly with the proteinuria as a result of the variable extent of tubular catabolism. The amount of compensatory increase in hepatic synthesis is also variable.

Oedema

An attractive hypothesis is that the oedema is driven by hypovolaemia caused by reduced plasma oncotic pressure, resulting in compensatory sodium retention. However, this simple explanation cannot be sustained in adults, although it may apply in children with minimal-change disease. Plasma volume is not reduced in untreated sodium-retaining adult nephritis; sodium retention does not correlate well with renin–angiotensin activation; and converting enzyme inhibitors are not natriuretic.

Epidemiology

The underlying histological diagnosis varies with age (Fig. 34). Not included are large numbers of people with diabetes who are

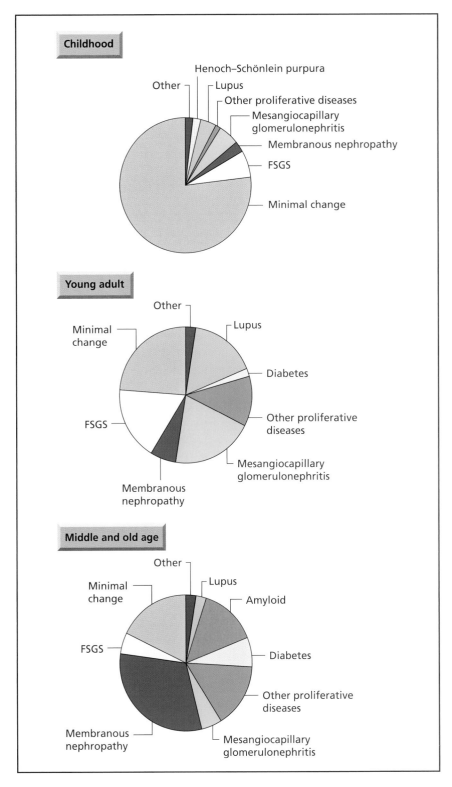

Fig. 34 Histological diagnoses of renal biopsies of 1,000 patients at Guy's Hospital, London, 1963–1990. FSGS, focal segmental glomerulosclerosis. (Redrawn with permission from Cameron JS. In: Davison AM *et al.*, eds. *Oxford Textbook of Clinical Nephrology*, 2nd edn. Oxford: Oxford University Press, 1998.)

technically late in the course of diabetic nephropathy, but in whom a renal biopsy would not be appropriate.

Most children with nephrotic syndrome are steroid responsive (minimal-change nephrotic syndrome or focal segmental glomerulosclerosis). For patients under the age of 10, it is therefore usual to treat with steroids and only biopsy non-responders.

Clinical presentation

- Usually with peripheral oedema.

- May be of gradual or sudden onset.

- Ranges from trivial to a major problem resistant to diuretics, etc.

- Some children present with abrupt onset of massive proteinuria, hypovolaemia and even collapse.

- Elderly patients with minimal-change nephrotic syndrome may present with acute renal failure.

- Sometimes the patient will notice frothy urine (Fig. 35).

Investigations

Investigations aim to do the following:

- confirm that the patient is nephrotic;

- assess the severity of the protein leak;

- obtain a histological diagnosis of the glomerular abnormality.

Investigations should include the following.

- Serum albumin and creatinine.

- Urinalysis and microscopy: the presence of some red cells does not rule out minimal change, but makes it less likely.

- A 24-hour urine collection to estimate protein excretion, or spot protein/creatinine ratio (see Section 3.1).

- Renal ultrasonography: scars suggest reflux nephropathy. Biopsy is relatively contraindicated if there is a single kidney.

- CXR.

- Protein electrophoresis: urine and serum.

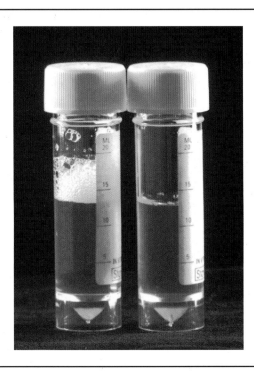

▲ **Fig. 35** Urine from a nephrotic patient with a protein content of 5 g/L (left) and a normal sample (right).

Other investigations could be refined on the basis of the histological diagnosis and/or other clinical information, the following being examples.

- Systemic lupus erythematosus gives positive antinuclear factor, antibodies to double-stranded DNA and low complement levels.

- Hepatitis B is associated with membranous nephropathy.

- Hepatitis C is associated with cryoglobulinaemia and mesangiocapillary glomerulonephritis.

- Adults (and children over the age of 10) will almost always have a renal biopsy.

Differential diagnosis

- Oedema commonly results from other factors, eg congestive cardiac failure (CCF).

- Proteinuria: dipstick testing of the urine is very sensitive and minor proteinuria occurs in many situations (eg CCF and fever).

- Hypoalbuminaemia is common in other circumstances (liver disease and chronic illness).

Treatment

Oedema

The success of symptomatic treatment is best monitored by daily weighing; aim to reduce the patient's weight by 0.5–1.0 kg/day. To achieve negative sodium balance, do the following.

- Restrict dietary sodium.

- Diuretics will almost always be necessary, usually furosemide/ bumetanide. Large doses are often required (partly because the drugs are sequestered by filtered protein in the tubular lumen). In resistant cases, additional diuretics that act synergistically, eg metolazone, may be needed; also potassium supplements and/or amiloride.

- Severe cases may be treated with the combination of intravenous 20% albumin and diuretics, or haemofiltration.

Reduction of proteinuria

- Where appropriate the underlying process is treated, eg steroids in minimal change.

- Angiotensin-converting enzyme inhibitors reduce proteinuria and slow deterioration in glomerular filtration rate (GFR), although their use may be restricted by hypotension.

- Refractory cases: NSAIDs or ciclosporin are sometimes used to reduce proteinuria in refractory cases. The effect results mainly from a reduction in GFR. Such cases should be distinguished from the use of ciclosporin to treat the underlying condition (relapsing minimal change or membranous glomerulonephritis). Nephrectomy and renal replacement therapy are only rarely justified in exceptional cases of refractory oedema.

Complications

Hyperlipidaemia

- Over half of nephrotic patients have cholesterol >7.5 mmol/L.

- High-density lipoprotein is often decreased.

- Low-density lipoprotein synthesis is increased and catabolism decreased.

It is not clear what impact hyperlipidaemia has on cardiovascular risk, but concern is obviously increased with increased duration of nephrotic syndrome. 3-Hydroxy-3-methylglutaryl (HMG) coenzyme A reductase inhibitors do lower cholesterol in this group and are

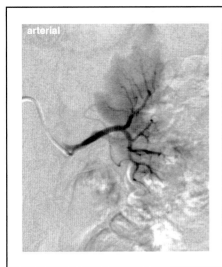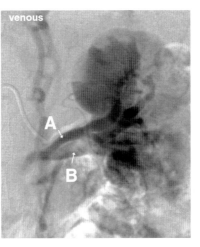

▲**Fig. 36** Digital subtraction angiography in a patient with membranous nephropathy. On the venous phase (b) there is defective filling of the inferior renal vein (B). The superior renal vein (A) fills normally.

considered on the basis of the overall risk profile (see Section 1.4).

Thrombosis

Between 10 and 40% of patients with the nephrotic syndrome develop deep venous thrombosis or renal vein thrombosis (Fig. 36). This is probably less common in minimal-change nephrotic syndrome. Prothrombotic abnormalities include reduced antithrombin III (urinary losses). Renal vein thrombosis may present with:

• pulmonary emboli (Fig. 37);

• decrease in GFR;

• flank pain and haematuria.

Thrombosis is diagnosed by selective venography, venous phase of renal angiogram (see Fig. 36), CT or MRI.

Prevention of thrombosis This involves both primary and secondary prevention.

• Primary prevention: oral anticoagulants may be considered in ambulant patients with severe nephrotic syndrome.

• Secondary prevention: after an episode of thrombosis,

anticoagulation should continue as long as the patient remains nephrotic.

Infections

• Primary peritonitis (usually with *Streptococcus pneumoniae*)

can occur in children. Low concentrations of complement factor B (55 kDa), which is necessary for alternative pathway activation, might explain this propensity. Most adults are probably protected by antibodies to capsular antigens. Consider prophylactic penicillin in children.

• Cellulitis is frequent, presumably as a result of immunological factors and skin fragility/oedema.

Deterioration in renal function

Minimal-change nephrotic syndrome does not lead to chronic deterioration in renal function. Other histological categories carry a substantial risk of progressive loss of GFR, which varies according to histological diagnosis (see Section 2.3).

Prognosis

This varies with the histological diagnosis (see Section 2.3).

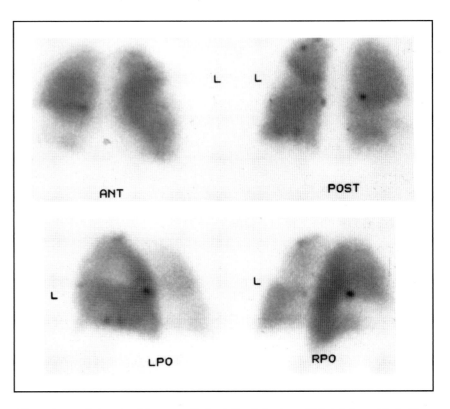

▲**Fig. 37** Lung perfusion scan of the same patient as in Fig. 36 showing multiple defects consistent with pulmonary emboli.

FURTHER READING

Donckerwolcke RAMG and
Cameron JS. The nephrotic syndrome:
management, complications and
pathophysiology. In: Davison AM,
Cameron JS, Grünfeld J-P, *et al*., eds.
Oxford Textbook of Clinical Nephrology,
3rd edn. Oxford: Oxford University
Press, 2005: 415–38.

2.2 Renal replacement therapy

Renal replacement therapy is
necessary in order to sustain
and/or maintain quality of life
once renal function is no longer
sufficient. Three modalities of
renal replacement therapy are
available:

- haemodialysis;

- peritoneal dialysis;

- renal transplantation.

Choice of treatment modality

Renal transplantation is the
modality of choice for most
patients where it is possible because
both quality of life and survival are
improved compared with dialysis.
However, transplantation is
restricted by the availability of
donor organs, the suitability of
patients to undergo the transplant
operation and postoperative long-
term immunosuppression.

Haemodialysis and peritoneal
dialysis are poorly tolerated by some
patients. In those with substantial
comorbidity, renal replacement
therapy may be considered
inappropriate by the patient and
the family. This should preferably
be discussed well before end-stage
renal disease occurs. Conservative

management to alleviate
symptomatic complications of renal
failure may include erythropoietin,
management of fluid balance with
diuretics and potassium restriction.
With more advanced renal failure
a symptomatic approach is taken
similar to that given to patients with
any other terminal illnesses.

The relative advantages and
disadvantages of haemodialysis and
peritoneal dialysis are outlined in
Table 14.

2.2.1 Haemodialysis

Principle

Haemodialysis involves circulating
the patient's blood through an
extracorporeal circulation where
it is exposed to an isotonic buffered
dialysis solution across a semi-
permeable membrane. The patient's
blood is obtained via a form of
vascular access.

The removal of toxins occurs
principally through diffusion (Fig. 38).

TABLE 14 ADVANTAGES AND DISADVANTAGES OF HAEMODIALYSIS AND PERITONEAL DIALYSIS

	Advantages	Disadvantages
Haemodialysis	Responsibility lies with renal staff Intermittent, allowing 'time off treatment' Dialysis is separate from home environment	Hospital based and so requires travel Requires vascular access Attached to a machine Stringent dietary restrictions Stringent fluid restrictions Imposes restrictions on travel Haemodynamically stressful Higher risk of bacteraemia
Peritoneal dialysis	In control of own treatment Less frequent visits to hospital Ease of travel Can usually be integrated into work Less stringent dietary and fluid restrictions Haemodynamically gentle compared with haemodialysis	May be unsuitable for patients with large muscle mass Episodes of acute peritonitis Sclerosing peritonitis is uncommon but very serious Technique survival usually <10 years

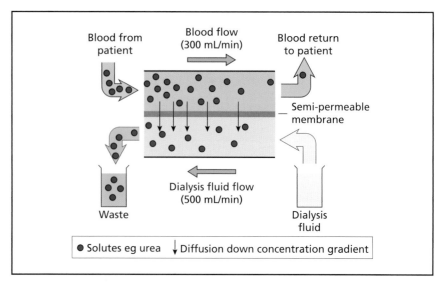

▲ **Fig. 38** Haemodialysis: clearance of toxins by diffusion.

Waste products at a high concentration in the patient's blood travel down a concentration gradient across the semi-permeable membrane into the dialysis solution.

Removal of fluid occurs principally by ultrafiltration (Fig. 39). Water moves from the circulation down a pressure gradient across the semi-permeable membrane into the dialysis solution. Dialysis machines control fluid removal by regulating transmembrane pressure. Some solute molecules move with water by convection.

Practical details

The basic haemodialysis circuit is shown in Fig. 40. Most patients in the UK receive three treatments of about 4 hours each week. There is evidence for a threshold amount of dialysis below which morbidity and mortality increase. There are national targets for measured dialysis adequacy, which are based on urea (small molecule) clearance. Increasing dialysis delivery for a patient requires either an increase in time on dialysis or greater dialysis efficiency. Improved dialysis efficiency may be achieved by using dialysis membranes with a larger surface area or by increasing blood flow through the dialysis circuit (where possible).

Apart from dialysis adequacy, the major parameters to consider in haemodialysis patients include the following.

- Fluid balance: removal of salt and water during dialysis to achieve a target 'dry' weight. BP control should ideally be obtained by manipulation of dry weight in dialysis patients.

- Electrolyte balance: different dialysis solutions are available in which the concentration of sodium, potassium, calcium and bicarbonate varies.

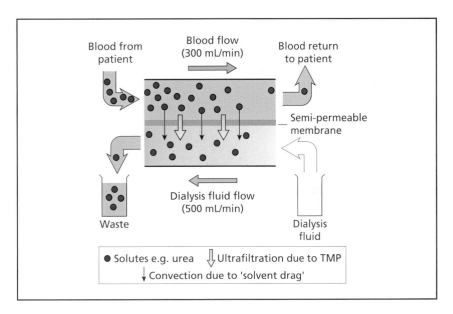

▲ **Fig. 39** Haemodialysis: ultrafiltration (fluid removal) is driven by the transmembrane pressure (TMP) across the semi-permeable membrane.

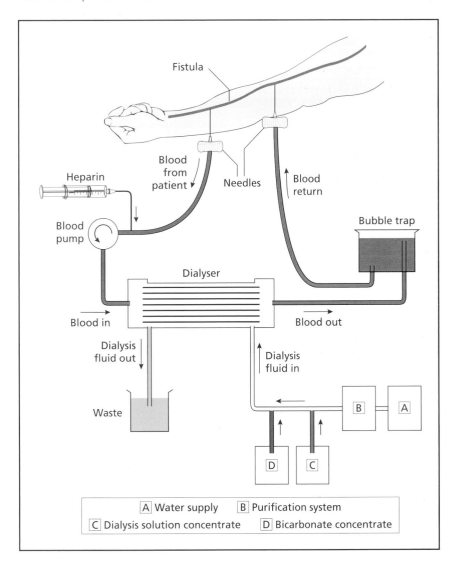

▲ **Fig. 40** Basic haemodialysis circuit.

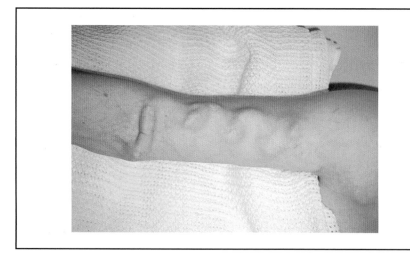

▲ **Fig. 41** Well-developed brachial arteriovenous fistula.

• Removal of larger 'middle' molecules: high-flux dialysis membranes clear middle molecules such as β_2-microglobulin with greater efficiency.

Vascular access is required for haemodialysis. The preferred form of vascular access is the arteriovenous fistula (AVF) (Fig. 41). Formation of an AVF requires an operation in which the radial or brachial artery is anastamosed to a vein, which is not always possible or successful. An AVF must 'mature' (involving an increase in flow arterialisation of the vein) before it can be used: this takes at least 6 weeks and the operation should therefore be planned well before dialysis is required. Other forms of vascular access, all of which are less safe than an AVF, include the following.

• Temporary dialysis catheter: large-bore dual-lumen catheters inserted into the internal jugular (Fig. 42) or femoral veins. Used for acute inpatient dialysis, but not suitable for outpatient use.

• Tunnelled dialysis catheter: large-bore dual-lumen catheters inserted into the internal jugular vein and tunnelled subcutaneously to an exit point on the chest wall (Fig. 43). A dacron cuff that sits in the 'tunnel' reduces infection rates, although infection remains a very significant problem. Suitable for outpatient use. Can also be placed in subclavian veins, femoral veins or the inferior vena cava.

• Polytetrafluoroethylene graft: if native veins are unsuitable for anastomosis to an artery, then a graft can be used. However, there is a significant risk of infection if this route is chosen.

Blood circulating in the extracorporeal system requires anticoagulation (usually with heparin) and many nephrologists prescribe regular low-dose aspirin for patients with an AVF as prophylaxis against thrombosis.

Complications
Table 15 shows the major complications of haemodialysis.

2.2.2 Peritoneal dialysis

Principle
As with haemodialysis, peritoneal dialysis exposes the patient's blood to a buffered dialysis solution across a semi-permeable membrane. However, the blood remains within the body and the semi-permeable membrane is the peritoneum. Dialysis fluid is introduced via a peritoneal dialysis catheter (Fig. 44).

Removal of toxins occurs through diffusion and convection. Small molecules diffuse across the

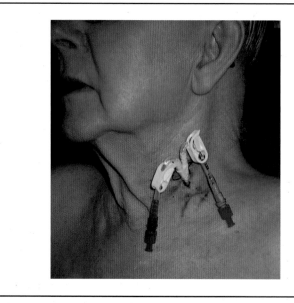

▲ **Fig. 42** Temporary dialysis line inserted in the left internal jugular vein.

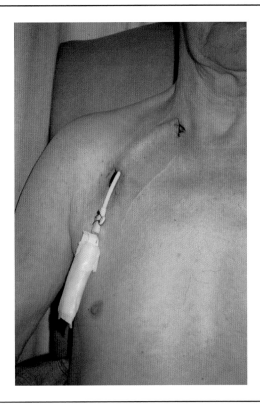

▲ **Fig. 43** Semi-permanent dialysis line inserted into the right internal jugular vein.

Timing	Nature of complication
TABLE 15 MAJOR COMPLICATIONS OF HAEMODIALYSIS	
Acute	Hypotension Access-related: infection, thrombosis, inadequate flow for dialysis, steal syndrome related to reduced distal flow Haemorrhage: may be related to anticoagulation
Chronic	Accelerated cardiovascular disease (the usual cause of death in dialysis patients)

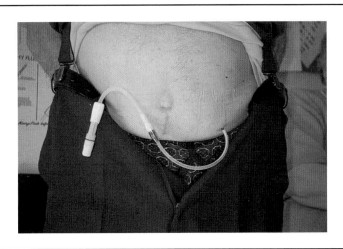

▲ **Fig. 44** Tenckhoff dialysis catheter.

peritoneal membrane down the concentration gradient between the blood and the intraperitoneal dialysis fluid. Larger molecules tend to move through convection associated with the movement of fluid.

Removal of fluid (ultrafiltration) occurs by osmosis. Water moves to equilibrate the osmolalities between the two compartments (Fig. 45). Peritoneal dialysis fluids are manufactured to be hyperosmolar, using dextrose as the usual osmotic agent. Different concentrations of the osmotic agent enable control of fluid removal.

The rate at which solutes cross the peritoneal membrane varies, and depends on the individual characteristics of a patient's membrane. Broadly, patients fall into two groups (Fig. 46).

- Low transporters have a slow rate of solute removal and so require long dwell times, ie continuous ambulatory peritoneal dialysis (CAPD).

- High transporters have a fast rate of solute removal and therefore require short dwell times. High transporters tend to rapidly absorb the dextrose, thus losing the osmotic gradient and leading to poor ultrafiltration. Best suited to automated peritoneal dialysis (APD).

With more time on peritoneal dialysis the peritoneum tends to move towards higher transport.

Practical details
Relative contraindications of peritoneal dialysis include previous major abdominal surgery, diverticulitis, the presence of hernias or chronic respiratory disease, and an inability to learn the technique.

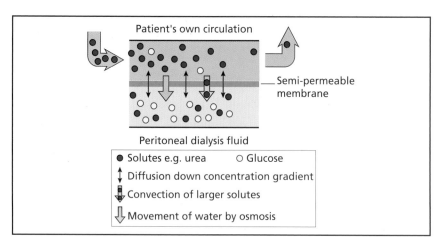

▲ **Fig. 45** Mechanisms underlying peritoneal dialysis.

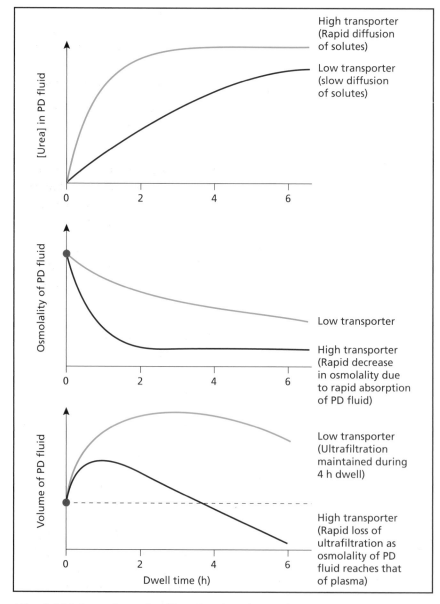

▲ **Fig. 46** Solute transport properties of the peritoneal membrane. High transporters rapidly clear toxins but also quickly experience a fall in dialysis fluid osmolality as a result of the rapid uptake of glucose, which leads to poor ultrafiltration. Low transporters take longer to clear toxins, but their ultrafiltration is good because glucose uptake from the dialysis fluid is slower.

CAPD is illustrated in Fig. 47. There are usually four exchanges of 1.5–3.0 L/day. The majority of patients receiving peritoneal dialysis in the UK are on a CAPD system. APD is illustrated in Fig. 48. The regimen involves continuous cyclic peritoneal dialysis with several exchanges of 2–2.5 L overnight, each with short dwell times. After the last cycle, fluid is left in during the daytime. Often one manual daytime exchange is necessary.

As in haemodialysis, clearance on peritoneal dialysis can be measured, and below a certain minimum level mortality appears to be increased. Increasing the amount of dialysis on CAPD usually involves exchanging five times daily (ie an additional daily exchange), but many patients cannot achieve adequate dialysis with CAPD as their residual renal function declines. Some achieve targets by switching to APD but the majority require a switch to haemodialysis.

A recent advance is specialised fluid using polymerised dextran (icodextrin) instead of glucose. The polymer is not transported across the peritoneum, so ultrafiltration is greatly improved in fast transporters. It is more expensive.

Patient survival on peritoneal dialysis is probably equivalent to that with haemodialysis. However, technique survival is markedly inferior to haemodialysis. The following factors are frequently involved in the failure of peritoneal dialysis:

- ultrafiltration failure may be due to increased peritoneal membrane permeability (convert to APD) or membrane sclerosis (convert to haemodialysis);

- recurrent peritonitis;

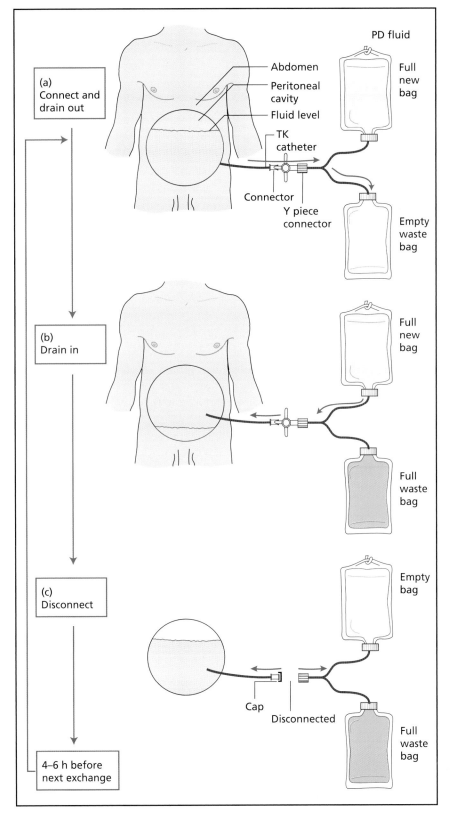

PD fluid

Full new bag

Abdomen
Peritoneal cavity
Fluid level
TK catheter

(a) Connect and drain out

Connector
Y piece connector

Empty waste bag

(b) Drain in

Full new bag

Full waste bag

(c) Disconnect

Empty bag

Cap

Disconnected

Full waste bag

4–6 h before next exchange

▲ **Fig. 47** CAPD. (**a**) A Y connector with an empty waste bag and a bag containing fresh dialysis fluid is attached to the Tenckhoff (TK) catheter. Used dialysis fluid is drained into the waste bag. (**b**) The Y connector is switched to drain in the fresh dialysis fluid. (**c**) The Y connector is removed. The patient is now free until the next exchange in 4–6 hours.

- inability to achieve dialysis adequacy may develop as residual renal function declines.

Complications
Table 16 shows the major complications of peritoneal dialysis.

2.2.3 Renal transplantation

Principle
The principle is to implant a functioning healthy kidney that may be from the following sources.

- Living related donor: sibling to sibling and parent to child are the most common pairings. Long-term graft survival is better with living than cadaveric kidneys.

- Living unrelated donor (eg spouse or friend): becoming more common in the UK.

- Cadaveric: heart-beating donors who satisfy the criteria of brain death. This has been the main source of organs in the UK.

- Cadaveric: non-heart-beating donors. Results are less good with high rates of delayed graft function.

Practical details and complications
The possibility of renal transplantation should be considered in nearly all patients requiring renal replacement therapy. Suitability for transplantation depends on the following,

- Patient survival issues: for example, coronary artery disease is common in patients with end-stage renal failure, may be asymptomatic and is associated with a high risk of early postoperative mortality. It should be sought in high-risk patients and intervention should take place prior to transplantation.

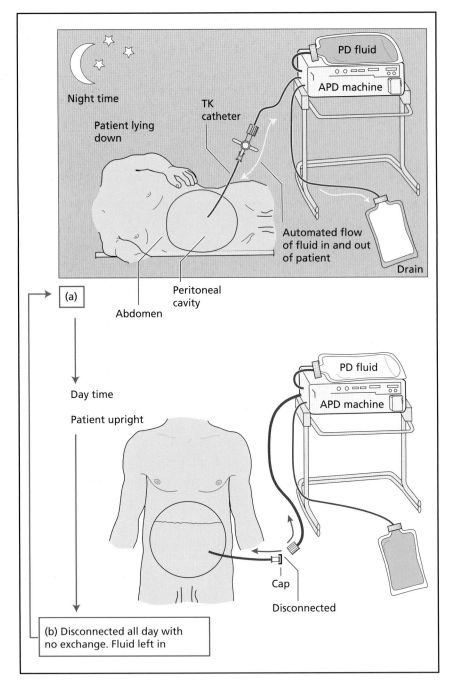

(a)

Night time

Patient lying
down

TK
catheter

PD fluid

APD machine

Automated flow
of fluid in and out
of patient

Drain

Peritoneal
cavity

Abdomen

Day time

Patient upright

PD fluid

APD machine

Cap

Disconnected

(b) Disconnected all day with
no exchange. Fluid left in

▲ **Fig. 48** APD. **(a)** At bedtime the patient connects to the machine with sufficient dialysis solution for the
night. The machine delivers and drains fluid automatically throughout the night. **(b)** In the morning the
patient disconnects. Fluid is left inside the peritoneal cavity. The patient may need one manual exchange
in the daytime, but is otherwise free until bedtime.

- Graft survival issues: for example,
  there is a significant risk of
  disease recurrence and graft loss
  in patients with focal segmental
  glomerulosclerosis.

- Resource allocation: balance
  between maximising benefit to
  each patient and the financial

benefit of maximising potential
life achieved through each graft
(ie death with a functioning
transplant is not financially
cost-effective).

The UK transplant register is
managed by the UK Transplant
Support Service Authority and

enrols all potential transplant
recipients. Allocation from the
national pool of organs is on a
points system, according to human
leucocyte antigen (HLA) matching,
donor/recipient relative age, time
on waiting list, etc. Preoperatively,
recipient serum and donor
lymphocytes are cross-matched to
detect preformed antibodies that
would preclude transplantation.

The transplant kidney is placed
extraperitoneally in the iliac fossa
and vessels are anastomosed usually
to the external iliac artery and vein.
The ureter is implanted into the
bladder and a J-J stent is usually
left in situ, which is typically
removed after 6 weeks.

Various immunosuppression
regimens are used to prevent
rejection of the donor kidney by the
recipient's immune system. Most
units tailor immunosuppression
regimens according to the perceived
risk of transplant rejection.
Increasingly, a depleting monoclonal
antibody may be given at the time of
transplantation as induction therapy.
Nearly all regimens contain steroids
initially, but many units now
withdraw steroids within
the first year. A standard
immunosuppression regimen would
include a calcineurin inhibitor
(ciclosporin or tacrolimus), steroids
and an inhibitor of purine synthesis
(azathioprine or mycophenolate
mofetil). Other therapies may
include aspirin to reduce the risk
of thrombosis, co-trimoxazole
prophylaxis against *Pneumocystis
carinii* pneumonia and antibiotic
prophylaxis.

The complications of renal
transplantation are summarised
in Table 17.

Outcome

The 5-year graft survival rate for first
cadaveric transplantation in

TABLE 16 COMPLICATIONS OF PERITONEAL DIALYSIS

Timing	Nature of complication
Acute	Peritonitis: the main acute problem associated with peritoneal dialysis. Occurs about once per 18 patient months. Usually responds to intraperitoneal antibiotics Poor drainage of dialysis fluid, usually due to constipation or poorly positioned catheter Hernias are relatively common Fluid leak, typically through the diaphragm causing pleural effusion
Chronic	Accelerated cardiovascular disease (as in haemodialysis) Sclerosing peritonitis, usually diagnosed more than 5 years after commencement of peritoneal dialysis. Poorly understood, very limited response to treatment and sometimes fatal. Some nephrologists advocate a switch from peritoneal dialysis to haemodialysis at around 5 years for all patients

TABLE 17 SHORT- AND LONG-TERM COMPLICATIONS OF RENAL TRANSPLANTATION

Timing	Nature of complication
Short term	Surgical problems: renal or arterial thrombosis, ureteric necrosis or stenosis, lymphocele Delayed graft function: occurs in up to 30% of patients. More common in non-heart-beating donor kidneys Acute rejection (Fig. 50a): occurs in up to 30% of patients and its presence probably reduces long-term graft survival; usually reversible Infection: cytomegalovirus is the commonest major problem. Infection of renal tubular cells by the human polyoma virus BK results in progressive graft dysfunction and may be stabilised by reducing immunosuppression (Fig. 50b). Fungal pathogens are uncommon but frequently fatal
Long term	Cardiovascular disease: very common Diabetes: develops in up to 10% of patients, and in an even higher proportion of those receiving an immunosuppressive regimen containing tacrolimus and steroids Chronic allograft nephropathy: involves immunological and non-immunological mechanisms. Average graft survival is about 10–12 years and has not increased in recent years Malignancy: skin cancers are very common. Post-transplant lymphoproliferative disorder is a particular concern and is related to the intensity of immunosuppression. The incidence of most solid tumours is also significantly increased

the UK is 64–72% and is partly dependent on the degree of HLA matching (Fig. 49). Graft and patient survival with living related transplantation is superior to that with cadaveric transplantation regardless of HLA matching. There is a definite survival benefit with transplantation compared with remaining on the transplant waiting list, although there is an initial increase in mortality in the first year after transplantation. Relative to remaining dialysis-dependent, patients with diabetes benefit most from transplantation despite poorer absolute survival than other patient group following transplantation.

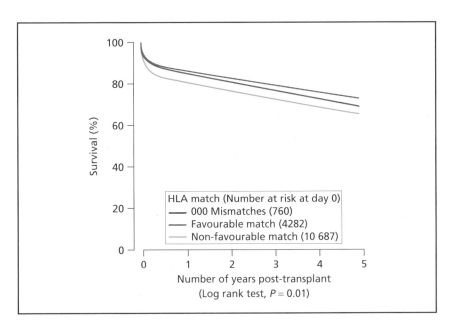

▲ Fig. 49 Transplant survival in the UK for first cadaveric kidney grafts, 1990–97, stratified by HLA mismatches. (Reproduced with permission from UK Transplant Support Service Authority.)

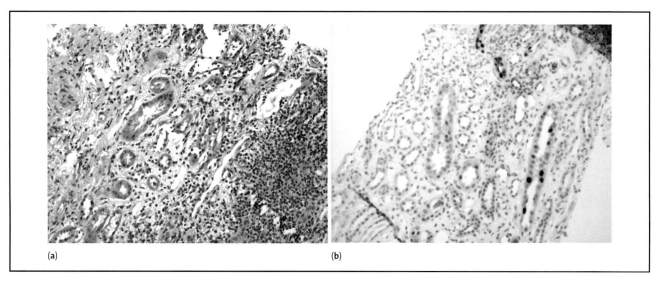

▲**Fig. 50** Renal transplant biopsy: (**a**) interstitial infiltrate, tubulitis and atypical tubular cell nuclei (H&E); (**b**) immunohistochemistry showing a BK protein in the tubular cell nuclei.

2.3 Glomerular diseases

Although many different diseases act on the glomeruli, the effects of glomerular damage are limited and include the following:

- reduced glomerular filtration;

- proteinuria and haematuria;

- hypertension;

- sodium retention causing oedema.

Glomerular disease can seem confusing, partly because it can be classified according to clinical features, histopathological appearance or the underlying disease process. Glomerular disease can affect one or more of the components of the glomerulus:

- glomerular basement membrane;

- glomerular cells;

- intraglomerular vessels;

- mesangium.

Important pathological terms that describe the histopathological appearances include the following.

- Proliferative disease: there is proliferation of cells within the glomerulus. In severe cases, proliferation of cells, especially macrophages within Bowman's capsule, causes an appearance known as a crescent.

- Mesangial disease: there is excess production of mesangial matrix.

- Membranous disease: the glomerular basement membrane is damaged and thickened.

- Membranoproliferative disease: there is both thickening of the glomerular basement membrane and cellular proliferation, usually of mesangial cells.

The pattern of glomerular involvement is further classified on the basis of whether all glomeruli are involved, and whether the whole of each glomerulus is involved.

- Focal disease affects only some glomeruli.
- Diffuse disease affects all the glomeruli.
- Segmental disease affects only part of the glomerulus.
- Global disease affects the whole glomerulus.

FURTHER READING

O'Callaghan CA. *The Renal System at a Glance.* Oxford: Blackwell Publishing, 2006.

2.3.1 Primary glomerular disease

Minimal-change nephropathy

Aetiology/pathophysiology/ pathology
The cause is unknown but is associated with atopy. The findings are as follows.

- Light microscopy and immunofluorescence: normal or nearly normal.

- Electron microscopy: glomerular epithelial podocyte foot process fusion (Fig. 51).

Epidemiology
This disease constitutes 80% of childhood nephrotic syndromes and 25% of adult nephrotic syndromes, with an incidence of 2 per 100,000. The peak age of incidence is between 2 and 7 years, but all ages can be affected.

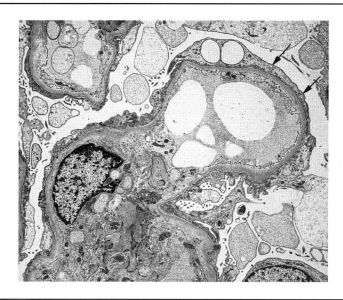

▲ Fig. 51 Electron micrograph of glomerular changes in minimal-change disease. Note the fusion of epithelial cell foot processes (arrows) (×6200).

Clinical presentation

Nephrotic syndrome often follows upper respiratory tract infection. In older people minimal-change disease may be associated with acute renal failure.

Physical signs

- Oedema.

- Often facial swelling in children.

Investigations

- Urinalysis: check nephrotic range in protein on 24-hour collection or check protein/creatinine ratio.

- Plasma: check for hypoalbuminaemia and hyperlipidaemia.

- Renal biopsy: children are often treated with a trial of steroids without a biopsy (Fig. 51).

Differential diagnosis

The differential diagnosis is from other causes of the nephrotic syndrome, especially focal segmental glomerulosclerosis (FSGS) and membranous nephropathy, amyloidosis, diabetic nephropathy, lupus and, rarely, congenital nephrotic syndrome.

Treatment

- Steroids: if there are frequent relapses or a poor response, then cyclophosphamide, ciclosporin or tacrolimus can be useful.

- Diuretics for oedema.

- Lipid-lowering drugs (usually statins) if there is prolonged nephrotic syndrome with hyperlipidaemia.

- Penicillin prophylaxis may be given to prevent streptococcal infection.

Complications

Complications are those of the nephrotic syndrome (see Section 2.1.4).

Prognosis

Nearly all patients (98% of children, 94% of adults) respond to steroids; 10–20% of these relapse several times, of whom 40–50% relapse frequently.

Disease associations

- Lymphoma.

- NSAID use.

Focal segmental glomerulosclerosis

Aetiology/pathophysiology/pathology

This is of unknown aetiology, apart from rare familial cases due to mutations in defined genes (*NPHS2* encoding podocin, *ACTN4* encoding α-actinin-4, and *TRPC6* encoding a cation channel). Minimal-change nephropathy and FSGS share similarities and may be different points on a spectrum of disease. Damage to the glomerular filtration barrier causes protein leak and nephrotic syndrome. The findings are as follows.

- Light microscopy: focal and segmental glomerular sclerosis (Fig. 52).

- Immunofluorescence: IgM and C3 in scars.

- Electron microscopy: glomerular epithelial podocyte foot process fusion.

Epidemiology

FSGS accounts for 15% of adult nephrotic syndrome. It is also a common finding in individuals with non-nephrotic proteinuria and can occur if there is hyperfiltration due to any cause.

Clinical presentation

Clinical presentations may include:

- proteinuria;

- nephrotic syndrome;

- hypertension;

- chronic renal impairment.

Physical signs

- Hypertension.

- Oedema if nephrotic.

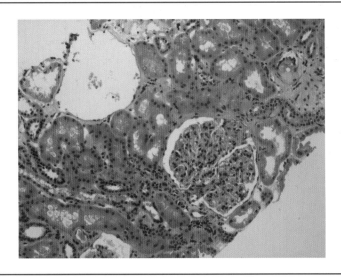

▲ **Fig. 52** Renal biopsy showing a glomerulus with segmental sclerosis. Note that the sclerosis is at the tip of the glomerulus, opposite the vascular pole near the origin of the proximal tubule. This 'tip' variant of FSGS generally responds well to steroids.

Investigations

- Urinalysis: protein ± blood.

- Plasma: hypoalbuminaemia and renal impairment.

- Renal biopsy.

Differential diagnosis

The differential diagnosis is from other causes of nephrotic syndrome or renal impairment (if present).

Treatment

- Steroids will induce a remission in many nephrotic individuals with FSGS, but the time to remission is longer than in minimal-change disease.

- Ciclosporin or cyclophosphamide may be beneficial.

- Symptomatic treatment: diuretics, angiotensin-converting enzyme (ACE) inhibitors or angiotensin receptor blockers to control BP and reduce proteinuria, and lipid-lowering agents if required.

Complications

Complications are those of the nephrotic syndrome and chronic renal impairment (see Section 2.1.2). Often recurs in transplanted kidneys.

Prognosis

Between 40 and 60% of patients develop end-stage renal disease within 10 years of being diagnosed with FSGS. Up to 40% of both adults and children remit in response to steroids: those who do respond have a much better prognosis for renal survival.

Disease associations

FSGS is associated with obesity, and also occurs at increased frequency in black ethnic groups, those who are infected with HIV and in intravenous drug users.

Membranous nephropathy

Aetiology/pathophysiology/pathology

The aetiology is unknown. Damage to the glomerular filtration barrier causes protein leak and nephrotic syndrome. The findings are as follows.

- Light microscopy: thickening of the glomerular basement membrane (GBM).

- Immunofluorescence: immunoglobulin and complement deposition.

- Electron microscopy: subepithelial membrane deposits.

Epidemiology

This is the most common cause of nephrotic syndrome in older patients in the UK. The peak age is 30–50 years.

Clinical presentation

Clinical presentations may include:

- nephrotic syndrome;

- chronic renal impairment;

- asymptomatic proteinuria;

- hypertension.

Physical signs

- Oedema if nephrotic.

- Hypertension.

Investigations

- Urinalysis: protein ± blood.

- Plasma: for signs of hypoalbuminaemia and renal impairment.

- Renal biopsy (Fig. 53).

Differential diagnosis

The differential diagnosis is from other causes of nephrotic syndrome or renal impairment (if present). Exclude systemic lupus erythematosus (SLE).

Treatment

- Symptomatic treatment: diuretics, ACE inhibitors to control BP and lipid-lowering agents.

- Steroids and chlorambucil or a calcineurin inhibitor may be effective in those who are severely

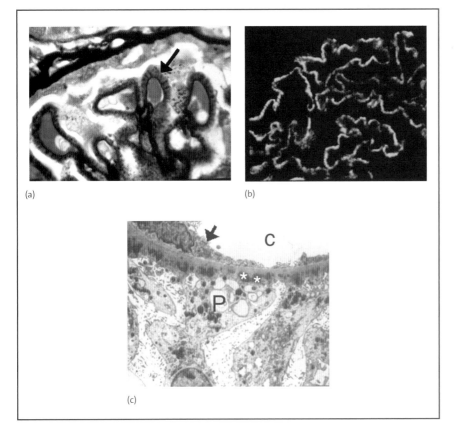

(a)

(b)

(c)

▲ **Fig. 53** Characteristics of membranous nephropathy. (**a**) Silver-stained section: the basement membrane is widened, with spikes. (**b**) Immunofluorescence for IgG: part of the glomerulus is shown and there is granular fluorescence along the basement membrane. (**c**) Electron micrograph of capillary loop: the basement membrane is seen adjacent to the capillary (C) lined by an endothelial cell (arrow); within the basement membrane are electron-dense deposits (*) and a podocyte (P) is also visible. (Courtesy of Dr D. Davies, Oxford Radcliffe Hospitals.)

nephrotic or have declining renal function, but these agents are not used unless membranous nephropathy is causing such problems (Fig. 54).

Complications

Complications are those of the nephrotic syndrome, chronic renal impairment and hyperlipidaemia if present.

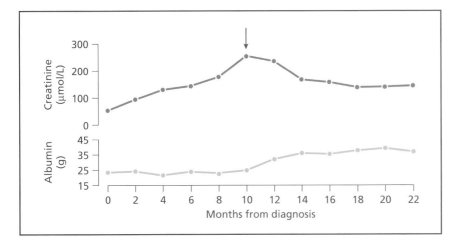

▲ **Fig. 54** Creatinine and albumin in a patient with membranous nephropathy. Renal function deteriorated progressively over the 10 months following diagnosis and the patient was then treated with immunosuppression (intermittent chlorambucil and prednisolone for 6 months). This resulted in remission of the nephrotic syndrome and the creatinine returned to normal.

Prognosis

Between 20 and 30% of patients remit spontaneously; 40% have a partial remission or remain stable and around 30% develop progressive renal failure.

Disease associations

- Hepatitis B.

- Malignancy.

- SLE.

- Drugs and toxins (gold, penicillamine and mercury).

IgA nephropathy

Aetiology/pathophysiology/pathology

The aetiology is unknown, but it is associated with abnormal glycosylation of the hinge region of bone marrow-derived IgA. Renal IgA deposition may trigger complement-mediated damage. The findings are as follows.

- Light microscopy: mesangial matrix expansion and mesangial cell proliferation (Fig. 55).

- Immunofluorescence: IgA deposits in mesangium (Fig. 56).

Epidemiology

IgA nephropathy is relatively common: the prevalence of overt nephropathy is approximately 2 per 10,000. The peak incidence of IgA nephropathy is in the second and third decades. The male to female ratio is 3.6:1. Post-mortem studies reveal mesangial IgA deposits in as many as 2–5% of all individuals, ie IgA deposition is much commoner than overt nephropathy.

Clinical presentation

There may be macroscopic haematuria at the same time as,

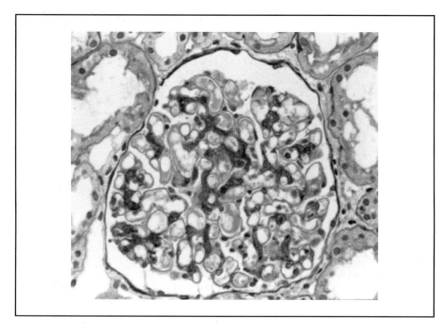

▲ **Fig. 55** Light microscopy of a glomerulus. The Section has been stained by the periodic acid–Schiff method and shows expansion of the mesangium.

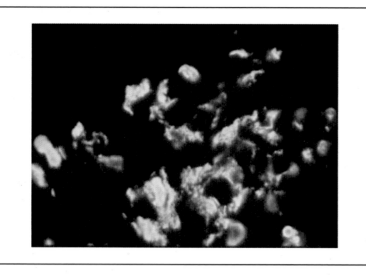

▲ **Fig. 56** Immunofluorescence of part of a glomerulus for IgA showing mesangial deposition of IgA.

or 1–2 days after, a sore throat (synpharyngitic). Most patients will have microscopic haematuria. Hypertension is common and there may be renal impairment. There may be a vasculitic skin rash (Henoch–Schönlein purpura). Less common presentations include nephrotic syndrome (in 10% of cases) and, rarely, acute nephritis.

Physical signs

- Hypertension.

Investigations

- Urinalysis: blood and protein.

- Plasma: for renal impairment; serum IgA is raised in 50% of cases.

- Renal biopsy.

Differential diagnosis

The differential diagnosis is from other forms of glomerulonephritis, eg SLE, poststreptococcal glomerulonephritis and antineutrophil cytoplasmic antibody (ANCA)-associated vasculitis.

Treatment

The role of specific treatment is unclear. However, strict BP control, typically with ACE inhibitors or angiotensin receptor blockers, reduces the risk of progression of renal impairment. Hypercholesterolaemia should be controlled with statins. There is likely to be a small benefit from fish oils, although this is controversial. Also remember the following:

- steroids may be given if nephrotic;

- aggressive disease with crescent formation may be treated with steroids, cyclophosphamide or mycophenolate mofetil;

- symptomatic treatment should include diuretics, ACE inhibitors to control BP and lipid-lowering agents.

Complications

Complications are those of the nephrotic syndrome or chronic renal impairment (if present).

Prognosis

Highly variable. Ranges from spontaneous clinical remission to rapid progression to end-stage renal disease: 15% of patients develop end-stage renal disease within 10 years of diagnosis, 20–30% by 20 years.

Disease associations

- Liver disease: alcoholic and viral hepatitis.

- HIV.

- Coeliac disease.

Mesangiocapillary glomerulonephritis (or membranoproliferative glomerulonephritis)

Aetiology/pathophysiology/pathology

The aetiology is often unclear. If cryoglobulinaemia is present, hepatitis C is often the underlying cause. Rarely there is an autoantibody resulting in complement activation (C3 nephritic factor).

The disease is subclassified into types I and II. Type I is usually associated with SLE, infection or cryoglobulinaemia. The findings are as follows.

- Light microscopy: types I and II show mesangial expansion and mesangial cell proliferation, also thickening of the GBM.

- Immunofluorescence: type I, immunoglobulins and complement; type II, some C3.

- Electron microscopy: type I, subendothelial deposits; type II, intramembranous deposits and subepithelial deposits.

Epidemiology

The disease is declining in developed countries, and 80% of the cases that do occur are of type I. It accounts for 10–20% of biopsies performed for presumed primary glomerulonephritis.

Clinical presentation

Presentation varies from asymptomatic haematuria or proteinuria to acute nephritis or severe nephrotic syndrome.

Physical signs

- Hypertension.

- Oedema.

Investigations

- Urinalysis: blood and protein.

- Plasma: renal impairment, hypoalbuminaemia and low complement levels, especially C3. In type II disease there may be antibodies to the C3 convertase C3bBb, resulting in complement activation.

- Renal biopsy.

Differential diagnosis

The differential diagnosis is from other causes of chronic renal impairment and of nephrotic syndrome (if present). Both postinfectious glomerulonephritis and SLE also cause renal disease and hypocomplementaemia.

Treatment

Treat any underlying cause.

- Although steroids and cytotoxic agents have been used, their benefit has not been proved in adults.

- Symptomatic treatment: diuretics, ACE inhibitors to control BP and lipid-lowering agents.

Complications

Complications are those of the nephrotic syndrome or chronic renal impairment (if present). There is a high recurrence rate following renal transplantation.

Prognosis

Half of all patients develop end-stage renal disease within 10 years of diagnosis; 90% develop it by 20 years.

Disease associations

- Infection, especially with hepatitis B and C viruses.

- Autoimmune disease, especially SLE.

- Complement deficiency: partial lipodystrophy is associated with type II disease.

- Hypogammaglobulinaemia.

Diffuse proliferative glomerulonephritis (or acute endocapillary glomerulonephritis)

Aetiology/pathophysiology/pathology

This may be idiopathic or secondary to infection, typically poststreptococcal, but also in the context of chronic infections. The findings are as follows.

- Light microscopy: endothelial and mesangial cell proliferation, and glomerular infiltration with neutrophils and monocytes.

- Immunofluorescence: complement and immunoglobulins.

- Electron microscopy: subepithelial deposits.

Epidemiology

This disease is declining in developing countries. The peak age of incidence is 2–12 years, and the male to female ratio is 2:1. It accounts for 10% of glomerular disease in developed countries and is the most common histological presentation of intrinsic renal disease in developing countries.

Clinical presentation

Presentation is typically 1–2 weeks after a streptococcal throat infection or 3–6 weeks after a streptococcal skin infection. It varies from asymptomatic microscopic haematuria to acute nephritic syndrome with frank haematuria, oedema, hypertension and oliguria.

Physical signs

- Hypertension.

- Oedema.

- Signs of preceding infection.

Investigations

- Urinalysis: blood (all cases), sometimes protein and often red blood cell casts.

- Plasma: impaired renal function; serological evidence of infection such as raised antistreptolysin O titres and anti-DNase B. Also low complement levels, especially C3.

Differential diagnosis

- Mesangiocapillary glomerulonephritis.

- SLE.

Treatment

- Ensure that any focus of infection is eradicated (using antibiotics and surgery).

- Symptomatic treatment: diuretics, hypertension (ACE inhibitors) and lipid-lowering agents.

Complications

Complications are those of the ongoing infection, uncontrolled oedema or hypertension.

Prognosis

Good: only 0.1–1% of patients have progressive renal impairment.

Antiglomerular basement membrane disease (or Goodpasture's disease)

Aetiology/pathophysiology/pathology

Autoantibodies to the basement membrane in glomeruli and alveoli cause renal and pulmonary damage.

The antigen is usually part of the non-collagenous domain of the α_3 component of type IV collagen. The signs are as follows.

- Light microscopy: focal segmental proliferative glomerulonephritis, often with necrosis and crescents.

- Immunofluorescence: antibody deposition (usually IgG) along the GBM.

Epidemiology

Rare: 0.5–1 per million per year. It occurs mainly in white patients, and in more men than women.

Clinical presentation

The presentation is with lung haemorrhage in 50–70% of patients, causing cough, haemoptysis or shortness of breath. Renal involvement is initially asymptomatic, but can cause loin pain, frank haematuria, oliguria and acute renal failure.

Physical signs

- Lung signs resemble pulmonary oedema or infection.

Investigations

- Urinalysis: blood and protein, and red cell casts.

- Plasma: renal impairment and anti-GBM antibodies.

- CXR: diffuse pulmonary haemorrhage may resemble pulmonary oedema or infection.

- Lung function: gas transfer (Kco) is raised by the absorption of carbon monoxide by the blood in the alveoli if haemorrhage has occurred recently.

- Renal biopsy.

Differential diagnosis

- Systemic vasculitis.

- Another glomerulonephritis with pulmonary oedema or infection.

Treatment

If the patient's kidneys have not failed completely, do the following.

- Plasma exchange is used to remove the pathogenic antibody.

- Immunosuppression with steroids and cyclophosphamide is used to inhibit further antibody production and reduce inflammatory damage. Azathioprine may be substituted for cyclophosphamide in the later stages of treatment.

- If the patient requires dialysis at presentation, then most nephrologists would not give immunosuppression.

Complications

- Respiratory failure, secondary pulmonary infection, and treatment toxicity.

Prognosis

Untreated, most patients die. Patients who require dialysis before treatment is started do not usually recover renal function and morbidity from immunosuppression is high (if it is given at all). Of those patients whose plasma creatinine is below 600 μmol/L before treatment, 80–90% recover independent renal function.

Disease associations

There is a strong association with human leucocyte antigen (HLA)-DR15 and a weaker association with HLA-DR4. Pulmonary haemorrhage is more common if the patient is a smoker, has pulmonary infection or oedema, or there is exposure to other inhaled toxins.

Crescentic glomerulonephritis (or rapidly progressive glomerulonephritis, focal necrotising glomerulonephritis or renal microscopic polyangiitis)

Aetiology/pathophysiology/pathology

The aetiology varies. The findings are as follows.

- Light microscopy: proliferative glomerulonephritis with fibrinoid necrosis often with crescents (inflammatory cells in Bowman's capsule) and possibly small-vessel vasculitis.

- Immunofluorescence: see below.

This condition is subclassified as follows.

- Anti-GBM disease.

- Renal microscopic vasculitis: immunofluorescence shows scant or absent immunoglobulins. Serum ANCA is usually positive (see Sections 1.4.5 and 2.7.6) and there may or may not be extrarenal manifestations.

- Complicating a pre-existing glomerulonephritis, a systemic disorder or an infection: immunofluorescence often shows immunoglobulin deposition (associations include lupus, Henoch–Schönlein purpura, IgA nephropathy, mesangiocapillary glomerulonephritis and postinfectious glomerulonephritis).

Epidemiology

Accounts for 2–5% of renal biopsies; the male to female ratio is 2:1.

Clinical presentation

Renal disease is often asymptomatic but can result in oliguria and acute renal failure. Manifestations of associated or underlying systemic diseases may be present. There may be systemic symptoms such as fever, weight loss and general malaise.

Physical signs

Manifestations of systemic disease may be present, such as rashes or joint lesions.

Investigations

- Urinalysis: blood, protein and red blood cell casts.

- Plasma: renal impairment; raised inflammatory markers such as C-reactive protein, erythrocyte sedimentation rate, white cell count and platelet count; positive serological tests for associated systemic diseases, especially ANCA or anti-GBM antibody.

- Renal biopsy.

Differential diagnosis

- Other forms of acute glomerulonephritis.

- Other causes of acute renal failure.

Treatment

- Immunosuppression with prednisolone and cyclophosphamide; azathioprine may be substituted for cyclophosphamide after 3 months.

- Plasma exchange is used for anti-GBM antibody disease. Therapy for rapidly progressive glomerulonephritis is often supplemented with adjuvant methylprednisolone or plasma exchange.

Complications

Complications are those of immunosuppression and acute renal failure.

Prognosis

Less than 25% of patients escape dialysis but, with treatment, the 5-year survival rate once off dialysis is 60–80%.

Disease associations

See Aetiology above.

FURTHER READING

Cameron JS. The patient with glomerular disease. In: Davison AM, Cameron JS, Grünfeld J-P, *et al.*, eds. *Oxford Textbook of Clinical Nephrology*, 3rd edn. Oxford: Oxford University Press, 2005: 347–658.

2.3.2 Secondary glomerular disease

Glomerular disease can be secondary to many conditions, including those discussed in Section 2.7. Malignancy and infection-associated glomerular disease are considered here.

Aetiology/pathophysiology/pathology

Malignancy-associated glomerulonephritis

The mechanism is unclear, but renal disease may improve with treatment of the malignancy. Most patterns of glomerulonephritis can occur.

Infection-related glomerulonephritis

The mechanism is usually unclear; pathogen antigens can trigger an aberrant immune response causing renal damage. Most patterns of glomerulonephritis can occur.

Epidemiology

Malignancy-associated glomerulonephritis

Of patients with malignancy, 15–58% have urinary abnormalities. Up to 17% of patients with solid tumours have histologically evident glomerular changes. Membranous nephropathy is the most common histological type.

Infection-related glomerulonephritis

Significant glomerulonephritis can be associated with viral infection (hepatitis C, hepatitis B and HIV), bacterial infection (streptococcal and endocarditis) and other infections (malaria and syphilis).

Clinical presentation and physical signs

Malignancy-associated glomerulonephritis

This varies from asymptomatic urinary abnormality to nephrotic syndrome or acute renal failure. Physical signs depend on the tumour and renal pathology.

Infection-related glomerulonephritis

This is highly variable, depending on the infection and the associated renal disease.

Investigations

These are as for other glomerular disease (see Section 2.3.1). Investigations will also be directed towards the malignancy or infection.

Differential diagnosis

Malignancy-associated glomerulonephritis

The differential diagnosis is from either primary glomerulonephritis or other tumour-related causes of renal dysfunction, including obstruction, invasion of the renal tract, renal vein thrombosis, urate nephropathy, hypercalcaemia and drug toxicity.

Infection-related glomerulonephritis

Differential diagnosis is from unrelated primary

glomerulonephritis. With chronic infection, amyloid A amyloidosis can occur. In treated infections, consider drug toxicity.

Treatment

Treat the malignancy in malignancy-associated glomerulonephritis.

Eradicate, where possible, the infection in infection-related glomerulonephritis.

Complications

Malignancy-associated glomerulonephritis

The complications are those of the malignancy and its therapy, and also of the nephrotic syndrome, hypertension or renal impairment if these are present.

Infection-related glomerulonephritis

The complications are those of the underlying infection, and also of the nephrotic syndrome, hypertension and renal impairment if these are present.

Prognosis

This depends on the infection or malignancy. Generally, renal involvement is associated with a worsened prognosis for the malignancy.

Disease associations

In infection-related glomerulonephritis, these could potentially include the following.

- Hepatitis B: membranous nephropathy, mesangiocapillary glomerulonephritis (type I) and IgA nephropathy.

- Hepatitis C: mesangiocapillary glomerulonephritis (type I) and mixed essential cryoglobulinaemia type II.

- HIV: focal segmental glomerulosclerosis.

- Epstein–Barr virus: microscopic haematuria and proteinuria.

- Streptococcal infection: poststreptococcal (diffuse proliferative) glomerulonephritis.

- Staphylococcal infection (endocarditis, shunt infections and general sepsis): diffuse proliferative glomerulonephritis, focal segmental proliferative glomerulonephritis or type I mesangiocapillary glomerulonephritis.

- *Salmonella* infections: mesangiocapillary glomerulonephritis or IgA nephropathy.

- Tuberculosis: amyloidosis.

- Leprosy: amyloidosis, diffuse proliferative glomerulonephritis or mesangiocapillary glomerulonephritis.

- Malaria and syphilis: membranous nephropathy.

- *Escherichia coli* and other enteric infections can cause haemolytic–uraemic syndrome (see Section 2.7.3).

- Leptospirosis causes an acute tubulointerstitial nephritis.

FURTHER READING

Daghestani L and Pomeroy C. Renal manifestations of hepatitis C infection. *Am. J. Med.* 1999; 106: 347–54.

Humphreys MH. Human immunodeficiency virus-associated glomerulosclerosis. *Kidney Int.* 1995; 48: 311–20.

Norris SH. Paraneoplastic glomerulopathies. *Semin. Nephrol.* 1993; 13: 258–72.

2.4 Tubulointerstitial diseases

2.4.1 Acute tubular necrosis

Aetiology/pathophysiology

Acute tubular necrosis (ATN) occurs when there is tubular cell injury and death. This usually results from renal hypoperfusion, referred to as ischaemic ATN. Drugs may also directly damage tubular cells, referred to as nephrotoxic ATN (eg contrast media and aminoglycosides).

In ischaemic ATN, reduced renal blood flow results in cortical vasoconstriction and medullary hypoxia (Fig. 57). Cells of the proximal convoluted tubule and thick ascending limb of the loop of Henle have high oxygen requirements and are particularly susceptible to hypoxic damage. Thus cell necrosis results, mediated by oxygen free radicals and calcium, and cells are shed into the tubular lumen, forming casts that obstruct urine flow. Loss of tubular integrity produces back-leak of glomerular filtrate and hence reabsorption of water and toxins. Vascular endothelial cells within the medulla are also damaged, further impairing blood flow.

When renal perfusion is compromised, exposure to NSAIDs inhibits cyclooxygenases and further decreases perfusion. This is a common contributing factor to ATN in clinical practice.

Remarkably, the kidney can recover from ATN. Once blood supply and oxygen delivery are normalised, tubular cells still adherent to the basement membrane can divide and regenerate a functional epithelium. Glomerular filtration is reinitiated through mechanisms that are unclear. However, at this point tubular function may not have sufficiently recovered to enable fluid reabsorption, resulting in a 'polyuric phase' during recovery from ATN.

Epidemiology

Acute renal failure (ARF) has an annual incidence of 170 per million adult population and over 50% of these are caused by ATN. Elderly people are much more at risk.

Clinical presentation

- Presentation is usually in the context of an obvious illness (eg the initial presentation may be with pneumonia and dehydration).

- ATN is often part of the multiorgan failure syndrome and is relatively common in patients in the intensive care unit (ICU).

- Occasionally patients present with ARF due to ATN without an obvious episode of hypoperfusion.

- It may occur on the background of known or previously unrecognised chronic renal impairment (acute-on-chronic renal failure).

Investigations

- Urine may show low-grade (trace/1+) proteinuria and/or haematuria, but heavy proteinuria/haematuria and cellular casts raise doubt about the diagnosis.

- Ultrasonography shows normal-sized unobstructed kidneys.

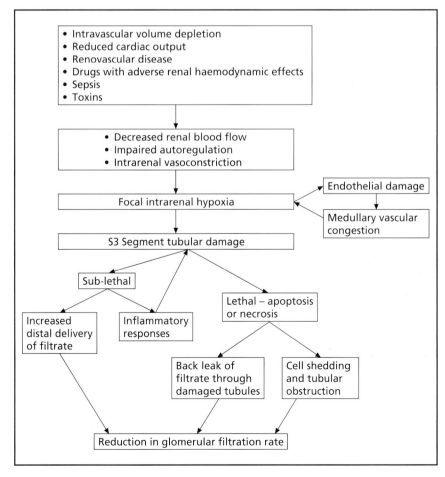

▲**Fig. 57** Pathophysiology of ATN.

- Renal biopsy is not usually necessary, but if performed shows tubular necrosis, sometimes with evidence of regeneration.

Treatment

- The first priority is treatment of life-threatening complications (see Section 1.4.1).

- Supportive treatments: maintain circulation and oxygenation, and avoid further nephrotoxic drugs.

- If ATN is suspected, refer early to a nephrologist. ICU input is also often required, especially in the patient with multiorgan failure.

- The precipitating condition must be treated vigorously.

Prognosis

Approximately 60% of all patients who require renal replacement therapy for ATN will survive. Of the survivors, 60% will regain full renal function, but 30% will have residual chronic renal failure and 10% will have end-stage renal failure, and will need to remain on long-term dialysis. The likelihood of recovery is lower in elderly people.

FURTHER READING

Lameire N, Van Biesen W and Vanholder R. Acute renal failure. *Lancet* 2005; 365: 417–30.

2.4.2 Acute interstitial nephritis

Aetiology

Some cases are idiopathic, but a recognised precipitating cause (most often drugs, particularly NSAIDs) can be identified in most patients.

Causes of acute interstitial nephritis

- Idiopathic.
- Drugs, eg NSAIDs (most common cause), penicillin, rifampicin, allopurinol, cephalosporins, sulphonamides, furosemide, thiazide diuretics, cimetidine, amphotericin.
- Infections: viral (eg Hanta virus), bacterial (eg leptospirosis) and mycobacterial.

Clinical presentation

This is usually with mild renal impairment and hypertension or, in more severe cases, acute renal failure, which is often non-oliguric. Systemic manifestations may include fever, arthralgia and skin rash.

Investigations

- Urinalysis is usually unremarkable (eg minor proteinuria, some blood is commonly detected); urinary eosinophils may be present.

- Differential FBC may show an eosinophilia and serum IgE can be raised.

- Renal biopsy typically shows oedema of the interstitium with an acute inflammatory infiltrate (plasma cells, lymphocytes and eosinophils) (Fig. 58).

Treatment

- Withdraw the causative agent (eg drugs).

- Moderate-dose oral steroids (eg prednisolone 30 mg od) are commonly given.

Prognosis

Most patients make a complete renal recovery.

FURTHER READING

Rossert JA and Fischer EA. Acute interstitial nephritis. In: Johnson RJ and Feehally J, eds. *Comprehensive Clinical Nephrology*, 2nd edn. Edinburgh: Mosby, 2003: 769–77.

2.4.3 Chronic interstitial nephritis

Aetiology

Diverse systemic or renal conditions and drugs can result in chronic inflammation within the tubulointerstitium.

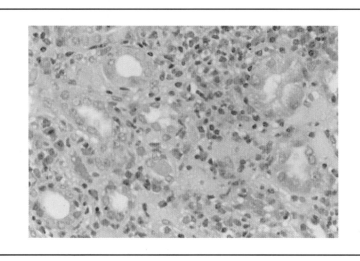

▲ **Fig. 58** Histological appearance of acute interstitial nephritis. There is a diffuse inflammatory infiltrate with plasma cells and lymphocytes; tubular architecture is well preserved (H&E, ×200).

Causes of chronic interstitial nephritis

- Immunological diseases: systemic lupus erythematosus, Sjögren's syndrome, rheumatoid arthritis, systemic sclerosis.
- Granulomatous disease: Wegener's granulomatosis, tuberculosis (TB), sarcoidosis.
- Drugs: ciclosporin, cisplatin, lithium, iron, analgesics.
- Haematological disorders: myeloma, light-chain nephropathy, sickle cell disease.
- Heavy metals: lead and cadmium.
- Hereditary disorders: nephronophthisis, Alport's syndrome.
- Metabolic disorders: hypercalcaemia, hypokalaemia, hyperuricaemia.
- Endemic disease: Balkan nephropathy.
- Other: irradiation, chronic transplant rejection.

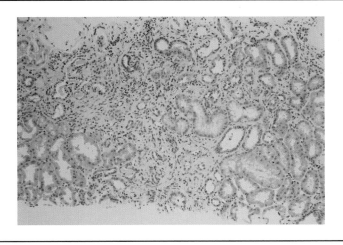

▲ **Fig. 59** Histological appearance of chronic interstitial nephritis. Alongside the inflammatory infiltrate, there is evidence of chronic tubulointerstitial damage, with scarring and tubular atrophy (H&E, ×80).

Clinical presentation

Patients present with chronic renal failure or end-stage renal failure. Some patients may also manifest renal tubular acidosis (usually type 1), nephrogenic diabetes insipidus or salt-wasting states.

Investigations

Renal biopsy shows a chronic inflammatory infiltrate within the interstitium, often with extensive scarring and tubular loss (Fig. 59); the latter indicates irreversible renal damage. Other histological features may be specific to the underlying disorder:

- tubular casts with myeloma or light-chain nephropathy;

- granulomas in TB or sarcoidosis.

Treatment

Treat the underlying condition. Withdraw any drugs/toxins.

Prognosis

This depends on the cause and the severity of damage at the time of diagnosis. If the cause can be treated (eg connective tissue disorder) or removed (eg drugs), then progression of chronic renal failure may be prevented. However, extensive tubulointerstitial fibrosis usually predicts a progressive decline to end-stage renal failure.

2.4.4 Specific tubulointerstitial disorders

Balkan nephropathy

Aetiology
This was initially thought to be due to an environmental toxin (eg trace metals in drinking water) or a viral infection. Recent evidence suggests the cause is chronic exposure to a fungal toxin.

Epidemiology
This is a chronic interstitial renal disease endemic in villages along the tributaries of the river Danube (eg in Romania, Bulgaria, Bosnia and Herzegovina, and Croatia).

Clinical presentation
Presentation is with chronic renal failure (CRF) or end-stage renal failure.

Physical signs
Patients have coppery-yellow pigmentation of the palms and soles.

Investigations
Imaging reveals small smooth kidneys.

Treatment
There is currently no specific treatment. Proceed with the appropriate treatment for CRF and renal replacement.

Complications
Urothelial malignancy is increased 200-fold.

Analgesic nephropathy

Aetiology
Chronic analgesic use (previously compound analgesics containing phenacetin, now NSAIDs).

Epidemiology
Between 1950 and 1970, analgesic nephropathy was the most common cause of CRF in parts of Europe and Australia. The condition is now in decline, especially since the withdrawal of phenacetin. It affects women more often than men.

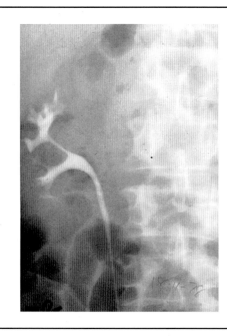

▲**Fig. 60** IVU of papillary necrosis. There is clubbing of right upper polar calyces with typical 'cup and spill' deformities.

Clinical presentation

There is a history of chronic analgesic use, eg for backache, pelvic inflammatory disease and headache. There may be loin pain associated with papillary necrosis. Presentation is often with CRF or end-stage renal failure.

Investigations

The classic radiological appearance is of 'cup and spill' calyces, resulting from papillary necrosis, with renal scarring seen on an intravenous urogram (IVU) (Fig. 60). Renal biopsy is not of diagnostic value.

Treatment

As for CRF and end-stage renal failure. Complete cessation of analgesic consumption. Initiate prompt treatment of infection/obstruction.

Complications

The risk of urothelial malignancy is increased.

Renal tubular acidosis

Aetiology

- Distal or type 1 renal tubular acidosis (RTA) results from impaired urinary acidification.

- Proximal or type 2 RTA is caused by a failure of bicarbonate reabsorption.

- Type 4 RTA (hyporeninaemic hypoaldosteronism) describes a metabolic acidosis that is associated with hyperkalaemia and mild renal impairment, with glomerular filtration rate (GFR) usually >30 mL/min.

The causes of different forms of RTA are shown in Table 18.

Epidemiology

- Distal RTA is fairly common and can complicate many renal parenchymal disorders.

- Proximal RTA is uncommon.

Clinical presentation

- Distal RTA can present with acidosis, hyperventilation and muscular weakness (due to hypokalaemia). It is also associated with growth failure and rickets in children and osteomalacia in adults. A majority (70%) of sufferers

	TABLE 18 CAUSES OF RTA	
Type of RTA	**Causes**
Distal RTA	Primary: genetic (dominant) or idiopathic Secondary to autoimmune diseases: systemic lupus erythematosus, Sjögren's syndrome Tubulointerstitial disease: chronic pyelonephritis, transplant rejection, obstructive uropathy, chronic interstitial nephritis Nephrocalcinosis: medullary sponge kidney, hypercalcaemia Drugs and toxins: lithium, amphotericin, toluene
Proximal RTA	Occurring alone: idiopathic With Fanconi's syndrome: Wilson's disease, cystinosis, fructose intolerance, Sjögren's syndrome Tubulointerstitial disease: interstitial nephritis, myeloma, amyloidosis Drugs and toxins: outdated tetracyclines, streptozotocin, lead and mercury (and other heavy metals), acetazolamide, sulphonamides
Type IV RTA	Diabetic nephropathy Gouty nephropathy Urinary tract obstruction Drugs: NSAIDs or potassium-sparing diuretics

have nephrocalcinosis or urinary stones.

- Proximal RTA can present with growth failure and rickets (children), osteomalacia (adults) and proximal myopathy. Polyuria and polydipsia can be seen.

Physical signs

The diagnosis of RTA depends on demonstrating that in the presence of normal or near-normal GFR the renal tubules cannot excrete acid normally. In many cases formal testing is not required because the patient is already acidaemic.

A formal acidification test involves determination of the minimum urinary pH after ingestion of a standardised dose of ammonium chloride. Urine pH should fall to less than 5.5. Specific signs include the following.

- Distal RTA: plasma bicarbonate tends to be very low (<12 mmol/L) and urinary pH is always >5.5. There may be severe hypokalaemia. Abdominal radiograph may show nephrocalcinosis/urinary stones.

- Proximal RTA: when plasma bicarbonate falls sufficiently, urinary pH can fall to normal minimum (<5.5). Proximal RTA is almost always associated with Fanconi's syndrome (phosphaturia, glycosuria, aminoaciduria and uricosuria). Nephrocalcinosis and urinary stones are not seen. Hypokalaemia is common.

Treatment

- Distal RTA: the acutely acidotic patient is usually very hypokalaemic. Acutely, potassium should be given before bicarbonate. Chronic acidosis responds well to oral sodium bicarbonate (1–3 mmol/kg daily)

- Proximal RTA: very large doses of oral sodium bicarbonate (3–20 mmol/kg daily) are required, usually with potassium supplementation.

Complications

- Distal RTA: nephrocalcinosis (Fig. 61), calculi and growth failure.

- Proximal RTA: rickets and osteomalacia (caused by phosphate wasting).

Reflux nephropathy (or chronic pyelonephritis)

Aetiology

Childhood vesicoureteric reflux (VUR) and infection cause renal scarring and nephropathy (Fig. 62). There is a genetic predisposition: children of parents with reflux nephropathy have an approximately 25% risk of VUR.

Epidemiology

- Common during the first 5 years of life (when almost all scarring occurs).

- Reflux diminishes with age.

- Accounts for about 15% of patients entering dialysis programmes.

Clinical presentation

- Young children: urinary tract infection.

- Adults: hypertension, proteinuria or chronic renal impairment. Often there will be a history of bed-wetting in late childhood and/or urinary tract infections (UTIs). Renal impairment due to reflux nephropathy is always accompanied by proteinuria. Haematuria is not expected and should prompt further investigation (eg cystoscopy).

Investigations

Scarring can be demonstrated by ultrasonography or ^{99m}Tc-dimercaptosuccinic acid scintigraphy. The presence of scars in an adult without another explanation is taken as evidence of childhood VUR and scarring. Further investigations are not

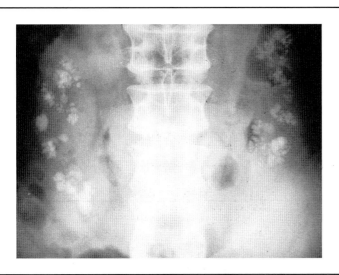

▲ **Fig. 61** Plain abdominal radiograph of nephrocalcinosis in a patient with RTA. There is gross calcification within the outer medullary and cortical regions of the kidneys.

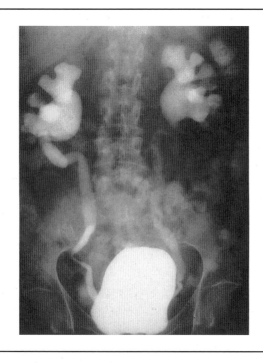

▲**Fig. 62** Micturating cystogram showing severe reflux nephropathy (grade 3).

usually performed. Reflux does not usually persist in adults.

It is recommended that offspring or siblings (if a child) of affected patients undergo screening for VUR. Diagnosis of VUR is by micturating cystography. Reflux can be classified on a scale from grade I (reflux into the ureter only) to grade V (gross dilatation and tortuosity of ureter, renal pelvis and calyces) (Fig. 63).

Treatment

Renal scarring results from infection in young children. To prevent this, children with reflux are given antibiotic prophylaxis. Surgery for VUR is not proved to protect against scarring and its role is therefore controversial. Operations that are performed include:

• endoscopic injection of collagen behind the intravesical ureter;

• lengthening of the submucosal ureteric tunnel;

• ureteric reimplantation.

As with all forms of chronic and potentially progressive renal disorders, control of hypertension is of vital importance in retarding progression.

Prevention

• Of children with a UTI, 15–60% will have VUR and about 10% will have evidence of reflux nephropathy.

• All children with a UTI should be investigated for VUR.

• If VUR is present, treatment with prophylactic antibiotics is recommended.

2.5 Diseases of renal vessels

2.5.1 Renovascular disease

Aetiology

The overwhelming majority of patients with renal artery stenosis have atheromatous renovascular disease (ARVD). Depending on the distribution of the atheroma, this may produce discrete narrowing of the renal arteries at their origin (renal artery stenosis) or, more commonly, diffuse atherosclerotic disease of the renal arteries and smaller vessels. Fibromuscular dysplasia is a rare cause of renal artery stenosis and hypertension in young patients.

Epidemiology

ARVD is associated with generalised vascular disease. It is present in up to 30% of patients undergoing coronary angiography and affects up

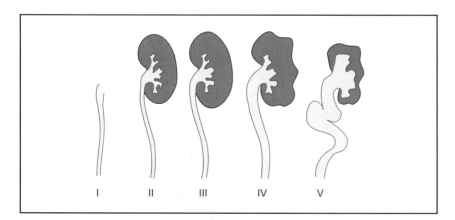

▲**Fig. 63** Classification of VUR: grade I, ureter only; grade II, up to pelvis and calyces but with no dilatation; grade III, mild-to-moderate dilatation but with only minimal blunting of fornices; grade IV, moderate dilatation with obliteration of sharp angles of fornices; grade V, gross dilatation, tortuosity of the ureter and pelvicalyceal system, and calyces severely clubbed.

to 60% of patients with peripheral vascular disease and about 30% of those with congestive heart failure aged >70 years. As older patients are now readily admitted to dialysis programmes, ARVD is an increasing cause of end-stage renal failure (about 20%) in this population.

Clinical presentation

Presentation is with hypertension (ARVD accounts for 80% of all cases of secondary hypertension, ie 4% of all cases of hypertension), chronic renal failure or end-stage renal failure. Less commonly, there is 'flash' pulmonary oedema and angiotensin-converting enzyme (ACE) inhibitor-related acute renal failure.

Predominant symptoms usually relate to coexisting extrarenal vascular disease (eg intermittent claudication). Clinical examination may demonstrate vascular disease elsewhere (reduced or absent peripheral pulses, arterial leg ulcers or carotid and femoral bruits); renal artery bruits are occasionally present.

Investigations

Investigations are aimed at identifying atheromatous disease in the renal arteries, particularly if a discrete stenosis can be found.

- Ultrasonography: a discrepancy in renal length >2 cm is strongly predictive of renovascular disease. Imaging will also give an indication of how much chronic damage there is and exclude obstruction. Doppler ultrasonography is time-consuming, highly observer dependent and not usually suitable as a screening tool.

- Magnetic resonance angiography (MRA) of the renal arteries has

become the most commonly used screening test. It avoids the use of radiocontrast media and exposure to ionising radiation, but tends to overestimate the severity of stenoses.

- CT angiography: its disadvantages are risks of allergy, contrast nephropathy and radiation exposure, although it may be appropriate if MRA is not available or contraindicated (eg there is a pacemaker *in situ*).

- Captopril renography: this is of limited value if there is significant renal dysfunction. It cannot delineate the anatomy of stenoses, but is very useful for determining the relative contribution to function of each kidney prior to intervention.

- Renal angiography: this remains the definitive investigation for renovascular disease (Fig. 64). Often angiography and treatment (angioplasty with or without stenting) will be performed as part of the same procedure. Risks include volume overload and/or

acute renal dysfunction related to contrast, cholesterol emboli, bleeding (both at the site of catheter introduction and retroperitoneally) and dissection of the artery.

Treatment

All patients should receive aspirin and cholesterol-lowering therapy for their general atherosclerotic risk, hypertension should be controlled and smoking (an independent risk factor for the progression of renal disease) should be stopped.

Patients with significant stenoses, especially ostial lesions, can be treated with angioplasty with or without a stent, but this is controversial and the subject of ongoing trials. In most patients it is not proven that revascularisation procedures are beneficial, but most nephrologists would recommend angioplasty for:

- bilateral stenoses with acute deterioration in renal function, especially in the context of ACE inhibitors;

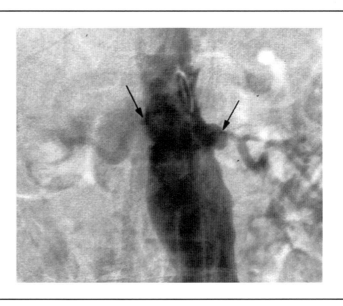

▲ **Fig. 64** Aortic aneurysm in association with ARVD. An infrarenal aneurysm with bilateral renal artery stenoses (arrows) are shown on this intravenous digital subtraction angiogram.

- when there is a small kidney on one side and tight stenosis affecting the opposite kidney;

- episodes of flash pulmonary oedema not explained by left ventricular dysfunction.

Angioplasty may also be considered for:

- resistant hypertension;

- significant stenosis with other indications for the use of ACE inhibitors;

- renal impairment;

Complicated lesions (eg related to aortic aneurysm) may be treated surgically. Autotransplantation is rarely an option because of widespread arterial disease.

Prognosis

This is poor as a result of comorbid vascular events; the 5-year survival rate on dialysis is less than 20%.

FURTHER READING

Safian RD and Textor SC. Renal-artery stenosis. *N. Engl. J. Med.* 2001; 344: 431–42.

2.5.2 Cholesterol atheroembolisation

Pathophysiology

Embolisation of cholesterol crystals occurs in patients with widespread atheromatous disease, often following trauma to the vessels, such as:

- vascular surgery, especially to the abdominal aorta;

- angiography or stenting procedures (usually coronary).

Ruptured or unstable plaques release showers of cholesterol crystals that embolise to the kidneys and other distal vessels (eg feet and skin of the lower extremities). This results in arteriolar occlusion and ischaemic injury. Systemic anticoagulation may cause or exacerbate the condition by preventing the formation of stable thrombus on atheromatous plaques.

Clinical presentation

- Patients present with acute renal failure.

- There may be skin changes (see below) and systemic upset: cholesterol atheroembolism can mimic a vasculitic illness with acute renal failure, rash and fever, etc.

- There may be a history of recent vascular surgery or angiography.

- Unlike contrast nephropathy (in which peak creatinine level occurs at 1–3 days, with evidence of recovery at 5 days), acute renal failure may present much later (occasionally weeks or months after an insult) and persists for longer. Cholesterol emboli probably contribute to the chronic renal failure seen in patients with renovascular disease.

Physical signs

- Evidence of generalised vascular disease in 90%.

- Livedo reticularis.

- Purple cyanotic toes ('trash foot').

- Ulceration in areas of skin involvement.

- Low-grade fever.

Investigations

- Cholesterol crystals ('cholesterol clefts') within vessels on renal biopsy (Fig. 65).

- Skin biopsy is less invasive and may demonstrate a similar appearance.

- Non-diagnostic findings include elevated erythrocyte sedimentation rate, hypocomplementaemia and eosinophilia.

Treatment

Treatment is supportive. Anticoagulation should be

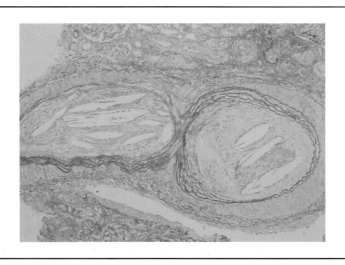

▲ **Fig. 65** Intrarenal cholesterol emboli. Large cholesterol crystals are seen within renal arterioles, producing the appearance of 'cholesterol clefts' (H&E, ×120).

withdrawn if implicated. Statin therapy may be beneficial (purported to stabilise atheromatous plaques). Avoid further angiography.

Prognosis

- Prognosis is poor because of underlying vascular disease.

- Chronic renal failure may stabilise if precipitating factors can be removed.

- Some patients never recover renal function.

2.6 Postrenal problems

2.6.1 Obstructive uropathy

Aetiology/pathophysiology/pathology

Obstruction can arise at any point along the urinary tract (Fig. 66). If pressure rises proximal to the obstruction, then the glomerular filtration rate will fall and renal damage may occur.

Obstruction can arise:

- within the lumen of the urinary tract (eg stones);
- within the wall of the system (eg urothelial tumours);
- outside the system (eg pressure from a pelvic tumour).

Epidemiology

Lower tract obstruction is common in elderly people, mainly in older men with prostatic disease.

Clinical presentation

Acute obstruction, especially with stones, can cause severe pain in the areas to which the urinary tract refers pain, from the loin down to the external genitalia (see Section 1.4.6).

Chronic obstruction is often asymptomatic until there is substantial renal impairment. A poor urinary stream suggests significant obstruction in a patient with prostatic disease: hesitancy, terminal dribbling and urinary frequency also occur.

Always consider prostatic obstruction in an older man with renal impairment or urinary tract infection.

Physical signs

- Prostate enlargement.

- Large palpable residual bladder volume.

- Note that urinary obstruction does not cause the kidneys to become palpable.

Investigations

- Imaging of the renal tract, usually by ultrasonography.

- Further imaging to define the site and nature of the obstruction.

- Plasma: check for evidence of renal impairment.

- Specific tests may be relevant, such as prostate-specific antigen.

Differential diagnosis

The differential diagnosis is from other causes of renal impairment.

Treatment

- Surgical or radiological relief of obstruction.

- Endocrine treatment of benign prostatic disease with 5α-reductase inhibitors may be of some benefit.

Complications

- End-stage renal disease.

- Infection.

- Stone formation in static urine.

Prognosis

The renal prognosis depends on the amount of renal damage caused by the obstruction before it is relieved.

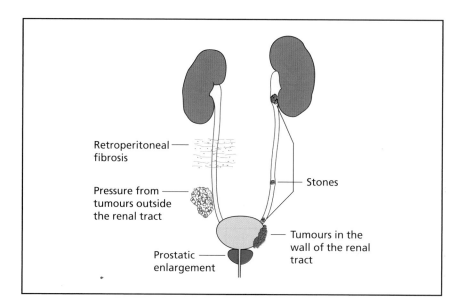

▲ **Fig. 66** Urinary tract obstruction can arise from outside the wall of the urinary tract, within the wall or within the lumen of the urinary system. The major sites at which obstruction to the urinary tract can occur are shown.

Labels: Retroperitoneal fibrosis; Pressure from tumours outside the renal tract; Prostatic enlargement; Stones; Tumours in the wall of the renal tract

Disease associations

- Tumours.

- Retroperitoneal fibrosis.

- Stones.

Pelviureteric junction obstruction
Quite commonly a ring of fibrous tissue where the renal pelvis joins the ureter can obstruct the renal pelvis and calyces. This can correct spontaneously, but if there is pain or evidence of declining renal function then surgery is needed.

2.6.2 Stones

Aetiology/pathophysiology/pathology

Stones form when the concentration of stone-forming substances in the urine exceeds their solubility. Conditions that raise urinary concentrations of stone-forming substances or lower urinary levels of stone-inhibiting compounds therefore predispose an individual to stones. In particular, if urine volume is reduced then the concentration of stone-forming substances rises and stone formation increases. Compounds such as citrate reduce stone formation by chelating stone substances.

Hypercalciuria occurs in 65% of patients with stones and is usually idiopathic. It is associated with obesity and hypertension. Major causes of stone formation are shown in Table 19.

Major sites of stone obstruction in the ureters are:

- the pelviureteric junction;
- the point where the ureters cross over the rim of the pelvic bones;
- the entry site of the ureters into the bladder.

TABLE 19 MAJOR CAUSES OF STONE FORMATION	
Stone type	**Causes**
Calcium stones (80%)	Hypercalciuria: disorders that cause hypercalcaemia, especially primary hyperparathyroidism; idiopathic Hyperoxaluria: primary hyperoxaluria, excess intake, ileal disease and ileal bypass Hypocitraturia: distal tubular disease
Uric acid stones (10%)	Acid urine causes uric acid precipitation High purine intake High cell turnover: tumours and tumour lysis
Cystine stones (2%)	Cystinuria: autosomal recessive defect in dibasic amino acid transporter
Infection stones (5%)	Chronic infection with urea-splitting organisms causes stones made of magnesium ammonium phosphate and calcium phosphate
Other stones (3%)	Xanthine stones in xanthinuria Rare renal chloride channel mutations can cause stone formation

Epidemiology
Stones are common, with a prevalence of up to 10% in men and 5% in women. They are much commoner in hot climates. There is a strong familial predisposition, with first-degree relatives having a relative risk of 2.5 compared with controls. After one stone, there is a greater than 50% chance of having a second stone in the following 10 years.

Clinical presentation
The clinical presentation varies:

- asymptomatic haematuria and uncomplicated passage of small stones or gravel;

- acute renal colic with loin pain, nausea, vomiting and sometimes frank haematuria (see Section 1.4.6);

- incidentally demonstrated on imaging.

Physical signs
Obstruction may cause renal tenderness.

Investigations

Acute setting

- Urine: look for microscopic or macroscopic blood.

- Imaging by plain radiography, ultrasonography, radiographic contrast studies (intravenous urogram, CT, antegrade or retrograde ureterography): calcium and infection stones are radio-opaque, cystine stones weakly radio-opaque, and urate stones radiolucent.

- Culture urine to exclude infection.

Outpatient setting
To identify a predisposing metabolic disorder, do the following.

- Analyse any stone passed to determine its constituents.

- Perform a spot urinalysis: check pH, specific gravity, microscopy for crystals, culture and qualitative test for cystine (if there is a radiolucent stone). A pH >7 with phosphate crystals is suggestive of magnesium ammonium phosphate/calcium phosphate 'infection stones'; hexagonal cystine crystals are diagnostic of cystine stones.

- Check serum sodium, potassium, creatinine, urea, calcium, phosphate, albumin, urate and bicarbonate.

- Collect a 24-hour urine sample with acid preservative: check volume, creatinine, calcium, magnesium, sodium, potassium, phosphate, oxalate and citrate.

- Collect a 24-hour urine sample in plain container (no preservative): check volume, creatinine, pH, protein, urate and cystine (qualitative test).

Consider an anatomical as well as a biochemical predisposition to stone formation: stones can form because of urinary stasis, infection or around catheters. Ultrasonography is a good screening test for an anatomical abnormality.

> Hypercalciuria, usually idiopathic, is found in 65% of patients with urinary stones.

Differential diagnosis

- Clot retention.
- Papillary necrosis.
- Tumours.

Treatment
Asymptomatic stones not associated with obstruction or infection require conservative treatment only (see Prevention). Symptomatic, obstructing or large stones may be removed by percutaneous or surgical intervention, or by extracorporeal shock-wave lithotripsy.

Complications

- Infection.
- Urinary obstruction.
- Permanent renal damage.

Prognosis
Half of those who pass a urinary stone will do so again. Untreated or repeated obstruction can cause chronic renal failure, most commonly in those with infection stones.

Prevention of stone recurrence

> The most important preventive measure is to increase fluid intake.

- All types of stones: maintain a high fluid intake to keep the urinary concentration of stone-forming substances low. Patients who form urinary stones should be told to drink enough liquids to ensure a urine output of at least 2–3 L/day. In those with frequent stones, it can be useful to suggest that they drink a pint of water before going to bed, which typically means they will have to get up during the night to pass urine and they should then drink another pint at that point.

- Eradicate (if possible) any chronic infection.

- Potassium citrate: helpful in most stone-forming situations because the citrate chelates calcium, as well as causing alkalinisation.

- Calcium stones: correct hyperparathyroidism if present. Avoid excesses of animal protein (meat, fish and poultry), oxalate-containing foods (rhubarb and spinach), salt and refined sugar (increase intestinal calcium

absorption) or calcium intake. Do not advise avoidance of dairy products, which can do more harm than good: a low dietary calcium intake causes an increase in intestinal absorption of oxalate and can thereby increase the risk of stone formation. Thiazide diuretics can be used to increase urine volume and inhibit calcium excretion.

- Urate stones: alkalinisation of the urine with potassium citrate or sodium bicarbonate; reduce purine intake; and reduce urate production (allopurinol).

- Cystine stones: alkalinisation of the urine; penicillamine, which cleaves cystine to soluble cysteine products; and captopril, which binds cystine.

2.6.3 Retroperitonal fibrosis or periaortitis

Aetiology/pathophysiology/pathology
This is an autoimmune periaortitis, possibly triggered by material leaking out of atheromatous plaques. Histologically there is atheroma, thinning of the media, increased adventitia and inflammatory infiltration of the vessel wall. The lower and middle thirds of the ureters become embedded in fibrous tissue and can become obstructed.

Epidemiology

- Peak age of incidence is 50–70 years.
- Male to female ratio is 3:1.

Clinical presentation
With flank or abdominal pain, or as an incidental finding when investigating impaired renal function or vascular disease.

Physical signs
There may be hypertension and signs of vascular disease.

Investigations

- CT or MRI.

- Raised erythrocyte sedimentation rate and normochromic/normocytic anaemia are common.

- Intravenous urogram or retrograde contrast studies may show characteristic medial deviation of the ureters.

Differential diagnosis

- Other causes of urinary tract obstruction.

- Malignancy with obstruction.

Treatment

Steroids reduce inflammation and, if still necessary, the ureters can be stented or surgically freed from the fibrotic tissue (ureterolysis).

Prognosis

With treatment the prognosis for renal function is good.

Disease associations

This disease can be triggered by methysergide, and possibly by beta-blockers and methyldopa.

2.6.4 Urinary tract infection

Aetiology/pathophysiology/pathology

Infection usually enters the urinary tract through the urethra, but blood-borne infection can deposit in the kidney. The higher incidence in women is attributed to easier access for pathogens through the shorter female urethra.

- The usual organisms are Gram-negative *Escherichia coli*, *Klebsiella* and *Proteus* species.
- Lower urinary tract infection is restricted to the bladder and urethra, usually involves only the superficial mucosa and has no long-term effects.
- Upper urinary tract infection affects the kidney or ureters, involves the deep renal medullary tissue and can permanently damage the kidney.

During pregnancy the ureters are relatively dilated and have a lower tone, which increases the risk of infection ascending to the kidneys.

Infection of the urinary tract by *Mycobacterium tuberculosis* is uncommon in the UK but is a cause of sterile pyuria (white cells in the urine, but no organism grown in standard culture conditions). Early-morning urine samples should be cultured specifically for mycobacteria when this diagnosis is considered.

2.7 The kidney in systemic disease

2.7.1 Myeloma

Pathology

The commonest cause of renal dysfunction in patients with myeloma is cast nephropathy or 'myeloma kidney', which is characterised by the renal biospy finding of intratubular cast deposition (Fig. 67). Other renal biopsy findings in patients with myeloma include glomerular lesions, amyloidosis or chronic interstitial nephritis.

Pathophysiology

In cast nephropathy, κ or λ light chains form casts that obstruct the distal tubules and collecting ducts. The proteinaceous casts may be directly toxic to the tubules and are usually associated with an interstitial infiltrate, often with multinucleated giant cells (Fig. 67). Acute tubular necrosis and tubular atrophy also occur.

Epidemiology

Acute renal failure occurs in about 5% of those with myeloma; the prevalence of myeloma patients on dialysis programmes is about 2%.

Clinical presentation

Acute renal failure (ARF) is frequently associated with cast nephropathy; however, hypercalcaemia, hyperuricaemia, sepsis and radiocontrast agents may

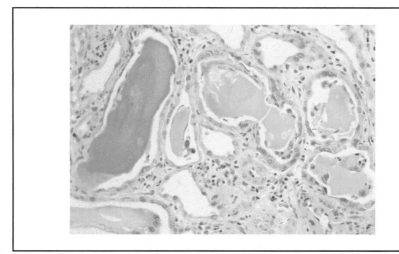

▲ **Fig. 67** Myeloma kidney showing dense intratubular casts with accompanying tubular cell atrophy (H&E, ×200).

also contribute. Renal AL (primary) amyloidosis associated with myeloma usually presents with proteinuria (which may be massive) and/or renal impairment.

Treatment

- ARF in myeloma may sometimes be reversed by vigorous rehydration, treatment of hypercalcaemia and sepsis, and chemotherapy for the myeloma.

- Most cases of myeloma presenting with subacute or chronic renal failure progress to end-stage renal failure despite chemotherapy.

- Renal transplantation is not appropriate, but dialysis should be considered unless the patient is terminally ill.

Prognosis

The presence of renal failure in patients with myeloma is a poor prognostic factor and median survival in myeloma patients requiring renal replacement therapy is around 18 months. Most patients die from sepsis.

FURTHER READING

Ronco PM, Aucouturier P and Mougenot B. Kidney involvement in plasma cell dyscrasias. In: Davison AM, Cameron JS, Grünfeld J-P, *et al.*, eds. *Oxford Textbook of Clinical Nephrology*, 3rd edn. Oxford: Oxford University Press, 2005: 709–32.

2.7.2 Amyloidosis

Aetiology

Amyloid deposits consist of proteins that have adopted an abnormal fibrillar conformation and non-fibrillar constituents that include serum amyloid P (SAP) component and the glycosaminoglycans, heparan and dermatan sulphate.

Type of amyloid	Amyloid protein involved	Underlying cause
Systemic AL (primary) amyloidosis	Monoclonal immunoglobulin Light chains	Plasma cell dyscrasia
Systemic amyloid A (AA) amyloidosis	Serum amyloid A protein (SAA)	Chronic inflammatory illness, eg rheumatoid arthritis
Hereditary amyloidosis	Fibrinogen Aα chain Apolipoprotein AI Lysozyme	Mutations in the genes encoding the relevant proteins Autosomal dominant inheritance

TABLE 20 TYPES OF AMYLOID THAT AFFECT THE KIDNEYS

There are many types of amyloidosis, which are classified according to the protein from which the amyloid fibrils are derived. The types of amyloid that typically affect the kidneys are shown in the Table 20.

Clinical presentation

Renal amyloid presents with proteinuria, nephrotic syndrome or chronic kidney disease.

Investigations

- Renal ultrasonography demonstrates normal-sized or enlarged, echogenic kidneys.

- Renal biopsy demonstrates extracellular amorphous material that may be within the mesangium, interstitium and/or vessel walls, and which shows red–green birefringence when stained with Congo red and viewed under cross-polarised light (Fig. 68).

- SAP scintigraphy scan is useful for demonstrating whole-body amyloid load, delineating organ involvement and monitoring response to treatment.

Treatment

Treatment of amyloidosis aims to suppress production of the fibril precursor protein and is therefore type specific.

- AL (primary) amyloidosis is treated with cytotoxic chemotherapy to suppress the production of monoclonal light chains.

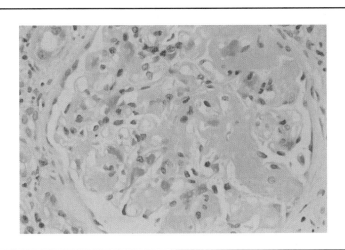

▲ **Fig. 68** Renal amyloidosis. Renal biopsy specimen showing diffuse material staining with Congo red within the glomeruli; the patient had rheumatoid arthritis for 25 years (H&E, ×250).

- AA amyloidosis is treated by control of the underlying inflammatory or infective process, thereby suppressing SAA production.

- Liver transplantation may remove production of all (fibrinogen) or a proportion (apolipoprotein AI) of the mutant proteins that are amyloidogenic.

With the above treatments, amyloid deposits can sometimes slowly regress and proteinuria can improve. Some patients progress to end-stage renal failure. Patients with end-stage renal failure due to amyloidosis should be considered for renal transplantation, but not all are suitable.

Prognosis

The prognosis depends on the amyloid type. AL (primary) amyloidosis has a relatively poor prognosis (median survival <5 years), whereas AA and hereditary amyloidosis usually have a markedly better prognosis.

2.7.3 Thrombotic microangiopathy (haemolytic–uraemic syndrome)

Pathology

- Intraglomerular thrombi with ischaemia (Fig. 69).

- Arteriolar lesions.

Epidemiology

Children aged under 4 years account for 90% of cases.

- In children, haemolytic–uraemic syndrome (HUS) is frequently associated with diarrhoea, of which one-third of UK cases are caused by verotoxin-producing *Escherichia coli*.

- Other causes of thrombotic microangiopathy include drugs (eg ciclosporin), HIV, pregnancy and accelerated-phase hypertension.

- Familial forms of thrombotic microangiopathy have recently been described and are associated with mutations in the genes encoding the complement regulatory proteins, eg complement regulatory proteins factor H or factor I, or the matrix metalloprotease ADAMTS13, which cleaves multimers of von Willebrand factor. A common finding in all types of thrombotic microangiopathy is dysregulated endothelial activation.

Clinical presentation

- Presentation is with acute renal failure (ARF) and microangiopathic haemolytic anaemia (HUS is the most common cause of ARF in children).

- There is frequently severe hypertension.

- There may be severe anaemia and thrombocytopenia due to haemolysis and platelet consumption.

- Neurological disease may occur in patients with thrombotic microangiopathy. This has traditionally been termed 'thrombotic thrombocytopenic purpura'.

Investigations

The haematological abnormalities are characteristic: microangiopathic haemolytic anaemia with anaemia, red blood cell fragments and schistocytes, etc. Renal biopsy may confirm the diagnosis.

Treatment

Treatment depends on the aetiology but may include fresh frozen plasma (replacing complement regulatory

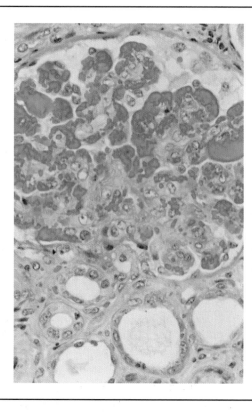

▲ **Fig. 69** HUS. Typical renal histological appearance with intraglomerular thrombi (H&E, ×300).

proteins) and/or plasma exchange (removing antibodies against ADAMTS13 protein).

Prognosis

The overall mortality rate is 10%. The prognosis is worse in adults and particularly in 'atypical' cases, in which chronic renal failure may be insidious and progress to end-stage renal failure. Atypical HUS may recur after renal transplantation leading to graft loss.

FURTHER READING

Taylor CM and Neild GH. Acute renal failure associated with microangiopathy. In: Davison AM, Cameron JS, Grünfeld J-P, *et al.*, eds. *Oxford Textbook of Clinical Nephrology*, 3rd edn. Oxford: Oxford University Press, 2005: 1545–63.

2.7.4 Sickle cell disease

Pathophysiology

Homozygous sickle cell disease can cause:

- glomerular disease (thought to result from hyperfiltration injury in childhood);

- ischaemic injury to the renal medulla (from papillary necrosis as a result of sickle-related occlusion of the vasa rectae).

Clinical presentation

- Enuresis occurs in about 40% of cases (poor concentrating ability).

- Haematuria, resulting from papillary necrosis, occurs in both homozygotes and sickle cell trait.

- Chronic kidney disease in adult homozygotes, especially those aged over 40 years.

- Nephrotic syndrome can occur but is less common.

Investigations

An intravenous urogram may show the 'cup and spill' calyceal deformities of papillary necrosis (see Fig. 60). Renal biopsy findings in those with chronic kidney disease typically demonstrate widespread nephron loss and glomerulosclerosis.

FURTHER READING

Allon M. Renal abnormalities in sickle cell disease. *Arch. Intern. Med.* 1990; 150: 501–4.

2.7.5 Autoimmune rheumatic disorders

Most autoimmune rheumatic disorders can cause renal disease, but most commonly renal problems are seen in:

- rheumatoid arthritis;

- systemic lupus erythematosus (SLE);

- systemic sclerosis;

- Sjögren's syndrome.

Rheumatoid arthritis

Pathology

Renal disease may be caused by amyloid A (AA) amyloidosis, a proliferative glomerulonephritis or as a complication of drug therapy. Gold and penicillamine can cause membranous glomerulonephritis and NSAIDs may cause interstitial nephritis. A rheumatoid-related mesangioproliferative glomerulonephritis (with IgM deposition) can occur.

Clinical presentation

Presentation is with proteinuria, nephrotic syndrome (especially amyloid) or renal impairment. Patients with mesangioproliferative glomerulonephritis will have microscopic haematuria and an 'active' urine sediment with red cell casts.

Treatment

Withdraw offending drugs. Attempt to avoid NSAIDs in all cases of renal impairment (although this is not always possible). In cases of AA amyloidosis, take vigorous measures to suppress the inflammation associated with rheumatoid arthritis. Standard management of chronic kidney disease (CKD) and end-stage renal failure is applicable.

Prognosis

Patients with amyloidosis and chronic interstitial nephritis may progress to end-stage renal failure. Drug-related glomerulonephritis usually resolves within 6 months of withdrawing the offending agent.

Systemic lupus erythematosus

Pathology

Several patterns of renal disease may be seen on histological examination of the kidneys in patients with SLE (Table 21; Figs 70 and 71):

- 'wire-loop' lesions (thickened capillary walls, electron microscopy shows electron-dense deposits) are characteristic of SLE (Fig. 71);

- immunofluorescence is often positive for most immunoglobulins (IgG, IgM, IgA) and complement components (C3, C4, C1q) in SLE.

> In SLE nephrits there is usually a 'full house' of immunoglobulins and complement components on the renal biopsy.

Epidemiology

Of patients with SLE, 40% have evidence of some renal involvement

TABLE 21 ABBREVIATED CLASSIFICATION OF LUPUS NEPHRITIS (INTERNATIONAL SOCIETY OF NEPHROLOGY/RENAL PATHOLOGY SOCIETY 2003)

Class	Biopsy findings	Frequency
I	Minimal mesangial lupus nephritis	5–10%
II	Mesangial proliferative lupus nephritis	10%
III	Focal lupus nephritis	10%
IV	Diffuse segmental (IV-S) or global (IV-G) lupus nephritis	50%
V	Membranous lupus nephritis	20%
VI	Advanced sclerosing lupus nephritis	0–5%

Class V lupus nephritis may occur in combination with class III or IV, in which case both are diagnosed.

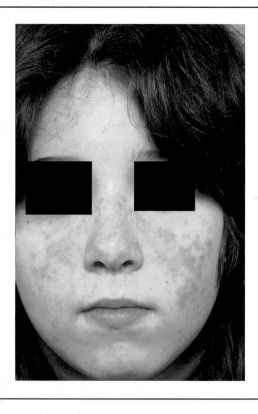

▲ **Fig. 70** Typical rash of SLE.

at presentation; lupus nephritis is more common in black patients and in women (male to female ratio 1:10).

Clinical presentation
Renal disease in patients with SLE can present in a variety of ways that reflect the different pathologies, eg asymptomatic proteinuria, nephrotic syndrome and rapidly progressive renal failure.

Treatment
Treatment depends on the class of lupus nephritis, disease activity and the degree of chronic damage. Rapidly progressive glomerulonephritis is usually due to class III or IV lupus nephritis and is treated with immunosuppressive agents such as cyclophosphamide, mycophenolate mofetil, azathioprine and steroids. Randomised trials support the use of oral steroids with intermittent intravenous cyclophosphamide. Membranous lupus nephritis is usually responsive to steroids and azathioprine. General management is as for CKD and end-stage renal disease.

Prognosis
The pattern of renal histological damage is of prognostic value:

- membranous (class V) lesions have a favourable renal outcome;

- class III and IV (proliferative) lupus nephritis predicts the worst renal prognosis.

Systemic sclerosis

Pathology
Prominent pathological changes occur in interlobular arteries (severe intimal proliferation with deposition of mucopolysaccharides, forming an 'onion skin'); fibrinoid necrosis of afferent arterioles and secondary glomerular ischaemia are common (Fig. 72).

Clinical presentation
Renal disease is almost invariably accompanied by hypertension. In classic 'scleroderma renal crisis' there is accelerated-phase hypertension, microangiopathic haemolytic anaemia and acute renal failure.

Treatment
Treatment is with angiotensin-converting enzyme inhibitors for control of hypertension and may include prostaglandin analogues. Management is as for CKD and end-stage renal disease.

Prognosis
In many patients renal failure is irreversible. Renal impairment may

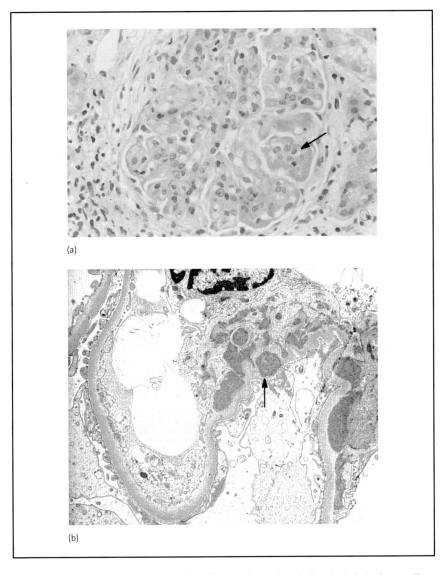

▲ **Fig. 71** Renal histological changes in SLE. (**a**) Proliferative glomerulonephritis: a typical wire-loop capillary is arrowed (H&E, ×200). (**b**) Electron microscopy reveals subendothelial deposits (arrow) (×20,000).

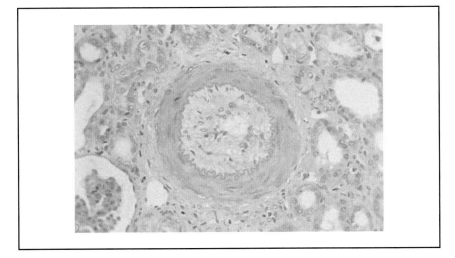

▲ **Fig. 72** Vascular changes in scleroderma. Renal biopsy specimen showing obliterative arteriolar lesions with 'onion skin' appearance and intimal hyperplasia (H&E, ×250).

improve after months of dialysis but the prognosis is still poor due to the frequency of extrarenal disease involvement (especially restrictive cardiomyopathy, pulmonary fibrosis and bowel involvement).

Sjögren's syndrome

Pathology
The most common renal abnormality is interstitial nephritis.

Clinical presentation
Presentation is with proteinuria, CKD or renal tubular dysfunction such as renal tubular acidosis, which may be proximal and/or distal.

Treatment
The condition responds to steroids and cyclophosphamide, but these are rarely required for renal manifestations alone.

FURTHER READING

Emery P and Adu D. Rheumatoid arthritis, mixed connective tissue disease, and polymyositis. In: Davison AM, Cameron JS, Grünfeld J-P, *et al.*, eds. *Oxford Textbook of Clinical Nephrology*, 3rd edn. Oxford: Oxford University Press, 2005: 855–70.

- - - - - - - - - - - - - - - - - -

Shapiro AP and Medsger TA. Renal involvement in sysemic sclerosis. In: Schrier R and Gottschalk C, eds. *Disease of the Kidney*, 4th edn. Boston: Little, Brown, 1988: 2272–83.

2.7.6 Systemic vasculitis
The term 'vasculitis' refers to a group of diseases characterised by the presence of inflammation in the blood vessels, resulting in tissue ischaemia. The spectrum of disease is wide and is classified according to the size of blood vessels affected. The kidney is commonly involved in small-vessel vasculitides, which are

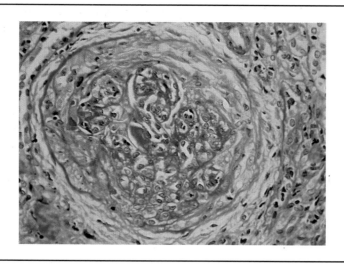

▲ **Fig. 73** Crescentic glomerulonephritis. The crescent derives from the epithelial cells of Bowman's capsule (periodic acid–Schiff, ×300). This appearance is recognised in many forms of aggressive glomerulonephritis, including Goodpasture's disease, ANCA-positive vasculitis and idiopathic rapidly progressive glomerulonephritis.

usually associated with the presence of antineutrophil cytoplasmic antibodies (ANCAs). ANCA-negative small-vessel vasculitides include cryoglobulinaemia, various autoimmune rheumatic disorders and Henoch–Schönlein purpura.

Pathology

ANCA-associated vasculitis includes a spectrum of disease entities previously described as microscopic polyangiitis, Wegener's granulomatosis, polyarteritis nodosa and Churg–Strauss syndrome. Renal histology typically shows necrotising glomerulitis, associated with focal proliferative and/or crescentic glomerulonephritis (Fig. 73). Necrotising granulomas are characteristic in Wegener's granulomatosis. Vasculitis is typically 'pauci-immune', ie there is little or no detectable immunoglobulin deposition by immunohistochemistry. Findings in polyarteritis nodosa, which is a medium-sized arterial vasculitis, may show renal infarction rather than glomerulonephritis.

Clinical presentation

Patients with renal vasculitis classically present with acute nephritic syndrome, but may also present with extrarenal manifestations of vasculitis and be discovered incidentally to have renal involvement. A purpuric vasculitic skin rash is common. Pulmonary involvement is most frequent in

Wegener's granulomatosis (Fig. 74), where there may be characteristic necrotising granulomas in the upper respiratory tract with sinusitis and nasal discharge. Pulmonary haemorrhage may be life-threatening. In polyarteritis nodosa, patients may present with acute renal failure, usually associated with severe hypertension. Pulmonary infiltrates and haemorrhage, gastrointestinal ischaemia, mononeuritis multiplex, cutaneous vasculitis (Fig. 75) and systemic features (myalgia and pyrexia of unknown origin) may occur.

Investigations

- Microscopic polyangiitis is typically associated with perinuclear ANCA (pANCA) staining. The antibodies are usually directed against myeloperoxidase. Cytoplasmic ANCA (cANCA) staining can also be seen, directed specifically against proteinase 3 (PR3).

- Wegener's granulomatosis is strongly associated (90% of cases) with cANCA, with antibodies specific for PR3.

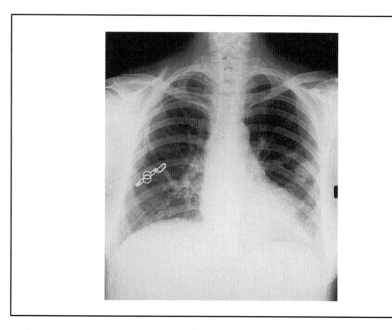

▲ **Fig. 74** CXR showing pulmonary vasculitis in Wegener's granulomatosis. Diffuse infiltrates are seen in the lower zones.

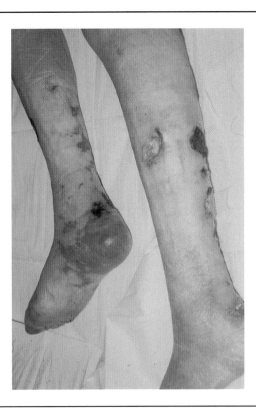

▲ **Fig. 75** Vasculitic skin ulcers in polyarteritis nodosa. The ulcers are deep, 'punched-out' and caused by necrosis.

- Polyarteritis nodosa is associated with ANCA in approximately 50% of cases (more commonly pANCA). There may be an eosinophilia. About 30% of cases are positive for hepatitis B surface antigen. Mesenteric angiography characteristically shows microaneurysms (Fig. 76) in polyarteritis nodosa.

- Renal or other tissue biopsy is usually necessary in cases of suspected vasculitis to confirm the diagnosis.

Treatment

- Immunosuppressive therapy: standard therapy would be corticosteroids and cyclophosphamide for 3 months, followed by azathioprine and low-dose steroid maintenance.

- There is evidence for the use of plasma exchange in patients with

ANCA-associated vasculitis who present with a serum creatinine >500 μmol/L and in those with pulmonary haemorrhage.

- Vasculitis can relapse at any time and patients need careful lifelong monitoring after the initial diagnosis.

FURTHER READING

Gaskin G. Systemic vasculitis. In: Davison AM, Cameron JS, Grünfeld J-P, et al., eds. *Oxford Textbook of Clinical Nephrology*, 3rd edn. Oxford: Oxford University Press, 2005: 766–96.

2.7.7 Diabetic nephropathy

Pathology
Initially there is hyperfiltration and enlargement of the glomeruli. In established diabetic nephropathy, Kimmelstiel–Wilson nodules (focal glomerular sclerosis) are characteristic, but mesangial matrix expansion and diffuse glomerular sclerosis with vascular changes are more common (Fig. 77).

Epidemiology
Diabetic nephropathy is the most common cause of end-stage renal failure in the Western world. About

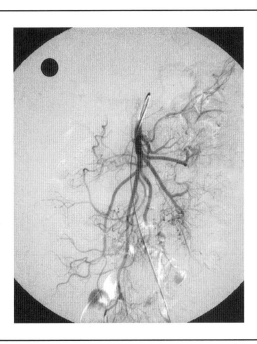

▲ **Fig. 76** Mesenteric angiogram showing microaneurysms in polyarteritis nodosa.

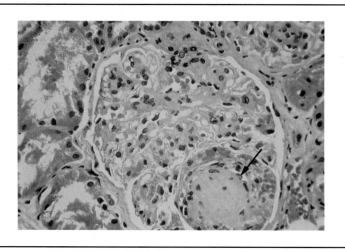

▲ **Fig. 77** Diabetic nephropathy. A classic Kimmelstiel–Wilson nodule (arrow) is present with a background of diffuse mesangial sclerosis (H&E, ×250).

- The mainstay of management of established diabetic nephropathy is tight BP control with ACE inhibitors and angiotensin II receptor blockers, which slow disease progression. Tight glycaemic control is recommended.

- Risk factors for cardiovascular disease should be corrected wherever possible.

- Pancreatic transplantation (either at the time of renal transplantation or as a separate procedure) is now feasible in selected patients with type 1 diabetes mellitus.

40% of patients with type 1 diabetes mellitus have nephropathy 20–40 years after diagnosis and about 25% of patients with type 2 diabetes mellitus develop nephropathy. Type 2 diabetes is much commoner, so most patients with diabetic nephropathy are type 2 diabetics.

Clinical presentation

- The earliest finding is microalbuminuria (albumin excretion 20–200 µg/min or 30–300 mg/day), but this is not reliably detected by standard dipstick.

- The majority of patients with microalbuminuria develop overt diabetic nephropathy with proteinuria >0.5 g/day (Fig. 78), and subsequently develop hypertension and chronic renal failure. About 30% of patients with diabetic nephropathy become frankly nephrotic.

- Diabetic nephropathy is usually associated with retinopathy (common basement membrane pathology).

- Macrovascular disease (ie renal artery stenosis) should

be considered in all diabetics with renal impairment.

Treatment

- Angiotensin-converting enzyme (ACE) inhibitors and angiotensin II receptor blockers can prevent progression from microalbuminuria to overt nephropathy.

Prognosis

Once there is renal impairment in diabetic nephropathy, decline to end-stage renal failure is usually inexorable. Mortality is high: patients with type 1 diabetes have a 20-fold greater mortality than the general population, and relative risk is increased further in those with proteinuria, largely due to cardiovascular disease.

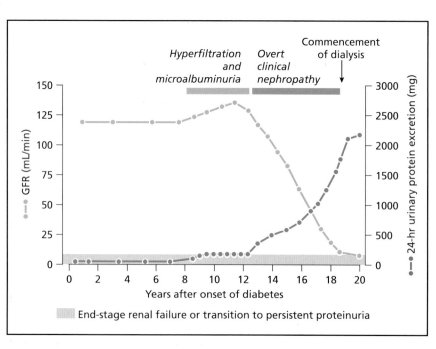

▲ **Fig. 78** The clinical course of diabetic nephropathy (in a patient with type 1 diabetes). This demonstrates the typical temporal relationship between the development of microalbuminuria, proteinuria and progressive decline in glomerular filtration rate.

With all modalities of renal replacement therapy, survival among diabetic patients is reduced compared with other causes of end-stage renal failure (eg 2-year mortality rate of 30% in diabetic patients with end-stage renal failure). However, diabetic patients obtain substantial survival benefit from renal transplantation.

FURTHER READING

Watts GF and Shaw KM. Diabetic nephropathy. In: Raman GV and Golper TA, eds. *Renal Disease: Prevention and Treatment*. London: Chapman & Hall, 1998: 137–71.

2.7.8 Hypertension

Hypertension is a major cause of kidney disease and may cause progressive renal failure. Renal disease is an important cause of secondary hypertension, in which some of the following mechanisms may play a role:

- renin release and activation of the renin–angiotensin–aldosterone axis;

- reduced natriuretic capacity;

- disorganisation of intrarenal vascular structures.

Pathology

- Characteristic findings on renal biopsy specimens in hypertensive subjects include vascular wall thickening and luminal obliteration, with interstitial fibrosis and glomerulosclerosis (hypertensive nephrosclerosis).

- Accelerated-phase hypertension is characterised by arterial fibrinoid necrosis with tubular and glomerular ischaemia (Fig. 79).

- A wide range of renal pathologies can be complicated by hypertension.

Epidemiology

Hypertension affects up to 15% of the population, and is of unknown aetiology (essential hypertension) in the vast majority. It is more common in certain ethnic groups than others (eg black people). Renal disease is the most common cause of secondary hypertension. Among patients approaching end-stage renal failure, 80% are hypertensive.

Clinical presentation

- Patients with essential hypertension may develop proteinuria or chronic kidney disease (hypertensive nephrosclerosis).

- Accelerated-phase hypertension is a cause of acute renal failure.

Physical signs

- Essential hypertension can cause end-organ damage: heart (left ventricular hypertrophy, cardiac failure); kidneys (proteinuria, elevated creatinine); eyes (grade I and II retinopathy); brain (stroke).

- The characteristic finding in accelerated-phase hypertension is grade III or IV retinopathy (grade III, haemorrhages and exudates; grade IV, papilloedema) (Fig. 80); end-organ damage is as for essential hypertension but occurs with higher frequency. There may be thrombotic microangiopathy.

Investigations

Investigate for end-organ damage and consider a secondary cause. All hypertensive patients should have serum creatinine checked and dipstick urinalysis. Factors that increase clinical suspicion of a secondary cause for hypertension include young age, absence of family history, accelerated-phase hypertension and low serum potassium.

Treatment

Treatment of hypertension involves general measures such as regular exercise and reduction in salt intake, as well as modification of cardiovascular risk factors. There are many different classes of antihypertensive agent, but in patients with associated renal disease, particularly proteinuria, angiotensin-converting enzyme inhibitors and angiotensin II receptor blockers are the treatments of choice.

▲ **Fig. 79** Accelerated-phase hypertension. Renal biopsy showing severe arteriolar lesions with intimal hyperplasia and fibrinoid necrosis of the media (arrow). (H&E, x200.)

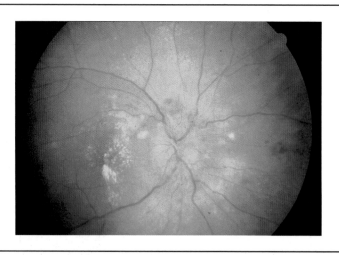

▲ **Fig. 80** The retina in accelerated-phase hypertension. There is papilloedema, cotton-wool spots and hard retinal exudates, as well as haemorrhage (grade IV hypertensive retinopathy).

FURTHER READING

De Wardener HE. The primary role of the kidney and salt intake in the aetiology of essential hypertension: part 1. *Clin. Sci.* 1990; 79: 193–200.

- - - - - - - - - - - - - - -

Kincaid-Smith P. Malignant hypertension. *J. Hypertens.* 1991; 9: 893–9.

- - - - - - - - - - - - - - -

Klahr S. The kidney in hypertension: villain or victim. *N. Engl. J. Med.* 1989; 320: 731–3.

2.7.9 Sarcoidosis

Epidemiology

Hypercalciuria occurs in 65% of patients with sarcoidosis and hypercalcaemia in about 20%. Clinically significant renal failure is uncommon.

Clinical presentation

This is usually with renal impairment in the context of other features of sarcoidosis. Tubular proteinuria, Fanconi's syndrome and distal or proximal renal tubular acidosis are all recognised. Nephrocalcinosis sometimes occurs, but renal calculi are not common.

Investigation

Among patients with chronic kidney disease, renal biopsy usually shows a granulomatous interstitial nephritis (Fig. 81). Sarcoid-related glomerulopathy (usually membranous glomerulonephritis) is rare.

Treatment

Both hypercalcaemia and interstitial nephritis respond to corticosteroids in moderate dosage.

FURTHER READING

Mery JP. The patient with sarcoidosis. In: Davison AM, Cameron JS, Grünfeld J-P, *et al.*, eds. *Oxford Textbook of Clinical Nephrology*, 3rd edn. Oxford: Oxford University Press, 2005: 733–40.

2.7.10 Hepatorenal syndrome

Pathophysiology

Severe liver disease is associated with marked intrarenal hypoperfusion secondary to excessive renal vasoconstriction. Renal parenchymal damage generally does not occur and if normal hepatic function is restored by liver transplantation, renal function usually recovers completely.

Epidemiology

Hepatorenal syndrome occurs in about 10% of patients with cirrhosis and ascites who are admitted to hospital. It is also common in jaundiced patients requiring major surgery for biliary or pancreatic disease.

Clinical presentation

Usually with acute renal failure in the context of severe liver disease

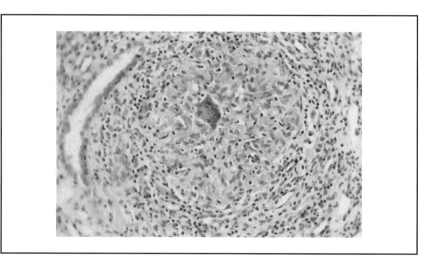

▲ **Fig. 81** Sarcoidosis. Typical renal histological appearance with chronic interstitial nephritis and giant-cell granulomatous change (H&E, ×160).

and hyperbilirubinaemia. Precipitants include hypovolaemia and sepsis.

Investigations

Other causes of renal failure in the context of liver disease, of which there are several, always need to be excluded to make the diagnosis of hepatorenal syndrome. Urinary biochemistry in hepatorenal syndrome characteristically shows a very low sodium concentration (<10 mmol/L).

Treatment

Renal replacement therapy and other types of intensive support are appropriate only in patients with potentially remediable liver disease, or in candidates for liver transplantation.

Prognosis

The mortality of hepatorenal syndrome is high. Median survival of patients who present with rapidly deteriorating renal function is 2 weeks and virtually all are dead within 10 weeks of the onset of renal failure. Median survival among patients with gradual reduction of glomerular filtration rate due to hepatorenal syndrome is 3–6 months.

FURTHER READING

Sweny P. The hepatorenal syndrome. In: Rainford D and Sweny P, eds. *Acute Renal Failure*. London: Farrand Press, 1990: 83–112.

2.7.11 Pregnancy and the kidney

Circulatory and other physiological changes during pregnancy affect the kidneys:

- glomerular filtration rate (GFR) increases by up to 50% in the first trimester of normal pregnancy;

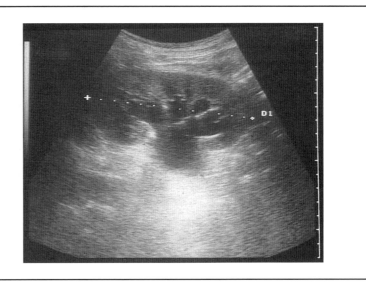

▲ **Fig. 82** Hydronephrosis of pregnancy: typical ultrasonographic appearance.

- ureters and renal pelvis become dilated (Fig. 82) and the risk of lower urinary tract infection is increased.

Pre-eclampsia constitutes new-onset hypertension and proteinuria, and manifests after the twentieth week of pregnancy. It is the most common medical complication of pregnancy, affecting 5–7% of expecting mothers and is associated with increased fetal morbidity and mortality. Placental abruption, thrombotic microangiopathy and severe pre-eclampsia are all causes of acute renal failure (ARF) in the latter stages of pregnancy: irreversible cortical necrosis can occur, although reversible acute tubular necrosis (ATN) is more common (Fig. 83).

Chronic kidney disease (CKD) of any sort before pregnancy has major implications for both the fetus and the mother (Table 22). Patients with reflux nephropathy may be at particularly high risk of pregnancy-related problems (Table 23). If

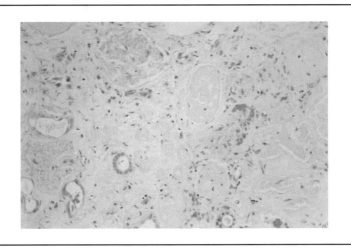

▲ **Fig. 83** Renal biopsy showing cortical necrosis. There is complete necrosis of the majority of visible structures (including glomeruli) (H&E, ×160).

TABLE 22 PREGNANCY-RELATED PROBLEMS IN WOMEN WITH PRE-EXISTING RENAL DISEASE

Impairment of renal function before pregnancy or in the first trimester	Maternal complications	Fetal loss
Mild (creatinine <125 μmol/L)	Common (~25%)	Rare (<5%)
Moderate (creatinine 125–250 μmol/L)	Very common (~50%)	Uncommon (<10%)
Severe (creatinine >250 μmol/L)	Nearly all (~90%)	Very common (~50%)

TABLE 23 PREGANCY-RELATED PROBLEMS IN WOMEN WITH REFLUX NEPHROPATHY

Impairment of renal function	Deterioration in renal function (%)	Pre-eclampsia (%)	Fetal loss (%)
Mild (creatinine <110 μmol/L)	2	13	8
Moderate (creatinine >110 μmol/L)	18	30	18

pregnant women with CKD have hypertension, the risks of renal deterioration, intrauterine growth retardation and preterm delivery all increase considerably.

Epidemiology

- Asymptomatic bacteriuria occurs in up to 5% of pregnancies. If untreated, symptomatic infection develops in about 25% of these cases.

- Pre-eclampsia occurs in 5–7% of pregnancies and is more common in first pregnancies.

- ARF complicates 1 in 6,000 pregnancies.

Clinical presentation

This is with urinary infection, pre-eclampsia or ARF. In proteinuric disease, it is important to distinguish between pre-existing renal disease and pre-eclampsia by determining the timing of onset of proteinuria.

Idiopathic postpartum ARF may be associated with severe hypertension and disseminated intravascular coagulation.

Investigations

Proteinuria most commonly occurs in the context of pre-eclampsia. This typically resolves within 3 months of delivery and requires further investigation if it does not.

Peripartum ARF is usually haemodynamically mediated and recovery is anticipated. If recovery does not occur after delivery, renal perfusion can be assessed by radionuclide scintigraphy and renal biopsy should be considered.

Treatment

- Patients with significant bacteriuria should receive antibiotics.

- Hypertension should be tightly controlled in pre-eclampsia. Suitable agents include

methyldopa, hydralazine, nifedipine and labetalol. Treatment is to deliver the fetus.

Prognosis

Pre-eclampsia is the second leading cause of maternal mortality, accounting for 12–18% of pregnancy-related maternal deaths. It is also associated with increased fetal morbidity and mortality, usually as a result of iatrogenic prematurity. In patients with ARF during pregnancy, renal recovery is anticipated in those with ATN, but not in those with cortical necrosis. ARF in the mother is associated with a high perinatal fetal mortality rate. In patients with CKD, the chance of a successful pregnancy declines as GFR falls and is unusual with a GFR of <20 mL/min.

FURTHER READING

Davison JM. Renal complications that may occur in pregnancy. In: Davison AM, Cameron JS, Grünfeld J-P, et al., eds. *Oxford Textbook of Clinical Nephrology*, 3rd edn. Oxford: Oxford University Press, 2005: 2233–42.

Davison JM and Baylis C. Pregnancy in patients with underlying renal disease. In: Davison AM, Cameron JS, Grünfeld J-P, et al., eds. *Oxford Textbook of Clinical Nephrology*, 3rd edn. Oxford: Oxford University Press, 2005: 2243–60.

2.8 Genetic renal conditions

2.8.1 Autosomal dominant polycystic kidney disease

Aetiology/pathophysiology

There is progressive development of renal cysts (Fig. 84). Two genetic loci have been described:

▲ **Fig. 84** Macroscopic appearance of a polycystic kidney. (Courtesy of Dr D. Peat.)

- *PKD1* on chromosome 16 (85% of cases) encodes polycystin 1, a large transmembrane molecule likely to be involved in cell–matrix interactions;

- *PKD2* on chromosome 4 (10% of cases) encodes polycystin 2, which tends to produce a milder disease than *PKD1*.

Polycystin 1 and 2 proteins probably form a physical complex, and are important in the function of the primary cilium, a hair-like appendage that is thought to sense the flow of urine along the tubule.

Note that autosomal recessive polycystic kidney disease is distinct from autosomal dominant polycystic kidney disease (**ADPKD**). The autosomal recessive form is a rare disease (1 in 10,000 to 1 in 40,000) that typically presents in infancy and is frequently associated with congenital hepatic fibrosis, characterised by cysts, fibrosis and portal hypertension.

Epidemiology

- The most common inherited renal disease.

- Accounts for 5–10% of end-stage renal disease.

- Prevalence 1 in 400 to 1 in 1,000.

Clinical presentation

Common features

- Discovered through screening of an affected family (an increasingly likely way for these patients to present).

- Acute abdominal pain (usually due to bleeding into a cyst or cyst infection) in 30% of cases. Chronic abdominal pain may occur.

- Hypertension in 20% of cases.

- Gross haematuria in 20% of cases.

- Urinary tract infection in 5–40% of cases; this is more common in women.

- Incidental discovery of an abdominal mass.

Uncommon features

- End-stage renal failure.

Rare features

- Intracranial haemorrhage.

Physical signs

- Palpable kidneys and/or liver.

- Hypertension.

- Murmurs associated with mitral regurgitation or mitral valve prolapse (mitral valve prolapse occurs in 20% of patients with polycystic kidney disease).

Investigations
Diagnosis is by detection of multiple bilateral renal cysts and a positive family history.

- Ultrasonography: in *PKD1* families, diagnostic criteria are age-related (two cysts in those <30 years old, at least two cysts in each kidney in those aged 30–59, and four cysts in each kidney for those aged over 60). Normal ultrasonography after the age of 30 (but not before) excludes the diagnosis. Associated cysts in the liver and pancreas can be helpful in supporting the diagnosis.

- Genetic linkage studies can make the diagnosis or exclude it. Can be useful in younger patients where imaging is not conclusive. Requires blood from at least two affected family members.

- Cranial magnetic resonance angiography: in patients with a family history of intracranial aneurysm. In other families with polycystic kidney disease, screening for cerebral aneurysms is controversial.

Other investigations are as for chronic renal disease.

Differential diagnosis
Simple renal cysts.

Treatment

- Antihypertensives reduce cardiovascular complications but probably do not slow the progression of renal disease.

- Treat urinary tract infections. It is often difficult to eradicate infection in a cyst. Sometimes cyst drainage is helpful.

- Analgesia: occasionally drainage or deroofing of large cysts may give long-term relief in those whose kidneys are painful.

Complications/prognosis

- Renal: end-stage renal failure will occur in at least 75% of cases. In *PKD1*, this occurs typically at about 50–60 years of age, in *PKD2* at about 65–75 years of age. The age at which end-stage failure is reached is more similar within families than between families. Urinary tract infections and bleeds into cysts are also common.

- Cardiovascular disease: associated with hypertension and chronic renal failure. Cardiac valve abnormalities, most commonly mitral valve prolapse or aortic regurgitation, occur in 25% of patients.

- Cerebrovascular disease: ruptured intracranial aneurysm complicates 5–10% of patients with ADPKD and is more common in some families than others.

- Liver disease: the incidence of hepatic cysts increases with age (<10% if younger than 30, >40% if over 60) and they are found more commonly in patients with significant renal disease. Apart from pain in some cases, these do not usually cause symptoms.

- Colonic diverticulae.

- Herniae, both abdominal wall and inguinal.

2.8.2 Alport's syndrome

Aetiology/pathophysiology
Alport's syndrome consists of:

- nephritis and progressive renal impairment;

- sensorineural deafness (in two-thirds of cases);

- eye abnormalities (in one-third of cases).

The defect is in type IV collagen, a key component of the glomerular basement membrane (GBM). There are a number of different forms.

- X-linked dominant (85–90% of cases): mutations in the *COL4A5* gene encoding the α5 chain of type IV collagen. This alteration prevents integration of the α3 chain into the GBM. The α3 chain contains the Goodpasture antigen. Affected males develop progressive renal failure.

- Autosomal recessive (10% of cases): similar to X-linked disease but equally severe in females. Due to mutations in *COL4A3* or *COL4A4*.

- Autosomal dominant: uncommon; due to dominant-negative mutations in *COL4A3* or *COL4A4*.

Benign familial haematuria is also due to mutations in *COL4A3* and *COL4A4*.

Epidemiology

- Gene frequency is 1 in 5,000 to 1 in 10,000.

- Of European dialysis patients, 0.6% have Alport's syndrome.

Clinical presentation
This can typically include:

- microscopic or macroscopic haematuria;

- renal impairment;

- hearing loss;

- visual problems.

Physical signs

- High-tone sensorineural hearing loss.

- Bilateral anterior lenticonus (protrusion of the lens into the anterior chamber).

Investigations

- Audiometry.

- Slit-lamp examination of the eye.

- Renal biopsy: look for structural abnormalities of the GBM under electron microscopy.

- In suspected X-linked Alport's syndrome, a defect in *COL4A5* can be established on skin biopsy in affected males or as a mosaic in carrier females, thus avoiding the need for renal biopsy.

Treatment
There is no specific treatment.

Complications/prognosis

- End-stage renal failure (ESRF): all affected males with X-linked disease progress to ESRF, usually by age 30. Most carrier females never reach ESRF, but do have persistent haematuria and/or proteinuria. Some develop ESRF at 45–60 years of age.

- Progressive hearing loss.

- Visual impairment through lens rupture and cataract formation.

- Following transplantation, patients may develop antibodies to type IV collagen and anti-GBM disease.

2.8.3 X-linked hypophosphataemic vitamin-D resistant rickets

Aetiology/pathophysiology
This is the most common hereditary form of isolated renal phosphate wasting. Hypophosphataemia,

together with a functional defect in osteoblasts, leads to abnormal mineralisation of growing bone. The defect is in the *PHEX* gene, which codes for a zinc metallopeptidase. The pathogenesis is unclear.

Clinical presentation

- Growth delay is usually noted by 6 months.

- Rickets, which develops after the child starts walking.

- Bone pain.

Physical signs

- Small stature.

- Rickets.

Investigations

- Low serum phosphate with inappropriate phosphaturia.

- Normal serum calcium, potassium, glucose, bicarbonate and parathyroid hormone: these (and the absence of glycosuria and proteinuria on urinalysis) exclude syndromes with other renal tubular defects or nutritional rickets.

- Bone radiographs: rickets.

Treatment

- High-dose oral 1,25-dihydroxyvitamin D (calcitriol).

- Oral phosphate supplements are often poorly tolerated as a result of associated diarrhoea.

- Recombinant growth hormone may reduce growth delay.

Complications

Treatment-associated hypercalcaemia can cause nephrocalcinosis and renal damage.

Prognosis

- A sufferer's growth rate can be improved, although final stature is usually abnormal.

- Females are less severely affected.

3.1 Examination of the urine

3.1.1 Urinalysis

Indications

Urinalysis should be performed in all patients with renal disease/dysfunction. In addition, it is appropriate as a screening test in almost any clinical setting because:

- the consequences of renal failure are serious;

- substantial loss of renal function occurs in a wide range of clinical settings with no specific clinical symptoms;

- serious renal disease is virtually excluded if urinalysis is negative and glomerular filtration rate is normal.

Practical details

Urinalysis for blood and protein provides a sensitive, cheap and non-invasive screening test.

Estimation of protein content

This can be done by a dipstick at the bedside, or formal quantification can be performed in the laboratory. Standard dipsticks are more sensitive to albumin than other proteins. The threshold for albumin is 150–300 mg/L.

Dipstick tests Dipstick tests for urinary protein can be interpreted as follows.

- A negative does not exclude immunoglobulin light chain excretion.

- Measures concentration, not rate of protein loss; for the same rate of protein loss, concentrations will be lower when urine is dilute (eg after loop diuretic).

- Contamination with skin cleanser/antiseptics (eg chlorhexidine) can give false-positive results.

- Trace results, especially in concentrated urine, are usually not clinically significant.

- Positive results should usually be followed by quantitative urine protein determination.

Dipstick for microalbuminuria In people with diabetes, development of microalbuminuria (20–200 mg/L) identifies a group at high risk of progressive renal failure. This degree of albuminuria is not reliably detected by standard urine dipsticks, but is with antibody (rather than chemical) detection (eg Micral-Test II).

Laboratory determination of protein content Laboratory tests for urinary protein can be interpreted as follows.

- Used to quantify protein excretion, eg after positive dipstick urinalysis.

- Methods used are equally sensitive to different proteins: they measure total protein concentration (immunoglobulins and light chains, etc. in addition to albumin).

- Can give protein excretion rate from a sample of known volume, produced over a known time.

- Alternatively, protein excretion rate can be predicted from protein/creatinine ratio (thereby avoiding need for timed collections) because creatinine excretion is about 8.8 mmol/day per 1.73 m^2.

- The normal value for protein/creatinine ratio in a spot urine sample is <20 mg/mmol.

Testing for haem

The urine dipstick threshold for haemoglobin is 150 µg/L, equivalent to 5,000 red cells/mL.

- The test will be positive with red cells, haemoglobin or myoglobin.

- A negative test effectively excludes the presence of abnormal numbers of red cells in the urine.

All people excrete some red cells in the urine, hence positive tests are common: 2.5–4% of healthy adult men in population-based studies. The possibility that these results could be caused by serious renal or urological disease (eg transitional cell carcinoma) should always be considered (see Section 1.1.1).

Intact red cells will sediment on centrifugation, whereas haemoglobin or myoglobin will not. In haemoglobinuria or myoglobinuria, the supernatant will remain pink/red and positive on dipstick testing, whereas in haematuria it will not (Fig. 85).

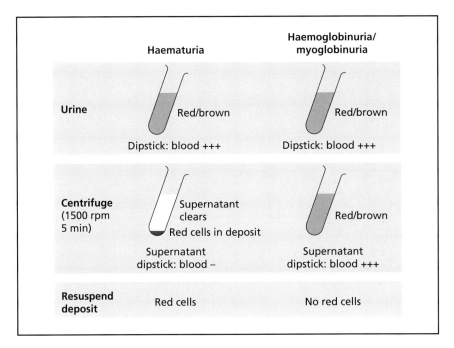

▲ **Fig. 85** Distinguishing haematuria (red cells in urine) from haemoglobinuria/myoglobinuria.

Other selected urine tests

- Urinalysis for nitrites: screening test for urine infection.

- Urinalysis for leucocytes: screening for infection; is also positive when white cells present in sterile urine (eg interstitial nephritis).

- Urinalysis for glucose: glucose will be present if there is a lowered renal threshold for glucose or elevated blood glucose concentration.

- Urine sodium content: 24-hour excretion is useful in assessing sodium intake and can be useful in establishing that renal failure is prerenal.

- Urine osmolality: used in diagnosis of diabetes insipidus and syndrome of inappropriate secretion of antidiuretic hormone.

- Urine pH: for diagnosis of renal tubular acidosis; monitor in situations where a particular urine pH is desirable (eg preventing urate deposition in tumour lysis).

- Urine electrophoresis: for light chains (Bence Jones protein).

- Urine calcium, oxalate and citrate determination in those with stones.

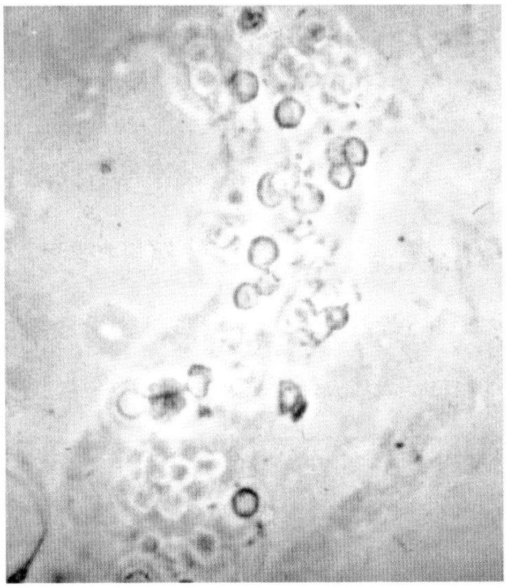

3.1.2 Urine microscopy

Principle

- Centrifuge a 10-mL urine sample at 1,500 rpm for 5 minutes. This will sediment the cellular elements, casts and crystals.

- Resuspend sediment in 1 mL of the sample (with a staining agent if desired).

- View under microscope.

- Red cell casts are particularly important in establishing that there is glomerular inflammation (Fig. 86).

Indications

- Reduced glomerular filtration rate.

- Abnormality on dipstick urinalysis.

3.2 Estimation of glomerular filtration rate

Principle

An ideal marker for glomerular filtration rate (GFR) would have the following characteristics:

- steady-state level in plasma;

▲ **Fig. 86** Red cell cast from the urine of a patient with glomerulonephritis, viewed with phase contrast.

- glomerulus represents no barrier to its filtration;

- no tubular absorption or secretion;

- no extrarenal clearance.

GFR = (concentration in urine × urine production rate)/ concentration in plasma

Accurate determinations for research and certain clinical purposes are based on the administration of various filtered markers including inulin, iohexol, or radiolabelled ethylenediaminetetra-acetic acid (EDTA) or diethylenetriaminepenta-acetic acid (DTPA).

In routine clinical practice the GFR marker used is creatinine, a waste product of muscle metabolism that is the closest endogenous approximation to an ideal marker for GFR that is relatively easily measured. It is not a perfect marker of GFR because there is:

- some tubular secretion of creatinine in addition to glomerular filtration;

- extrarenal clearance of about 2 mL/min.

Practical details

Estimated GFR
There are many formulae that can be used to estimate a patient's GFR based on serum creatinine, age, sex and (sometimes) weight and/or race. The most widely used is the abbreviated 'modification of diet in renal disease' (MDRD) equation that, in the form typically used by clinical chemistry laboratories, reports estimated GFR (eGFR) based on the patient's serum creatinine, age and sex (with the standing instruction that the value should be multiplied by 1.21 if the patient is black, in order to account for higher muscle

mass). Many laboratories now routinely report eGFR in conjunction with any measurement of serum creatinine made in a non-acute setting (see Section 2.1.2).

When considering eGFR as derived by the abbreviated MDRD equation it is important to recognise the following.

- It is an estimate not a precise value, eg it will be inaccurate in people with extreme body types, underestimating true GFR in those with big muscles and overestimating true GFR in those with little muscle.

- Creatinine level must be stable: eGFR calculations are not valid if serum creatinine is changing.

- It is not valid in pregnant women or children (aged <18 years).

Creatinine clearance
GFR can be predicted from measurement of creatinine clearance. Before routine calculation of eGFR, this was often used in clinical practice to give a more precise estimate of GFR than measurement of serum creatinine alone, but a substantial problem with the technique is its dependence on timing and completeness of urine collection, which are often unreliable.

> Incomplete urine collections will underestimate creatinine clearance.

> Plasma creatinine will be normal (for a short time) even if there is no glomerular filtration. In cases of acute renal failure, creatinine will be accumulating rapidly in the plasma but this cannot be discerned from a single value. GFR can be predicted only if plasma creatinine is stable.

FURTHER READING
Cockcroft DW and Gault MH. Prediction of creatinine clearance from serum creatinine. *Nephron* 1976; 16: 31–41.

The Renal Association. The short chronic kidney disease e-guide: online resource adapted from the full UK Chronic Kidney Disease Guidelines. Available at http://www.renal.org/eGFR/eguide.html

3.3 Imaging the renal tract

By far the most commonly used method is ultrasonography, which is cheap, reliable and non-invasive. Other tests are used in specific clinical settings.

Ultrasonography
This should be performed in all those with reduced glomerular filtration rate (GFR) or abnormal urinary findings. Important findings on ultrasonography include:

- renal size (Fig. 87);

- obstruction (Fig. 88);

- scars (reflux nephropathy);

- cysts (autosomal dominant polycystic kidney disease);

- renal tumours;

- renal stones;

- thickness of renal cortex.

> Occasionally, obstruction is not evident on ultrasonography, usually when it has occurred rapidly, recently and the patient is volume depleted. If there is a high index of suspicion, repeat ultrasonography after correcting the volume depletion. Negative ultrasound findings can also occur when obstruction is caused by malignant encasement of the kidneys.

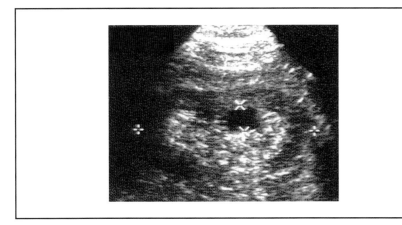

▲ **Fig. 87** Ultrasonogram of the kidney in chronic renal failure. The length is reduced (8.15 cm), the cortex thinned and there is a simple cyst (1.1 cm).

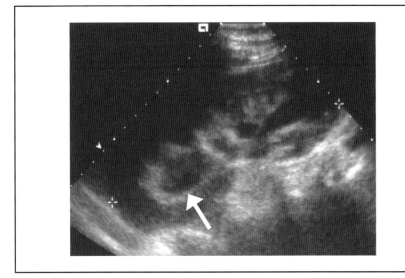

▲ **Fig. 88** Ultrasonogram of an obstructed kidney. Its length is enlarged at 14 cm, calyces are dilated (arrow) and cortical thickness is preserved.

Plain abdominal radiograph

This is useful in detecting calculi and nephrocalcinosis (Fig. 89a). Distinction of ureteric stones from phleboliths may require an intravenous urogram (IVU).

Intravenous urography

Radiographic contrast medium is injected, which is filtered by the glomerulus and concentrated in the tubule. The contrast medium is radio-opaque and is visible on radiographs as it passes through the kidney, ureter and bladder (Fig. 89b).

Indications

- In many circumstances, IVU has been superseded by ultrasonography and/or cross-sectional imaging.

- IVU is useful mainly for imaging the ureters (eg for stones or transitional cell carcinoma), which are not reliably visualised on ultrasonography.

- Also useful in demonstrating renal scars.

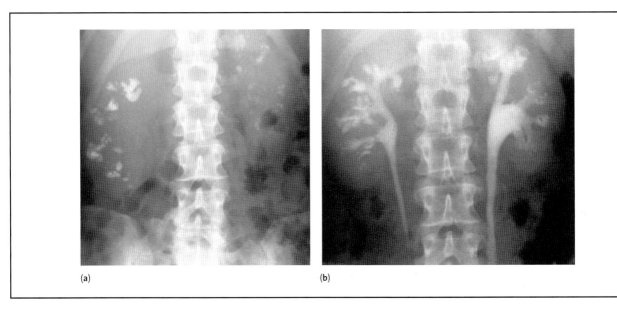

(a) (b)

▲ **Fig. 89** (a) Plain abdominal radiograph and (b) IVU of a patient with medullary sponge kidney with marked nephrocalcinosis.

Contraindications

- Patient sensitivity to contrast agents.

- IVU is less informative as GFR falls because clearance and concentration of the contrast medium are reduced.

Retrograde ureterography

Radiographic contrast medium is injected into the ureter from below using a cystoscope (Fig. 90). This technique is indicated for imaging the ureter when GFR is too low for IVU to be useful.

Isotopic imaging

The following compounds are often used.

- ^{99m}Tc-dimercaptosuccinic acid (DMSA): filtered by the glomerulus and then taken up by the tubules. Useful in detecting renal scars (particularly in children).

- ^{99m}Tc-mercaptoacetyltriglycine (MAG3): secreted by the tubules.

- ^{99m}Tc-DTPA: filtered by the glomerulus.

Indications

- Detection of renal scars: DMSA used for screening children with suspected reflux nephropathy or urinary tract infection for scars. More sensitive than IVU.

- Assessment of contribution to GFR of each kidney: DMSA or DTPA scan, eg before nephrectomy (Fig. 91).

- Screening for renal artery stenosis: DTPA or MAG3. Sensitivity will be enhanced by the administration of captopril 1 hour previously. Renal artery stenosis is indicated by a decreased, delayed uptake by one kidney. This screening would not be useful if GFR is substantially reduced.

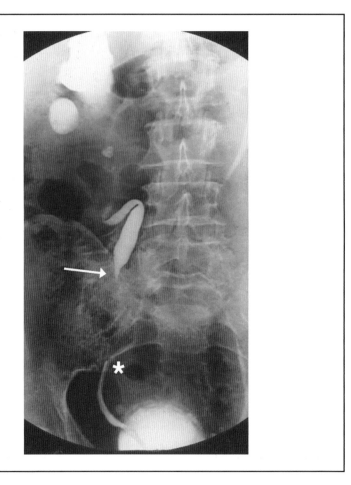

▲ **Fig. 90** Retrograde ureterogram. A catheter is inserted in the lower ureter from the bladder (*). Contrast outlines a tapered stricture (arrow) and the obstructed calyceal system.

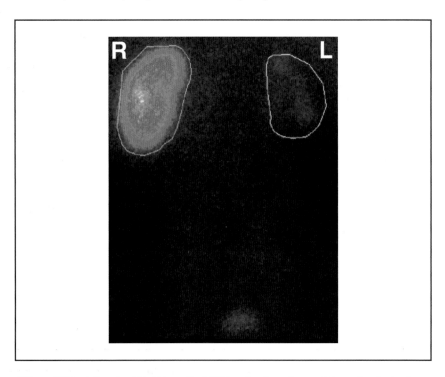

▲ **Fig. 91** DMSA scintigraphy of the kidneys. The left kidney is not seen because it is non-functioning; it was subsequently removed.

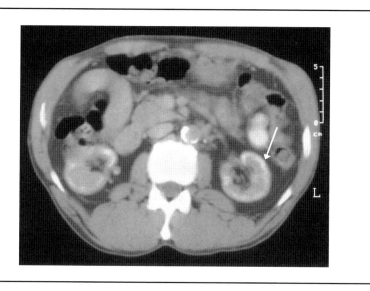

▲ **Fig. 92** CT scan of the abdomen without contrast showing calcification of the renal cortex. This patient had acute cortical necrosis during an episode of acute pancreatitis.

Renal angiography

- Establishes the anatomy of renal vessels in living kidney donors.

- Diagnoses renal artery stenosis and fibromuscular hyperplasia (Fig. 93a).

- Establishes (and potentially embolises) site of bleeding in the kidney, eg after renal biopsy or percutaneous nephrostomy (Fig. 93b).

- Renal venography (or venous phase of intra-arterial digital subtraction angiography) for diagnosis of renal vein thrombosis.

Magnetic resonance imaging

This is useful for evaluation of many space-occupying lesions and for screening for renovascular disease.

Computed tomography

- Evaluation of space-occupying lesions in the kidney or to meet requirement for detailed anatomical knowledge (Fig. 92).

- Investigation of extrinsic problems impinging on the renal tract (eg ureteric compression in retroperitoneal fibrosis).

- Spiral CT can be used to examine the renal arteries.

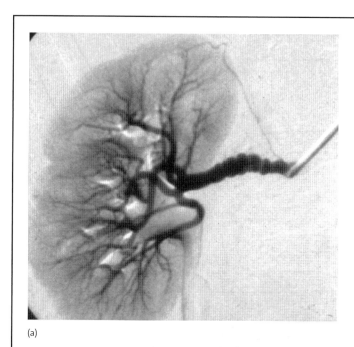

(a)

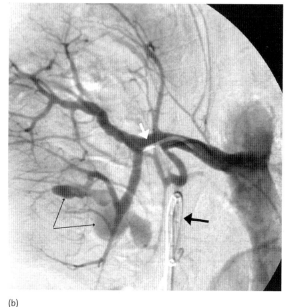

(b)

▲ **Fig. 93** (a) Renal angiogram showing fibromuscular hyperplasia. (b) Renal angiogram showing a fistula from the renal circulation into the pelvicalyceal system after percutaneous nephrostomy. A catheter is seen in the renal artery (white arrow). Also seen is the upper end of a ureteric stent (heavy black arrow). Contrast is seen to enter the dilated pelvicalyceal system (fine black arrows). The fistula was successfully embolised along with resolution of the haematuria.

3.4 Renal biopsy

Principle

Needle biopsies of the kidney are taken and processed as follows (Fig. 94).

- Paraffin: for haematoxylin and eosin staining, and also special stains (eg silver stain and Congo red).

- Frozen sections: immunofluorescence for immunoglobulins and complement components.

- Resin embedding: for electron microscopy.

Indications

- Investigation of unexplained acute and chronic renal disease.

- Most frequently useful in the diagnosis of glomerular disease.

- Should be performed only if the result could alter management.

- Expert renal histology must be available.

Contraindications

These are relative rather than absolute. The decision will depend on the clinical setting.

- Single kidney: possibility of losing the kidney.

- Reduced renal size: biopsy is less likely to be diagnostic and more likely to cause a significant bleed.

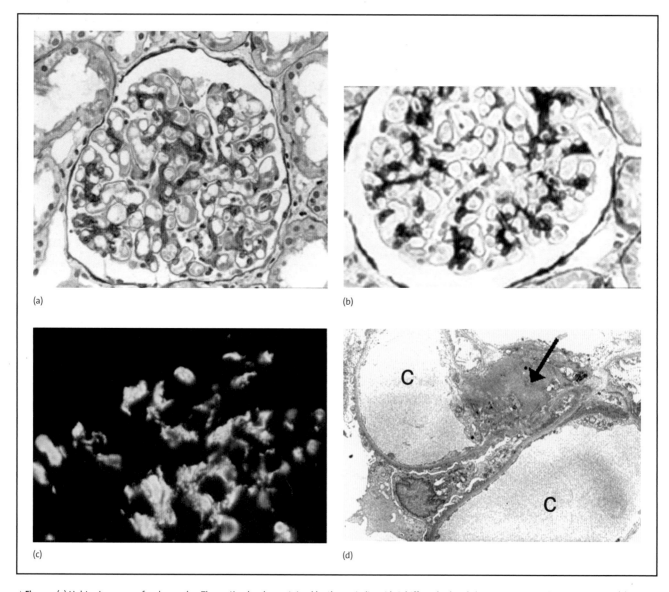

(a)

(b)

(c)

(d)

▲**Fig. 94** (**a**) Light microscopy of a glomerulus. The section has been stained by the periodic acid–Schiff method and shows expansion of the mesangium. (**b**) Silver-stained section of a glomerulus showing mesangial expansion characteristic of IgA nephropathy. (**c**) Immunofluorescence of part of a glomerulus for IgA: there is mesangial deposition of IgA. (**d**) Electron micrograph showing dense deposits in the mesangium between capillary loops (C). (Courtesy of Dr D. Davies, Oxford Radcliffe Hospitals.)

- Difficulty in breath-holding.

- Hypertension: increased risk of haemorrhage, so should be corrected before biopsy.

- Reduced platelet count, reduced haematocrit and abnormal coagulation tests: these increase the risk of haemorrhage and should be corrected before biopsy.

Practical details

Before the investigation

- Ultrasonography or other formal imaging to determine size, location and number of kidneys.

- FBC, coagulation screen, blood group and save.

- Appropriate premedication.

- In severe renal impairment, consider desmopressin acetate (DDAVP) infusion (raises levels of von Willebrand factor and factor VIII, and ameliorates the bleeding tendency related to uraemia).

The investigation

1. The patient lies prone.

2. The lower pole of the kidney is localised using ultrasonography.

3. The kidney moves down with inspiration, and the operator directs the patient's respiration.

4. A spinal needle is used to anaesthetise the track and to localise the kidney. It is advanced only when the patient is breath-holding so that the kidney is stationary.

5. When the kidney is reached, the patient is asked to breathe and the needle is seen to swing.

6. The spinal needle is replaced with a biopsy needle, which is passed into the lower pole of the kidney.

7. Usually two cores of tissue are taken.

Special handling of biopsy material is sometimes needed.

- Oxalate nephropathy: alcohol-containing fixative.

- Culture for *Mycobacterium tuberculosis*: no fixative.

After the investigation

- Bed-rest (typically up to 16 hours).

- Monitor pulse, BP and urine colour.

Complications

The major complication is haemorrhage. Perirenal haematoma is also very common (>30% of cases) if looked for by ultrasonography. There is macroscopic haematuria in about 8% of cases. Up to 2% of patients require blood transfusion, and <1% need embolisation/nephrectomy.

Acknowledgements

The authors are grateful to Drs R.M. Hilton, J.E. Scoble, J.A. Amess and E.C. Morris for their help in sourcing some of the medical images in this book. The editor would also like to thank Dr D. Davies.

NEPHROLOGY: SECTION 4
SELF-ASSESSMENT

4.1 Self-assessment questions

Question 1

Clinical scenario

A 48-year-old man with alcoholic chronic liver disease presents with renal failure.

Question

Which of the following findings would make a diagnosis of hepatorenal syndrome unlikely?

Answers

A Urine sodium concentration <10 mmol/L
B Normal urine dipstick
C Recent infection
D Urine output >2 L per 24 hours
E Severe jaundice

Question 2

Clinical scenario

A 65-year-old diabetic woman is discovered to have a plasma creatinine of 150 µmol/L.

Question

Which one of the following findings would offer the strongest support for diabetic nephropathy being the cause of her renal impairment?

Answers

A History of hypertension for many years
B History of peripheral vascular disease
C Normal urinalysis
D Proliferative diabetic retinopathy
E Femoral bruit on examination

Question 3

Clinical scenario

A patient is referred to the renal team with nephrotic syndrome and her renal biopsy shows amyloid A (AA) amyloid deposits.

Question

Which of the following underlying diagnoses is most likely to have caused this?

Answers

A Monoclonal gammopathy of undetermined significance
B Systemic lupus erythematosus
C Sarcoidosis
D Rheumatoid arthritis
E Multiple myeloma

Question 4

Clinical scenario

A 60-year-old man presents acutely with a recent history of oedema, proteinuria of 10 g per 24 hours and serum albumin of 20 g/L.

Question

Which of the following diagnoses is most consistent with the presentation?

Answers

A Amyloidosis
B Sarcoidosis
C Wegener's granulomatosis
D Acute interstitial nephritis
E Hepatorenal syndrome

Question 5

Clinical scenario

A 28-year-old man is admitted with haemoptysis and renal failure.

Question

Which of the following is the *least* likely underlying diagnosis?

Answers

A Wegener's granulomatosis
B Systemic lupus erythematosus
C Goodpastures disease
D Tuberculosis
E IgA nephropathy

Question 6

Clinical scenario

You are called to see a woman who is in her thirtieth week of pregnancy and has proteinuria.

Question

Which of the following findings would make you suspect that the renal protein leak is not due to pre-eclampsia?

Answers

A Hypertension
B Proteinuria at the pregnancy booking visit
C Oedema
D High serum urate
E It is her first pregnancy

Question 7

Clinical scenario

A pregnant woman with pre-eclampsia has severe hypertension.

Question

Which of the following is the definitive treatment for the condition?

Answers

A Delivery of her baby
B Control of BP with diuretics

C Aspirin
D Control of BP with labetalol
E Treatment with antiepileptic agents to prevent eclampsia

Question 8

Clinical scenario

A man with known haemolytic–uraemic syndrome presents with a recurrence of his disease.

Question

Which of the following investigative findings is *not* typical of the diagnosis?

Answers

A Red cell fragments on the blood film
B Abnormal clotting profile
C Elevated lactate dehydrogenase
D Low platelet count
E Low haptoglobins

Question 9

Clinical scenario

A 60-year-old woman is referred with creatinine 350 µmol/L. Two years previously it was 220 µmo/L. Renal ultrasound shows she has symmetrical, smooth kidneys of reduced size.

Question

Which of the following is most likely to have caused her renal impairment?

Answers

A Type 2 diabetes mellitus
B Amyloidosis
C Glomerulonephritis
D Polycystic kidney disease
E Reflux nephropathy

Question 10

Clinical scenario

A 55-year-old man with long-standing ankylosing spondylitis is referred for investigation to determine whether he has amyloid A (AA) amyloidosis.

Question

Which two of the following findings are typical of systemic AA amyloidosis?

Answers

A Macroglossia
B Periorbital purpura
C Amyloid plaques in the brain
D Splenic enlargement due to amyloid infiltration
E Cardiac failure due to amyloid infiltration of the heart
F Amyloid autonomic neuropathy
G Proteinuria
H Carpal tunnel syndrome
I Raynaud's phenomenon
J Jaw claudication

Question 11

Clinical scenario

A 24-year-old woman presents with a history of swollen legs for the past 4 weeks. She is otherwise well, with no significant past medical history and no abnormal physical signs apart from oedema. Her GP has tested her urine and found proteinuria 3+ and haematuria 1+. Her serum albumin is low at 28 g/dL.

Question

Which are the two most likely causes?

Answers

A Lupus nephritis
B Cholesterol emboli
C Minimal-change disease
D Autosomal dominant polycystic kidney disease (ADPKD)
E IgA nephropathy
F Fibromuscular dysplasia of the renal arteries
G Membranous glomerulonephritis
H Amyloidosis
I Diabetic nephropathy
J Wegener's granulomatosis

Question 12

Clinical scenario

A 47-year-old man with known nephrotic syndrome due to focal segmental glomerulosclerosis attends hospital with acute flank pain, proteinuria 3+ and haematuria 3+ on urinalysis, and a rise in creatinine from 115 to 167 µmol/L. He is taking prednisolone, ciclosporin, frusemide and ramipril.

Question

What is the most likely underlying cause of his presentation?

Answers

A Acute interstitial nephritis
B Spontaneous bacterial peritonitis
C Renal vein thrombosis
D Ciclosporin nephrotoxicity
E Renal artery stenosis

Question 13

Clinical scenario

A 28-year-old woman with biopsy-proven IgA nephropathy and a stable serum creatinine of ~130 µmol/L informs you that she has done a pregnancy test and that it is positive.

Question

She is taking the following medications. Which is most important to stop and substitute with a safer alternative?

Answers

A Folic acid
B Lisinopril
C Ranitidine
D Aspirin
E Nifedipine

Question 14

Clinical scenario

A 19-year-old man is brought into the Emergency Department after having been found collapsed at home. He is drowsy but rousable, with a BP of 82/51 mmHg, heart rate of 130 bpm and a tense, swollen right calf. You cannot feel any pulses in his right foot. Blood tests demonstrate acute renal failure, with hyperkalaemia (K+ 7.2 mmol/L; normal range 3.5–5.0) and a very high creatine kinase level (30,200 U/L; normal <195).

Question

Which of the following is *least* appropriate as part of his immediate management?

Answers

A Urgent surgical referral regarding possible compartment syndrome
B Insulin/dextrose infusion
C Insertion of a central venous catheter to guide fluid replacement
D Bladder catheterisation
E ECG monitoring

Question 15

Clinical scenario

A 44-year-old man is admitted under the acute medical team after being found by the police semi-conscious in a local park. He is obtunded and cannot give a coherent history. No past medical history is known. Examination is unremarkable. Investigations demonstrate rhabdomyolysis with an elevated creatine kinase, acute renal failure, hyperkalaemia, hyperphosphataemia and hypocalcaemia.

Question

What are the two most likely underlying diagnoses?

Answers

A Cocaine overdose
B Femoral artery embolism
C Cerebrovascular event
D Heroin overdose
E Malignant hyperpyrexia
F Meningitis
G Alcohol overdose
H Myocardial infarction

I Multiple myeloma
J McArdle's syndrome

Question 16

Clinical scenario

A 37-year-old man is referred to the renal team 2 days after admission to hospital. He is a motorcyclist who was involved in a road-traffic accident in which he sustained multiple injuries with significant blood loss. On arrival in the Emergency Department his BP was 74/51 mmHg. He was fluid resuscitated, taken to theatre and then transferred to the intensive treatment unit. He is now oligoanuric with a rapidly rising creatinine. A clinical diagnosis of acute tubular necrosis (ATN) has been made.

Question

Which one of the following statements regarding ATN do you disagree with?

Answers

A Elderly patients are at greater risk of ATN
B The podocytes are the renal cells most at risk from ischaemic damage
C Urinalysis usually only demonstrates low-grade haematuria and/or proteinuria

D Renal ultrasonography is usually normal
E Only 40–50% of patients who require renal replacement therapy and ventilation for respiratory failure will survive

Question 17

Clinical scenario

A 67-year-old man presents with increasing lethargy over the course of 1 week and a skin rash. Blood tests are performed, which demonstrate acute renal impairment with a urea of 18.1 mmol/L and creatinine 274 μmol/L (previously normal). He is referred to the renal team and undergoes a renal biopsy. A haematoxylin and eosin-stained section is shown in Fig. 95.

Question

What is most likely to be useful in establishing the cause of his renal failure?

Answers

A Assay for antibodies to neutrophil cytoplasmic antigens
B Blood cultures
C Assay for antibodies to double-stranded DNA
D Immunofluorescence on the biopsy specimen
E A full drug history

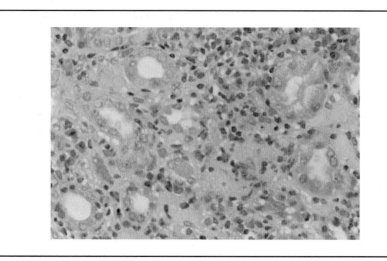

▲ **Fig. 95** Question 17.

Question 18

Clinical scenario

A 74-year-old man who is a smoker and has peripheral vascular disease is referred to the nephrology clinic following an episode of sudden-onset pulmonary oedema, despite having good left ventricular function on echocardiography. He has moderately impaired renal function (creatinine 160 µmo/L) and an ultrasound has demonstrated kidneys measuring 9.1 and 10.9 cm in length. The referral letter raises the question as to whether he may have renovascular disease causing 'flash' pulmonary oedema. On examination he has poor pedal pulses and a left carotid bruit.

Question

What is the most appropriate investigation to pursue the possibility that he has renovascular disease?

Answers

A CT
B Captopril renography
C Intravenous urography
D Magnetic resonance angiography
E Doppler ultrasonography

Question 19

Clinical scenario

A 67-year-old man is referred to the acute medical team. He has complained of feeling unwell for 2 weeks, with fevers, anorexia and a purple rash on his legs. Blood tests performed by his GP have shown a rise in creatinine from 127 to 254 µmol/L (normal <115 µmol/L), together with an elevated erythrocyte sedimentation rate of 72. He has a past medical history of ischaemic heart disease, peptic ulceration and diverticulitis, and had also undergone diagnostic coronary angiography 1 month previously.

Question

What is the most likely diagnosis?

Answers

A Henoch–Schönlein purpura
B Churg–Strauss syndrome
C Cholesterol emboli
D Multiple myeloma
E Contrast nephropathy

Question 20

Clinical scenario

A 51-year-old woman with polycystic kidney disease and a slowly rising creatinine, which was 320 µmol/L at her last clinic visit 3 weeks ago, is brought into casualty having been found collapsed at home by her partner. She is now fully conscious but complains of a headache.

Question

What is the most likely diagnosis?

Answers

A Aortic dissection
B Subarachnoid haemorrhage
C Uraemic encephalopathy
D Pulmonary embolism
E Renal cyst infection

Question 21

Clinical scenario

A 26-year-old woman presents with a creatinine of 160 µmol/L, dipstick proteinuria 2+, BP 145/90 mmHg and a history of repeated urinary tract infections as a young child.

Question

Which of the following is the most appropriate initial investigation to establish a diagnosis of reflux nephropathy?

Answers

A Micturating cystogram
B Ultrasonography
C Renal biopsy
D CT
E Microscopy and culture of a midstream urine specimen

Question 22

Clinical scenario

A man aged 60 years with a 10-year history of diabetes mellitus and a previous history of proliferative retinopathy and gout is referred for a renal opinion because investigation reveals serum creatinine 170 µmol/L and proteinuria 0.8 g per 24 hours. Two years previously he had microalbuminuria and normal plasma creatinine, but then stopped attending the clinic. He had been intolerant of angiotensin-converting enzyme inhibitors in the past because of a cough. His current medication is metformin, allopurinol 300 mg od and amlodipine 5 mg od. His BP is 142/85 mmHg and his BMI is 32. Recently he has had a poor appetite and lost weight.

Question

Which one of the following statements is *not* correct?

Answers

A Metformin is contraindicated in renal impairment and it would be advisable to stop this
B The history is consistent with diabetic nephropathy and a renal · biopsy is unlikely to alter management
C The dose of allopurinol should be decreased in view of his renal impairment
D Rather than increase his amlodipine there is a strong case for starting an angiotensin receptor blocker
E His recent poor appetite suggests that he may need renal replacement therapy

Question 23

Clinical scenario

A man aged 50 years has stable chronic renal impairment with a creatinine of 200 µmol/L. At a routine clinic visit his creatinine is unexpectedly 280 µmol/L. He has recently started on new medication.

Question

Which of the following medicines is well recognised as increasing creatinine in the absence of a change in glomerular filtration rate (GFR)?

Answers

A Ranitidine
B Trimethoprim
C Allopurinol
D Metformin
E Ibuprofen

Question 24

Clinical scenario

A 38-year-old man with known Alport's syndrome and renal impairment has plasma creatinine 695 µmol/L, and says he feels more tired than usual and that his appetite is poor. His last creatinine measurement 2 months previously was 640 µmol/L. His haemoglobin level is 10.8 g/dL, potassium 5.4 mmol/L, corrected calcium 2.25 mmol/L and phosphate 1.9 mmol/L. He is currently treated with calcium carbonate, an angiotensin-converting enzyme inhibitor and recombinant human erythropoietin. His BP is 138/84 mmHg. His parathyroid hormone level is 22 pmol/L (normal range 1–5.5).

Question

Which of the following is indicated to improve his sense of fatigue?

Answers

A Renal replacement therapy
B Commencing alfacalcidol
C Reducing his dose of angiotensin-converting enzyme inhibitor
D Strict avoidance of foods and drinks containing potassium
E Increasing his dose of recombinant erythropoietin

Question 25

Clinical scenario

A 42-year-old woman presents with nephrotic syndrome and a renal biopsy is reported as showing membranous glomerulonephritis. She has two children aged 20 and 22 years. Currently her creatinine is 130 µmol/L and she has proteinuria 6 g per 24 hours. She has moderate peripheral oedema and her BP is 122/74 mmHg without medication.

Question

Which one of the following statements do you agree with?

Answers

A There is an approximately 75% likelihood that her nephrotic syndrome will go into complete remission over the next year without immunosuppressive treatment
B There is an approximately 75% likelihood that she has an underlying malignancy and investigation should include upper and lower gastrointestinal endoscopy
C Treatment with an angiotensin-converting enzyme inhibitor is indicated and would be expected to reduce proteinuria
D Her children should be screened for renal disease
E It is important that she drinks at least 2 L of clear fluid a day

Question 26

Clinical scenario

A 28-year-old man is found to have dipstick haematuria at a medical performed for life insurance purposes. His BP is 118/75 mmHg. There is no proteinuria and his plasma creatinine is normal. There is no other significant history, except that his mother died of a

stroke aged 35 years. He has two healthy children aged 3 and 5 years. A renal ultrasound shows three cysts in his left kidney and two cysts in his right kidney.

Question

Which one of the following statements do you agree with?

Answers

A He should be told that it is very unlikely that there is a link between the cysts in the kidney and his mother's early death
B He should commence taking an angiotensin-converting enzyme inhibitor to prevent deterioration of his renal function
C He should have a renal biopsy and the most likely diagnosis is IgA nephropathy
D His children should be offered renal ultrasound
E The probable diagnosis is autosomal dominant polycystic kidney disease

Question 27

Clinical scenario

A 70-year-old man who has previously been well has developed ankle oedema over approximately 2 months. Apart from oedema, his physical examination is normal, with BP 105/60 mmHg. Urinalysis shows blood 1+ and protein 3+, and a spot urine protein/creatinine ratio is 620 mg/mmol (normal <20 mg/mmol). Blood tests show creatinine 110 µmol/L and albumin 28 g/L. Renal ultrasound shows slightly enlarged kidneys that are echogenic.

Question

Which two statements do you most agree with?

Answers

A A high-protein diet is indicated to help compensate for the loss of protein in the urine

B He should be started on warfarin because of his increased risk of venous thromboembolism

C A renal biopsy is most likely to show mesangiocapillary glomerulonephritis

D The risk of a percutaneous renal biopsy leading to loss of one kidney is approximately 5%

E There is insufficient information to establish a diagnosis of nephrotic syndrome

F Prior to a renal biopsy he should have a therapeutic trial of prednisolone 1 mg/kg for 4 weeks

G AL (primary) amyloid is a likely diagnosis

H He should be screened for a mutation in the gene encoding nephrin

I Renal biopsy is indicated

J A blood film will probably show microangiopathy

Question 28

Clinical scenario

A 63-year-old man who is a smoker presents with hypertension (BP 160/100 mmHg) and renal impairment (creatinine 170 µmol/L). He has intermittent claudication and a history of ischaemic heart disease. Renal ultrasound shows kidneys of 11.2 cm on the right and 9.1 cm on the left.

Question

Which investigation would you perform next?

Answers

A Radionuclide scan with ^{99m}Tc-dimercaptosuccinic acid

B Doppler ultrasound of the renal arteries

C Percutaneous biopsy of the right kidney

D Magnetic resonance angiography of the renal arteries

E Percutaneous biopsy of the left kidney

Question 29

Clinical scenario

A 70-year-old man with recent fatigue is found to have a serum creatinine of 800 µmol/L and potassium 6.2 mmol/L. Renal ultrasound shows urine in the bladder following micturition (estimated volume 600 mL) and bilateral pelvicalyceal dilatation. His BP is 110/80 mmHg, there is no peripheral oedema, his JVP is not elevated and his chest is clear on auscultation.

Question

Which of the following do you think is the most appropriate initial treatment?

Answers

A Haemodialysis

B Bilateral antegrade nephrostomies

C Transurethral prostatectomy

D Urethral catheterisation

E 0.9% sodium chloride 500 mL iv

Question 30

Clinical scenario

A 60-year-old man has autosomal dominant polycystic kidney disease and renal impairment, with creatinine 550 µmol/L. He is blood group A.

Question

Which two statements do you most agree with?

Answers

A Dietary restrictions are unlikely to be necessary at this level of renal impairment.

B A kidney transplant from his wife, who is blood group O and willing to donate a kidney, should be considered

C He is less likely to need treatment with erythropoietin than a man with the same degree of renal impairment due to diabetic nephropathy

D Bilateral native nephrectomies will need to be performed prior to renal transplantation

E He should be screened for pheochromocytoma in view of a 10-fold increased risk of this tumour in patients with polycystic kidney disease (PKD)

F Continuous ambulatory peritoneal dialysis is not feasible in patients with PKD

G He should have annual cystoscopies in view of the 10-fold increased risk of bladder cancer in patients with PKD

H He should have annual cross-sectional abdominal imaging because of the 10-fold increased risk of renal cancer in patients with PKD

I Calcineurin inhibitors have been shown to reduce the rate of progression of PKD

J Calcium channel antagonists have been shown to reduce the rate of progression of PKD

Question 31

Clinical scenario

A 27-year-old man complains of recurrent episodes of renal colic. On one occasion he sieved his urine and found a small stone.

Question

Which of the following would *not* be a predisposition to urinary tract stone formation?

Answers

A A high urinary urate level

B A high urinary calcium level

C A high urinary citrate level

D A high urinary oxalate level

E A high urinary cystine level

Question 32

Clinical scenario

A 31-year-old woman presents with seizures. On examination she has a facial rash. There is blood and protein in her urine on dipstick analysis. Serum creatinine is 575 µmol/L (normal range 60–115). On immunological testing she has antibodies to double-stranded DNA.

Question

Which of the following conditions is a well-recognised renal feature of systemic lupus erythematosus?

Answers

A Nephrocalcinosis
B Membranous nephropathy
C IgA nephropathy
D Amyloidosis
E Renal cell cancer

Question 33

Clinical scenario

A 76-year-old man presents with general malaise and is found to have creatinine 256 µmol/L (normal range 60–115), plasma calcium 2.9 mmol/L (normal range 2.15–2.55), haemoglobin 9.5 g/dL (normal range 12–17) and erythrocyte sedimentation rate (ESR) 80 mm/hour (normal range <20).

Question

Which of the following is the most likely diagnosis?

Answers

A Secondary hyperparathyroidism
B Myeloma
C Scleroderma
D Systemic lupus erythematosus
E Paget's disease

Question 34

Clinical scenario

A 19-year-old woman, who is normally well, attends her local Emergency Department complaining of a burning sensation on passing urine. She also mentions that the urine looks cloudy and has an unpleasant smell.

Question

Which of the following statements is true?

Answers

A Urinary tract infection with a fungus is the likely explanation
B Urinary tract stones are probably present
C An urgent potassium level should be obtained
D Urinary tract infection with a streptococcal species is a common cause of this clinical presentation
E An underlying anatomical abnormality is not usually present in women of this age with this clinical presentation

Question 35

Clinical scenario

A 58-year-old man presents with severe right loin pain. He is obese, with a BMI of 42, and his BP is 186/93 mmHg when measured with an appropriately large cuff. On urine dipstick analysis he has haematuria 2+ and proteinuria 2+. His plasma creatinine is 213 µmol/L (normal <115 µmol/L).

Question

Which one of the following statements is *false*?

Answers

A Renal impairment can arise as a result of obesity
B He could have diabetic nephropathy
C He could have renal impairment as a result of hypertensive renal damage
D The analgesic of choice in his case is an NSAID
E His pain may result from urinary tract stone disease

Question 36

Clinical scenario

An otherwise well 68-year-old man is found to have an IgG λ

paraprotein. His plasma creatinine is 312 µmol/L (normal range 60–115) and subsequent investigations confirm that he has myeloma.

Question

Which of the following is *not* a cause of a raised plasma creatinine associated with myeloma?

Answers

A Hypercalcaemia
B Minimal-change nephropathy
C Light chain deposition in the kidneys
D Amyloidosis
E Cast nephropathy

Question 37

Clinical scenario

A 24-year-old man presents with a 4-day history of progressive swelling of both ankles. On examination his BP is 115/72 mmHg and he has pitting oedema to his mid calves. His urine contains protein 3+ on dipstick analysis, but no blood.

Question

Which two of following statements are most likely to be true?

Answers

A He has nephritic syndrome
B The likely diagnosis is membranous nephropathy
C Myeloma must be excluded urgently
D His plasma ionised calcium level is likely to be very low
E Daily monitoring of serum amylase is mandatory
F He should be placed on a cardiac monitor immediately
G The likely diagnosis is minimal-change nephropathy
H NSAIDs could cause this clinical presentation
I He should be given broad-spectrum intravenous antibiotics
J The likely cause is an infectious agent

Question 38

Clinical scenario

A 56-year-old man with known chronic renal failure is admitted with general malaise to the Emergency Department. He complains of itching and nausea. His BP is 175/110 mmHg and plasma creatinine 952 µmol/L (normal range 60–115)

Question

Which two of the following would be the most important reasons for initiating urgent haemodialysis in this man?

Answers

A Hyperchloridaemia
B A high plasma hydrogen ion concentration
C Itch
D Hyperkalaemia
E Headache
F Poor appetite
G Skin pigmentation
H Anaemia
I A diastolic BP above 98 mmHg
J A low magnesium level

Question 39

Clinical scenario

A 30-year-old woman is noted to have haematuria on a routine health check. Her plasma creatinine is 112 µmol/L. Six months previously she had a successful pregnancy that was complicated by hypertension and proteinuria at 34 weeks. For this reason, she underwent induction of labour at 37 weeks and gave birth to a healthy baby boy. She was well before and after the delivery. At her first booking appointment at 8 weeks she was noted to have a BP of 156/91 mmHg and again at 10 weeks this was 162/93 mmHg, but this fell to a normal level over the next few weeks and was only noted to be high again at 34 weeks.

Question

Which two of the following statements are most likely to be true?

Answers

A Systemic vascular resistance typically rises during pregnancy
B Pre-eclampsia usually presents in early pregnancy
C Haematuria in this woman is consistent with a diagnosis of IgA nephropathy
D BP typically rises in early pregnancy but falls in mid pregnancy
E Proteinuria is a normal finding in pregnant women
F This woman is unlikely to have had pre-eclampsia during her pregnancy
G Cardiac output falls during pregnancy
H Renal vascular resistance normally rises during pregnancy
I The haematuria is not likely to indicate an underlying glomerulonephritis
J It is likely that this woman had a higher than average BP before her pregnancy

Question 40

Clinical scenario

A 38-year-old man has been on regular maintenance haemodialysis for 3 years. His underlying diagnosis is focal segmental glomerulosclerosis. His blood group is O. A renal transplant is planned using a kidney that his wife will donate.

Question

Which two of the following statements are the most important considerations in this case?

Answers

A She must be a blood relation
B She must be seronegative for cytomegalovirus
C His systolic BP must be below 130 mmHg
D They must both have the same human leucocyte antigen (HLA) type (tissue type)
E She should not have blood group B
F The focal glomerulosclerosis may recur in the transplanted kidney
G He must never have received any previous blood transfusions
H She must receive a cash payment for the kidney
I She should not have blood group A
J He must have one of his own kidneys removed first

Question 41

Clinical scenario

A 68-year-old man presents with a red itchy rash over his trunk and limbs that has been present for 5 days. His plasma creatinine is 327 µmol/L (normal range 60–115), but had been only 98 µmol/L a month ago. He brought a large bag of drugs with him.

Question

Which two of the following drugs are the most likely causes of his acute renal failure?

Answers

A Thyroxine
B Prednisolone
C Atenolol
D Allopurinol
E Simvastatin
F Doxazosin
G Digoxin
H Amlodipine
I Amoxicillin
J Aspirin

Question 42

Clinical scenario

A 36-year-old woman is sent to the Emergency Department because she is disorientated and drowsy. Blood tests give the following results:
Na^+ 133 mmol/L (normal range

135–145), K$^+$ 4.6 mmol/L (normal range 3.8–5.2), urea 28 mmol/L (normal range 4–7), creatinine 470 µmol/L (normal range 90–115), chloride 97 mmol/L (normal range 95–105) and bicarbonate 16 mmol/L (normal range 22–28). An arterial blood sample gives the following results: pH 7.1 (normal range 7.36–7.44), P_{O_2} 92 mmHg (normal range 80–95), P_{CO_2} 19 mmHg (normal range 36–44) and bicarbonate 7 mEq/L (normal range 22–26).

Question
Which two of the following diagnoses do you think are most likely in this patient?

Answers
A Laxative abuse
B Previous bowel surgery with ureteric diversion
C Ethylene glycol intoxication
D Multiple myeloma with type 2 renal tubular acidosis
E Bulimia nervosa
F Diabetic ketoacidosis
G Severe chronic obstructive pulmonary disease
H A glaucoma sufferer using acetazolamide
I Primary hyperventilation
J Opioid overdose

Question 43

Clinical scenario
A 54-year-old man presents to the Emergency Department with acute renal failure and haemoptysis. He has had arthralgia for the last 2 months, but in the past has been completely well. He had an insurance medical 8 months previously at which his BP was normal and urinalysis was negative.

Question
Which single test listed below is most likely to be helpful in establishing a precise diagnosis?

Answers
A Bronchoscopy and lavage
B Identifying a mutation in a gene encoding one of the α chains of type IV collagen
C CT scan of chest and abdomen
D Assay for circulating antineutrophil cytoplasmic antibodies (ANCA)
E Examination of a renal biopsy by electron microscopy

Question 44

Clinical scenario
A 37-year-old woman suffers from recurrent *Klebsiella* urinary tract infections. She now presents to the Emergency Department complaining of severe right-sided flank pain. A spiral CT scan reveals a stone in the right ureter.

Question
What is the most likely chemical composition of the stone?

Answers
A Struvite (magnesium ammonium phosphate)
B Potassium citrate
C Cystine
D Calcium acetate
E Uric acid

Question 45

Clinical scenario
A 33-year-old woman originally from Central Africa presents with sudden onset of severe right-sided loin pain and haematuria. She explains that she is HIV positive and is being treated with various medicines from a genitourinary clinic, including indinavir and zidovudine.

Question
What is the most likely diagnosis?

Answers
A Bladder involvement with *Schistosoma mansoni*
B Collapsing focal segmental glomerulosclerosis due to HIV-associated nephropathy
C Bladder involvement with *Schistosoma haematobium*
D Renal stone disease related to indinavir
E Acute papillary necrosis caused by zidovudine

Question 46

Clinical scenario
A 58-year-old white man presents to hospital with renal dysfunction, earache and coughing. He has an episode of fresh haemoptysis and a CXR shows bilateral diffuse alveolar shadowing.

Question
Which of the following tests is likely to be diagnostic of the cause of his bilateral diffuse alveolar shadowing?

Answers
A High-resolution CT scan
B Bronchoscopy
C Echocardiogram
D Spirometry
E Transfer coefficient (K_{CO})

Question 47

Clinical scenario
A 63-year-old man who has received a renal transplant for polycystic kidney disease 5 years previously presents with significantly worsening renal function. He is immunosuppressed with ciclosporin and mycophenolate mofetil. His creatinine has risen from 120 to 300 µmol/L (normal range 90–115). Recently he attended his GP, who treated him with a course of clarithromycin for a cough.

Question
What is the most likely cause for his deterioration in renal function?

Answers
A Acute allergic interstitial nephritis

B Ciclosporin toxicity

C Dehydration

D Pulmonary–renal syndrome associated with circulating antibodies to glomerular basement membrane

E Pyelonephritis

Question 48

Clinical scenario

A 38-year-old man with a family history of autosomal dominant polycystic kidney disease is referred with renal impairment and hypertension. An ultrasound scan of the abdomen confirms bilateral large cystic kidneys. He has a question concerning the risk to his children.

Question

'What do you think the chance is that both of my two children will have polycystic kidney disease?'

Answers

A 0%

B 25%

C 33.3%

D 50%

E 75%

Question 49

Clinical scenario

A 52-year-old woman with systemic lupus erythematosus who had a renal transplant 3 years previously attends the Emergency Department. She is shocked (BP 80/40 mmHg) and has a pyrexia of 39.5°C.

Question

Which of the following would *not* be recommended in the initial period following admission?

Answers

A Fluid resuscitation

B Broad-spectrum antibiotics

C Stop maintenance immunosuppression

D Intravenous corticosteroids

E CXR

Question 50

Clinical scenario

A 20-year-old man comes to your clinic. His father, who had end-stage renal failure due to adult polycystic kidney disease, died after a subarachnoid haemorrhage secondary to a berry aneurysm. The patient has recently had an ultrasound scan that confirms that he has several renal cysts. He wants to talk about what other problems the genetic mutation underlying his polycystic kidneys could cause.

Question

Which one of the following is *not* associated with autosomal dominant polycystic kidney disease?

Answers

A Mitral valve prolapse

B Aortic regurgitation

C Colonic diverticulae

D Congenital hepatic fibrosis

E Inguinal herniae

Question 51

Clinical scenario

A 56-year-old man complains of generalised swelling for the past 2 months. On examination he has marked peripheral oedema. Urine dipstick testing reveals proteinuria 4+ with no other abnormalities. Blood tests show a normal serum urea and creatinine, although his albumin is low at 30 g/dL (normal range 35–40).

Question

Which management strategy is most appropriate?

Answers

A Initiation of steroid therapy for presumed glomerulonephritis

B Urgent admission for initiation of further investigations

C Referral to local renal services as an outpatient

D Placement of central venous line for fluid assessment

E Infusion of 20% human albumin solution via a peripheral vein

4.2 Self-assessment answers

Answer to Question 1

D

In hepatorenal syndrome the patient is usually oligoanuric, with low urinary sodium concentration. Often he or she will be severely jaundiced and there will have been recent decompensation of the liver disease, triggered by an event such as infection.

Answer to Question 2

D

In diabetic nephropathy there is almost always some evidence of diabetic retinopathy. Proteinuria will always be present on dipstick testing. Evidence of peripheral vascular disease increases the likelihood of renovascular disease.

Answer to Question 3

D

Monoclonal gammopathy of undetermined significance and multiple myeloma are associated with paraproteinaemia and could give rise to AL (primary) amyloid. Chronic rheumatoid arthritis is an important cause of AA amyloid because of the associated persistent inflammatory response.

Answer to Question 4

A

Renal amyloidosis typically presents with nephrotic syndrome and accounts for a significant proportion of all nephrotic presentations in the elderly. None of the other conditions typically present with nephrotic syndrome, although they are all important causes of renal disease.

Answer to Question 5

E

In Wegener's granulomatosis, systemic lupus erythematosus and Goodpasture's disease, pulmonary haemorrhage causing haemoptysis is well recognised. In tuberculosis haemoptysis is common and renal failure could be due to several different causes, including glomerulonephritis or tubulointerstitial nephritis. IgA nephropathy is not associated with haemoptysis.

Answer to Question 6

B

Pre-eclampsia is commoner in first pregnancies, and is characterised by oedema, proteinuria, hypertension and an elevated serum urate. Proteinuria at the booking visit indicates underlying renal disease that was present before the pregnancy.

Answer to Question 7

A

In pre-eclampsia diuretics are not recommended for BP control. Labetalol, aspirin and antiepileptic medication may all be appropriate, but the definitive treatment is to deliver the baby. The timing of this depends on balancing the risks to the baby of premature birth against the risk to the mother and baby of postponing delivery.

Answer to Question 8

B

In haemolytic–uraemic syndrome, there is red cell fragmentation and

platelet consumption. The haemolysis causes raised circulating lactate dehydrogenase and reduced haptoglobins. Coagulation tests are not usually affected.

Answer to Question 9

C

In diabetic nephropathy and amyloidosis the kidneys are typically of normal or increased size. In polycystic kidneys there are multiple cysts and the kidneys are of increased size. In reflux nephropathy there would be evidence of scarring, and the kidneys are often of different sizes. Important causes of chronic renal failure with symmetrical, smooth small kidneys are glomerulonephritis and tubulointerstitial nephritis.

Answer to Question 10

D and G

Macroglossia and cardiac involvement are much more common in AL (primary) amyloid. Carpal tunnel syndrome is typical of dialysis-related amyloid. AA amyloid typically presents with heavy proteinuria and hepatosplenomegaly. It is important to consider the possibility of adrenal infiltration, which is also common and can lead to cortisol deficiency.

Answer to Question 11

C and G

She has nephrotic syndrome. Common causes in this age group are minimal-change disease and membranous glomerulonephritis. Haematuria 1+ does not exclude minimal change. Lupus nephritis is also relatively common as a cause of nephrotic syndrome in young women, but is usually accompanied by other symptoms. Cholesterol emboli, fibromuscular dysplasia and

ADPKD present quite differently. IgA nephropathy, diabetic nephropathy, amyloidosis and Wegener's granulomatosis are unlikely or would be expected to result in other features.

Answer to Question 12

C

Nephrotic syndrome predisposes to renal vein thrombosis, which typically presents with flank pain, haematuria and a rise in creatinine.

Answer to Question 13

B

Angiotensin-converting enzyme inhibitors are contraindicated in pregnancy, especially in the second and third trimester due to increased fetal malformations.

Answer to Question 14

C

He almost certainly has a decreased circulating volume. Inserting a central venous catheter is unlikely to give useful information and there are more important immediate manoeuvres to perform, including A, B, D and E.

Answer to Question 15

D and G

Rhabdomyolysis may be due to an underlying metabolic disorder, but this is uncommon. Common causes are alcohol excess and opioid overdose.

Answer to Question 16

B

Older patients are at much higher risk of ATN. The tubular epithelial cells are the most susceptible to ischaemic damage. Mortality remains high in patients who require renal replacement therapy in the setting of ATN.

Answer to Question 17

E

The biopsy shows normal glomeruli and the interstitium is abnormal with infiltration by inflammatory cells. This is most commonly related to drugs, especially NSAIDs and antibiotics.

Answer to Question 18

D

The clinical suspicion of renovascular disease is high in this case. Magnetic resonance angiography avoids exposure to ionising radiation and is a sensitive method for detecting renal artery stenosis.

Answer to Question 19

C

The history is typical of cholesterol embolisation following instrumentation in a man with established arterial disease. As in this case, it can occur after an interval of days to weeks. The differential diagnosis is wide and would include antineutrophil cytoplasmic antibody-associated vasculitis and an acute interstitial nephritis.

Answer to Question 20

B

There is an important association between berry aneurysms and polycystic kidney disease. This history is highly suggestive of a subarachnoid haemorrhage.

Answer to Question 21

B

This is a typical presentation of reflux nephropathy, and the

diagnosis will be confirmed by the detection of renal scarring on ultrasound. Usually reflux of urine up the ureters does not persist beyond childhood, so a micturating cystogram would be negative; if there is persistent reflux present, this would not usually alter management. Renal biopsy is not appropriate unless another diagnosis is considered plausible.

Answer to Question 22

E

This history is entirely consistent with diabetic nephropathy: key features are the known proliferative retinopathy, proteinuria and previous microalbuminuria. Although diabetics commonly need renal replacement therapy a little earlier than other chronic kidney disease patients, this man has an estimated glomerular filtration rate (38 mL/min) well above the threshold at which this is likely to be appropriate and another cause for his weight loss should be considered.

Answer to Question 23

B

Trimethoprim interferes with the tubular secretion of creatinine and so will increase plasma creatinine in the absence of a change in GFR. Cimetidine also has this effect, but ranitidine does not. It is important to reduce the dose of allopurinol in renal impairment, and metformin is relatively contraindicated. NSAIDs typically reduce GFR due to altered renal haemodynamics.

Answer to Question 24

A

Commencing alfacalcidol would be likely to increase calcium, phosphate, and calcium phosphate product. His slightly low

haemoglobin may contribute to his tiredness and would almost certainly be corrected by increasing his dose of erythropoietin. However, the loss of appetite and level of creatinine both suggest that it is time to commence renal replacement therapy.

Answer to Question 25

C

Typical complete remission rate without treatment is about 30%. In this age group an underlying malignancy is very unlikely. There is no recognised genetic predisposition to membranous glomerulonephritis and her children are not expected to be at increased risk of renal disease. Angiotensin-converting enzyme inhibitors are usually very effective in reducing proteinuria in this setting, and should be used (if tolerated) in patients who are normotensive.

Answer to Question 26

E

Five cysts on ultrasound at this age satisfy the diagnostic criteria for polycystic kidney disease, and his mother's death would be consistent with a subarachnoid haemorrhage. Therefore it is likely that he has autosomal dominant polycystic kidney disease. Ultrasound on his children is not useful for excluding the diagnosis at this age, since most individuals with *PKD1* or *PKD2* mutations develop cysts much later.

Answer to Question 27

G and I

This presentation satisfies the criteria for nephrotic syndrome. AL (primary) amyloid is one of the more common causes of nephrotic syndrome in the elderly, and would also account for enlarged, echobright kidneys on ultrasound. A renal biopsy is indicated to establish a diagnosis and determine what treatment to give. For example, if it shows minimal-change glomerulonephritis, then treatment with steroids would be appropriate. The risk of losing a kidney following percutaneous renal biopsy is substantially less than 1%.

Answer to Question 28

D

The clinical history and findings on examination strongly suggest renal artery stenosis. Magnetic resonance angiography is a sensitive test for this.

Answer to Question 29

D

He should be catheterised and then given intravenous fluids. He may well become polyuric when his obstruction is relieved. In some cases there is obstruction of the ureters as well as bladder outflow (eg with infiltrating bladder carcinoma), in which case nephrostomies may be needed if an upper tract obstruction is not relieved with an indwelling catheter.

Answer to Question 30

B and C

A transplant from his wife, who is blood group compatible, should certainly be considered. Polycystic patients often have relative preservation of native erythropoietin production. Patients with autosomal dominant polycystic kidney disease do not have a significantly increased risk of bladder or adrenal tumours. Mammalian TOR (target of rapamycin) inhibitors may reduce the progression of cysts, but this does not apply to calcineurin inhibitors or calcium channel

blockers. Nephrectomies are difficult in PKD patients and are not routinely necessary prior to transplantation. Continuous ambulatory peritoneal dialysis can be performed in patients with polycystic kidneys.

Answer to Question 31

C

A high concentration of any stone-forming substance in the urine will promote urinary tract stone formation. Stone-forming substances include calcium, phosphate, oxalate, urate and cystine. Citrate chelates calcium and reduces the formation of stones containing calcium. A low citrate level predisposes to stone formation.

Answer to Question 32

B

Systemic lupus erythematosus can affect the kidney in a number of different ways. Typical patterns of renal involvement include focal or diffuse proliferative, membranous, mesangiocapillary (membranoproliferative) and crescentic glomerulonephritides. Interstitial damage, tubular defects and ultimately glomerular fibrosis and sclerosis can also occur.

Answer to Question 33

B

The combination of renal impairment, hypercalcaemia, anaemia and a raised ESR is highly suggestive of myeloma. Systemic lupus erythematosus can cause a raised ESR, anaemia and renal impairment, but does not typically cause hypercalcaemia and is very much less likely. Secondary hyperparathyroidism occurs in response to a low calcium level.

Answer to Question 34

E

This clinical presentation is common and is typical of lower urinary tract infection. Common organisms include *Escherichia coli*, and *Proteus* and *Klebsiella* species. Fungal urinary tract infection is very rare, and in a younger woman with urinary tract infection the presence of stones or an anatomical abnormality would be unusual.

Answer to Question 35

D

Obesity can result in renal impairment due to focal segmental glomerulosclerosis. Obesity is associated with type 2 diabetes mellitus, which is a common cause of nephropathy. NSAIDs are contraindicated in patients with renal impairment as they can further reduce renal perfusion and glomerular filtration rate.

Answer to Question 36

B

Many patients with myeloma develop renal impairment. This can arise from hypercalcaemia and associated dehydration. AL (primary) amyloidosis is a potential long-term consequence of myeloma. Light chains can deposit in the kidneys causing renal damage (light-chain deposition disease). Cast nephropathy occurs when paraprotein casts form in the tubules resulting in renal impairment.

Answer to Question 37

G and H

He has heavy proteinuria and peripheral oedema that suggest the nephrotic (not nephritic) syndrome. Other features of this syndrome are hypoalbuminaemia and hyperlipidaemia. His BP is normal and he has no haematuria, both of which are present in the nephritic syndrome. The commonest cause of nephrotic syndrome in this age group is minimal-change nephropathy, which can be associated with NSAID use.

Answer to Question 38

B and D
The key reasons for initiating urgent renal replacment therapy when renal function is severely compromised are hyperkalaemia, metabolic acidosis, pulmonary oedema and severe uraemic syndrome (such as a severe confusional state or uraemic pericarditis). Relatively milder symptoms, such as poor appetite, lethargy and nausea, may prompt the elective initiation of renal replacement therapy in patients with chronic renal impairment, but they do not require urgent action.

Answer to Question 39

C and J
During pregnancy, systemic vascular resistance falls due to the effects of prostaglandins produced by the placenta. This lowers systemic BP despite a rise in cardiac output. BP falls to a nadir in the second trimester and slowly rises towards full term. If BP is relatively high in early pregnancy, this usually suggests that there was pre-existing chronic hypertension. Commonly in this situation, BP will fall in mid pregnancy but rise again in the third trimester. Chronic hypertension before pregnancy increases the risk of superimposed pre-eclampsia during the pregnancy. Proteinuria is not normal in pregnancy and is a feature of pre-eclampsia. Haematuria and hypertension are

both features that can occur with IgA nephropathy.

Answer to Question 40

E and I
Living donation is commonly undertaken and there is no requirement for the recipient and donor to be related. Spousal donation is legal in the UK. It is essential that the blood group of the transplanted kidney is compatible with that of the recipient or rapid aggressive rejection will occur. Other factors such as HLA type may reduce the likelihood of rejection but are much less important than the blood group. Focal segmental glomerulosclerosis can recur in transplanted kidneys, but would not be such an important consideration as blood group compatibility.

Answer to Question 41

D and I
He has a rash and recent-onset renal impairment. The most likely cause is an acute interstitial nephritis. Common causes of this are antibiotics (particularly penicillins, cephalosporins, sulphonamides and rifampicin), NSAIDs and allopurinol.

Answer to Question 42

C and F
This patient has severe metabolic acidosis with partial compensation through hyperventilation. The anion gap is increased. The acidosis is more marked than expected for this level of renal dysfunction. Important possible explanations include diabetic ketoacidosis and ethylene glycol intoxication. Another possibility might be a salicylate overdose. Bulimia and laxative abuse are characterised by alkalosis. If the patient has severe chronic obstructive pulmonary disease, this

might result in hypoxia, CO_2 retention and respiratory acidosis, but not the picture seen here. Acetazolamide can rarely cause metabolic acidosis, but this is much less likely.

Answer to Question 43

D
The history is consistent with an ANCA-associated vasculitis. Bronchoscopy and lavage would be very hazardous. A renal biopsy may be appropriate, especially if ANCA are not detected in the blood, but light microscopy and immunofluorescence are more likely to be useful than the electron microscopic appearance. A genetic test for Alport's syndrome is not appropriate here.

Answer to Question 44

A
Struvite (magnesium ammonium phosphate) stones occur in patients with chronic infections with bacteria expressing urease. They account for about 10% of all instances of stones. The most common type of urinary stone is calcium oxalate.

Answer to Question 45

D
Urinary stones are well recognised with the antiretroviral protease inhibitor indinavir. The sudden onset of severe loin pain and haematuria would be consistent with a stone in the ureter.

Answer to Question 46

E
This history is suggestive of pulmonary haemorrhage in the context of antineutrophil cytoplasmic antibody-associated

vasculitis. The Kco will be elevated in acute pulmonary haemorrhage.

Answer to Question 47

B

Clarithromycin inhibits CYP3A4 and, if the dose has not been adjusted, ciclosporin levels will have increased dramatically.

Answer to Question 48

B

Assuming he has autosomal dominant polycystic kidney disease, each child has a 50% risk of being affected, so the risk of both them being affected is 25%.

Answer to Question 49

C

Immunosuppression should not be stopped as it may precipitate acute rejection. She should be resuscitated and given broad-spectrum antibiotics and intravenous corticosteroids to cover the possibility of adrenal insufficiency in a patient who has been on steroid therapy in the past.

Answer to Question 50

D

Mitral valve prolapse, aortic regurgitation, colonic diverticulae and inguinal herniae are all associated with autosomal dominant polycystic kidney disease.

Answer to Question 51

C

This patient has nephrotic syndrome. A renal biopsy is indicated to establish a diagnosis. This should be done soon, but does not require immediate admission. A loop diuretic (eg furosemide) will alleviate the peripheral oedema in the interim.

THE MEDICAL MASTERCLASS SERIES

Scientific Background to Medicine 1

GENETICS AND MOLECULAR MEDICINE

Nucleic Acids and Chromosomes 3

Techniques in Molecular Biology 11

Molecular Basis of Simple Genetic Traits 17

More Complex Issues 23

Self-assessment 30

BIOCHEMISTRY AND METABOLISM

Requirement for Energy 35

Carbohydrates 41

Fatty Acids and Lipids 45

3.1 Fatty acids 45
3.2 Lipids 48

Cholesterol and Steroid Hormones 51

Amino Acids and Proteins 53

5.1 Amino acids 53
5.2 Proteins 56

Haem 59

Nucleotides 61

Self-assessment 66

CELL BIOLOGY

Ion Transport 71

1.1 Ion channels 72
1.2 Ion carriers 79

Receptors and Intracellular Signalling 82

Cell Cycle and Apoptosis 88

Haematopoiesis 94

Self-assessment 97

IMMUNOLOGY AND IMMUNOSUPPRESSION

Overview of the Immune System 103

The Major Histocompatibility Complex, Antigen Presentation and Transplantation 106

T Cells 109

B Cells 112

Tolerance and Autoimmunity 115

Complement 117

Inflammation 120

Immunosuppressive Therapy 125

Self-assessment 130

ANATOMY

Heart and Major Vessels 135

Lungs 138

Liver and Biliary Tract 140

Spleen 142

Kidney 143

Endocrine Glands 144

Gastrointestinal Tract 147

Eye 150

Nervous System 152

Self-assessment 167

PHYSIOLOGY

Cardiovascular System 171

1.1 The heart as a pump 171
1.2 The systemic and pulmonary circulations 176
1.3 Blood vessels 177
1.4 Endocrine function of the heart 180

Respiratory System 182

2.1 The lungs 182

131

Gastrointestinal System 187

3.1 The gut 187
3.2 The liver 190
3.3 The exocrine pancreas 193

Brain and Nerves 194

4.1 The action potential 194
4.2 Synaptic transmission 196
4.3 Neuromuscular transmission 199

Endocrine Physiology 200

5.1 The growth hormone–insulin-like growth factor 1 axis 200
5.2 The hypothalamic–pituitary–adrenal axis 200
5.3 Thyroid hormones 201
5.4 The endocrine pancreas 203
5.5 The ovary and testis 204
5.6 The breast 206
5.7 The posterior pituitary 207

Renal Physiology 209

6.1 Blood flow and glomerular filtration 209
6.2 Function of the renal tubules 211
6.3 Endocrine function of the kidney 217

Self-assessment 220

Scientific Background to Medicine 2

CLINICAL PHARMACOLOGY

Introducing Clinical Pharmacology 3

1.1 Risks versus benefits 4
1.2 Safe prescribing 4
1.3 Rational prescribing 5
1.4 The role of clinical pharmacology 5

Pharmacokinetics 7

2.1 Introduction 7
2.2 Drug absorption 7
2.3 Drug distribution 11
2.4 Drug metabolism 12
2.5 Drug elimination 17
2.6 Plasma half-life and steady-state plasma concentrations 19
2.7 Drug monitoring 20

Pharmacodynamics 22

3.1 How drugs exert their effects 22
3.2 Selectivity is the key to the therapeutic utility of an agent 25
3.3 Basic aspects of the interaction of a drug with its target 27
3.4 Heterogeneity of drug responses, pharmacogenetics and pharmacogenomics 31

Prescribing in Special Circumstances 33

4.1 Introduction 33
4.2 Prescribing and liver disease 33
4.3 Prescribing in pregnancy 36
4.4 Prescribing for women of childbearing potential 39
4.5 Prescribing to lactating mothers 39
4.6 Prescribing in renal disease 41
4.7 Prescribing in the elderly 44

Adverse Drug Reactions 46

5.1 Introduction and definition 46
5.2 Classification of adverse drug reactions 46
5.3 Clinical approach to adverse drug reactions 47
5.4 Dose-related adverse drug reactions (type A) 48
5.5 Non-dose-related adverse drug reactions (type B) 51
5.6 Adverse reactions caused by long-term effects of drugs (type C) 56
5.7 Adverse reactions caused by delayed effects of drugs (type D) 57
5.8 Withdrawal reactions (type E) 58
5.9 Drugs in overdose and use of illicit drugs 59

Drug Development and Rational Prescribing 60

6.1 Drug development 60
6.2 Rational prescribing 65
6.3 Clinical governance and rational prescribing 66
6.4 Rational prescribing: evaluating the evidence for yourself 68
6.5 Rational prescribing, irrational patients 68

Self-assessment 70

STATISTICS, EPIDEMIOLOGY, CLINICAL TRIALS AND META-ANALYSES

Statistics 79

Epidemiology 86

2.1 Observational studies 87

Clinical Trials and Meta-Analyses 92

Self-assessment 103

Clinical Skills

CLINICAL SKILLS FOR PACES

Introduction 3

History-taking for PACES (Station 2) 6

Communication Skills and Ethics for PACES (Station 4) 11

Examination for PACES Stations 1, 3 and 5: General Considerations 13

Station 1: Respiratory System 16

Station 1: Abdominal System 21

Station 3: Cardiovascular System 27

Station 3: Central Nervous System 36

Station 5: Skin, Locomotor System, Endocrine System and Eyes 54

PAIN RELIEF AND PALLIATIVE CARE

PACES Stations and Acute Scenarios 61

1.1 **History-taking** 61
   1.1.1 Pain 61
   1.1.2 Constipation/bowel obstruction 63

1.2 **Communication skills and ethics** 65
   1.2.1 Pain 65
   1.2.2 Breathlessness 66
   1.2.3 Nausea and vomiting 67
   1.2.4 Bowel obstruction 69
   1.2.5 End of life 70
1.3 **Acute scenarios** 71
   1.3.1 Pain 71
   1.3.2 Breathlessness 74
   1.3.3 Nausea and vomiting 76
   1.3.4 Bowel obstruction 79

Diseases and Treatments 82

2.1 **Pain** 82
2.2 **Breathlessness** 87
2.3 **Nausea and vomiting** 88
2.4 **Constipation** 89
2.5 **Bowel obstruction** 90
2.6 **Anxiety and depression** 91
2.7 **Confusion** 93
2.8 **End-of-life care: the dying patient** 94
2.9 **Specialist palliative care services** 96

Self-assessment 98

MEDICINE FOR THE ELDERLY

PACES Stations and Acute Scenarios 107

1.1 **History-taking** 107
   1.1.1 Frequent falls 107
   1.1.2 Recent onset of confusion 110
   1.1.3 Urinary incontinence and immobility 114
   1.1.4 Collapse 116
   1.1.5 Vague aches and pains 119
   1.1.6 Swollen legs and back pain 121
   1.1.7 Failure to thrive: gradual decline and weight loss 127

1.2 **Clinical examination** 129
   1.2.1 Confusion (respiratory) 129
   1.2.2 Confusion (abdominal) 130
   1.2.3 Failure to thrive (abdominal) 131
   1.2.4 Frequent falls (cardiovascular) 131
   1.2.5 Confusion (cardiovascular) 132
   1.2.6 Frequent falls (neurological) 132
   1.2.7 Confusion (neurological) 134
   1.2.8 Impaired mobility (neurological) 135
   1.2.9 Confusion (skin) 135
   1.2.10 Frequent falls (locomotor) 136
   1.2.11 Confusion (endocrine) 136
   1.2.12 Confusion (eye) 136
1.3 **Communication skills and ethics** 137
   1.3.1 Frequent falls 137
   1.3.2 Confusion 138
   1.3.3 Collapse 139
1.4 **Acute scenarios** 141
   1.4.1 Sudden onset of confusion 141
   1.4.2 Collapse 143

Diseases and Treatments 147

2.1 **Why elderly patients are different** 147
2.2 **General approach to management** 149
2.3 **Falls** 151
2.4 **Urinary and faecal incontinence** 155
   2.4.1 Urinary incontinence 155
   2.4.2 Faecal incontinence 157
2.5 **Hypothermia** 158
2.6 **Drugs in elderly people** 161
2.7 **Dementia** 162
2.8 **Rehabilitation** 165
2.9 **Aids, appliances and assistive technology** 166
2.10 **Hearing impairment** 168
2.11 **Nutrition** 170

2.12 Benefits 174
2.13 Legal aspects of elderly care 175

Investigations and Practical Procedures 178

3.1 Diagnosis vs common sense 178
3.2 Assessment of cognition, mood and function 178

Self-assessment 181

Acute Medicine

ACUTE MEDICINE

PACES Stations and Acute Scenarios 3

1.1 Communication skills and ethics 3
  1.1.1 Cardiac arrest 3
  1.1.2 Stroke 4
  1.1.3 Congestive cardiac failure 5
  1.1.4 Lumbar back pain 6
  1.1.5 Community-acquired pneumonia 7
  1.1.6 Acute pneumothorax 7
1.2 Acute scenarios 8
  1.2.1 Cardiac arrest 8
  1.2.2 Chest pain and hypotension 12
  1.2.3 Should he be thrombolysed? 15
  1.2.4 Hypotension in acute coronary syndrome 20
  1.2.5 Postoperative breathlessness 21
  1.2.6 Two patients with tachyarrhythmia 23
  1.2.7 Bradyarrhythmia 27
  1.2.8 Collapse of unknown cause 30
  1.2.9 Asthma 33
  1.2.10 Pleurisy 36

  1.2.11 Chest infection/ pneumonia 39
  1.2.12 Acute-on-chronic airways obstruction 42
  1.2.13 Stridor 44
  1.2.14 Pneumothorax 46
  1.2.15 Upper gastrointestinal haemorrhage 48
  1.2.16 Bloody diarrhoea 51
  1.2.17 Abdominal pain 54
  1.2.18 Hepatic encephalopathy/ alcohol withdrawal 56
  1.2.19 Renal failure, fluid overload and hyperkalaemia 59
  1.2.20 Diabetic ketoacidosis 62
  1.2.21 Hypoglycaemia 65
  1.2.22 Hypercalcaemia 67
  1.2.23 Hyponatraemia 69
  1.2.24 Addisonian crisis 71
  1.2.25 Thyrotoxic crisis 74
  1.2.26 Sudden onset of severe headache 75
  1.2.27 Severe headache with fever 77
  1.2.28 Acute spastic paraparesis 79
  1.2.29 Status epilepticus 81
  1.2.30 Stroke 83
  1.2.31 Coma 86
  1.2.32 Fever in a returning traveller 89
  1.2.33 Anaphylaxis 90
  1.2.34 A painful joint 91
  1.2.35 Back pain 94
  1.2.36 Self-harm 96
  1.2.37 Violence and aggression 97

Diseases and Treatments 100

2.1 Overdoses 100
  2.1.1 Prevention of drug absorption from the gut 100
  2.1.2 Management of overdoses of specific drugs 100

Investigations and Practical Procedures 103

3.1 Central venous lines 103
  3.1.1 Indications, contraindications, consent and preparation 103

  3.1.2 Specific techniques for insertion of central lines 104
  3.1.3 Interpretation of central venous pressure measurements 106
3.2 Lumbar puncture 106
3.3 Cardiac pacing 107
3.4 Elective DC cardioversion 109
3.5 Intercostal chest drain insertion 109
3.6 Arterial blood gases 112
  3.6.1 Measurement of arterial blood gases 112
  3.6.2 Interpretation of arterial blood gases 113
3.7 Airway management 113
  3.7.1 Basic airway management 113
  3.7.2 Tracheostomy 116
3.8 Ventilatory support 117
  3.8.1 Controlled oxygen therapy 117
  3.8.2 Continuous positive airway pressure 117
  3.8.3 Non-invasive ventilation 118
  3.8.4 Invasive ventilation 118

Self-assessment 120

Infectious Diseases and Dermatology

INFECTIOUS DISEASES

PACES Stations and Acute Scenarios 3

1.1 History-taking 3
  1.1.1 A cavitating lung lesion 3
  1.1.2 Fever and lymphadenopathy 5
  1.1.3 Still feverish after 6 weeks 7
  1.1.4 Chronic fatigue 10

1.1.5   A spot on the penis 12
1.1.6   Penile discharge 15
1.1.7   Woman with a genital
        sore 17
1.2 **Communication skills and
    ethics 20**
1.2.1   Fever, hypotension and
        confusion 20
1.2.2   A swollen red foot 21
1.2.3   Still feverish after
        6 weeks 22
1.2.4   Chronic fatigue 23
1.2.5   Malaise, mouth ulcers
        and fever 24
1.2.6   Don't tell my wife 25
1.3 **Acute scenarios 27**
1.3.1   Fever 27
1.3.2   Fever, hypotension and
        confusion 30
1.3.3   A swollen red foot 33
1.3.4   Fever and cough 34
1.3.5   Fever, back pain and
        weak legs 37
1.3.6   Drug user with fever and
        a murmur 40
1.3.7   Fever and heart failure
        44
1.3.8   Persistent fever in the
        intensive care unit 47
1.3.9   Pyelonephritis 49
1.3.10 A sore throat 52
1.3.11 Fever and headache 55
1.3.12 Fever with reduced
        conscious level 60
1.3.13 Fever in the neutropenic
        patient 62
1.3.14 Fever after renal
        transplant 65
1.3.15 Varicella in pregnancy
        68
1.3.16 Imported fever 70
1.3.17 Eosinophilia 74
1.3.18 Jaundice and fever after
        travelling 76
1.3.19 A traveller with
        diarrhoea 78
1.3.20 Malaise, mouth ulcers
        and fever 81
1.3.21 Breathlessness in a
        HIV-positive patient 83
1.3.22 HIV positive and blurred
        vision 86

1.3.23 Abdominal pain and
        vaginal discharge 88
1.3.24 Penicillin allergy 91

Pathogens and Management 94

2.1 **Antimicrobial prophylaxis 94**
2.2 **Immunisation 95**
2.3 **Infection control 97**
2.4 **Travel advice 99**
2.5 **Bacteria 100**
2.5.1   Gram-positive
        bacteria 101
2.5.2   Gram-negative
        bacteria 104
2.6 **Mycobacteria 108**
2.6.1   Mycobacterium
        tuberculosis 108
2.6.2   Mycobacterium leprae
        113
2.6.3   Opportunistic
        mycobacteria 114
2.7 **Spirochaetes 115**
2.7.1   Syphilis 115
2.7.2   Lyme disease 117
2.7.3   Relapsing fever 118
2.7.4   Leptospirosis 118
2.8 **Miscellaneous bacteria 119**
2.8.1   *Mycoplasma* and
        Ureaplasma 119
2.8.2   Rickettsiae 120
2.8.3   *Coxiella burnetii*
        (Q fever) 120
2.8.4   Chlamydiae 121
2.9 **Fungi 121**
2.9.1   *Candida* spp. 121
2.9.2   *Aspergillus* 123
2.9.3   *Cryptococcus
        neoformans* 124
2.9.4   Dimorphic fungi 125
2.9.5   Miscellaneous fungi
        126
2.10 **Viruses 126**
2.10.1 Herpes simplex
        viruses 127
2.10.2 Varicella-zoster virus
        128
2.10.3 Cytomegalovirus 130
2.10.4 Epstein–Barr virus
        130
2.10.5 Human herpesviruses
        6 and 7 130

2.10.6 Human herpesvirus 8
        131
2.10.7 Parvovirus 131
2.10.8 Hepatitis viruses 132
2.10.9 Influenza virus 133
2.10.10 Paramyxoviruses 134
2.10.11 Enteroviruses 134
2.10.12 Coronaviruses and
        SARS 135
2.11 **Human immunodeficiency
     virus 135**
2.11.1 Prevention following
        sharps injury 140
2.12 **Travel-related viruses 142**
2.12.1 Rabies 142
2.12.2 Dengue 143
2.12.3 Arbovirus infections
        143
2.13 **Protozoan parasites 144**
2.13.1 Malaria 144
2.13.2 Leishmaniasis 145
2.13.3 Amoebiasis 146
2.13.4 Toxoplasmosis 147
2.14 **Metazoan parasites 148**
2.14.1 Schistosomiasis 148
2.14.2 Strongyloidiasis 149
2.14.3 Cysticercosis 150
2.14.4 Filariasis 151
2.14.5 Trichinosis 151
2.14.6 Toxocariasis 152
2.14.7 Hydatid disease 152

**Investigations and Practical
Procedures 154**

3.1 **Getting the best from the
    laboratory 154**
3.2 **Specific investigations 154**

Self-assessment 159

DERMATOLOGY

**PACES Stations and Acute
Scenarios 175**

1.1 **History taking 175**
1.1.1   Blistering disorders 175
1.1.2   Chronic red facial rash
        177

1.1.3 Pruritus 178
1.1.4 Alopecia 180
1.1.5 Hyperpigmentation 181
1.1.6 Hypopigmentation 183
1.1.7 Red legs 185
1.1.8 Leg ulcers 187
1.2 **Clinical examination 189**
1.2.1 Blistering disorder 189
1.2.2 A chronic red facial rash 193
1.2.3 Pruritus 198
1.2.4 Alopecia 200
1.2.5 Hyperpigmentation 202
1.2.6 Hypopigmentation 205
1.2.7 Red legs 207
1.2.8 Lumps and bumps 210
1.2.9 Telangiectases 212
1.2.10 Purpura 214
1.2.11 Lesion on the shin 216
1.2.12 Non-pigmented lesion on the face 217
1.2.13 A pigmented lesion on the face 219
1.2.14 Leg ulcers 221
1.2.15 Examine these hands 223
1.3 **Communication skills and ethics 225**
1.3.1 Consenting a patient to enter a dermatological trial 225
1.3.2 A steroid-phobic patient 227
1.3.3 An anxious woman with a family history of melanoma who wants all her moles removed 228
1.3.4 Prescribing isotretinoin to a woman of reproductive age 229
1.4 **Acute scenarios 231**
1.4.1 Acute generalised rashes 231
1.4.2 Erythroderma 238

2.4 **Bullous pemphigoid 246**
2.5 **Dermatomyositis 248**
2.6 **Dermatitis herpetiformis 249**
2.7 **Drug eruptions 249**
2.8 **Atopic eczema 251**
2.9 **Contact dermatitis 252**
2.10 **Erythema multiforme, Stevens–Johnson syndrome and toxic epidermal necrolysis 253**
2.11 **Erythema nodosum 254**
2.12 **Fungal infections of skin, hair and nails (superficial fungal infections) 255**
2.13 **HIV and the skin 257**
2.14 **Lichen planus 258**
2.15 **Lymphoma of the skin: mycosis fungoides and Sézary syndrome 260**
2.16 **Pemphigus vulgaris 261**
2.17 **Psoriasis 263**
2.18 **Pyoderma gangrenosum 265**
2.19 **Scabies 266**
2.20 **Basal cell carcinoma 268**
2.21 **Squamous cell carcinoma 270**
2.22 **Malignant melanoma 271**
2.23 **Urticaria and angio-oedema 274**
2.24 **Vitiligo 275**
2.25 **Cutaneous vasculitis 276**
2.26 **Topical therapy: corticosteroids and immunosuppressants 277**
2.27 **Phototherapy 278**
2.28 **Retinoids 279**

Investigations and Practical Procedures 281

3.1 **Skin biopsy 281**
3.2 **Direct and indirect immunofluorescence 282**
3.3 **Patch tests 282**
3.4 **Obtaining specimens for mycological analysis 284**

Self-assessment 285

Haematology and Oncology

HAEMATOLOGY

PACES Stations and Acute Scenarios 1

1.1 **History-taking 3**
1.1.1 Microcytic hypochromic anaemia 3
1.1.2 Macrocytic anaemia 5
1.1.3 Lymphocytosis and anaemia 8
1.1.4 Thromboembolism and fetal loss 11
1.1.5 Weight loss and thrombocytosis 12
1.2 **Clinical examination 14**
1.2.1 Normocytic anaemia 14
1.2.2 Thrombocytopenia and purpura 14
1.2.3 Jaundice and anaemia 16
1.2.4 Polycythaemia 17
1.2.5 Splenomegaly 18
1.3 **Communication skills and ethics 19**
1.3.1 Persuading a patient to accept HIV testing 19
1.3.2 Talking to a distressed relative 20
1.3.3 Explaining a medical error 22
1.3.4 Breaking bad news 23
1.4 **Acute scenarios 25**
1.4.1 Chest syndrome in sickle cell disease 25
1.4.2 Neutropenia 27
1.4.3 Leucocytosis 29
1.4.4 Spontaneous bleeding and weight loss 31
1.4.5 Cervical lymphadenopathy and difficulty breathing 32
1.4.6 Swelling of the leg 35

Diseases and Treatments 243

2.1 **Acne vulgaris 243**
2.2 **Acanthosis nigricans 245**
2.3 **Alopecia areata 245**

Diseases and Treatments 37

2.1 Causes of anaemia 37
2.1.1 Thalassaemia syndromes 38
2.1.2 Sickle cell syndromes 39
2.1.3 Enzyme defects 41
2.1.4 Membrane defects 41
2.1.5 Iron metabolism and iron-deficiency anaemia 43
2.1.6 Vitamin B_{12} and folate metabolism and deficiency 44
2.1.7 Acquired haemolytic anaemia 44
2.1.8 Bone-marrow failure and inflitration 46
2.2 Haematological malignancy 46
2.2.1 Multiple myeloma 46
2.2.2 Acute leukaemia: acute lymphoblastic leukaemia and acute myeloid leukaemia 49
2.2.3 Chronic lymphocytic leukaemia 52
2.2.4 Chronic myeloid leukaemia 54
2.2.5 Malignant lymphomas: non-Hodgkin's lymphoma and Hodgkin's lymphoma 55
2.2.6 Myelodysplastic syndromes 58
2.2.7 Non-leukaemic myeloproliferative disorders (including polycythaemia vera, essential thrombocythaemia and myelofibrosis) 60
2.2.8 Amyloidosis 62
2.3 Bleeding disorders 64
2.3.1 Inherited bleeding disorders 64
2.3.2 Aquired bleeding disorders 67
2.3.3 Idiopathic throbocytopenic purpura 68
2.4 Thrombotic disorders 69
2.4.1 Inherited thrombotic disease 69
2.4.2 Acquired thrombotic disease 72
2.5 Clinical use of blood products 74
2.6 Haematological features of systemic disease 76
2.7 Haematology of pregnancy 79
2.8 Iron overload 80
2.9 Chemotherapy and related therapies 82
2.10 Principles of bone-marrow and peripheral blood stem-cell transplantation 85

Investigations and Practical Procedures 87

3.1 The full blood count and film 87
3.2 Bone-marrow examination 89
3.3 Clotting screen 91
3.4 Coombs' test (direct antiglobulin test) 91
3.5 Erythrocyte sedimentation rate versus plasma viscosity 92
3.6 Therapeutic anticoagulation 92

Self-assessment 94

ONCOLOGY

PACES Stations and Acute Scenarios 109

1.1 History-taking 109
1.1.1 A dark spot 109
1.2 Clinical examination 110
1.2.1 A lump in the neck 110
1.3 Communication skills and ethics 111
1.3.1 Am I at risk of cancer? 111
1.3.2 Consent for chemotherapy (1) 113
1.3.3 Consent for chemotherapy (2) 114
1.3.4 Don't tell him the diagnosis 116
1.4 Acute scenarios 117
1.4.1 Acute deterioration after starting chemotherapy 117
1.4.2 Back pain and weak legs 119
1.4.3 Breathless, hoarse, dizzy and swollen 121

Diseases and Treatments 124

2.1 Breast cancer 124
2.2 Central nervous system cancers 126
2.3 Digestive tract cancers 129
2.4 Genitourinary cancer 132
2.5 Gynaecological cancer 136
2.6 Head and neck cancer 139
2.7 Skin tumours 140
2.8 Paediatric solid tumours 144
2.9 Lung cancer 146
2.10 Liver and biliary tree cancer 149
2.11 Bone cancer and sarcoma 151
2.12 Endocrine tumours 157
2.13 The causes of cancer 159
2.14 Paraneoplastic conditions 162

Investigations and Practical Procedures 167

3.1 Investigation of unknown primary cancers 167
3.2 Investigation and management of metastatic disease 169
3.3 Tumour markers 171
3.4 Screening 173
3.5 Radiotherapy 175
3.6 Chemotherapy 176
3.7 Immunotherapy 179
3.8 Stem-cell transplantation 180
3.9 Oncological emergencies 180

Self-assessment 185

Cardiology and Respiratory Medicine

CARDIOLOGY

PACES Stations and Acute Scenarios 3

1.1 History-taking 3
- **1.1.1** Paroxysmal palpitations 3
- **1.1.2** Palpitations with dizziness 6
- **1.1.3** Breathlessness and ankle swelling 9
- **1.1.4** Breathlessness and exertional presyncope 12
- **1.1.5** Dyspnoea, ankle oedema and cyanosis 14
- **1.1.6** Chest pain and recurrent syncope 16
- **1.1.7** Hypertension found at routine screening 19
- **1.1.8** Murmur in pregnancy 23

1.2 Clinical examination 25
- **1.2.1** Irregular pulse 25
- **1.2.2** Congestive heart failure 27
- **1.2.3** Hypertension 29
- **1.2.4** Mechanical valve 29
- **1.2.5** Pansystolic murmur 30
- **1.2.6** Mitral stenosis 31
- **1.2.7** Aortic stenosis 32
- **1.2.8** Aortic regurgitation 33
- **1.2.9** Tricuspid regurgitation 34
- **1.2.10** Eisenmenger's syndrome 35
- **1.2.11** Dextrocardia 36

1.3 Communication skills and ethics 37
- **1.3.1** Advising a patient against unnecessary investigations 37
- **1.3.2** Explanation of uncertainty of diagnosis 38
- **1.3.3** Discussion of the need to screen relatives for an inherited condition 38
- **1.3.4** Communicating news of a patient's death to a spouse 39
- **1.3.5** Explanation to a patient of the need for investigations 40
- **1.3.6** Explanation to a patient who is reluctant to receive treatment 41

1.4 Acute scenarios 42
- **1.4.1** Syncope 42
- **1.4.2** Stroke and a murmur 46
- **1.4.3** Acute chest pain 49
- **1.4.4** Hypotension following acute myocardial infarction 52
- **1.4.5** Breathlessness and collapse 54
- **1.4.6** Pleuritic chest pain 57
- **1.4.7** Fever, weight loss and a murmur 60
- **1.4.8** Chest pain following a 'flu-like illness 64

Diseases and Treatments 69

2.1 Coronary artery disease 69
- **2.1.1** Stable angina 69
- **2.1.2** Unstable angina and non-ST-elevation myocardial infarction 71
- **2.1.3** ST-elevation myocardial infarction 72

2.2 Cardiac arrhythmia 76
- **2.2.1** Bradycardia 76
- **2.2.2** Tachycardia 78

2.3 Cardiac failure 82

2.4 Diseases of heart muscle 86
- **2.4.1** Hypertrophic cardiomyopathy 86
- **2.4.2** Dilated cardiomyopathy 89
- **2.4.3** Restrictive cardiomyopathy 89
- **2.4.4** Arrhythmogenic right ventricular cardiomyopathy 90
- **2.4.5** Left ventricular non-compaction 90

2.5 Valvular heart disease 90
- **2.5.1** Aortic stenosis 90
- **2.5.2** Aortic regurgitation 92
- **2.5.3** Mitral stenosis 93
- **2.5.4** Mitral regurgitation 95
- **2.5.5** Tricuspid valve disease 97
- **2.5.6** Pulmonary valve disease 98

2.6 Pericardial disease 98
- **2.6.1** Acute pericarditis 98
- **2.6.2** Pericardial effusion 100
- **2.6.3** Constrictive pericarditis 102

2.7 Congenital heart disease 104
- **2.7.1** Acyanotic congenital heart disease 105
  - **2.7.1.1** Atrial septal defect 105
  - **2.7.1.2** Isolated ventricular septal defect 107
  - **2.7.1.3** Patent ductus arteriosus 107
  - **2.7.1.4** Coarctation of the aorta 108
- **2.7.2** Cyanotic congenital heart disease 109
  - **2.7.2.1** Tetralogy of Fallot 109
  - **2.7.2.2** Complete transposition of great arteries 111
  - **2.7.2.3** Ebstein's anomaly 112
- **2.7.3** Eisenmenger's syndrome 113

2.8 Infective diseases of the heart 114
- **2.8.1** Infective endocarditis 114
- **2.8.2** Rheumatic fever 119

2.9 Cardiac tumours 120

2.10 Traumatic heart disease 122

2.11 Disease of systemic arteries 124

    2.11.1 Aortic dissection 124

2.12 Diseases of pulmonary arteries 126

    2.12.1 Primary pulmonary hypertension 126

    2.12.2 Secondary pulmonary hypertension 129

2.13 Cardiac complications of systemic disease 130

    2.13.1 Thyroid disease 130

    2.13.2 Diabetes 131

    2.13.3 Autoimmune rheumatic diseases 131

    2.13.4 Renal disease 132

2.14 Systemic complications of cardiac disease 133

    2.14.1 Stroke 133

2.15 Pregnancy and the heart 134

2.16 General anaesthesia in heart disease 136

2.17 Hypertension 136

    2.17.1 Hypertensive emergencies 140

2.18 Venous thromboembolism 141

    2.18.1 Pulmonary embolism 141

2.19 Driving restrictions in cardiology 145

Investigations and Practical Procedures 147

3.1 ECG 147

    3.1.1 Exercise ECGs 151

3.2 Basic electrophysiology studies 152

3.3 Ambulatory monitoring 154

3.4 Radiofrequency ablation and implantable cardioverter defibrillators 156

    3.4.1 Radiofrequency ablation 156

    3.4.2 Implantable cardioverter defibrillator 157

    3.4.3 Cardiac resynchronisation therapy 158

3.5 Pacemakers 159

3.6 Chest radiograph in cardiac disease 161

3.7 Cardiac biochemical markers 163

3.8 CT and MRI 164

    3.8.1 Multislice spiral CT 164

    3.8.2 MRI 165

3.9 Ventilation–perfusion imaging 166

3.10 Echocardiography 167

3.11 Nuclear cardiology 170

    3.11.1 Myocardial perfusion imaging 170

    3.11.2 Radionuclide ventriculography 170

    3.11.3 Positron emission tomography 171

3.12 Cardiac catheterisation 171

    3.12.1 Percutaneous coronary intervention 172

    3.12.2 Percutaneous valvuloplasty 173

Self-assessment 176

RESPIRATORY MEDICINE

PACES Stations and Acute Scenarios 191

1.1 History-taking 191

    1.1.1 New breathlessness 191

    1.1.2 Solitary pulmonary nodule 193

    1.1.3 Exertional dyspnoea with daily sputum 195

    1.1.4 Dyspnoea and fine inspiratory crackles 197

    1.1.5 Nocturnal cough 199

    1.1.6 Daytime sleepiness and morning headache 202

    1.1.7 Lung cancer with asbestos exposure 204

    1.1.8 Breathlessness with a normal chest radiograph 206

1.2 Clinical examination 209

    1.2.1 Coarse crackles: bronchiectasis 209

    1.2.2 Fine crackles: interstitial lung disease 210

    1.2.3 Stridor 212

    1.2.4 Pleural effusion 213

    1.2.5 Wheeze and crackles: chronic obstructive pulmonary disease 215

    1.2.6 Cor pulmonale 216

    1.2.7 Pneumonectomy/lobectomy 217

    1.2.8 Apical signs: old tuberculosis 218

    1.2.9 Cystic fibrosis 219

1.3 Communication skills and ethics 220

    1.3.1 Lifestyle modification 220

    1.3.2 Possible cancer 221

    1.3.3 Potentially life-threatening illness 222

    1.3.4 Sudden unexplained death 224

    1.3.5 Intubation for ventilation 225

    1.3.6 Patient refusing ventilation 226

1.4 Acute scenarios 228

    1.4.1 Pleuritic chest pain 228

    1.4.2 Unexplained hypoxia 232

    1.4.3 Haemoptysis and weight loss 234

    1.4.4 Pleural effusion and fever 237

    1.4.5 Lobar collapse in non-smoker 239

    1.4.6 Upper airway obstruction 241

Diseases and Treatments 243

2.1 Upper airway 243

    2.1.1 Sleep apnoea 243

2.2 Atopy and asthma 245

    2.2.1 Allergic rhinitis 245

    2.2.2 Asthma 246

2.3 Chronic obstructive pulmonary disease 251

2.4 Bronchiectasis 253

2.5 **Cystic fibrosis** 256
2.6 **Occupational lung disease 258**
   2.6.1 Asbestosis and the pneumoconioses 258
2.7 **Diffuse parenchymal lung disease 261**
   2.7.1 Usual interstitial pneumonia 261
   2.7.2 Cryptogenic organising pneumonia 262
   2.7.3 Bronchiolitis obliterans 263
2.8 **Miscellaneous conditions 264**
   2.8.1 Extrinsic allergic alveolitis 264
   2.8.2 Sarcoidosis 265
   2.8.3 Respiratory complications of rheumatoid arthritis 267
   2.8.4 Pulmonary vasculitis 269
   2.8.5 Pulmonary eosinophilia 270
   2.8.6 Iatrogenic lung disease 272
   2.8.7 Smoke inhalation 274
   2.8.8 Sickle cell disease and the lung 276
   2.8.9 Human immunodeficiency virus and the lung 278
2.9 **Malignancy 279**
   2.9.1 Lung cancer 279
   2.9.2 Mesothelioma 283
   2.9.3 Mediastinal tumours 285
2.10 **Disorders of the chest wall and diaphragm 287**
2.11 **Complications of respiratory disease 288**
   2.11.1 Chronic respiratory failure 288
   2.11.2 Cor pulmonale 289
2.12 **Treatments in respiratory disease 290**
   2.12.1 Domiciliary oxygen therapy 290
   2.12.2 Continuous positive airways pressure 292

2.12.3 Non-invasive ventilation 292
2.13 **Lung transplantation 294**

Investigations and Practical Procedures 297

3.1 **Arterial blood gas sampling 297**
3.2 **Aspiration of pleural effusion or pneumothorax 298**
3.3 **Pleural biopsy 298**
3.4 **Intercostal tube insertion 300**
3.5 **Fibreoptic bronchoscopy and transbronchial biopsy 302**
   3.5.1 Fibreoptic bronchoscopy 302
   3.5.2 Transbronchial biopsy 302
3.6 **Interpretation of clinical data 302**
   3.6.1 Arterial blood gases 302
   3.6.2 Lung function tests 304
   3.6.3 Overnight oximetry 306
   3.6.4 Chest radiograph 306
   3.6.5 Computed tomography scan of the thorax 307

Self-assessment 312

Gastroenterology and Hepatology

GASTROENTEROLOGY AND HEPATOLOGY

PACES Stations and Acute Scenarios 3

1.1 **History-taking 3**
   1.1.1 Heartburn and dyspepsia 3
   1.1.2 Dysphagia and feeding difficulties 5
   1.1.3 Chronic diarrhoea 8
   1.1.4 Rectal bleeding 10

   1.1.5 Weight loss 14
   1.1.6 Chronic abdominal pain 16
   1.1.7 Abnormal liver function tests 18
   1.1.8 Abdominal swelling 21
1.2 **Clinical examination 24**
   1.2.1 Inflammatory bowel disease 24
   1.2.2 Chronic liver disease 24
   1.2.3 Splenomegaly 25
   1.2.4 Abdominal swelling 26
1.3 **Communication skills and ethics 27**
   1.3.1 A decision about feeding 27
   1.3.2 Limitation of management 29
   1.3.3 Limitation of investigation 30
   1.3.4 A patient who does not want to give a history 31
1.4 **Acute scenarios 32**
   1.4.1 Nausea and vomiting 32
   1.4.2 Acute diarrhoea 36
   1.4.3 Haematemesis and melaena 39
   1.4.4 Acute abdominal pain 46
   1.4.5 Jaundice 50
   1.4.6 Acute liver failure 54

Diseases and Treatments 60

2.1 **Oesophageal disease 60**
   2.1.1 Gastro-oesophageal reflux disease 60
   2.1.2 Achalasia and oesophageal dysmotility 62
   2.1.3 Oesophageal cancer and Barrett's oesophagus 63
2.2 **Gastric disease 66**
   2.2.1 Peptic ulceration and *Helicobacter pylori* 66
   2.2.2 Gastric carcinoma 68
   2.2.3 Rare gastric tumours 69
   2.2.4 Rare causes of gastrointestinal haemorrhage 70

2.3 **Small bowel disease 71**
- **2.3.1** Malabsorption 71
  - **2.3.1.1** Bacterial overgrowth 71
  - **2.3.1.2** Other causes of malabsorption 72
- **2.3.2** Coeliac disease 73

2.4 **Pancreatic disease 75**
- **2.4.1** Acute pancreatitis 75
- **2.4.2** Chronic pancreatitis 78
- **2.4.3** Pancreatic cancer 80
- **2.4.4** Neuroendocrine tumours 82

2.5 **Biliary disease 83**
- **2.5.1** Choledocholithiasis 83
- **2.5.2** Primary biliary cirrhosis 85
- **2.5.3** Primary sclerosing cholangitis 87
- **2.5.4** Intrahepatic cholestasis 89
- **2.5.5** Cholangiocarcinoma 89

2.6 **Infectious diseases 92**
- **2.6.1** Food poisoning and gastroenteritis 92
- **2.6.2** Bacterial dysentery 93
- **2.6.3** Antibiotic-associated diarrhoea 94
- **2.6.4** Parasitic infestations of the intestine 94
- **2.6.5** Intestinal and liver amoebiasis 95
- **2.6.6** Intestinal features of HIV infection 95

2.7 **Inflammatory bowel disease 95**
- **2.7.1** Crohn's disease 95
- **2.7.2** Ulcerative colitis 98
- **2.7.3** Microscopic colitis 101

2.8 **Functional bowel disorders 101**

2.9 **Large bowel disorders 103**
- **2.9.1** Adenomatous polyps of the colon 103
- **2.9.2** Colorectal carcinoma 104
- **2.9.3** Diverticular disease 107
- **2.9.4** Intestinal ischaemia 108
- **2.9.5** Anorectal diseases 109

2.10 **Liver disease 109**
- **2.10.1** Acute viral hepatitis 109
  - **2.10.1.1** Hepatitis A 109
  - **2.10.1.2** Other acute viral hepatitis 112
- **2.10.2** Chronic viral hepatitis 113
  - **2.10.2.1** Hepatitis B 113
  - **2.10.2.2** Hepatitis C 114
- **2.10.3** Acute liver failure 115
- **2.10.4** Alcohol-related liver disease 116
- **2.10.5** Drugs and the liver 118
  - **2.10.5.1** Hepatic drug toxicity 118
  - **2.10.5.2** Drugs and chronic liver disease 120
- **2.10.6** Chronic liver disease and cirrhosis 120
- **2.10.7** Focal liver lesion 124
- **2.10.8** Liver transplantation 127

2.11 **Nutrition 129**
- **2.11.1** Defining nutrition 129
- **2.11.2** Protein–calorie malnutrition 133
- **2.11.3** Obesity 133
- **2.11.4** Enteral and parenteral nutrition and special diets 134

Investigations and Practical Procedures 136

3.1 **General investigations 136**
3.2 **Tests of gastrointestinal and liver function 137**
3.3 **Diagnostic and therapeutic endoscopy 138**
3.4 **Diagnostic and therapeutic radiology 139**
3.5 **Rigid sigmoidoscopy and rectal biopsy 140**
3.6 **Paracentesis 143**
3.7 **Liver biopsy 144**

Self-assessment 147

Neurology, Ophthalmology and Psychiatry

NEUROLOGY

PACES Stations and Acute Scenarios 3

1.1 **History-taking 3**
- **1.1.1** Episodic headache 3
- **1.1.2** Facial pain 6
- **1.1.3** Funny turns/blackouts 8
- **1.1.4** Increasing seizure frequency 11
- **1.1.5** Numb toes 12
- **1.1.6** Tremor 15
- **1.1.7** Memory problems 17
- **1.1.8** Chorea 19
- **1.1.9** Muscle weakness and pain 20
- **1.1.10** Sleep disorders 21
- **1.1.11** Dysphagia 24
- **1.1.12** Visual hallucinations 26

1.2 **Clinical examination 27**
- **1.2.1** Numb toes and foot drop 27
- **1.2.2** Weakness in one leg 28
- **1.2.3** Spastic legs 32
- **1.2.4** Gait disturbance 33
- **1.2.5** Cerebellar syndrome 36
- **1.2.6** Weak arm/hand 37
- **1.2.7** Proximal muscle weakness 40
- **1.2.8** Muscle wasting 41
- **1.2.9** Hemiplegia 42
- **1.2.10** Tremor 44
- **1.2.11** Visual field defect 45
- **1.2.12** Unequal pupils 47
- **1.2.13** Ptosis 48
- **1.2.14** Abnormal ocular movements 51
- **1.2.15** Facial weakness 53
- **1.2.16** Lower cranial nerve assessment 55
- **1.2.17** Speech disturbance 57

1.3 **Communication skills and ethics 60**

1.3.1 Genetic implications 60
1.3.2 Explanation of the diagnosis of Alzheimer's disease 61
1.3.3 Prognosis after stroke 62
1.3.4 Conversion disorder 63
1.3.5 Explaining the diagnosis of multiple sclerosis 64
1.4 Acute scenarios 65
1.4.1 Acute weakness of legs 65
1.4.2 Acute ischaemic stroke 67
1.4.3 Subarachnoid haemorrhage 71
1.4.4 Status epilepticus 73
1.4.5 Encephalopathy/coma 78

Diseases and Treatments 81

2.1 Peripheral neuropathies and diseases of the lower motor neuron 81
2.1.1 Peripheral neuropathies 81
2.1.2 Guillain–Barré syndrome 85
2.1.3 Motor neuron disease 87
2.2 Diseases of muscle 89
2.2.1 Metabolic muscle disease 89
2.2.2 Inflammatory muscle disease 91
2.2.3 Inherited dystrophies (myopathies) 91
2.2.4 Channelopathies 93
2.2.5 Myasthenia gravis 93
2.3 Extrapyramidal disorders 95
2.3.1 Parkinson's disease 95
2.4 Dementia 99
2.4.1 Alzheimer's disease 99
2.5 Multiple sclerosis 101
2.6 Headache 104
2.6.1 Migraine 104
2.6.2 Trigeminal neuralgia 107
2.6.3 Cluster headache 108
2.6.4 Tension-type headache 109

2.7 Epilepsy 110
2.8 Cerebrovascular disease 116
2.8.1 Stroke 116
2.8.2 Transient ischaemic attacks 120
2.8.3 Intracerebral haemorrhage 122
2.8.4 Subarachnoid haemorrhage 125
2.9 Brain tumours 127
2.10 Neurological complications of infection 131
2.10.1 New variant Creutzfeldt–Jakob disease 131
2.11 Neurological complications of systemic disease 132
2.11.1 Paraneoplastic conditions 132
2.12 Neuropharmacology 133

Investigations and Practical Procedures 139

3.1 Neuropsychometry 139
3.2 Lumbar puncture 140
3.3 Neurophysiology 142
3.3.1 Electroencephalography 142
3.3.2 Evoked potentials 142
3.3.3 Electromyography 142
3.3.4 Nerve conduction studies 143
3.4 Neuroimaging 143
3.4.1 Computed tomography and computed tomography angiography 143
3.4.2 Magnetic resonance imaging and magnetic resonance angiography 144
3.4.3 Angiography 145
3.5 Single-photon emission computed tomography and positron emission tomography 145
3.6 Carotid Dopplers 147

Self-assessment 148

OPHTHALMOLOGY

PACES Stations and Acute Scenarios 161

1.1 Clinical scenarios 161
1.1.1 Examination of the eye 161
1.2 Acute scenarios 164
1.2.1 An acutely painful red eye 164
1.2.2 Two painful red eyes and a systemic disorder 166
1.2.3 Acute painless loss of vision in one eye 168
1.2.4 Acute painful loss of vision in a young woman 170
1.2.5 Acute loss of vision in an elderly man 171

Diseases and Treatments 173

2.1 Iritis 173
2.2 Scleritis 174
2.3 Retinal artery occlusion 175
2.4 Retinal vein occlusion 178
2.5 Optic neuritis 179
2.6 Ischaemic optic neuropathy in giant-cell arteritis 180
2.7 Diabetic retinopathy 181

Investigations and Practical Procedures 186

3.1 Fluorescein angiography 186
3.2 Temporal artery biopsy 186

Self-assessment 188

PSYCHIATRY

PACES Stations and Acute Scenarios 195

1.1 History-taking 195
1.1.1 Eating disorders 195
1.1.2 Medically unexplained symptoms 197

1.2 Communication skills and ethics 199

1.2.1 Panic attack and hyperventilation 199

1.2.2 Deliberate self-harm 200

1.2.3 Medically unexplained symptoms 201

1.3 Acute scenarios 202

1.3.1 Acute confusional state 202

1.3.2 Panic attack and hyperventilation 205

1.3.3 Deliberate self-harm 207

1.3.4 The alcoholic in hospital 208

1.3.5 Drug abuser in hospital 210

1.3.6 The frightening patient 212

Diseases and Treatments 215

2.1 Dissociative disorders 215

2.2 Dementia 215

2.3 Schizophrenia and antipsychotic drugs 217

2.3.1 Schizophrenia 217

2.3.2 Antipsychotics 218

2.4 Personality disorder 220

2.5 Psychiatric presentation of physical disease 221

2.6 Psychological reactions to physical illness (adjustment disorders) 222

2.7 Anxiety disorders 223

2.7.1 Generalised anxiety disorder 225

2.7.2 Panic disorder 226

2.7.3 Phobic anxiety disorders 228

2.8 Obsessive–compulsive disorder 229

2.9 Acute stress reactions and post-traumatic stress disorder 231

2.9.1 Acute stress reaction 231

2.9.2 Post-traumatic stress disorder 231

2.10 Puerperal disorders 233

2.10.1 Maternity blues 233

2.10.2 Postnatal depressive disorder 233

2.10.3 Puerperal psychosis 233

2.11 Depression 235

2.12 Bipolar affective disorder 237

2.13 Delusional disorder 238

2.14 The Mental Health Act 1983 239

Self-assessment 241

Endocrinology

ENDOCRINOLOGY

PACES Stations and Acute Scenarios 3

1.1 History-taking 3

1.1.1 Hypercalcaemia 3

1.1.2 Polyuria 5

1.1.3 Faints, sweats and palpitations 8

1.1.4 Gynaecomastia 12

1.1.5 Hirsutism 14

1.1.6 Post-pill amenorrhoea 16

1.1.7 A short girl with no periods 17

1.1.8 Young man who has 'not developed' 20

1.1.9 Depression and diabetes 21

1.1.10 Acromegaly 23

1.1.11 Relentless weight gain 24

1.1.12 Weight loss 26

1.1.13 Tiredness and lethargy 29

1.1.14 Flushing and diarrhoea 32

1.1.15 Avoiding another coronary 34

1.1.16 High blood pressure and low serum potassium 37

1.1.17 Tiredness, weight loss and amenorrhoea 39

1.2 Clinical examination 42

1.2.1 Amenorrhoea and low blood pressure 42

1.2.2 Young man who has 'not developed' 43

1.2.3 Depression and diabetes 45

1.2.4 Acromegaly 45

1.2.5 Weight loss and gritty eyes 47

1.2.6 Tiredness and lethargy 48

1.2.7 Hypertension and a lump in the neck 48

1.3 Communication skills and ethics 50

1.3.1 Explaining an uncertain outcome 50

1.3.2 The possibility of cancer 51

1.3.3 No medical cause for hirsutism 52

1.3.4 A short girl with no periods 53

1.3.5 Simple obesity, not a problem with 'the glands' 54

1.3.6 I don't want to take the tablets 55

1.4 Acute scenarios 56

1.4.1 Coma with hyponatraemia 56

1.4.2 Hypercalcaemic and confused 60

1.4.3 Thyrotoxic crisis 61

1.4.4 Addisonian crisis 63

1.4.5 'Off legs' 65

Diseases and Treatments 68

2.1 Hypothalamic and pituitary diseases 68

2.1.1 Cushing's syndrome 68

2.1.2 Acromegaly 71

2.1.3 Hyperprolactinaemia 73

2.1.4 Non-functioning pituitary tumours 76

2.1.5 Pituitary apoplexy 77

2.1.6 Craniopharyngioma 78

2.1.7 Diabetes insipidus 80

2.1.8 Hypopituitarism and hormone replacement 83

2.2 Adrenal disease 85

 2.2.1 Cushing's syndrome 85

 2.2.2 Primary hyperaldosteronism 85

 2.2.3 Virilising tumours 87

 2.2.4 Phaeochromocytoma 89

 2.2.5 Congenital adrenal hyperplasia 92

 2.2.6 Primary adrenal insufficiency 94

2.3 Thyroid disease 97

 2.3.1 Hypothyroidism 97

 2.3.2 Thyrotoxicosis 100

 2.3.3 Thyroid nodules and goitre 105

 2.3.4 Thyroid malignancy 107

2.4 Reproductive disorders 107

 2.4.1 Delayed growth and puberty 107

 2.4.2 Male hypogonadism 111

 2.4.3 Oligomenorrhoea/ amenorrhoea and premature menopause 113

 2.4.4 Turner's syndrome 115

 2.4.5 Polycystic ovarian syndrome 116

 2.4.6 Hirsutism 118

 2.4.7 Erectile dysfunction 120

 2.4.8 Infertility 123

2.5 Metabolic and bone diseases 125

 2.5.1 Hyperlipidaemia/ dyslipidaemia 125

 2.5.2 Porphyria 128

 2.5.3 Haemochromatosis 130

 2.5.4 Osteoporosis 131

 2.5.5 Osteomalacia 134

 2.5.6 Paget's disease 136

 2.5.7 Hyperparathyroidism 137

 2.5.8 Hypercalcaemia 140

 2.5.9 Hypocalcaemia 141

2.6 Diabetes mellitus 143

 2.6.1 Management of hyperglycaemic emergencies 145

 2.6.2 Management of hypoglycaemic emergencies 147

 2.6.3 Short- and long-term management of diabetes 147

 2.6.4 Complications 153

 2.6.5 Important information for patients 160

2.7 Other endocrine disorders 162

 2.7.1 Multiple endocrine neoplasia 162

 2.7.2 Autoimmune polyglandular endocrinopathies 163

 2.7.3 Ectopic hormone syndromes 164

Investigations and Practical Procedures 165

3.1 Stimulation tests 165

 3.1.1 Short Synacthen test 165

 3.1.2 Corticotrophin-releasing hormone test 166

 3.1.3 Thyrotrophin-releasing hormone test 166

 3.1.4 Gonadotrophin-releasing hormone test 167

 3.1.5 Insulin tolerance test 167

 3.1.6 Pentagastrin stimulation test 168

 3.1.7 Oral glucose tolerance test 169

3.2 Suppression tests 169

 3.2.1 Overnight dexamethasone suppression test 169

 3.2.2 Low-dose dexamethasone suppression test 170

 3.2.3 High-dose dexamethasone suppression test 170

 3.2.4 Oral glucose tolerance test in acromegaly 171

3.3 Other investigations 171

 3.3.1 Thyroid function tests 171

 3.3.2 Water deprivation test 172

Self-assessment 174

Nephrology

NEPHROLOGY

PACES Stations and Acute Scenarios 3

1.1 History-taking 3

 1.1.1 Dipstick haematuria 3

 1.1.2 Pregnancy with renal disease 5

 1.1.3 A swollen young woman 8

 1.1.4 Rheumatoid arthritis with swollen legs 11

 1.1.5 A blood test shows moderate renal failure 13

 1.1.6 Diabetes with impaired renal function 16

 1.1.7 Atherosclerosis and renal failure 18

 1.1.8 Recurrent loin pain 20

1.2 Clinical examination 22

 1.2.1 Polycystic kidneys 22

 1.2.2 Transplant kidney 23

1.3 Communication skills and ethics 23

 1.3.1 Renal disease in pregnancy 23

 1.3.2 A new diagnosis of amyloidosis 24

 1.3.3 Is dialysis appropriate? 25

1.4 Acute scenarios 26

 1.4.1 A worrying potassium level 26

 1.4.2 Postoperative acute renal failure 30

 1.4.3 Renal impairment and a multisystem disease 33

 1.4.4 Renal impairment and fever 36

 1.4.5 Renal failure and haemoptysis 38

 1.4.6 Renal colic 41

 1.4.7 Backache and renal failure 43

 1.4.8 Renal failure and coma 47

Diseases and Treatments 49

2.1 Major renal syndromes 49
- 2.1.1 Acute renal failure 49
- 2.1.2 Chronic renal failure 51
- 2.1.3 End-stage renal failure 58
- 2.1.4 Nephrotic syndromes 60

2.2 Renal replacement therapy 64
- 2.2.1 Haemodialysis 64
- 2.2.2 Peritoneal dialysis 66
- 2.2.3 Renal transplantation 69

2.3 Glomerular diseases 72
- 2.3.1 Primary glomerular disease 72
- 2.3.2 Secondary glomerular disease 79

2.4 Tubulointerstitial diseases 81
- 2.4.1 Acute tubular necrosis 81
- 2.4.2 Acute interstitial nephritis 82
- 2.4.3 Chronic interstitial nephritis 82
- 2.4.4 Specific tubulointerstitial disorders 83

2.5 Diseases of renal vessels 86
- 2.5.1 Renovascular disease 86
- 2.5.2 Cholesterol atheroembolisation 88

2.6 Postrenal problems 89
- 2.6.1 Obstructive uropathy 89
- 2.6.2 Stones 90
- 2.6.3 Retroperitonal fibrosis or periaortitis 91
- 2.6.4 Urinary tract infection 92

2.7 The kidney in systemic disease 92
- 2.7.1 Myeloma 92
- 2.7.2 Amyloidosis 93
- 2.7.3 Thrombotic microangiopathy (haemolytic–uraemic syndrome) 94
- 2.7.4 Sickle cell disease 95
- 2.7.5 Autoimmune rheumatic disorders 95
- 2.7.6 Systemic vasculitis 97
- 2.7.7 Diabetic nephropathy 99
- 2.7.8 Hypertension 101
- 2.7.9 Sarcoidosis 102
- 2.7.10 Hepatorenal syndrome 102
- 2.7.11 Pregnancy and the kidney 103

2.8 Genetic renal conditions 104
- 2.8.1 Autosomal dominant polycystic kidney disease 104
- 2.8.2 Alport's syndrome 106
- 2.8.3 X-linked hypophosphataemic vitamin-D resistant rickets 106

Investigations and Practical Procedures 108

3.1 Examination of the urine 108
- 3.1.1 Urinalysis 108
- 3.1.2 Urine microscopy 109

3.2 Estimation of glomerular filtration rate 109

3.3 Imaging the renal tract 110

3.4 Renal biopsy 114

Self-assessment 116

Rheumatology and Clinical Immunology

RHEUMATOLOGY AND CLINICAL IMMUNOLOGY

PACES Stations and Acute Scenarios 3

1.1 History-taking 3
- 1.1.1 Recurrent chest infections 3
- 1.1.2 Recurrent meningitis 5
- 1.1.3 Recurrent facial swelling and abdominal pain 7
- 1.1.4 Recurrent skin abscesses 9
- 1.1.5 Flushing and skin rash 12
- 1.1.6 Drug-induced anaphylaxis 14
- 1.1.7 Arthralgia, purpuric rash and renal impairment 16
- 1.1.8 Arthralgia and photosensitive rash 19
- 1.1.9 Cold fingers and difficulty swallowing 23
- 1.1.10 Dry eyes and fatigue 25
- 1.1.11 Breathlessness and weakness 27
- 1.1.12 Low back pain 30
- 1.1.13 Chronic back pain 32
- 1.1.14 Recurrent joint pain and stiffness 33
- 1.1.15 Foot drop and weight loss in a patient with rheumatoid arthritis 35
- 1.1.16 Fever, myalgia, arthralgia and elevated acute-phase indices 38
- 1.1.17 Non-rheumatoid pain and stiffness 40
- 1.1.18 Widespread pain 42

1.2 Clinical examination 44
- 1.2.1 Hands (general) 44
- 1.2.2 Non-rheumatoid pain and stiffness: generalised osteoarthritis 45
- 1.2.3 Rheumatoid arthritis 46
- 1.2.4 Psoriatic arthritis 47
- 1.2.5 Systemic sclerosis 49
- 1.2.6 Chronic tophaceous gout 49
- 1.2.7 Ankylosing spondylitis 50
- 1.2.8 Deformity of bone: Paget's disease 51
- 1.2.9 Marfan's syndrome 51

1.3 Communication skills and ethics 52
- 1.3.1 Collapse during a restaurant meal 52
- 1.3.2 Cold fingers and difficulty swallowing 54
- 1.3.3 Back pain 55
- 1.3.4 Widespread pain 56
- 1.3.5 Explain a recommendation to start a disease-modifying antirheumatic drug 57

1.4 Acute scenarios 59

1.4.1 Fulminant septicaemia in an asplenic woman 59

1.4.2 Collapse during a restaurant meal 61

1.4.3 Systemic lupus erythematosus and confusion 64

1.4.4 Acute hot joints 66

1.4.5 A crush fracture 69

Diseases and Treatments 72

2.1 Immunodeficiency 72

2.1.1 Primary antibody deficiency 72

2.1.2 Combined T-cell and B-cell defects 75

2.1.3 Chronic granulomatous disease 77

2.1.4 Cytokine and cytokine-receptor deficiencies 78

2.1.5 Terminal pathway complement deficiency 80

2.1.6 Hyposplenism 81

2.2 Allergy 82

2.2.1 Anaphylaxis 82

2.2.2 Mastocytosis 84

2.2.3 Nut allergy 85

2.2.4 Drug allergy 87

2.3 Rheumatology 88

2.3.1 Carpal tunnel syndrome 88

2.3.2 Osteoarthritis 89

2.3.3 Rheumatoid arthritis 91

2.3.4 Seronegative spondyloarthropathies 94

2.3.5 Idiopathic inflammatory myopathies 98

2.3.6 Crystal arthritis: gout 99

2.3.7 Calcium pyrophosphate deposition disease 101

2.3.8 Fibromyalgia 101

2.4 Autoimmune rheumatic diseases 103

2.4.1 Systemic lupus erythematosus 103

2.4.2 Sjögren's syndrome 105

2.4.3 Systemic sclerosis (scleroderma) 106

2.5 Vasculitides 109

2.5.1 Giant-cell arteritis and polymyalgia rheumatica 109

2.5.2 Wegener's granulomatosis 111

2.5.3 Polyarteritis nodosa 113

2.5.4 Cryoglobulinaemic vasculitis 114

2.5.5 Behçet's disease 115

2.5.6 Takayasu's arteritis 117

2.5.7 Systemic Still's disease 119

Investigations and Practical Procedures 121

3.1 Assessment of acute-phase response 121

3.1.1 Erythrocyte sedimentation rate 121

3.1.2 C-reactive protein 121

3.2 Serological investigation of autoimmune rheumatic disease 122

3.2.1 Antibodies to nuclear antigens 122

3.2.2 Antibodies to double-stranded DNA 123

3.2.3 Antibodies to extractable nuclear antigens 124

3.2.4 Rheumatoid factor 125

3.2.5 Antineutrophil cytoplasmic antibody 125

3.2.6 Serum complement concentrations 125

3.3 Suspected immune deficiency in adults 126

3.4 Imaging in rheumatological disease 129

3.4.1 Plain radiology 129

3.4.2 Bone densitometry 130

3.4.3 Magnetic resonance imaging 131

3.4.4 Nuclear medicine 131

3.4.5 Ultrasound 132

3.5 Arthrocentesis 132

3.6 Corticosteroid injection techniques 133

3.7 Immunoglobulin replacement 135

Self-assessment 138

INDEX

Note: page numbers in *italics* refer to figures, those in **bold** refer to tables.

A

abdominal examination 23
abdominal imaging
  computed tomography *16, 113*
  radiography 111, *111*
  see also imaging
abdominal pain 4
ACE inhibitors 10–11, 12, 18, 53
  in pregnancy 117, 126
  in renovascular disease 19
acidosis 123–4, 129
  chronic renal failure 55
  dialysis **30**
acute endocapillary glomerulonephritis
    see diffuse proliferative
    glomerulonephritis
acute interstitial nephritis 82, *82*, 123,
    129
acute renal failure 36, 49–51
  aetiology/pathology 49
  causes *50*
  clinical presentation 49
  diagnosis 32, 49
  epidemiology 49
  investigations **15**, 49
  outcome 33
  postoperative 30–3
  prognosis 50–1
  treatment 49–50
acute scenarios 26–48
  backache and renal failure 43–7
  hyperkalaemia 26–30
  postoperative acute renal failure 30–3
  renal colic 41–3
  renal failure
    and coma 47–8
    and haemoptysis 38–41
  renal impairment
    and fever 36–8
    and multisystem disease 33–6
acute tubular necrosis 30, 37, 49, 81–2,
    118, 126–7
  aetiology/pathophysiology 81, *81*
  causes **31**
  clinical presentation 81
  epidemiology 81
  haemodynamically mediated **31**
  investigations 81–2
  prognosis 82
  toxic **31**
  treatment 82

ADAMTS13 protein 94, 95
allopurinol 56
Alport's syndrome 4, 9, 23, 106, 120,
    127
amyloidosis 9, 24–5, 93–4, 116, 120–1,
    125–6, 127–8
  aetiology 93, **93**
  clinical presentation 93
  investigations 93, *93*
  physical signs 117, 126
  prognosis 94
  treatment 93–4
anaemia in chronic renal failure 56
analgesic nephropathy 6, 83–4, *84*
ANCA-associated vasculitis 124, 129–30
angiotensin converting enzyme inhibitors
    see ACE inhibitors
ankylosing spondylitis 25
anticoagulants 10
anti-double-stranded DNA antibodies 35
anti-glomerular basement membrane
    disease *see* Goodpasture's syndrome
antihypertensives 54
antineutrophil cytoplasmic antibodies
    (ANCA) 9, 39
antinuclear antibodies 35
antinuclear cytoplasmic antibodies 98
antiplatelet agents 10
anuria 36
aortic regurgitation 38
aortic valve replacement 38, *39*
arterial blood gases 48
arteriovenous fistula *66*
ascites 22
aspirin 20
atherosclerosis with renal failure 18–20
autoimmune haemolysis 35
automated peritoneal dialysis 67, *70*
autosomal dominant polycystic kidney
    disease 104–6, 121, 128
  aetiology/pathophysiology 104–5, *105*
  clinical presentation 105
  complications 106
  differential diagnosis 105
  disease associations 125, 129
  epidemiology 105
  genetics 125, 130
  investigations 105
  physical signs 105
  prognosis 106
  treatment 105–6
azathioprine 35

B

backache 43–7
Balkan nephropathy 83
biliary colic 42
bisphosphonates 46
bladder
  enlarged **28**
  outflow obstruction 31
blood count 7
blood film 7
  microangiopathic haemolytic anaemia
    35
blood pressure control 18
blood tests 19, 21, 44–5
bone and mineral metabolism 55–6
bronchoalveolar lavage 40
bronchoscopy 40
bumetanide 10

C

calcium
  hyperkalaemia 27, **27**
  stones **90**, 91
  see also hypercalcaemia
captopril renography 87
cardiac dysfunction 31
carithromycin 124–5, 130
cellulitis 63
chest X-ray 10, 12
  pulmonary-renal syndrome *40*
cholesterol atheroembolisation 17, 88–9,
    119, 127
  clinical presentation 88
  investigations 88, *88*
  pathophysiology 88
  physical signs 88
  prognosis 89
  treatment 88–9
chronic interstitial nephritis 82–3
  aetiology 82–3
  clinical presentation 83
  investigations 83, *83*
  prognosis 83
  treatment 83
chronic renal failure 51–8
  acidosis 55
  aetiology/pathophysiology 51
  anaemia 56
  bone and mineral metabolism 55–6
  cardiovascular risk 56

chronic renal failure (*continued*)
  clinical presentation 52
  complications and treatment 53
  drugs in 57
  epidemiology 51–2
  gout 56
  hyperkalaemia 55
  hypertension 55
  investigations **15**, 53
  pregnancy in 56–7
  prognosis 57
  progression 53
  renal replacement therapy 57
  stages of **52**
Churg-Strauss syndrome 39
ciclosporin, side-effects 23
clinical examination 22–3
  polycystic kidneys 22–3
  transplant kidney 23
coma 47–8
communication skills 23–6
  amyloidosis 24–5
  renal disease in pregnancy 23–4
  renal failure 25–6
complement 9, 35
computed tomography *16*, 113, *113*
  abdominal *16*
computed tomography angiography 87
continuous ambulatory peritoneal
    dialysis 67, 69
C-reactive protein 9, 35
creatine kinase 48
creatinine clearance 6, *52*, 110
  chronic renal failure *54*
crescentic glomerulonephritis 79, *98*
crystalluria 21
cyclophosphamide 35
cystine stones 22, **90**, 91
cystoscopy 5
cytology 5

D

deep venous thrombosis 34
diabetes insipidus 109
diabetic nephropathy 16–18, 99–101,
    116, 119, 127
  clinical presentation 100, *100*
  epidemiology 99–100
  history 17
  investigations
    blood tests 17
    renal ultrasound 17–18
    urine tests 17
  management 18
  pathology 99, *100*
  prognosis 18, 100–1
  referral letter 16
  treatment 100
dialysis 26, 48
  indications for **30**

mortality *59*
  pregnant patients on 8
  see also haemodialysis; peritoneal
      dialysis
diffuse proliferative glomerulonephritis
    77–8
  aetiology/pathophysiology/pathology 77
  clinical presentation 77
  complications 78
  differential diagnosis 78
  epidemiology 77
  investigations 78
  physical signs 78
  prognosis 78
  treatment 78
dipstick haematuria 3–5, *3*, **3**
  differential diagnosis **3**
  drug history 4
  family history 4
  investigation and management *3*, 4–5
    blood tests 5
    imaging 5
    microscopy 4–5
    renal biopsy 5
    review 5
    urinary cytology and cystoscopy 5
  referral letter 3
  travel history 4
  urinary symptoms 4
dipstick tests 7, 17, 42
  microalbuminuria 108
  protein 108
  see also urinalysis
disodium pamidronate 46
diuretics 12
  loop 10
drug rash 31
dysuria 4

E

endocarditis 36–8
end-stage renal failure 58–60
  aetiology/pathophysiology/pathology
    58
  clinical presentation 58
  complications 59
  epidemiology 58
  investigations 59
  physical signs 59
  prevention 60
  prognosis 60
  treatment 59
enuresis 95
erythrocyte sedimentation rate 35
erythropoietin 15
  control of secretion *58*
Escherichia coli 94
ethics 23–6
external genitalia, pain 4
external shock-wave lithotripsy 22

F

fever 36–8
fingertip infarcts 37
fluid intake 20–1
fluid management 32
  myeloma 45–6
  rhabdomyolysis 48
fluid overload 31
fluid replacement 29–30
focal necrotizing glomerulonephritis *see*
    crescentic glomerulonephritis
focal segmental glomerulosclerosis 73–4
  aetiology/pathophysiology/pathology
    73, *74*
  clinical presentation 73
  complications 74
  differential diagnosis 74
  disease associations 74
  epidemiology 73
  investigations 74
  physical signs 73
  prognosis 74
  treatment 74
furosemide 10, 12

G

glomerular disease 36, 72
  secondary 79–80
  see also individual conditions
glomerular filtration rate 5, 6, 37, 51,
    109–10
  creatinine clearance 110
  estimated 110
  principle 109–10
glomerulonephritis 4, 49, 117, 126
  crescentic 79, *98*
  infection-related 79–80
  lupus 35, *36*
  malignancy-associated 79–80
  pauci-immune 41
  postinfective 4
  poststreptococcal 33
  segmental *41*
glycaemic control 18
Goodpasture's syndrome 39, 41, 78
gout 21, 56
groin pain 4

H

haematuria 4, 6, *109*
  dipstick *see* dipstick haematuria
  microscopic 3, 17
  sickle cell disease 95
  urinary tract stones 41–3
haemodialysis 32–3, 64–6, 123, 129
  advantages and disadvantages **64**
  arteriovenous fistula *66*
  basic circuit 65, *65*

haemodialysis (*continued*)
  complications **67**
  polytetrafluoroethylene graft 66
  principle of 64–5, *64*, *65*
  temporary line *66*
  tunnelled dialysis catheter 66, *67*
haemodynamically mediated acute
    tubular necrosis **31**
haemofiltration 32–3
haemolytic-uraemic syndrome *see*
    thrombotic microangiopathy
haemophilia 4
haemoptysis 38–41
hepatitis B 62
hepatitis C 62
hepatorenal syndrome 102–3
  diagnosis 116
history-taking 3–22
  atherosclerosis and renal failure
      18–20
  diabetes with impaired renal function
      16–18
  dipstick haematuria 3–5, *3*, **3**
  moderate renal failure 13–16, *14*, **15**,
      16
  oedema 8–11
  pregnancy with renal disease 5–8, *7*
  recurrent loin pain 20–2
  rheumatoid arthritis with swollen legs
      11–13, *12*
hockey-stick incision 22, *23*
hydralazine 33
hydronephrosis 31
hypercalcaemia 43, 45
  causes **44**
  symptoms and signs **45**
  treatment 46
hypercholesterolaemia 8, 9, 10
hypercoagulability 8
hyperfiltration 16
hyperkalaemia 15, 26–30, 48
  assessment of severity 26–7, *27*
  chronic renal failure 55
  dialysis **30**
  ECG changes *27*, **27**, *51*
  investigations
    blood tests 29
    chest X-ray 29
    ultrasound 29, *29*
  management 29–30, **30**
  treatment **27**
hyperlipidaemia 62–3
hypertension 10–11, 17, 101, *102*
  chronic renal failure 55
  epidemiology 101
  pathology 101, *101*
  physical signs 101, *102*
  treatment 101
hypoalbuminaemia 8, 60
hypoperfusion 30–1
  evidence of 31

IgA nephropathy 6, 33, 75–6, 116, 123,
    126, 129
  aetiology/pathophysiology/pathology
      75, *76*
  clinical presentation 75–6
  complications 76
  differential diagnosis 76
  disease associations 76
  epidemiology 75
  investigations 76
  physical signs 76
  prognosis 76
  treatment 76
imaging 110–13
  abdominal radiography 111, *111*
  computed tomography *16*, 113, *113*
  indications
    haematuria 5
    myeloma 45
    renal colic 42–3
  intravenous urography 111–12, *111*
  isotopic 112, *112*
  magnetic resonance angiography 87,
      121, 128
  magnetic resonance imaging 113
  renal angiography 87, 113, *113*
  retrograde ureterography 112, *112*
  ultrasound 7, 12, *14*, 17–18, 19–20,
      29, 87, 110–11, *111*
immunoglobulins 9, 12
immunosuppressants 70
  side-effects 23
infection 63
  urinary tract 92, 122, 128
infection-related glomerulonephritis 79–80
  aetiology/pathophysiology/pathology 79
  clinical presentation and physical
      signs 80
  complications 80
  differential diagnosis 80
  disease associations 80
  epidemiology 79–80
  prognosis 80
  treatment 80
'infection stones' 21, 22, **90**
interstitial nephritis 6, 19
intrarenal renal failure 31
intravenous urography 111–12, *111*
isotopic imaging 112, *112*
itching 13

joint pain 33–6

left ventricular hypertension 56
liver function tests 7

loin pain 4, 31
  recurrent 20–2
loop diuretics 10
lupus glomerulonephritis 35, *36*

macroalbuminuria 16
magnetic resonance angiography 87,
    121, 128
magnetic resonance imaging 113
malignancy-associated
    glomerulonephritis 79–80
  aetiology/pathophysiology/pathology
      79
  clinical presentation and physical signs
      80
  complications 80
  differential diagnosis 80
  disease associations 80
  epidemiology 780
  prognosis 80
  treatment 80
membranous glomerulonephritis 120,
    127
membranous nephropathy 74–5
  aetiology/pathophysiology/pathology 74
  clinical presentation 74
  complications 75
  differential diagnosis 74
  disease associations 75
  epidemiology 74
  investigations 74, *75*
  physical signs 74
  prognosis 75
  treatment 74–5, *75*
mesangiocapillary
    (membranoproliferative)
    glomerulonephritis 77
metolazone 12
microalbuminuria 16
  dipstick tests 108
microangiopathic haemolytic anaemia *35*
microscopic haematuria 3, 17
microscopic polyangiitis 39, *41*
minimal-change nephropathy 72–3
  aetiology/pathophysiology/pathology
      72, *73*
  clinical presentation 73
  complications 73
  differential diagnosis 73
  epidemiology 72
  investigations 73
  physical signs 73
  prognosis 73
  treatment 73
  see also nephrotic syndrome
moderate renal failure 13–16, *14*, **15**, *16*
monoclonal gammopathy 116, 125
mononeuritis multiplex 40
multisystem disease 14, 33–6, *37*

myalgia 33
Mycobacterium tuberculosis 92
mycophenolate mofetil 35
myeloma 43–7, *44*, 92–3, 122, 128
   blood film *45*
   bone marrow in *46*
   clinical presentation 92–3
   epidemiology 92
   pathology 92, *92*
   prognosis 93
   treatment 93

N

nephritis
   acute interstitial 82, *82*
   chronic interstitial 82–3
nephrocalcinosis 85, *85*
nephrotic syndrome 8–11, 33, 60–4, 117, 122, 125, 126, 128–9
   aetiology/pathophysiology/pathology
      hypoalbuminaemia 60
      oedema 60
      proteinuria 60
   anticoagulation 10
   clinical presentation 61, *62*
   complications 62–3
      deterioration in renal function 63
      hyperlipidaemia 62–3
      infections 63
      thrombosis 63, *63*
   differential diagnosis 62
   epidemiology 60–1, *61*
   history 8–9
   hypercholesterolaemia 10
   hypertension 10–11
   investigations 61–2
      bedside tests 9
      blood biochemistry 9
      proteinuria 9
      radiological tests 10
      renal biopsy 10
   management 10
   minimal-change 9
   prognosis 63
   referral letter 8, 11
   with rheumatoid arthritis 11–13, *12*
   self-monitoring 10
   susceptibility to infection 11
   treatment 62
neuropathy 17
nocturia 6, 13
NSAIDs 43
   and nephrotic syndrome 11

O

obesity 122, 128
obstructive nephropathy **28**
   symptoms 28
obstructive uropathy 49, 89–90, 121, 128

aetiology/pathophysiology/pathology 89, *89*
   clinical presentation 89
   complications 89
   differential diagnosis 89
   disease associations 90
   epidemiology 89
   investigations 89
   physical signs 89
   prognosis 89
   treatment 89
oedema 8, 11–13, *12*, 60
   treatment 62
oliguria 36
overdiuresis 12

P

parathyroid hormone 44–5, 55, *56*
pauci-immune glomerulonephritis 41
pelviureteric junction obstruction 90
pericardial fluid 34
pericarditis 33, 34
peritoneal dialysis 66–9
   advantages and disadvantages **64**
   automated 67, *70*
   complications **71**
   continuous ambulatory 67, *69*
   mechanisms of *68*
   practical details 67–9, *69*
   principle of 66–7, *67*, *68*
   Tenckhoff dialysis catheter *67*
peritoneal membrane, solute transport properties *68*
phosphorus, foods high in 56
plasmapheresis 41
pleuritic chest pain 33–6
   examination 33–4
   history 33
   investigations 34–5
polychromasia 35
polycystic kidney disease 4, 22–3, 120, 127
   autosomal dominant *see* autosomal dominant polycystic kidney disease
polytetrafluoroethylene graft 66
postoperative acute renal failure 30–3
   examination 31
   history 30–1
   investigations 31–2
   management 32–3
postrenal renal failure 31
   evidence of 31
poststreptococcal glomerulonephritis 33
potassium citrate 91
potassium, foods and drinks high in **55**
pre-eclampsia 5, 6, 7, 103, 116–17, 126
pregnancy, renal disease in 5–8, *7*, 103–4, 123, 129
   chronic renal failure 56–7
   clinical presentation 104
   communication 23–4

dialysis-dependent patients 8
   epidemiology 104
   history 6
   hydronephrosis *103*
   investigation 7
   investigations 104
   management 7
   pre-eclampsia 5, 6, 7, 103, 116–17, 126
   pre-existing renal disease **104**
   prognosis 104
   proteinuria 116, 126
   referral letter 5–6
   reflux nephropathy **104**
   risk to fetus 6
   risk to mother 6
   treatment 104
prerenal failure 19
proteinuria 4, 60
   in pregnancy 116, 126
   reduction of 62
pulmonary embolism 34
pulmonary oedema 29
   dialysis **30**
pulmonary-renal syndrome 38–41

R

radiography, abdominal 111, *111*
rapidly progressive glomerulonephritis *see* crescentic glomerulonephritis
rash 33
   vasculitic *40*
Raynaud's syndrome 33
red cell casts 4, 5
reflux nephropathy 6, 7–8, 23–4, 85–6, 119, 127
   aetiology 85
   clinical presentation 85
   epidemiology 85
   investigations 85–6, *86*
   in pregnancy **104**
   prevention 86
   treatment 86
renal angiography 87, 113, *113*
renal artery stenosis 20
renal biopsy 5, 10, 18, *61*, 114–15, *114*, 118, *118*, 127
   complications 115
   contraindications 114–15
   indications 114
   practical details 115
renal colic 20, 41–3, 121, 128
renal dialysis *see* dialysis
renal disease in pregnancy *see* pregnancy, renal disease in
renal failure 25–6
   acute *see* acute renal failure
   with atherosclerosis 18–20
   avoidance of 11
   and backache 43–7
   chronic *see* chronic renal failure

renal failure (*continued*)
  and coma 47–8
  end-stage 58–60
  and haemoptysis 38–41
  intrarenal 31
  mild, in pregnancy 6–8
  moderate 13–16, *14*, **15**, *16*
  postrenal 31
  symptoms 28
renal impairment
  and fever 36–8
  and multisystem disease 33–6
renal microscopic polyangiitis *see*
    crescentic glomerulonephritis
renal replacement therapy 64–72
  choice of treatment 64, **64**
  haemodialysis 32–3, 64–6
  peritoneal dialysis 66–9
  renal transplantation 69–72
renal transplantation 69–72, 123, 129
  biopsy *72*
  complications 70, **71**
  outcome 70–1
  practical details 69–70
  principle 69
  survival *71*
renal tubular acidosis 84–5
  aetiology 84, **84**
  clinical presentation 84–5
  complications 85, *85*
  epidemiology 84
  physical signs 85
  treatment 85
renal tumours 4
renal ultrasound 7, 12, *14*, 17–18, 19–20
  hydronephrosis *29*
renal vasculitis 36
renin-angiotensin axis blockade 18
renovascular disease 18–20, 36, 86–8,
    119, 127
  aetiology 86
  clinical presentation 87
  epidemiology 86–7
  history 19
  investigations 87, *87*
    blood tests 19
    management 20
    ultrasound 19–20
    urinalysis 19
  prognosis 88
  referral letter 18
  treatment 87–8
reticulocytosis 35
retinopathy 17
retrograde ureterography 112, *112*
retroperitoneal fibrosis (periaortitis) 91–2
  aetiology/pathophysiology/pathology 91
  clinical presentation 91
  differential diagnosis 92
  disease associations 92
  epidemiology 91

investigations 92
physical signs 91
prognosis 92
treatment 92
rhabdomyolysis *47*, 48, 118, 126
  causes **47**
rheumatoid arthritis 95
  with swollen legs 11–13, *12*
rituximab 35
Roth's spots 40

S
sarcoidosis 102, *102*
Schistosoma haematobium 4
secondary glomerular disease 79–80
segmental glomerulonephritis *41*
sepsis 31
sepsis, screening for 32, 45
septicaemia 37
serum creatinine 7
serum proteins *53*
sickle cell disease 95
sirolimus, side-effects 23
Sjögren's syndrome 97
splinter haemorrhage 39
staghorn calculus *43*
Staphylococcus aureus 37
statins 12, 20
steroids
  hypercalcaemia 46
  side-effects 23
stones 4, 20–2, 41–3, 90–1, 121, 124, 128,
    129
  aetiology/pathophysiology/pathology
    90, **90**
  clinical presentation 90
  complications 91
  differential diagnosis 91
  epidemiology 90
  history 20
  investigations
    acute setting 90
    blood tests 21
    chemical examination of stone 21
    imaging 21
    outpatient setting 90–1
  management 21–2
  obstruction
    with infection 43
    without infection 43
  physical signs 90
  prevention 91
  prognosis 91
  referral letter 20
  sites of *42*
  treatment 91
  see also individual types
Streptococcus pneumoniae 63
subarachnoid haemorrhage 119, 127
swollen legs 11–13, *12*

systemic lupus erythematosus 6, 9, 23,
    39, 62, 95–6, 121–2, 125, 128, 130
  classification **96**
  clinical presentation 96
  epidemiology 95–6
  management 35
  manifestations of *34*
  pathology 95, *96*, *97*
  prognosis 96
  treatment 96
  see also pleuritic pain
systemic sclerosis 96–7, *97*
  clinical presentation 98, *98*, *99*
  investigations 98–9, *99*
  pathology 98
  treatment 99
systemic vasculitis 4, 97–9
  pathology 98, *98*

T
Tenckhoff dialysis catheter 22, *67*
thromboembolism 33
thrombosis 12–13, 63, *63*
  prevention of 63
thrombotic microangiopathy 31, 94–5,
    117, 126
  clinical presentation 94
  epidemiology 94
  investigations 94
  pathology 94, *94*
  prognosis 95
  treatment 94–5
toxic acute tubular necrosis **31**
transplant kidney 23
'trash feet' 31
trimethoprim 119–20, 127
tubulointerstitial nephritis, acute 31
tunnelled dialysis catheter 66, *67*

U
ultrasound 7, 12, *14*, 17–18, 19–20, *29*,
    87, 110–11, *111*
  renovascular disease 87
uraemia 13
  dialysis **30**
uraemic toxins 58
urate stones 22, 43, **90**, 91
ureteric obstruction 31
urinalysis 19, 34, 108–9
  haem content 108–9, *109*
  indications 108
  leucocytes 109
  nitrites 109
  osmolality 109
  pH 109
  practical details 108
  protein content 108
  sodium 109
urinary alkalinisation 48

urinary frequency 4
urinary obstruction 19
urinary proteins *53*
urinary tract
   infection 92, 122, 128
   stones *see* stones
urine
   albumin/creatinine ratio 7
   cystoscopy 5
   cytology 5
   dipstick tests 7

   frothy 61, *62*
   microscopy 7, 109, *109*
   protein/creatinine ratio 7
uveitis 39

V

vasculitis 6, 14, 39, 41
   rash *40*
   renal 36
vitamin D metabolism *57*

von Willebrand's disease 4

W

Wegener's granulomatosis 39, 40, 98
weight loss 44

X

X-linked hypophosphataemic vitamin-D
   resistant rickets 106–7